CAPITALISM, CORONAVIRUS AND WAR

Capitalism, Coronavirus and War investigates the decay of neoliberal financialised capitalism as revealed in the crisis the novel coronavirus triggered but did not cause, a crisis that has been deepened by the conflict over Ukraine and its repercussions across the globe.

Leading domestically to economic and political breakdown, the pandemic accelerated the decline of the US-led capitalist world's imperial power, intensifying the tendency to lash out with aggression and militarism, as seen in the US-led West's New Cold War against China and the proxy war against Russia over Ukraine. The geopolitical economy of the decay and crisis of this form of capitalism suggests that the struggle with socialism that has long shaped the fate of capitalism has reached a tipping point. The author argues that mainstream and even many progressive forces take capitalism's longevity for granted, misunderstand its historical dynamics and deny its formative bond with imperialism. Only a theoretically and historically accurate account of capitalism's dynamics and historical trajectory, which this book provides, can explain its current failures and predicament. It also reveals why, though the pandemic—by revealing capitalism's obscene inequality and shocking debility—prompted the most serious critiques of capitalism to emerge in decades, hopes of 'building back better' were so quickly dashed. This book sheds searching light on the dominant narratives that have normalised the neoliberal financialised capitalism and the dollar creditocracy dominating the world economy, with even critics unable to link capitalism's neoliberal turn to its financialisations, historical decay, productive debility and international decline. It contends that only by appreciating the seriousness of the crisis and rectifying our understanding of capitalism can progressive forces thwart a future of chaos and/or authoritarianism and begin the long task of building socialism.

This book will be of great interest to students, scholars and researchers of international relations, international political economy, comparative politics and global political sociology.

Radhika Desai is Professor in the Department of Political Studies and Director of the Geopolitical Economy Research Group at the University of Manitoba, Canada, and Convenor of the International Manifesto Group.

Rethinking Globalizations

Edited by Barry K. Gills, *University of Helsinki, Finland* and Kevin Gray, *University of Sussex, UK*

This series is designed to break new ground in the literature on globalization and its academic and popular understanding. Rather than perpetuating or simply reacting to the economic understanding of globalization, this series seeks to capture the term and broaden its meaning to encompass a wide range of issues and disciplines and convey a sense of alternative possibilities for the future.

Global Political Leadership
In Search of Synergy
Małgorzata Zachara-Szymańska

Post-Covid Transformations
Edited by Kevin Gray and Barry Gills

Challenging Authoritarian Capitalism
The Transformative Power of the World Social Forum
Edited by Thomas Wallgren, Uddhab Pd. Pyakurel, Catalina Revollo Pardo and Teivo Teivainen

The Reconfiguration of Twenty-first Century Latin American Regionalism
Actors, Processes, Contradictions and Prospects
Edited by Rowan Lubbock and Ernesto Vivares

Capitalism, Coronavirus and War
A Geopolitical Economy
Radhika Desai

For more information about this series, please visit: www.routledge.com/Rethinking-Globalizations/book-series/RG

CAPITALISM, CORONAVIRUS AND WAR

A Geopolitical Economy

Radhika Desai

Routledge
Taylor & Francis Group
LONDON AND NEW YORK

Cover image: Black Square and Red Square (Painterly Realism of a Boy with a Knapsack–Color Masses in the Fourth Dimension) by Kazimir Malevich, 1915 (Public Domain)

First published 2023
by Routledge
4 Park Square, Milton Park, Abingdon, Oxon OX14 4RN

and by Routledge
605 Third Avenue, New York, NY 10158

Routledge is an imprint of the Taylor & Francis Group, an informa business

British Library Cataloguing-in-Publication Data
A catalogue record for this book is available from the British Library

Library of Congress Cataloging-in-Publication Data
Names: Desai, Radhika, 1963- author.
Title: Capitalism, coronavirus and war: a geopolitical economy / Radhika Desai.
Description: Abingdon, Oxon; New York, NY: Routledge, 2023. | Series: Rethinking globalizations | Includes bibliographical references and index.
Identifiers: LCCN 2022031777 (print) | LCCN 2022031778 (ebook) | ISBN 9781032059518 (hardback) | ISBN 9781032059501 (paperback) | ISBN 9781003200000 (ebook)
Subjects: LCSH: Capitalism—United States—History. | Neoliberalism—United States—History. | COVID-19 (Disease)—Economic aspects—United States. | Militarism—United States—History. | Imperialism—History.
Classification: LCC HB501.D434 2023 (print) | LCC HB501 (ebook) | DDC 330.12/2—dc23/eng/20220912
LC record available at https://lccn.loc.gov/2022031777
LC ebook record available at https://lccn.loc.gov/2022031778

ISBN: 978-1-032-05951-8 (hbk)
ISBN: 978-1-032-05950-1 (pbk)
ISBN: 978-1-003-20000-0 (ebk)

DOI: 10.4324/9781003200000

Typeset in Bembo
by Apex CoVantage, LLC

For Alan, my partner in love and politics and to new generations of socialists and communists worldwide, who face tasks made immense by the failures and mistakes of the past

The objective prerequisites for the proletarian revolution have not only 'ripened'; they have begun to get somewhat rotten.

Trotsky, 1938

CONTENTS

FIGURES

TABLES

PREFACE AND ACKNOWLEDGEMENTS

Capitalism is in an advanced state of decay. Nowhere is this more obvious than in the two countries that have played a leading role in giving it its current neoliberal financialised form, and where that form—the only form it can take if capitalism is to survive—is most fully developed, the United States and the United Kingdom. This book examines the ashen spectrum of that decay as refracted through the prisms of the pandemic set off by the novel coronavirus and current US-led international aggressions including the New Cold War on China and the proxy war on Russia over Ukraine, the latest two of the many crises that, in its state of decay, capitalism is guaranteed to be increasingly prone to.

The decay forms two riveting contrasts: with the vigour of socialist China and with the failure of the left in the homelands of capitalism to abandon its century-long proclivity to imagine capitalism to be capable of ceaseless productive advance, despite decades of capitalism's manifest decay. This book places the two contrasts in a single frame, a necessary task if the left in the major capitalist countries is to play its part in helping humanity break free from the death grip of capitalism and advance towards saner ways of organising society, combining individual freedoms with solidarity among people and peoples and the survival of their planetary home.

These arguments rest on two distinct foundations. The first is a decades-long intellectual evolution. It involved an ever-deeper and wider investigation of Marxist thought, its analytical possibilities for the understanding of economy, society, politics and culture historically, and its setting in and strong connections with the intellectual history that preceded and succeeded it. Perhaps the main line of that evolution was the absorption, followed by the critique, of Western Marxism, the form in which I first encountered Marxism as a graduate student in the mid-1980s in Canada. The critique was developed over the decades in diverse writings—on the United Kingdom, India and the United States, on Keynes and

Polanyi as well as Marx and the Marxist tradition, on Marx's understanding of capitalism as contradictory value production and the inability of 'Marxist economics' to understand either contradiction or value, on political and geopolitical economy of capitalism as well as its politics and culture, on financialisations and their connection with the dollar creditocracy, on nationalism and imperialism. The standpoint of this critique was, in ways discernible to me only in retrospect, my early intellectual formation in India at a time when the idea of its socialist development, whose distinctive connections with Eastern, that is to say Communist, traditions of Marxism that I absorbed only indirectly, was still alive. Many puzzles of the rather singular structure of the book and its argument will be unlocked by this key.

A major station in this evolution was my 2013 book, *Geopolitical Economy: After US Hegemony, Globalization and Empire*. In that book, I contested cosmopolitan understandings of capitalism that assume it to be capable of Promethean productive advance and seamless worldwide spread, arguing instead that capitalism's contradictions had led to a very different evolution. On the international plane, they set off the process of uneven and combined development, the struggle between dominant, imperialist, capitalist countries to maintain the unevenness of capitalism's development—*complementarity* between their own high-value production and subordinated countries' low-value production—and their potential or actual targets rejecting, if they can, such subordination and seeking, through state-led and protectionist or mercantilist 'combined development', the *similarity* of productive capacities. Whether in capitalist or, beginning in 1917, socialist forms, such 'combined development', not the expansion of markets or imperialism, has spread productive capacity around the world, leading to ever-greater multipolarity. A decade of further capitalist decay with austerity and political disarray domestically and socialist China's challenge internationally had already led me to expect a major crisis—for instance, I began a February 2020 public talk I gave on 'Does Capitalism Have a Future' by saying 'the short answer is no'—when the pandemic triggered it.

From the start, my focus, since at least *Geopolitical Economy*, on the domestic disarray and international decline of the major capitalist countries made it very clear to me that the principal issue was not the pandemic but capitalism. Whether adverse weather events lead to famine is a question of social organisation: well-organised societies invest in food storage and distributions systems to ensure that inevitable weather-related shortfalls in food production lead, at worst, to difficulties but not widespread hunger and death. Similarly, a pandemic only leads to economic and political disarray and international decline if social arrangements are already considerably weakened. This was already clear to me when I wrote 'The Unexpected Reckoning: Coronavirus and Capitalism', the first of my writings on the subject the weekend after the World Health Organization declared the novel coronavirus a global pandemic. Nothing was clearer to me than that the pandemic was going to rock the foundations of already weakened neoliberal financialised capitalism, accelerating its internal disarray and international decline. Amid the din of crashing asset markets and the clanging of businesses and organisations shuttering down,

> It became clear that whatever the origins, paths, and lethality of the virus now named COVID-19, it was going to sorely test Western capitalism and its coping mechanisms. Almost certainly, they were going to be found wanting. After all, problems and imbalances have accumulated in the Western capitalist system over four decades, essentially since it took the neoliberal road out of the 1970s crisis and kept going along it, heedless of the crises and problems it led to.

Secondly, this book and its arguments rest on the intense attention I gave to events, domestic and international, as the pandemic began. This attention took at least four important forms. First, over the past two years and more, I have been riveted to the mainstream media as well as the plentiful alternative information and media sources that are available today in the West and internationally in an effort to understand the pace and pattern of the unfolding crisis.

Secondly, beginning with 'The Unexpected Reckoning', I kept up a steady stream of journalism, written and spoken commentary, in many outlets, inter alia, Canadian Dimension, China Global Television Network, Sputnik, RT and The Real News Network. In these outlets, I tracked the domestic unfolding of the pandemic, particularly in the United States and the United Kingdom with their public health failures, financial ructions calmed by oceans of central bank liquidity that only re-set asset markets on the precipitous ascent that now diverged even more unreally from plunging economies, and deepening economic and political crises. I also tracked international developments, particularly the New Cold War on China declared by the Trump administration in mid-2020 and pursued by the Biden administration with equal if not greater zeal, including by withdrawing—in an inglorious spectacle of military, political and intelligence incompetence—from Afghanistan in order to concentrate resources on China and then targeting Russia from the fall of 2021 onwards.

Thirdly, in early June 2020, Dimitri Lascaris, the well-known lawyer and activist widely esteemed for his principled stance on many issues of international concern, from Palestine to Venezuela, asked me to be part of his team for his ecosocialist and anti-imperialist campaign for the Green Party of Canada leadership. Ending up as the chair of the Platform Committee, I oversaw, and largely drafted, his campaign platform, including all-important documents on economic, ecological, foreign, Indigenous, health and social equity policies. Doing this against the background of the pandemic only underlined the scale of the task before us if major capitalist societies had to be put on the path to ecosocialism.

The final and most important form was the International Manifesto Group. From the start of the pandemic, Dimitrios Konstantakopoulos, editor of Defend Democracy Press, and I were in increasing communication. Over a Skype conversation, we decided to start an international discussion group focused on understanding and analysing the fast-paced events we were living with a view to answering the eternal political question, 'What is to be done?'. This orientation suggested the name, International Manifesto Group (IMG), and we started meeting fortnightly that April. By the fall of 2020, we were publishing recordings of parts of our deliberations on the Geopolitical Economy Research Group website and, in the runup to the November 2020 US presidential elections, we began organising fortnightly webinars on topical subjects. By the spring of 2021, thanks to the simple but important suggestion from Glenn Michalchuk, we were writing our manifesto. 'Through Pluripolarity to Socialism: A Manifesto', the work of a drafting committee which I chaired and for which I served as the principal drafter, was launched in October 2021.

The IMG has been and remains a source of critical important intellectual, political and personal connections and I can only list the most important here. In the Manifesto Drafting Committee, I benefitted from wide-ranging and penetrating discussions with Jane Akatay, Keith Bennett, Claudia Chaufan, Bruno Drweski, Mick Dunford, Alan Freeman, Carlos Martinez and Jean Pierre Page while many others sent in detailed and illuminating comments including Arnold August, Renate Bridenthal, Michael Brie, Mick Burke, Jenny Clegg, Judith Dellheim, Salvatore Engel Di Mauro, Peter Fleissner, Dimitrios Konstantakopoulos, Chris Matlhako, Attila Melegh, Glenn Michalchuck, Carol Mowat, John Riddell, Ariela Ruiz Caro, Ken Stone and Suzanne Weiss.

In the intellectual and practical discussions that took place in the running of the IMG, I have benefitted greatly from the contributions of Jane Akatay, Arnold August, Oleg Barabanov, Keith Bennett, Roland Boer, Aleksandr Buzgalin, Jenny Clegg, Renfrey Clarke, Mick Dunford, Bruno Drweski, Paul Graham, Danny Haiphong, Brandon Love, Carlos Martinez, Attila Melegh, Glenn Michalchuk, Ben Norton, Jean-Pierre Page, John Riddell, John Ross, Joel Wendland Liu and Suzanne Weiss.

The work of the IMG also put me in touch with a host of intellectually fascinating and politically critical people and networks of anti-imperialist activism and scholarship: Ajamu Baraka and Margaret Kimberly of Black Agenda Report, Friends of Socialist China, Brian Becker of the Party of Socialism and Liberation, Qiao Collective, Nodutdol, No Cold War, Sara Flounders and Joe Lombardo of the United National Anti-War Coalition, Kiyul Chung and Ju-Hyun Park of Nodutdol, Derek Ford, Gabriel Rockhill, Circulo Bolivariano and Winnipeg Venezuela Peace Committee. Speakers, too many to thank individually, at the many and ongoing webinars made critical contributions. Let me end this already long list—it has been my very good fortune to compile—by apologising for any omission.

Finally, I would like to thank Keith Bennett for reading and commenting carefully, with his inimitable political savvy, on the entire manuscript in record time, Mick Dunford for his careful comments on the introduction, Henry Heller for his enthusiastic reaction and Barry Gills, the series editor, for his comments and support. Thanks also to Brendan Devlin and Aziz ul Hakim for their help with some tables and figures. Above all, my deepest gratitude for Natalie Braun's competent, intelligent and warm assistance with the references and many tables and figures. It was a great pleasure working with her.

I dedicate this book to Alan Freeman, my partner in life, love, thought and politics for a decade and a half. So many of the ideas and arguments presented here are inextricable from our many conversations and joint endeavours. And I It is a mark of his admirable political acuity and commitment that it was he who suggested that I also dedicate it to new generations of socialists and communists, some of whom we are fortunate to know, who are creating new understandings from hard practical struggles.

1

INTRODUCTION

Resumption of history, return of choice

Like lightning, crises can momentarily illuminate dark landscapes. The US-led North Atlantic Treaty Organization (NATO) proxy war against Russia over Ukraine, the latest of US-led capitalism's wars against countries not amenable to imperial subordination, did just that in early 2022. As self-proclaimed allies incited Kyiv from the sidelines, demonised Russia to the point of precluding the negotiations that must end wars, imposed sacrifice-lite sanctions on Russia and supplied profit-heavy weapons to Ukraine, recklessly risking a wider, even nuclear, conflagration, the edifice of capitalism was lit up by the lightning bolt of war.

It revealed an unexpectedly diminutive structure. For all the high-decibel rhetoric about a world-girding capitalism relentlessly expanded by 'globalising' markets and empires, two and a half centuries of capitalist expansion had left it quite compact. If measured by the countries following the US lead in imposing sanctions on Russia or giving lethal aid to Ukraine, as shown in Figure 1.1, it was confined to the North Atlantic, with a few toe- and foot-holds scattered across the Pacific: Japan, South Korea, Singapore, Australia and New Zealand, essentially the triad of North America, Western Europe and North-Eastern Asia with eastern and southern European and Pacific Ocean fringes.

True, the US-led West's immediate target was a capitalist country dominated by an oligarchical 'big-insider' capitalism (Dzarasov 2013). True also that the overwhelming majority of the world's governments, representing the overwhelming majority of its people, that did not impose sanctions or supply weapons were not distinguished by their commitment to socialism. However, not even the United States' Latin American 'backyard' or India, often ranked among the most pro-US countries in the Third World, joined the ranks of the capitalist world. Whatever the successes or failures of these countries' development projects, they had historically required deviations from capitalism—that is, economies in which private capitalists determine the pace and pattern of investment and polities in

DOI: 10.4324/9781003200000-1

which they hold the reins of political power. These projects had also required foreign policy commitments that leaned towards the Communist world through international organisations such as the Non-Aligned Movement or the Group of 77. In the twenty-first century, moreover, the capitalist world's unattractive imperialist offer had them inclining towards socialist China and most supported its call for a negotiated solution that took account of Russian security interests.

Gauged thus, the capitalist world had hardly expanded since its imperialist core was fully formed on the eve of the First World War. Notwithstanding either the 45-year Cold War the West fought against the Soviet Union for the allegiance of the Third World (Kolko and Kolko 1972; Desai and Heller 2019) or the demise of that first socialist system, the most fundamental threat the capitalist world faced was still/again a socialist country, China. When the Cold War ended, Francis Fukuyama had stunningly proclaimed that history, humankind's quest for the good society, had ended with 'the universalization of Western liberal democracy as the final form of human government' (Fukuyama 1992, 4). With socialism defeated, no alternatives remained. Barely two decades later, however, history appeared to have resumed and socialism was once again on humanity's horizon as the 2008 North Atlantic Financial Crisis sent the major capitalist economies into a mire of low growth and austerity while socialist China continued its historic growth spurt. Socialism remained capitalism's Big Other destined to absorb and annihilate it.

This crisis-illuminated reality of capitalism requires a serious reconsideration of its historical evolution. Cosmopolitan accounts of its relentless onward march subjecting the whole world to its laws, whether as 'globalisation' or 'US hegemony' or even 'empire' were never credible (Desai 2013; see also Duong 2017). Now that US-led capitalism's grip on the world is slipping and socialist China appears to be winning friends and influencing peoples all over—by 2018, for instance, 70% of the world's countries traded more with China than the United States, up from 20% in 2001 (Leng and Rajah 2019), capitalism's history appears less like triumphal advance than a parabolic trajectory. Its upward escape orbit was already slowing as capitalism entered its monopoly phase and, beginning with the Bolshevik Revolution, socialism emerged to add to the gravity, forcing it into its downward capture orbit, notwithstanding the most strenuous efforts of the United States, in particular, to reverse or at least slow the descent.

That is not all. The US-led proxy war against Russia also brought deep historical fractures within the capitalist world into play, particularly between the United States and the United Kingdom, the two countries most enthusiastically prosecuting the war (ably assisted by Canada) on the one hand, and Germany, France, Italy and Japan, on the other. The United Kingdom and the United States have historically, one after another, sought to create a seamlessly unified capitalist world economy under their domination, with the former remaining and the latter becoming more commercially and financially (as opposed to productively) oriented to do so. The latter group, particularly Germany and Japan, do not just have formatively different, regionally- and productively-focused orientations, but they also stand to lose more by imposing sanctions on Russia, thanks to deeper economic ties dating back to the height of the Cold War and more extensive

FIGURE 1.1 The capitalist world.

Sources: Data from Funakoshi, Minami; Lawson, Hugh; and Deka, Kannaki. 2022. 'Tracking sanctions against Russia', Reuters, 9 March (Accessed 5 June 2022) https://graphics.reuters.com/UKRAINE-CRISIS/SANCTIONS/byvrjenzmve/

Map created using AMCHARTS, www.amcharts.com/visited_countries/#AT,BE,BG,HR,CY,CZ,DK,EE,FI,FR,DE,GR,HU,IS,IE,IT,LV,LT,LU,MT,NL,NO,PL,PT,RO,SK,SI,ES,SE,CH,GB,BS,CA,US,JP,SG,KR,TW,AU,NZ

Compiled using Canva, www.canva.com

Created by Brendan Devlin, using Canva, used with permission.

productive economies. While the United States and the United Kingdom claim that the US-led proxy war on Russia has forged a new unity within the capitalist world, the historically rooted differences in the two sets of countries' approach to Russia—expressed best in the refusal of France and Germany in particular to stop talking to the Russians and Japan to maintain its energy investments in that country—remain clearly visible and will widen if, as seems increasingly likely, Russia achieves its announced military objectives in Ukraine.

The conflict over Ukraine revealed the capitalist world's finitude and division just when the still-unended pandemic had revealed its incapacity. In the leading capitalist countries, that incapacity turned a manageable, if serious, public health emergency into a chaotic combination of catastrophic public health failure, economic crisis, social division and political breakdown. It was the cumulative result of the neoliberal road these countries took out of the stagflationist crisis of the 1970s and kept going, ignoring mounting problems and contradictions, uncaring that, rather than reviving them, neoliberal policies were weakening their productive structures, while expanding predatory finance explosively. While the United States and the United Kingdom led the way, other capitalist countries followed, though with differences in enthusiasm and implementation. After the 2008 financial crisis, these economies went critical. The drip feed of fiscal austerity and monetary laxity kept the patient alive but without vigour, leading many to speak of 'zombie capitalism'. Public attitudes towards capitalism soured as popular protest worldwide was matched by corporate and business loss of faith with mass resignations of executives.

This was the capitalism that the novel coronavirus hit. The pandemic performance of capitalist countries, particularly the neoliberal leaders, the United States and the United Kingdom, formed a profoundly unflattering contrast with socialist countries, led by China. Its competent handling of the pandemic permitted continuing economic stability and growth[1] and even increased social cohesion and political legitimacy domestically and international influence abroad. Naturally, most public discourse and scholarship in capitalist countries refused to acknowledge the contrast, going from blaming China for the 'Wuhan virus' early on to blaming its dynamic zero COVID policies for the economic problems of the capitalist world. They failed, therefore, to locate the roots of the contrast in capitalism's neoliberal and financialised course. Worse, they also joined their governments' aggression against socialist countries, pre-eminently China, as President Trump escalated his trade and technology wars into a New Cold War against China a couple of months into the pandemic.

If Trump's actions raised the possibility of war, Biden's realised it. China remains the main target, but Russia has also been in the United States' sight. President Obama had already launched a New Cold War against Russia in 2014 for resisting the increasingly threatening eastward expansion of NATO. Flailing against the pandemic, Biden not only escalated it into his proxy war but linked it to a potential proxy war against China over Taiwan. When capitalism must risk its greatest war ever, a planet-annihilating nuclear war, to meet its challenges, it is surely facing its most profound, most existential crisis.

The gap between the capitalist world's capabilities and its challenges widened continuously over the neoliberal decades and may have reached breaking point. Neoliberalism was the only way capitalism could survive the crisis of the 1970s. It could not, however, address the economic crisis and prolonged it instead into a Long Downturn (Brenner 1998) of languishing production and thriving financialisations. Most fully at work, and on display, in its leading countries, the contradictions of prolonging capitalism's life through neoliberalism lie at the heart of the capitalist world's diminishing capabilities, whether in pandemic or war.

Neoliberalism was diminishing the capitalist world's economic dynamism just when market socialist China was clocking up some of the highest growth rates for any sizeable economy and some other countries, applying a modified neoliberalism as India did or reversing its more extreme elements after suffering deep setbacks, such as Russia or Brazil did, were also growing rapidly, shifting the world economy's

1 By growth, I mean the expansion of the production of goods and services that remains necessary to provide the world's people with an acceptable standard of living. I take it for granted that it is critical to achieve it while at the same time work to reverse climate warming, pollution and biodiversity loss. Arguments that pit environmental protection against growth forget that nearly all the indices of environmental destruction began rising steeply precisely in the neoliberal low growth era.

centre of gravity away from the United States and the West (O'Neill 2001). After 2008, these BRICS countries also institutionalised their cooperation in many ways that recalled a previous era of South–South cooperation, once again inflecting international economic governance away from the capitalist and imperialist directions that capitalist countries desired and even towards socialist China's attractive example (Desai 2020b), the foundation of a 'Beijing Consensus' opposed to the neoliberal 'Washington Consensus'. However, by the late 2010s, Brazil and India's growth slowed down under authoritarian neoliberal governments, and Russia was challenged by sanctions, while China's growth remained high and chalked up social, environmental and technological achievements. This only made the contest even more clearly one between an enervated neoliberal financialised capitalism and socialism. While the United States, once again aided by the United Kingdom, tried hard to reverse the resulting loss of world influence militarily, it failed.

The pandemic contrasts between capitalism and socialism's leading countries that so damn the former and the perilous wars they are leading to distract and compensate demand a reconsideration of the history of capitalism, and this book attempts to provide it. It rescues that history not only from the deceits of capitalist ideology but salvages it from under the debris that the intellectual irresponsibility and political compromises of the Western left and Western Marxism have heaped upon it. This is not an antiquarian exercise. It is critical for the future, of the denizens of the Western capitalist countries and, thanks to their power—dwindling but still capable of intolerable harm—of humanity as a whole. It is also critical if humanity is to understand where the international cooperation necessary to end the ecological emergency of climate warming, pollution and biodiversity loss is going to come from. After all, not only has US-led neoliberal financialised capitalism contributed the most to that emergency but the political disarray of these countries domestically and their wars internationally are setting back efforts to deal with it even as socialist countries have demonstrated their greater abilities to deal with it (Engel-Di Mauro 2021). Our reconsideration leads to some surprising and surprisingly simple conclusions for socialists simply because crises also clarify historical choices.

In this introduction, I first elaborate on what war and pandemic revealed about capitalism and socialism. Then, looking more closely at the latest phase of their intertwined history, I argue that neoliberal financialised capitalism, best exampled by its leading countries, the United States and the United Kingdom, is the only form in which capitalism—a society in which the state ensures that the investment prerogative remains in the hands capital, which today means monopoly and financialised capital—can exist today. The more productively oriented capitalism of the sort that still lingers in countries like Germany and Japan, had always been in danger of serving as a stepping stone to socialism. There follows a brief outline of the parlous position of the left in the major capitalist countries after four decades of neoliberalism as the background to its failures amid the twin crises of pandemic and war. These failures underline why this book's approach, which I then outline, is so necessary. The introduction ends with a brief outline of the book.

War clarifies

In retrospect, 1914 constituted the peak of the capitalist world. With the outbreak of the inter-imperialist Great War, it entered the great Thirty Years' Crisis (1914–1945). Spanning two world wars and a Great Depression, it was bookended by the first and second revolutions against capitalism, the greatest so far. Before this great crisis, imperial Britain had led the capitalist world. After its end, the United States sought to take over this role and to impose its order on the rest of the world. However, it lacked the military, economic, political resources to achieve this in even more unpropitious circumstances than ever, and failure was inevitable (Desai 2013, Kolko and Kolko 1972). The United States failed to intimidate the Soviet Union into submission by using atomic bombs on Hiroshima and Nagasaki (Alperovitz 1998; Desai 2022) and, in the ensuing the Cold War, countries ruled by Communist parties subtracted vast territories and populations from the ambit of capitalism entirely and supported the great 'revolt against the West' (Barraclough 1964) in which the Third World of countries emerging from colonialism sought, more and less successfully, to throw off colonial shackles through autonomous national development that was not only state-directed but often professedly socialist. In the major capitalist countries, capitalism had to be radically reformed and regulated with socialistic and welfare measures to avoid relapse into depression and to legitimise a discredited capitalism.

However, these socialistic measures had been mounted onto economies that remained capitalist and, inevitably, they ran into crisis. As additional productive capacity of the recovering and developing economies saturated even the expanded demand that the socialistic measures created (Desai 2015), enabling the three-decades-long post-war 'golden age' or Long Boom (Brenner 1998), capitalism entered the 'stagflation' of the 1970s, a multifaceted crisis of overproduction, saturated demand and inflation with wage and commodity price rises. Now, the United States and the United Kingdom led the neoliberal response, claiming that it would revive capitalism. Though initially this claim appeared credible, with even many critical observers believing it as late as the mid-2000s (Duménil and Lévy 2004), neoliberalism could not have reinvigorated capitalism.

Its free market doctrines—whether of Friedman or Hayek, of supply side economics or public choice theory—were rooted in neoclassical economics. It had arisen in the late nineteenth century to glorify competitive markets precisely when capitalism had outgrown them and entered its monopoly phase (Clarke 1991; Bukharin 1914/1972). While competition once developed the forces of production, however brutally and chaotically, it was now heavily dampened. Capitalism's monopoly phase, Marx anticipated and some of his must acute successors confirmed, marked the exhaustion of capitalism's historical utility: it had developed the forces of production as much as it possibly could and was now ripe for socialism. This view was not, moreover, confined to Marxists. As it culminated in the Thirty Years' Crisis (Mayer 1981) of 1919–1945, John Maynard Keynes, for one, proposed an end to liberal policy and market calculation in 'nationally self-sufficient' economises to solve the problems of capitalism the Great Depression had exposed, particularly unemployment (Keynes 1933). Discussing prescriptions for smoothing out capitalism's cyclical ups and downs, he warned that monetary policy would soon reach its limits and 'a somewhat comprehensive socialisation of investment' would become necessary (Keynes 1936/1967, 378). Karl Polanyi, for another, looked forward to the 'new pattern of international life' after the Second World War that was expected to 'greatly improve [the] chances of democratic socialism' (Polanyi 1944/1985, 1945) while the ideologically opposed Hayek warned of precisely this (Hayek 1944; Desai 2019 analyses the opposition between the latter two). More broadly, the experience of wartime planning generated public conviction that the days of capitalism were numbered and history was pointing towards socialistic national planning (Addison 1982).

These views were at least partially confirmed. The 'golden age' or Long Boom that capitalism enjoyed after the Second World War was possible only because 'the politicians, officials and even many of the businessmen' of the time were convinced that

> . . . a return to *laissez-faire* and the unreconstructed free market were out of the question. Certain policy objectives—full employment, the containment of communism, the modernization of lagging or declining or ruined economies—had absolute priority and justified the strongest government presence. Even regimes dedicated to economic and political liberalism now could, and had to, run their economies in ways which would once have been rejected as 'socialist'.
>
> *(Hobsbawm 1994, 272–3)*

It was the crisis of this post-war order that gave neoliberalism its chance. However, it failed to revive capitalism, inaugurating its Long Downturn instead, a slowly unfolding economic disaster of the capitalist world that also made its victory over Soviet socialism pyrrhic. Both the expectations at the end of the Cold War—that the world would be unified under a US-led capitalism and enjoy a peace dividend—were belied.

Expecting unipolarity assumed that neoliberalism was reviving capitalism when, in fact, capitalist economies malingered productively—growing slowly, boosting inequality, increasing misery, dividing societies, hampering meaningful politics and, not least, losing ground in terms of economic weight and world influence. Only their speculative and parasitical financial sectors prospered, worsening their other problems. While Germany and Japan were productively stronger, they could not correct the worldwide demand deficit that caused the Long Downturn and that neoliberalism exacerbated, particularly given that large elements of their own capitalist classes were sold on neoliberalism of one or another variety. The neoliberal capitalist world's failure to subordinate China, Russia and a widening circle of other countries became clear in the new century. On the other hand, emerging economies, led by socialist China, were growing precisely because, and to the extent that their economic policy deviated from neoliberalism (Desai 2013). As the world economy's centre of gravity moved away from the United States and the West, it accelerated the trend towards multipolarity that began in the late nineteenth century (Desai 2013, 265), a trend that Hugo Chavez more accurately termed pluripolarity to denote a world whose multiplying poles also sported meaningfully different economic systems, capitalist and socialist.

The peace dividend evaporated in tandem with fading prospects of unipolarity as never-ending US-led wars followed the removal of the deterrence exercised by the Soviet Union (Desai 2022) and, in the new century, as neoliberalism's economic toll grew heavier, these wars became desperate attempts to stall or reverse the displacement from the centre of the world economy that came with economic decline. This militarism has reached a peak in the war over Ukraine though another, in the form of an even more dangerous war against China over Taiwan, may yet be in the offing.

Until now, US militarism had targeted smaller powers, largely without success, and treated China and Russia with greater circumspection if also barely concealed hostility. However, New Cold Wars against Russia and China were formally launched in 2014 and 2020, respectively, and the current proxy war against Russia marks a dangerous new turn for an unexpected reason. It appears that, alongside war as a means to an end—that of stalling and reversing the decline of the United States and the West it still leads—war appears to have increasingly become an end in itself, with the profits of the US war industries, one of the handful of productive sectors that remain vital in the United States, as much a consideration as any military aim.

Desperation never ensured victory and the increasingly mixed motives of the United States are unlikely to help. It is already clear that the capitalist world has overplayed its hand even against Russia and can only fare worse in any analogous confrontations with China. Most broadly, rather than uniting some putative 'democratic' (in reality neoliberal financialised capitalist) world against Russia, with most of humanity refusing to participate in sanctions against Russia and lethal aid to Ukraine, US actions are accelerating the ongoing division of the world between a declining, economically unattractive and militarily aggressive neoliberal and financialised capitalism centred on the United States and a rising, economically attractive market socialist China whose programmes for building mutual prosperity have been widening its circle of friends.

Worse, even the shrunken capitalist world revealed by the lightning of crisis is cleft by historically deep fault lines. Capitalism had expanded not through 'globalisation' or successive 'imperial' hegemonies (Desai 2013) but through struggles between dominant and contender powers. In these dynamics, which Marx and Engels and later Marxists understood well but are best known by the label Trotsky gave, uneven and combined development (Trotsky 1934), dominant centres of capital accumulation are driven by capitalism's contradictions to maintain capitalism's uneven development, that is to say, to create and maintain the structures of imperialism. Countries threatened by these efforts challenge them, if they can, through state-directed and protectionist efforts at combined development to build national productive capacity. Initially capitalist, after 1917, combined development also began to take socialist forms.

This pattern of expansion has not only cleft the world into capitalist and socialist economies but ensured that the capitalist world is no seamless or uniform entity but a congeries of national capitalisms, each marked by its distinctive history and struggle to avoid subordination and achieve its own domination. Britain's original industrial and imperial dominance, based on empire and 'free trade', was challenged by contenders pursuing nationally distinct state-directed industrialisation behind protectionist walls, giving each capitalism distinct national and quite statist economic structures. As these struggles intensified in the late nineteenth century, they produced what Karl Polanyi called 'crustacean' nations (Polanyi 1944, 202), national economies with hard statist shells.

These capitalisms were also productively more powerful, emerging just when capitalism was entering its monopoly phase which, as Marx and anticipated, and Hilferding had argued (Marx 1894/1981, 567–73; Hilferding 1910/1981, 367–8), ripened and readied capitalism for socialist transition. However, with Britain remaining committed to free trade and the United States seeking to take over its role of imposing economic openness on the world as Britain's abilities were manifestly declining, capitalism's life was prolonged, albeit through resort to 'socialistic' measures. For a time, they made even the comparatively far more liberal United States and the United Kingdom resemble the statist economies though, as the United States and the United Kingdom led the way in rolling these measures back from the 1980s onwards, the diversity of capitalisms re-emerged to be studied by a veritable cottage industry of its models (Coates 2000) and varieties (Hall and Soskice 2001).

Among their many fascinating differences, one was fundamental. The original liberal economy, the United Kingdom, and the United States, which turned increasingly liberal as it continued its quest to emulate British nineteenth century dominance even after the failure of its first post-war attempt in 1971 in new ways, were the countries that advanced farthest down the neoliberal road that was also the road towards financialisation. Many others, while hardly unaffected by neoliberalism and financialisation, continued to prioritise their substantial productive sectors, pre-eminently Japan and Germany (Dore 2000; Hutton 1995; Lapavitsas 2013). This difference was, in turn, rooted in contrasting bank–industry relations, governing the key question of where profits are invested, in production or in predation and speculation.

While capitalist countries did band together in NATO against the Soviet challenge, differences between productively weaker liberal and productively superior statist economies often turned into tensions. For instance, statist France with persisting imperial ambitions and *Wirtschaftswunder* Germany sought to assert their autonomy in the international sphere, whether during the Cold War—in Willy Brandt's *Ostpolitik* or in France's absence from NATO military command structures from 1966 to 2009)—or after (van der Pijl 2006) in European attempts to build an autonomous security structure that, critically, included post-Communist Russia (Gowan 1999, 93). Japan too has often driven hard bargains with the United States, for instance, market access in return for financial support in the 1980s.

The much-trumpeted unity capitalist countries found in their war against Russia may have been aided by the election of compliant governments and unprincipled political leaders, but it papers over these historically rooted cleavages, which the conflict is deepening in critical ways. Capitalist countries have imposed very different sanctions and offered different types of lethal aid and pursued different aims in the conflict, depending on what suited their economies and international ambitions. While these differences prompt the United States to put greater pressure on them to comply, they also prevent them from doing so: Russian gas continued to arrive in Germany and Japan refused to cancel a major gas development with Russia (Lyon 2022). Meanwhile, the United States and the United Kingdom contributed the shrillest rhetoric aided by Baltic and East European countries while German and French preference for a negotiated settlement was expressed in their continued dialogue with Russia (Adams 2022).

Even the more limited unity of an 'Anglosphere' is likely to prove elusive. Essentially involving the United States and the United Kingdom pulling Canada, Australia and New Zealand into an alliance tighter than their intelligence-sharing Five Eyes alliance that dated back to the 1941 Atlantic Charter, it seemed to acquire greater definition with the formation of AUKUS in late 2021. However, the exclusion of Canada and New Zealand already indicated formative problems and Australia's willingness to sacrifice a beneficial relationship with China to US aims may prove fickle (Murphy 2021).

The uneven and combined development of capitalism had created a structure of world capitalism considerably more ramshackle than most dominant discourses allow. For decades, the United States, still its weightiest element, has pulled in the direction of neoliberal, financialised and militarised capitalism while most of the capitalist world's other tenuously articulated components are pulled by the momentum of their own histories and orientations, not to mention the need to maintain some modicum of political legitimacy, if not in the opposite direction, at least at tangents. As capitalism's crises unfold, this disarticulation can only become jolting.

Pandemic reveals

When the pandemic punched in, it caught societies claiming to be at the forefront of science unawares. Once hit, the leading neoliberal financialised capitalisms, the United States and the United Kingdom, proved so incompetent that ruinous nationwide lockdowns had to be imposed repeatedly, causing the worst economic slumps in decades, in the case of the United Kingdom, the worst ever, and among the worst cumulative death rates. The problems lay in the priorities and capacities of public authorities.

US and UK priorities, articulated as the need to balance 'saving lives and livelihoods', lay in protecting the interests of their financialised capitalist classes, chiefly through massive injections of liquidity into the financial sector and parts of the productive sector on which it relied for its choicest assets. After initially considering doing nothing on the public health front, letting the pandemic rip, taking whom it would, they settled for the still-murderous course of 'flattening the curve' because doing nothing would prove ruinous for their economies and overwhelm public health infrastructures already weakened by four decades of neoliberal cuts and corporatisation. The historically unprecedented fiscal outlays that led so many to think that neoliberalism had finally been abandoned aimed only to save its essentials without addressing either these economies' productive debility or their inequality, without even addressing the inadequacies of their public health infrastructure. The funds went chiefly to the biggest corporations and the wealthy, with ordinary workers aided only to repay debts and to keep demand from plunging unacceptably.

Hospital systems creaked and traumatised doctors and nurses had to perform rough and ready triage. Belly-up societies revealed undersides of obscene inequality and disgusting racism and misogyny. Thanks to the decades-long weakness of left forces and government mismanagement and misinformation magnified by unregulated social media, conspiracy theories proliferated and provoked uncomprehending opposition easily manipulated by the well-funded and -organised right. Politically insecure governments sitting atop unstable electoral coalitions—electoral or social—that had only just managed to put them in power were either immobilised before their protests against vaccines and restrictions or responded by invoking emergency powers that smacked of authoritarianism. Amid all this, having come to rely exclusively on vaccines to fight COVID-19, erecting a veritable vaccine apartheid internationally by appropriating the bulk of the world's vaccines in the process, they nevertheless remained exposed to dangers of new variants, thanks to substantial sections of their own populations and much of the rest of the world remaining unprotected hosts to the still-raging virus.

By the spring of 2022, eager to return to some sort of economic normalcy, that is, to restore capitalist accumulation, most Western capitalisms were lifting restrictions and claiming it was time to learn to 'live with the virus' against the warning of leading medical authorities. This was the strategy their capitalist and corporate paymasters now wanted, and they were willing to fund right-wing protests to reinforce their point (see, for instance, Lardner et al. 2022). However, much of the economic damage of the pandemic—disrupted supply chains, business closures, job losses, workforce shrinkage, increased public debt and, not least, the return of inflation—was here to stay.

Moreover, having already witnessed more than a century of attempts to build alternatives to capitalism, humanity was now to witness how the pandemic performance of these alternatives could not have contrasted more.

With a per capita income about a fourth that of the United States, disdained as much by the left as the ruling classes of Western capitalisms, China, the first country to face the full assault of the novel coronavirus not only overcame the initial shock of the outbreak and successfully suppressed COVID-19 in Wuhan city and Hubei province, its 'dynamic zero COVID strategy' kept infections to a minimum and eliminated occasional local outbreaks in short order through localised restrictions. With social and political life back to near normal levels, it managed to host a successful Winter Olympics, aid poor countries against the pandemic and, as even the International Monetary Fund (IMF) had to concede, lead world growth (See Figure 1.2).

China, now clearly the world's economic powerhouse, was not alone. As Table 1.1 shows, as of 22 July 2021, alongside China's 3.21 deaths per million,

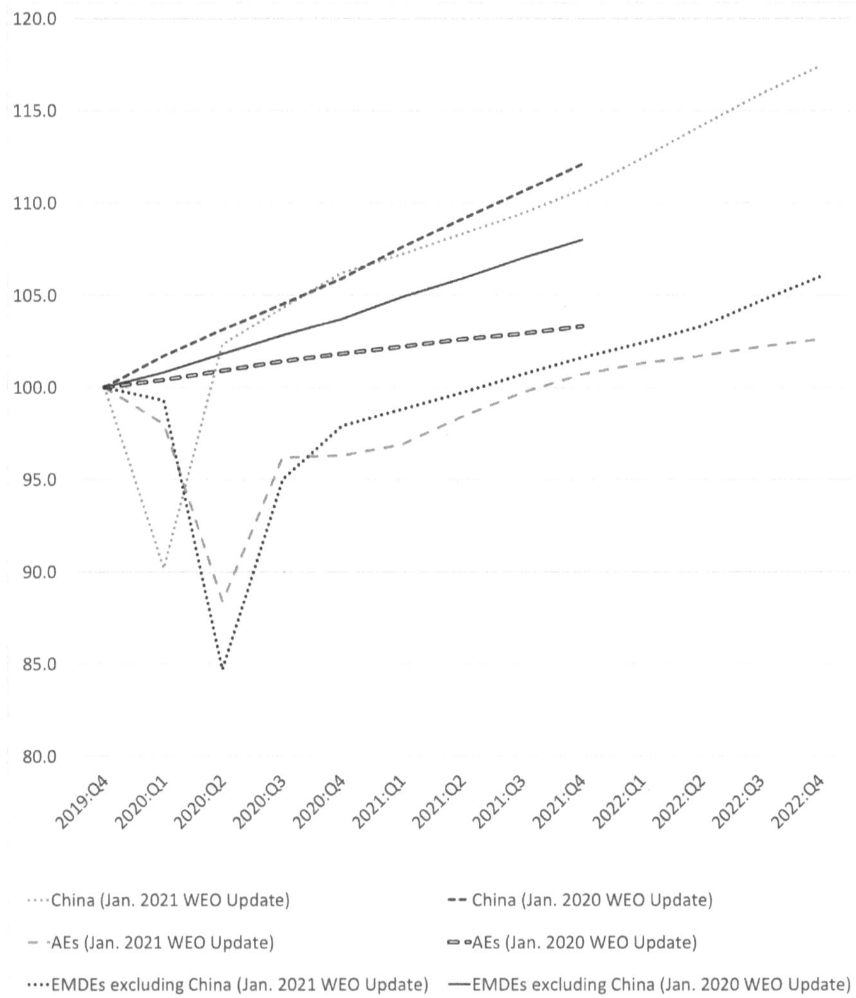

FIGURE 1.2 Divergent recoveries, 2019 Q4–2022 Q4.

Source: Data from International Monetary Fund. 2021. 'Policy Support and Vaccines Expected to Lift Activity', *World Economic Outlook*, World Economic Outlook Update, January. (Accessed 19 June 2022) www.imf.org/en/Publications/WEO/Issues/2021/01/26/2021-world-economic-outlook-update

Created by Natalie Braun, used with permission.

Note: AEs = advanced economies; EMDEs = emerging market and developing economies; WEO = World Economic Outlook.

TABLE 1.1 Cumulative COVID deaths per million: selected capitalist and socialist countries

Capitalist country	*Deaths Per million (22 July 2021)*	*Deaths Per million (17 June 2022)*	*Socialist country*	*Deaths per million (22 July 2021)*	*Deaths per million (17 June 2022)*
United States	1,824.25	3,043.89	China	3.21	3.62
United Kingdom	1,892.27	2,634.81	Vietnam	3.77	438.87
Canada	703.85	1,096.75	Cuba	188.82	753.61
France	1,655.08	2,211.56	Venezuela	119.94	199.41
Brazil	2,557.85	3,124.83	Nicaragua	28.95	35.96
Germany	1,090.08	1,670.74	Laos	0.68	102.58
Japan	119.85	245.93			
South Korea	40.27	476.11			

Source: Our World in Data.

https://ourworldindata.org/grapher/total-covid-cases-deaths-per-million?tab=table

Created by Natalie Braun and Aziz Hakim, used with permission.

Vietnam, Laos (the most bombed country in the world), Cuba, Venezuela and Nicaragua limited COVID-19 deaths per million to 3.77, 0.68, 188.82, 119.94 and 28.95, respectively. This is despite being far from perfect socialisms, despite some of these societies being quite poor and despite economically debilitating economic sanctions on some of them. Though, thanks to myriad difficulties, including sanctions and lower vaccine access, the performance of some of the socialist countries deteriorated thereafter; they still contrasted starkly with those of the major capitalist countries with 1,824.25, 1,892.27, 703.85 and 1,655.08 for the United States, United Kingdom, Canada and France, respectively, as of 21 July 2021 and 3,043.89, 2634.81, 1,096.75 and 2,211.56 as of 17 June 2022, respectively. Among capitalist countries, only the two major East Asian countries, Japan and South Korea, compared well with the socialist countries though they both performed worse than China. Though this was widely put down to 'Confucian' social cohesion, as we will see, their distinct, far more regulated, capitalisms played an important part. Developing capitalist countries, such as Brazil, fared far worse with 2,557.85 (3,124.83) deaths per million.

The pandemic's damning verdict on capitalism and extolling one on socialism is not incidental. It is deeply rooted in their *intertwined* history—a history of compulsive imperialism rooted in capitalism's contradictions and inevitable opposition to it, one that the ongoing war against Russia highlights. That history constitutes the most glaring indication that the more than century-long contest between capitalism and socialism has come to a (another, if one considers the Thirty Years' Crisis the first) tipping point where people and peoples must choose between reorienting their societies away from capitalism and towards some sort of socialism or endure more instalments of capitalist barbarity. The countries that embody the worst of what capitalism can inflict are the leading neoliberal financialised economies, the United States and the United Kingdom.

Neoliberal financialised capitalism: the end of the capitalist road

Their prominent role today has deep historical roots. The United Kingdom became committed to free trade when it achieved industrial supremacy (through statist and protectionist means, as Chang 2002 argued) and remained so even after the rise of its industrial challengers began eroding that supremacy. This was not, as often argued, because of its ideological commitment to free trade but because its originally agrarian capitalist class, which turned to financial and commercial activities and retained its dominance even as the industrial capitalist class rose (Anderson 1964; Ingham 1984; Leys 1990) and because the archaic, short-term financial system that capitalist Britain inherited formed the foundation of its commercial activities in the Empire and beyond and eventually of the gold-sterling standard. It too was imperial: surpluses extracted from non-settler colonies were turned into the famous 'capital exports' to the United States, Europe and settler colonies (Patnaik and Patnaik 2016). It was, however, was faltering well before the outbreak of the First World War thanks to the rise of challengers internationally (De Cecco 1984) and to the political assertion of working classes domestically (Desai 2015).

With the rise of its industrial challengers, with their vastly more productive, because state-directed, protectionist as well as more advanced, capitalisms, that had made the world pluripolar already in the late nineteenth century, Britain

> became caught between two strategies—securing its future by attempting to transform its loose and far-flung empire into a disciplined protectionist bloc in the world market, the equal of both Germany and the United States; and accepting the wider responsibilities of maintaining a liberal world economy that the success of commercial expansion and the adoption of free trade had imposed on Britain.
>
> *(Gamble 1994, 63)*

Its choice of the latter 'long after the conditions which had originally recommended it [Britain's industrial supremacy] had disappeared' determined a second choice: 'the decision to fight Germany rather than the United States' (Gamble 1994, 59) in the First World War. That choice was consequential: 'In two world wars the British helped destroy German ambitions to become the dominant world power. But instead of Britain's power being preserved, that of the United States was established' (Gamble 1994, 59). While the United Kingdom certainly lost power, how much power the United States acquired can be exaggerated.

It is true that, already in the early twentieth century, US business and political elites, witnessing the United Kingdom's faltering power, began nursing the ambition to replace it as the 'managing segment' of the world economy (Parrini 1969) in the new century. However, this would have to be done by replacing sterling with the dollar, not by acquiring a comparable empire, something that was now impossible.

It is also true that, in pursuit of this ambition the United States timed its late entry in both wars so as to maximise the benefit to its economy by acting as the unscathed supplier of war materiel (Lens 2003, 252–3) and the wager succeeded, with US GDP actually doubling between 1939 and 1945 (Desai 2013, 74–87). Even so, liberal victory against fascism in the Second World War, umbilically linked to the First by the Versailles settlement that settled little (Keynes 1919/2004), would not have been possible without Soviet Russia and Chinese Communist and nationalist forces.

So though, at the end of the Second World War, Karl Polanyi acutely intuited that, while most of the world was inclined in more or less socialist directions, the United States remained vested in capitalism's pre-1914 liberal, 'universal' (or imperialist) form (Polanyi 1945), new forces limited its abilities. The advance of pluripolarity had already weakened UK dominance (De Cecco 1984) and it continued advancing, now along Communist lines too, leaving the United States' memetic ambition unrealised, though not for lack of trying (Desai 2013). In the immediate post-war period, US power faced many constraints: the power of Communism and the associated need to permit recovering capitalist allies and the Third World emerging from colonialism many deviations from liberal economic policy. Indeed, retaining the productive advantages secured from war required the United States to adopt at least some of the socialistic measures widely adopted elsewhere (Desai 2013, 96–102). The United States was able to impose the dollar on the world by rejecting plans for the alternatives (Block 1977), though it had to promise to back it with gold. Without an empire comparable to Britain's, it was able to supply the world with liquidity only by running deficits, rather than exporting capital, subjecting the dollar's world role to the Triffin dilemma: the greater the deficits the greater the downward pressure on the dollar. Inevitably, European recovery and currency convertibility by 1958 led to a dollar glut and a drain on US gold reserves. After trying one device after another to save it through the 1960s, the link with gold had to be broken in 1971.

Only now were the foundations of the volatile and unstable dollar creditocracy (Desai and Hudson 2021) that has supported the dollar's world role since through a series of unstable and volatile financialisations—expansions of financial activity and asset bubbles—laid with the lifting of US capital controls in 1973 and the Volcker interest rate shock of the late 1970s. The resulting financial expansions would also aid, and shape, the shift to neoliberalism.

The crisis of the 1970s confronted the major capitalist countries with a choice. Deepening the socialistic measures that had enabled the Long Boom could have transcended the remaining limitations of capitalism as a productive system, but would certainly bring them closer to socialism. Freeing capital from its 'socialistic' fetters on the grounds that they were the problem, as the advocates of neoliberalism argued, promised productive redemption that was capitalist. While the distributional consequences would be criticised from the start, few foresaw that the neoliberal promise was empty. While, enhancing the capitalist character of these economies, neoliberalism would not restore productive dynamism.

Led by Thatcher and Reagan, major capitalist countries opted for the latter, inaugurating the neoliberal era. It was never about free markets and competition but about freeing capital, and in the late twentieth century even more than at its start, that meant freeing giant monopoly corporations, from state and social regulation and obligation, a freedom that required tremendous state effort to create and maintain as early and recent analysts observed (for instance, Gamble 1978, Crouch 2011). This effort is critical for capitalism's survival. Understood thus, neoliberal capitalism is nothing more or less than the only form in which capitalism can survive today. The alternative of a reformed 'socialistic' capitalism would put it back on the ramp to socialism.

Since freeing monopoly capital was never going to restore competitive vigour to capitalism and revive its productive economy, the slump of the 1970s turned into the Long Downturn from which the capitalist world is yet to recover. While the sharpest edge of neoliberalism's destructiveness was reserved for the Third World, much of which experienced economic havoc and retardation in the 1980s and 1990s, neoliberalism's record in major capitalist economies was, to say the least, woeful. Growth remained low, wages stagnated, inequality soared and public institutions and services were privatised, commodified and corporatised for private profit with visible declines in the quantity and quality of delivery. Worse, as the productive economy was increasingly outcompeted by lower cost producers elsewhere, facilitated by Western multinationals' outsourcing, financial activity exploded instead, indebting households, firms and governments and enriching an ever-narrowing elite through predation and plunder and through speculation in mushrooming asset bubbles, the greatest of which burst in 2008. Internationally, the expansion of financial activity supported the dollar's world role while domestically, it provided one financial fix after another to compensate for, rather than resolving, neoliberalism's demand problem (Streeck 2014).

The shifts to neoliberalism and financialisation were the results of the decisions of individual governments and not all major capitalist countries went as far as the United States and United Kingdom towards neoliberalism or financialisation. In the productively strongest economies like Germany and Japan, doing so would have been costly—to domestic capital historically oriented to production rather than finance and to political legitimacy. However, even they were affected by its international manifestations—saturated worldwide demand and the growth of international finance headquartered in New York and London. This book will focus on the United States and the United Kingdom as the leading and exemplary neoliberal financialised capitalisms, though suitably adapted, its arguments can also illuminate the experiences of other major capitalist countries.

Classes and nations against neoliberalism and towards socialism

Left forces capable of tackling capitalism's mounting contradictions were missing in action. Rather than producing a socialist critique of neoliberal financialised capitalism, having already forsaken socialism as the goal, the historic parties of working people in the major capitalist countries now capitulated to neoliberalism, moving their parties further rightwards and leaving vast swathes of working people with no serious political representation. Inevitably, some of their discontent found political expression, in a distorted and inadequate manner, in the morbid right-wing politics exemplified by Trump and Brexit. While often termed populist (Rodrik 2017; Eatwell and Goodwin 2018; Mudde and Kaltwasser 2017), these politics are better seen the hard edge of the right-wing resurgence that has gathered strength for decades.

Might the multifaceted crisis of pandemic and war in the capitalist world finally prompt genuine left opposition? In the early months of the pandemic, political hope rose, with much talk of not going back to the unbearable pre-pandemic normal and 'building back better'. More than two years into the crisis with a war making it even more urgent, however, a left critique of neoliberal governments' shambolic, not to say murderous, handling of the pandemic and cynical and hypocritical war was not much in evidence. While neoliberal politicians, such as Biden, appropriated the 'building back better' slogan, the hard right opposition made all the running in terms of a critique of governments' handling of the pandemic. As the United States led its war against Russia over Ukraine, not only did most historic parties of the left and working classes line up to support it, so did vast swathes of the farther left that have long denounced, in an 'anti-anti-imperialist' vein, all who those who support struggles against US and Western imperialism on the grounds that the countries leading them are 'authoritarian' or 'imperialist' or both. Too many who are still pleased to sport this or that left banner jump on to the 'democracy and human rights' bandwagon of Western imperialism, a tendency that remined strong enough for Jean-Luc Mélenchon to moderate his opposition to it in the 2022 French parliamentary elections.

Thus, pandemic and war seem only to have deepened the rut into which neoliberal financialised capitalisms have led the capitalist world for decades, increasing their domestic dysfunction and international malevolence while at the same time shrinking it back to its imperial core of 1914 with very few additions. Moreover, substantial parts of it feel the gravitational pull of China's socialist market economy. In the rest of the world, the emerging international alliance centred on China has been offering alternatives, to avowedly socialist countries and to those that simply seek to avoid subordination to the United States and the West.

Considering that actually existing socialisms are disdained by the Western left and Western Marxism as, at best, premature and insufficiently socialist and, at worst, authoritarian and dystopian, the domestic blockage of socialist politics in the capitalist world forms an ironic contrast with socialism's international prominence. The latter points to a rather different road map to socialism than the one the Western left and Western Marxism have been using, in which revolution must first occur in the homelands of capitalism and lead the rest of the world. The fall of the Berlin Wall and the demise of the Soviet Union appeared to vindicate it. However, three decades later, not only do large numbers in former Communist countries regret what they lost with the demise of socialism, not only has capitalism failed to integrate them into itself in an acceptable, let alone desirable manner, not only are major capitalist countries now at war with Russia to subordinate it, the challenge of actually existing socialism has returned with a vengeance.

It had to because it is rooted in the deeper logic of the international relations of the capitalist world, its geopolitical economy (Desai 2013), involving what Marx called 'the relations of producing nations' (Desai 2021), particularly the dialectic of uneven and combined development that has advanced pluripolarity since capitalism's beginnings. The principal drag on this to advance in recent decades has been the US attempt, dressed up in the ideology and rhetoric of 'US hegemony' or 'empire', to emulate the sort of dominance the United Kingdom briefly enjoyed over the world economy. It has never succeeded but, so far at least, the United States has persisted, even at the expense of its productive decline.

Pandemic and war have not only brought this challenge to the fore, they promise, underneath the much-trumpeted appearance of Western unity, to divide the Western alliance along historic lines, between the countries in the vanguard of the march towards neoliberalism and financialisation and others, such as the continental European countries or Japan, that remained more state regulated and production oriented.

This political configuration of the world—with the capitalist world in advanced decay and disarticulation, its domestic socialist forces missing in action and socialist societies' demonstrated competence against the pandemic and opposition to the US-led war—demands that the Western left re-visit its roadmap to socialism. The waskness of left analyses of the pandemic so far only underline the urgency of doing so.

The crisis and the opportunities?

That the pandemic was going to deal the financialised neoliberal capitalist economies of the Western world a historic blow was clear from the start. In Act I, Scene I of the coronavirus and capitalism drama, as markets for every kind of financial asset, risky and safe, nosedived even before the WHO upgraded the Public Health Emergency of International Concern to a global pandemic on 11 March 2020, nothing preoccupied public authorities in the United States and the United Kingdom more than saving asset values. The Federal Reserve responded with liquidity injections historic both in scale and variety (Brenner 2020; Leonard 2022). Corporate chief executive officers (CEOs) and governments went into huddles and announcements of bailouts and subsidies, and even some measure of income support for ordinary working people to keep demand from collapsing completely, came thick and fast.

The weekend after the WHO's declaration of the pandemic, it was already clear to me that the new virus

> was going to sorely test Western capitalism and its coping mechanisms. Almost certainly, they were going to be found wanting. After all, problems and imbalances have accumulated in the Western capitalist system over four decades, essentially since it took the neoliberal road out of the 1970s crisis and kept going along it, heedless of the crises and problems it led to.
> *(Desai 2020a)*

Over the previous decade, even the mainstream media had resonated with concern over the health of capitalism. After the private debt of the big financial institutions that caused the 2008 financial crisis was socialised, not that of ordinary people who lost homes and jobs, austerity followed. Public expenditure, already dwindling over the neoliberal decades, was cut even more drastically in preference to raising taxes on the rich, wages stagnated, public services decayed, inequality topped the list of public concerns and made Thomas Piketty's (2017) 1,000-page dry data-packed tome on the subject an international bestseller, popular protest mounted and at least one quite mainstream academic wrote a book titled *How Will Capitalism End?* (Streeck 2017). Inevitably, the advocates for this or that reform that had proliferated in this environment saw the new crisis as an opportunity for promoting their respective brands as reform.

In a short video for *The Intercept* on 16 March, Naomi Klein warned that the pandemic would become just another opportunity for 'disaster capitalism', the theme of her bestseller *The Shock Doctrine*, unless the public seized it to challenge corporate power and realise the Green New Deal (Klein 2020). For Mariana Mazzucato too, the pandemic was an opportunity to apply her preferred solution: to 'do capitalism differently' with governments not just fixing market failures but moving 'towards actively shaping and creating markets that deliver sustainable and inclusive growth' and partner with business for 'public interest, not profit' (Mazzucato 2020).

Meanwhile Paul Mason, who had been ploughing a rather different furrow in the putrid intellectual fields of decaying capitalisms, proclaimed his 'post-capitalism' thesis vindicated. Policies considered unthinkable because they would 'kill capitalism' had arrived as never before: 'Universal payments, state bailouts and the funding of state debts by central banks have all been adopted at a speed that has shocked even the usual advocates of these measures' (Mason 2020). His ultimate proof of post=capitalism? A wealth manager complaining that 'Conventional capitalism is dying, or at least mutating into something closer to a version of communism'. Mason's vision of capitalism spontaneously mutating into some sort of neo-Proudhonist 'post-capitalist' utopia is just another of the recently burgeoning imaginings of the Western professional managerial class (Desai 2011). In it, capitalism is doing so well, all that remains is to re-label it socialism. Changing anything is the farthest thing from their minds. Couched in apparently radical language, using terms like Communism and exploitation, they are, in reality, at once frivolous and deeply conservative.

Demand for writing on the pandemic was clearly rising as evidenced by rising news readership and the big publishing houses had to rush to fulfil it or others would challenge their dominant market position. At the same time, the pandemic had raised many uncertainties about the medium (paper or electronic), distribution (bookshops and launches or electronic) and even politics. So, sticking to authors they had already (literally) invested in, rather than critiques of capitalism they brought out a form of pandemic porn, claiming to feed the genuine appetite to understand the economically and emotionally painful crisis but incapable of providing anything more than a simulation of satisfaction.

Once such author, Adam Tooze, had turned from his world war histories to the 2008 crisis in *Crashed* (2018). In *Shutdown*, he grandly pronounced the 2020 crisis 'a comprehensive crisis of the neoliberal era—with regard to its environmental envelope, its domestic social, economic and political underpinnings, and the international order' and 'the end of an arc whose origin is to be found in the 1970s'. So far so good. However, he then disappointingly confined himself to 'the moment itself', pleading the necessity of 'coping with the intellectual and psychological stresses of a moment that was otherwise overwhelming' (Tooze 2021, 22). A survey of the public health emergency in various parts of the world was followed by discussion of economic and financial developments, providing details of the activities of the financial and monetary authorities and powers of neoliberal financialised world. Here Tooze had clearly graduated from a hesitant and none-too-analytical chronicler of the activities of powerful financial and political elites in *Crashed* to their court historian. His narrative, he claimed, was 'critical in intent' (Tooze 2021, 303) and 'cast as a "grand narrative"' (Tooze 2021, 304) that 'wrestle[s] with power and knowledge in time' (Tooze 2021, 304). However, by his own admission, it is also 'entangled and indeed complicit with its subject matter—the efforts of elites around the world to master the crisis' (Tooze 2021, 303). Complicity clearly trumps any wrestling in the breathlessly admiring 'grand narrative' of their actions (Chapter 6 on Federal Reserve Chairman Jay Powell's actions is an excellent example).

Niall Ferguson (2021) discoursed ponderously on the critical importance of human institutions to coping with a long historical line of great catastrophes. His lofty perch disguised his condescension towards non-Western and socialist societies only barely, while the apparent erudition of his existential reflections on death, unpredictability, science, globalisation and the international order simply drew attention away from the incompetence of neoliberal governments. Indeed, the book was little more than an attempt to exonerate the Western world and its leaders, even those of the worst performing of major capitalist countries, Trump and Johnson: 'to turn COVID-19 into a morality play—The Populists' Nemesis—is to miss the more profound systemic and societal failure that occurred, in a way that future historians will surely see as facile' (Ferguson 2021, 208). More interesting to him was '[t]he behaviour of ordinary people [, which] . . . can matter even more than the decisions of leaders or orders issued by governments in the event of a disaster. What leads some people to adapt rationally to a new threat, others to act passively as bystanders, and others to go into denial or revolt?' (Ferguson 2021, 10–11), preparing the way nicely for the neoliberal financialised capitalisms finally thrusting their responsibility onto individuals and blaming them for the failure to master the pandemic.

Nowhere in all this writing about the pandemic were capitalism's permanence and desirability questioned. After all, over the previous decade, a genre of literature had emerged to investigate and expose capitalisms' multiplying atrocities and scandals only to proclaim that no alternative was available.

The German sociologist Wolfgang Streeck exemplified it. After an impressively damning account of how neoliberal financialised capitalism had raised inequality and entrenched corporate power, undermined liberal democracy, disabled society's collective capacities and turned citizens into customers, Streeck threw up his hands in Weberian despair. Citizens of Western democracies can only look forward to 'a long and painful period of cumulative decay: of intensifying frictions, of fragility and uncertainty, and of a steady succession of 'normal accidents'—not necessarily but quite possibly on the scale of the global breakdown of the 1930s' (Streeck 2017, 72). He had a clear idea of how matters would unfold. Neoliberalism had hyper-individualised an already individualistic social order and only when 'the prevailing disorder will begin on a large scale and seriously to frustrate individual projects and ambitions' that 'a new order may emerge' (Streeck 2017, 46). However, he could not say what it might be.

Thomas Piketty had followed up his rather economistic analysis in *Capital in the Twenty-First Century* (2017) with a considerably more political one in early 2020 in which he came down in favour of 'participatory socialism'. However, distanced from any actually existing socialism, it referred to a hodgepodge of worker involvement through co-determination, steeply progressive taxes on inheritance and income to finance increased social services, a 'universal capital endowment' to every person attaining majority, educational justice and a vague internationalism that assumed that not only had liberal capitalism failed but so had nations. He was conscious these proposals were far from complete, showing only that 'human societies have yet to exhaust their capacity to imagine new ideological and institutional solutions' and that 'the political-ideological repertoire is vast' (Piketty 2020, 1034).

Some left analysts did go further. Grace Blakeley (2020) argued that the unprecedented scale and scope of government intervention in the major capitalist economies were transforming 'finance capitalism' into 'state monopoly capitalism'. It was a very centralised form of capitalism in which

> markets are dominated by a few large firms . . . state action is the only thing that stands between a firm and bankruptcy . . . [and] decisions about the production and allocation of resources are effectively made by a small number of people at the top of the world's largest corporations.
>
> *(Blakeley 2020, 32)*

Such capitalism was extended through 'the long arm of the imperial creditor' also to peripheral states 'subject to the discipline of capital' (Blakeley 2020, 52–3). In this context, admonished Blakeley, traditional socialist agitation against cuts in government spending and for more government intervention 'will ring hollow in the war economy created by the pandemic' and 'we must concern ourselves with how state power is being used—and who is wielding it' (Blakeley 2020, 35). The only way to 'wrest control back' from these elites is

> a radical democratization of national and international economic and political institutions, giving workers, consumers and communities a say in decision-making within public owned companies, central banks and

> throughout local government and the central state—and in giving the poorest states in the world a voice in international governance.
>
> *(Blakeley 2020, xvii)*

The apparent mountain of Blakeley's critique produced the mouse of 'radical democratization' to give people and the poorest nations 'a voice' in decision making. For Blakeley, socialism is associated with outdated demands while capitalism only needs radical democratisation. China is not discussed and imperialism is taken as a given.

None of these analyses recognised that the pandemic had made transforming capitalism into socialism (rather than just reforming it or doing it differently or radically democratising it) urgent. Nor did they recognise that attempts to do this may differ in detail from previous efforts to build socialism but not in their broad thrust and had to be organised in solidarity with them, however critical. Without recognising these things, even the best left-leaning analyses can, at most, serve as the mood music to the tempo of which the neoliberal political establishment will patching up the collapsing, systematically crisis-prone neoliberal, financialised capitalism for further disastrous decades. As Western governments swept the pandemic under the carpet of their hostilities against Russia and, through it, against the alternative pole of world economies open to socialist China, even questions of reform were swept off the table.

What the current crisis requires is a far more radical analysis of capitalism and its trajectory, one that Marxism can supply but only after decades of misinterpretation are removed from it, and its historical understanding of capitalism and relation to socialism re-established. This is what the book seeks to do.

Outline of the book

The next chapter argues that Marx and Engels's original understanding of capitalism as contradictory value production—of how it emerged and how its transition to the monopoly phase was ripening it for socialism—was historical in a dual sense. Capitalism was, of course, a historically specific form of social production. However, being contradictory, it was also historical in a second sense: its own history was driven forward, and its geography outwards as imperialism, by its many contradictions in processes managed by states. This was the understanding, of capitalism's political and geopolitical economy, that was eclipsed by the rise of a Marxist economics.

Marxist economics was the result of the failure to contest neoclassical economics, which emerged in the late nineteenth century, and was methodologically and theoretically antithetical to Marxism, designed to undermine it and its antecedent, classical political economy. Instead of contesting it, most Marxists sought to reconcile it with Marxism. Though they criticised many aspects of the new discipline, they accepted its fundamental wager: that capitalism had a self-regulating 'economy' separate from other social realms. Neither contradictory nor reliant on other social realms to cope with its contradictions, it needed neither state management nor imperialism. In reality, as the chapter argues, capitalism needed both and these needs have long propelled the unfolding of its profoundly historical political and geopolitical economy. The chapter ends with a systematic discussion of the myriad contradictions of capitalism arising in two forms along the two principal axes of value production, class struggle and competition, not only in the core realms of value production, production and realisation, but also beyond them in the various realms of society—money, finance, the natural environment, the state and the international—that capitalism transforms by putting contradictory demands on them. The last two sets of contradictions, arising from the realms of the state and the international, are left for the next chapter to form the theoretical framework for the discussion of the historical evolution of capitalism's political and geopolitical economy.

After that discussion, which emphasises the limits of capitalist states' abilities to manage contradictions and crises, and the dialectic of uneven and combined development capitalism sets off internationally, Chapter 3 goes on to outline the main lines of capitalism's evolution relevant to our argument, including its early entwinement with socialism. It covers the period from the mid-nineteenth century until the end of the post-war Long Boom. Early in that evolution, the historical transition to monopoly capitalism also proved a geographical one as the more advanced forms of capitalism emerged not in Britain, the original industrial capitalist country, but in her industrial challengers, chiefly Germany, the United States and Japan. As productive power migrated elsewhere, Britain reacted not by advancing hers in ways they had. Instead, she leaned more heavily on her empire to compensate for her decreasing competitiveness and to provide the surpluses that formed the foundation of her commercial and financial supremacy and of the gold-sterling standard. In doing so, Britain also prolonged the life of the archaic form of finance that had elsewhere been overtaken by forms of finance better able to facilitate the expansion of capitalist accumulation in the monopoly era of immense capital outlays.

Indeed, industrial and imperial competition of the now pluripolar world was challenging Britain's preeminent world role already in the early twentieth century, and US ruling circles had begun nursing the ambition to displace sterling with the dollar, when that competition erupted into the First World War. It set off the Thirty Years' Crisis of 1914–45, a veritable international civil war encompassing two world wars and the Great Depression. A crisis of both capitalism and imperialism, it released immense popular energies, socialist and nationalist, which transformed the world. Although the world did not turn to socialism, as many astute observers expected, it certainly took a marked turn to the left with socialistic reforms in the capitalist world that enabled capitalism's post-war Long Boom, Communist party ruled societies building socialism from Prague to Pyongyang and newly independent Third World countries embarked on autonomous national development, often at least avowedly socialist.

Though the United States styled itself the leader of the capitalist part of this world, its power was constrained. It had, for instance, to tolerate nearly worldwide economic interventionism and promise to keep the dollar convertible into gold even though it succeeded in thwarting alternatives to it at Bretton Woods.

Notwithstanding the socialistic turn taken by the major capitalist countries, their underlying character remained capitalist and the inevitable crisis—one involving constrained demand and falling profitability leading to low investment—arrived in the 1970s as productive capacity expanded, particularly in the recovering economies, faster than demand. As these economies took market shares from the United States and the United Kingdom, and demanded gold instead of the devalued dollars the United States issued to cover its current account deficits, the dollar was put on the rocky road to the end of convertibility in 1971.

The 'Second Slump' of the 1970s led to much contestation and placed the capitalist world before a choice: deepen that socialistic reform to continue and improve on the broad-based growth of the previous decades or roll back the reform and set capital free of the regulation and social obligations placed on it after the Second World War on the flimsy grounds that they had led to the crisis and that removing them would set capitalism free to create growth and prosperity. Since the former option would have taken the capitalist world even closer to socialism, the latter option was the only one if capitalism was to survive. Thanks to the intellectual and political weakness of the left, and the availability of a virulently free market version of neoclassical economics kept alive by small bands of true believers, the capitalist world, led by the United States and the United Kingdom, took the latter, intellectually vacuous, option, now labelled neoliberalism. It could not end the Slump (chiefly because capitalism had long ago ceased to be the competitive capitalism of the neoliberal imagination and entered its monopoly phase) and did not, prolonging it into the still-unended Long Downturn instead. That is the subject of Chapter 4.

Rather than resolving the problems of profitability and demand that had led to the crisis, neoliberalism exacerbated them. It provided capital the easy choices of financial investment and state-sponsored opportunities for risk-free profits absolving it from the need to invest and exacerbating the demand problem by increasing inequality and maldistributing income. At the same time, even as the fullest exercise of imperial power—which imposed economic retardation on much of the developing world in the 1980s and 1990s—could not prevent additions to capacity abroad. The greatest of them was, of course, in China, and the neoliberal era witnessed the shift in the centre of gravity of the world economy away from the major, chiefly Western, capitalist countries, and towards China.

It was probably fitting that the turn to neoliberalism was led by the United Kingdom, losing competitiveness for well over a century by the 1980s, and the United States, which had also been losing competitiveness since the 1950s. Other major capitalist economies, particularly the industrial powerhouses of Germany and Japan, applied the policy prescription less fully or enthusiastically not least because they sought to preserve their productive advantages and, particularly as the United States began deregulating its financial sector, effectively transforming it into something resembling the United Kingdom's archaic predatory and speculative financial system to give the dollar a new financial foundation, contrasts between them and the more productive and industrial capitalisms, particularly Germany and Japan, re-emerged.

In the leading neoliberal economies, neither growth nor profitability recovered and, while production languished, finance grew meteorically, drawing investment away from production into speculation and serving as the basis of the dollar creditocracy that now supported the dollar's world role by attracting funds into dollar-denominated financial activity and asset bubbles, thus counteracting the downward pressure on the dollar created by US deficits. Not only did their inevitable crash make more and more countries' financial regulators wary of the system, supported by the Federal Reserve, its deregulation and its support for asset markets, which became systematic by the 2000s, over time, these asset bubbles or financialisations became the sole motors of economic growth.

The parlous condition in which neoliberalism left the major capitalist economies and their public health system, especially in the two neoliberal leaders, the United States and the United Kingdom, set the stage for their failures in the face of the pandemic, failures that formed such a contrast with the successes of China and other socialist economies. They began with the choice of strategy. Discarding the murderous strategy of 'herd immunity', the United States and the United Kingdom settled for the only slightly less murderous one of 'flattening the curve' so as to not overwhelm weakened public health systems. Even this far-from-effective strategy was further compromised by the decision to balance the saving of lives with 'saving livelihoods', essentially saving what they could of the neoliberal financialised economy, particularly its financialised and corporate commanding heights. This doubly compromised strategy inevitably led to heavy losses of both lives and livelihoods because the unsuppressed virus returned in waves, requiring economically devastating lockdowns and restrictions to be imposed repeatedly, exposing shocking levels of fragility and inequality. Meanwhile, China, focused on saving lives by employing time-tested methods, saved its economy too.

The monetary and fiscal responses—the former now expanding the 'monetary policy' toolkit to include bailouts for the non-financial corporations whose debt was critical to the asset base of the financial sector and the latter focused on aiding corporations over people even under Biden with his 'build back better' campaign slogan—have only deepened the rut in which these neoliberal economies have been for decades, with no signs of productive revival and even the return of inflation, exacerbated by the war, to testify to their weakness and posing the choice between allowing it to rip or engaging in recession- and financial crisis-inducing monetary tightening that can only weaken the productive economy further.

All this was already clear when the proxy war against Russia began in early 2022 and definitively buried hopes of 'building back better' that arose early in the pandemic. It now appears as if, at best, those hopes and discourses will only grace moves to engineer a shift to a new phase of neoliberalism. What it might be is the subject of Chapter 6. It tackles debates over whether the fiscal and monetary policy responses heralded the end of neoliberalism and argues that, while there is no evidence that neoliberalism's essence—not competitive markets but the preservation of the power of capital, in our time big corporate, financialised capital—has changed, what we are witnessing efforts to shift to a new phase of neoliberalism. There have been previous such shifts, about one a decade. There were early signs that it could take a 'pseudo-civic' form, involving the state being the customer-in-chief for corporate capital producing allegedly 'essential' goods and services allegedly 'efficiently' for the state to provide to citizens free or very cheap. There is no doubt that powerful capitalist forces, such as the ubiquitous Bill Gates, have precisely such a scenario in mind. What is not clear is whether it will triumph.

The opposition to this form of neoliberal capitalism, the option favoured by the neoliberal establishment backed by 'house-trained' capitalists that have come to dominate all established parties, comes not from any left force, which was on the intellectual backfoot throughout the pandemic and has been pushed back further by the war, but from a new breed of 'warlord' or 'lumpen' capitalists bankrolling political forces even further to the right, forces that Trump and Johnson have brought to prominence. They are quite capable of tilting the political balance in favour of an even more authoritarian scenario than pseudo-civic neoliberalism. The likelihood is underlined by the alliance between the far-right politics of Trump and Johnson with fascistic mobs domestically, by their ability to pull the establishment towards their politics, as Biden's replication of so many aspects of Trump's politics shows, and by neoliberal financialised capitalisms' alliance with openly neo-Nazi forces in Ukraine, complete with media and scholarly discourses whitewashing them as mere nationalists and dangerously revising twentieth century history.

While the future of neoliberal capitalism hangs in this balance between an establishment pseudo-civic neoliberalism and an insurgent hard right domestically, internationally, it hangs in the balance of power between the surprisingly small capitalist world revealed by the proxy war on Russia and the rest of the world to whom socialist China increasingly provides leadership. Chapter 7 deals with how and why the proxy war against Russia and the New Cold War on China can be expected to tip the balance further against capitalism. As the latest in a long line of US wars waged for its impossible imperial project and, by the new century, in increasingly desperate attempts to compel militarily the dominance it has failed to secure economically, the war against Russia is not just failing but proving counterproductive vis-à-vis its principal goals. It is not destroying but strengthening the Russian economy and its ties with a stable and growing China while leading to intolerable inflation in the major capitalist economies. It is not demonstrating the power of the dollar creditocracy but undermining its already challenged structures further. It is not defeating Russia militarily but ensuring the dismemberment of Ukraine. It is not strengthening its alliances but, by putting far too much strain on them, it is testing them to breaking point. While the world watches its shabby treatment of Ukraine, the US-led West can only lose credibility in the rest of the world. As neoliberal failures, domestically against the pandemic and internationally in the war, mount, socialist China's economic successes and, very likely, Russia's economic resilience and military successes can only accelerate the shift of the world's economic centre of gravity from the West towards China and from capitalism to socialism.

As it does so, the conduct of the left in the homelands of capitalism will be critical and the conclusion addresses that matter. It argues that the weakness of left forces there was revealed by the timidity of the major proposals for social change that have been produced in the crisis set off by the pandemic, whether it was the 'mission economy' of 'doing capitalism differently, or modern monetary theory or universal basic income. Having exposed their timidity, and their likely conscription to the project of effecting transition to a new phase of neoliberalism, the conclusion goes on to outline the political trajectory that has brought the Western left to this point, that of ever greater compromises with capitalism, including neoliberal capitalism, along paths traced by the original compromise with neoclassical economics. Sociologically, that trajectory is also marked by the takeover of the major parties, including the historic parties of the left, by a professional managerial class converted to neoliberalism where their counterparts in earlier eras had been to socialism and Marxism. The result has been a left politics that, regards capitalism as the pinnacle of productive success against the arguments of Marxism and the evidence of history, attributes the prosperity of the major capitalist powers to capitalism's productive vigour, not their imperialism, and refuses to contemplate how to organise production in socialist societies and how to do so against the inevitable opposition of imperialism's remaining bastions. Refusing both socialist planning and party organisation, this left is neither capable of leading a truly socialist politics in the homelands of imperialism nor building alliances with actually existing socialisms that are so necessary to advancing the class and national forces building socialism in our time.

However, like all crises of capitalism, this one too is throwing up new forces and mobilisations which are quite capable of shedding long histories and taking new directions. If this work contributes to that, in however small a part, I will have achieved my purpose.

References

Adams, Paul. 2022. 'Ukraine War: How Long Can the Western Consensus Hold?', *BBC News*, 2 June, (Accessed 19 June 2022) www.bbc.com/news/world-europe-61664991

Addison, Paul. 1982. 'British Society Since 1945', *History*, 67(221), pp. 541–2.

Alperovitz, Gar. 1998. 'Historians Reassess: Did We Need to Drop the Bomb?', in Bird, Kai and Lifschultz, Lawrence (eds), *Hiroshima's Shadow: Writings on the Denial of History and the Smithsonian Controversy*, pp. 5–21. Stony Creek: Pamphleteer's Press.

Anderson, Perry. 1964. 'Origins of the Present Crisis', *New Left Review*, I/23, January–February, pp. 26–53. https://newleftreview.org/issues/i23/articles/perry-anderson-origins-of-the-present-crisis

Barraclough, Geoffrey. 1964. *An Introduction to Contemporary History*. London: Penguin. https://doi.org/10.1086/239693.

Blakeley, Grace. 2020. *The Corona Crash: How the Pandemic Will Change Capitalism*. London: Verso Books.

Block, Fred. 1977. *The Origins of International Economic Disorder: A Study of United States International Monetary Policy from World War II to the Present*. Berkeley, CA: University of California Press.

Brenner, Robert. 1998. 'The Looming Crisis of World Capitalism: From Neoliberalism to Depression?', *Against the Current*, 13(5), p. 22.

Brenner, Robert. 2020. 'Escalating Plunder', *New Left Review*, (123), pp. 5–22. https://newleftreview.org/issues/ii123/articles/robert-brenner-escalating-plunder

Bukharin, Nikolai. 1914/1972. *The Economic Theory of the Leisure Class*. New York: Monthly Review Press.

Chang, Ha-Joon. 2002. *Kicking Away the Ladder: Development Strategy in Historical Perspective*. London: Anthem.

Clarke, Simon. 1991. *Marx, Marginalism and Modern Sociology: From Adam Smith to Max Weber*. 2nd ed. Basingstoke: Macmillan Academic and Professional.

Coates, David. 2000. *Models of Capitalism: Growth and Stagnation in the Modern Era*. New York: Polity.

Crouch, Colin. 2011. *The Strange Non-Death of Neoliberalism*. Oxford: Polity.

De Cecco, Marcello. 1984. *The International Gold Standard: Money and Empire*. 2nd ed. London: Pinter.

Desai, Radhika. 2011. 'The New Communists of the Commons: 21st Century Proudhonists', *International Critical Thought*, 1(2), pp. 204–23. https://doi.org/10.1080/21598282.2011.584163

Desai, Radhika. 2013. *Geopolitical Economy: After US Hegemony, Globalization and Empire*. London: Pluto.

Desai, Radhika. 2015. 'Look Back in Hope? Reassessing Fordism today', in Van der Pijl, Kees (ed), *The International Political Economy of Production*, pp. 192–210. Cheltenham: Edward Elgar. https://doi.org/10.4337/9781783470211.00023

Desai, Radhika. 2019. 'Remastering the Smothered Clash of Titans: Hayek and Polanyi in 1944', in Munro, John and Freeman, Kirrily (eds), *Reading the Postwar Future: Textual Turning Points From 1944*, pp. 17–42. London: Bloomsbury.

Desai, Radhika. 2020a. 'The Unexpected Reckoning: Coronavirus and Capitalism', *Canadian Dimension*, 17 March, (Accessed 19 June 2022) https://canadiandimension.com/articles/view/the-unexpected-reckoning-coronavirus-and-capitalism

Desai, Radhika. 2020b. 'South–South Cooperation', in Ness, I. and Cope, Z. (eds), *The Palgrave Encyclopedia of Imperialism and Anti-Imperialism*. London: Palgrave.

Desai, Radhika. 2021. 'Marx's Geopolitical Economy: "The Relations of Producing Nations"', *Capital & Class*, 46(1), pp. 3–10. https://doi.org/10.1177/03098168211017433

Desai, Radhika. 2022. 'The Long Shadow of Hiroshima: Capitalism and Nuclear Weapons', *International Critical Thought*, 8 April, p. 1–21. https://doi.org/10.1080/21598282.2022.2051582

Desai, Radhika; and Heller, Henry. 2019. 'Cold War', in Ness, Immanuel and Cope, Zak (eds), *The Palgrave Encyclopedia of Imperialism and Anti-Imperialism*. London: Palgrave Macmillan.

Desai, Radhika; and Hudson, Michael. 2021. 'Beyond the Dollar Creditocracy: A Geopolitical Economy', *Real World Economic Review*, p. 97. https://doi.org/10.13169/worlrevipoliecon.6.4.0449

Dore, Ronald. 2000. *Stock Market Capitalism Versus Welfare Capitalism*. Oxford: Oxford University Press.

Duménil, Gérard; and Lévy, Dominique. 2004. *Capital Resurgent: Roots of the Neoliberal Revolution*. Cambridge, MA: Harvard University Press.

Duong, Thanh. 2017. *Hegemonic Globalisation: U.S. Centrality and Global Strategy in the Emerging World Order.* Abingdon, UK: Routledge.

Dzarasov, Ruslan. 2013. *The Conundrum of Russian Capitalism: The Post-Soviet Economy in the World System.* London: Pluto Press.

Eatwell, Roger; and Goodwin, Matthew. 2018. *National Populism: The Revolt Against Liberal Democracy.* London: Penguin.

Engel-Di Mauro, Salvatore. 2021. *Socialist States and the Environment.* London: Pluto.

Ferguson, Niall. 2021. *Doom: The Politics of Catastrophe.* London: Penguin.

Fukuyama, Francis. 1992. *The End of History and the Last Man.* New York: Free Press.

Funakoshi, Minami; Lawson, Hugh; and Deka, Kannaki. 2022. 'Tracking Sanctions Against Russia', *Reuters*, 9 March, (Accessed 5 June 2022) https://graphics.reuters.com/UKRAINE-CRISIS/SANCTIONS/byvrjenzmve/

Gamble, Andrew. 1978. 'Free Economy Strong State', in Miliband, R. and Saville, J. (eds), *The Socialist Register.* London: Merlin.

Gamble, Andrew. 1994. *Britain in Decline: Economic Policy, Political Strategy and the British State.* 4th ed. London: Macmillan.

Gowan, Peter. 1999. *The Global Gamble: Washington's Faustian Bid for World Dominance.* London: Verso.

Hall, Peter; and Soskice, David. 2001. *Varieties of Capitalism: The Institutional Foundations of Comparative Advantage.* Oxford: Oxford University Press.

Hayek, Friedrich A. von. 1944. *The Road to Serfdom.* Chicago: University of Chicago Press.

Hilferding, Rudolf. 1910/1981. *Finance Capital: A Study of the Latest Phase of Capitalist Development.* London: Routledge & Kegan Paul.

Hobsbawm, Eric J. 1994. *Age of Extremes: The Short Twentieth Century, 1914–1991.* London: Michael Joseph.

Hutton, Will. 1995. *The State We're In.* London: Jonathan Cape.

Ingham, Geoffrey K. 1984. *Capitalism Divided?: The City and Industry in British Social Development.* Basingstoke: Macmillan.

Keynes, John Maynard. 1919/2004. 'The Economic Consequences of the Peace', in *The End of Laissez Faire and the Economic Consequences of the Peace.* New York: Prometheus Books.

Keynes, John Maynard. 1933. 'National Self-Sufficiency', *The Yale Review*, 22(4), pp. 755–69.

Keynes, John Maynard. 1936/1967. *General Theory of Employment, Interest and Money.* London: Macmillan.

Klein, Naomi. 2020. 'Coronavirus Capitalism: And How to Beat It', *The Intercept*, 16 March, (Accessed 19 June 2022) https://theintercept.com/2020/03/16/coronavirus-capitalism/

Kolko, Joyce; and Kolko, Gabriel. 1972. *The Limits of Power: The World and United States Foreign Policy, 1945–1954.* New York: Harper & Row.

Lapavitsas, Costas. 2013. *Profiting Without Producing: How Finance Exploits Us All.* London: Verso.

Lardner, Richard; Smith, Michelle R.; and Swenson, Ali. 2022. 'How American Right-Wing Funding for Canadian Trucker Protests Could Sway U.S. Politics', *PBS News Hour*, 17 February, (Accessed 19 June 2022) www.pbs.org/newshour/world/how-american-right-wing-funding-for-canadian-trucker-protests-could-sway-u-s-politics

Leonard, Christopher. 2022. *The Lords of Easy Money: How the Federal Reserve Broke the American Economy.* New York: Simon & Schuster.

Leng, Alyssa; and Rajah, Roland. 2019. 'Global Trade Through a US–China lens', Sydney: Lowy Institute. www.lowyinstitute.org/the-interpreter/chart-week-global-trade-through-us-china-lens

Lens, Sidney. 2003. *The Forging of the American Empire.* London: Pluto Press.

Leys, Colin. 1990. 'Still a Question of Hegemony', *New Left Review*, I/181.

Lyon, Peter. 2022. 'Japan Balances Sanctions on Russia Against Need for Gas and Oil', *Forbes*, 31 March, (Accessed 19 June 2022) www.forbes.com/sites/peterlyon/2022/03/31/japan-balances-sanctions-on-russian-against-need-for-gas-and-oil/?sh=53ec82954ce5

Marx, Karl. 1894/1981. *Capital* (Vol. 3). London: Penguin.

Mason, Paul. 2020. 'Will Coronavirus Signal the End of Capitalism?', *Aljazeera*, 3 April, (Accessed 19 June 2022) www.aljazeera.com/opinions/2020/4/3/will-coronavirus-signal-the-end-of-capitalism

Mayer, Arno J. 1981. *The Persistence of the Old Regime: Europe to the Great War*. New York: Pantheon Books.

Mazzucato, Mariana. 2020. 'The Covid-19 Crisis Is a Chance to Do Capitalism Differently', *The Guardian*, 18 March, (Accessed 19 June 2022) www.theguardian.com/commentisfree/2020/mar/18/the-covid-19-crisis-is-a-chance-to-do-capitalism-differently

Mudde, Cas; and Kaltwasser, Cristóbal R. 2017. *Populism: A Very Short Introduction*. Oxford: Oxford University Press.

Murphy, Katharine. 2021. 'Essential Poll: Majority of Australians Back Aukus Submarine Pact, But Fear It Will Inflame Tensions With China', *The Guardian*, 27 September, (Accessed 19 June 2022) www.theguardian.com/australia-news/2021/sep/28/essential-poll-majority-of-australians-back-aukus-submarine-pact-but-fear-it-will-inflame-tensions-with-china

O'Neill, Jim. 2001. 'Building Better Economic BRICs', *Global Economics Paper no. 66*. New York: Goldman Sachs.

Our World in Data. 'COVID-19 Vaccinations, Cases, Excess Mortality, and Much More'. https://ourworldindata.org/grapher/total-covid-cases-deaths-per-million?tab=table

Parrini, Carl P. 1969. *Heir to Empire: United States Economic Diplomacy, 1916–1923*. Pittsburgh: University of Pittsburgh Press.

Patnaik, Utsa; and Patnaik, Prabhat. 2016. *A Theory of Imperialism*. New York: Columbia University Press.

Piketty, Thomas. 2017. *Capital in the Twenty-First Century*. Cambridge, MA: Belknap Press.

Piketty, Thomas. 2020. *Capital and Ideology*. Cambridge, MA: Harvard University Press.

Polanyi, Karl. 1944/1985. *The Great Transformation*. New York: Farrar & Rinehart.

Polanyi, Karl. 1945. 'Universal Capitalism or Regional Planning?', *The London Quarterly of World Affairs*, 10(3), pp. 86–91.

Rodrik, Dani. 2017. 'Populism and the Economics of Globalization', *Faculty Research Working Paper Series*, Kennedy School of Government, Harvard University.

Streeck, Wolfgang. 2014. *Buying Time: The Delayed Crisis of Democratic Capitalism*. London & New York: Verso.

Streeck, Wolfgang. 2017. *How Will Capitalism End? Essays on a Failing System*. London: Verso.

Tooze, Adam. 2018. *Crashed: How a Decade of Financial Crises Changed the World*. New York: Penguin.

Tooze, Adam. 2021. *Shutdown: How Covid Shook the World's Economy*. New York: Penguin.

Trotsky, Leon. 1934. *The History of the Russian Revolution*. London: Gollancz.

Van der Pijl, Kees. 2006. *Global Rivalries From the Cold War to Iraq*. London: Pluto Press.

2

CAPITALISM AS CONTRADICTORY VALUE PRODUCTION

Understanding the complex crisis the pandemic and war have cast capitalism into, its diminished capacity for addressing it, the surrender of the left in its homelands and elsewhere and the challenge of actually existing socialisms require us to discard the deeply flawed roadmap to socialism still brandished by Western Marxism, the Western left and important parts of the left internationally and the misinterpretation of Marxism—the most important intellectual resource the international left has—on which it rests. This map places the possibility of socialism at some indeterminate point in the future where capitalism has developed the forces of production to the fullest, with many even claiming, or at least assuming, that capitalism can do so ceaselessly (for instance, Cohen 1983). However, today, capitalism's crises are proliferating and its productive debility becoming more and more glaring even as its environmental depredations grow. The roadmap also assumes that Western working classes and their political organisations will make the world's leading socialist revolution though they remain at a low ebb despite 40 years of neoliberal attacks on them. The roadmap dismisses actually existing socialist revolutions as premature and flawed at a time when, 30 years after the end of the Cold War, not only has the confrontation between capitalism and socialism re-emerged to divide the world, the world's leading socialism is the work of a society that started from an even lower level of economic development, initially at least, faced more intense imperialism, than the Soviet Union, and today poses a more existential challenge to capitalism in its senility. And finally, the roadmap considers imperialism unnecessary to capitalism just when stiffening resistance to it, led but not exhausted by socialisms, has prompted the imperialist world to react with heightened militarism, complete with New Cold Wars against China and Russia, sanctions against the socialist countries, Cuba, North Korea and Venezuela, and a range of other countries including Belarus, Iran and Syria and the proxy war on Russia.

DOI: 10.4324/9781003200000-2

This flawed roadmap may claim authority from Marx and Engels but emerges from the intersection of three problems that mar the proper understanding of their work. First, inevitably given the scale and ambition of what they sought to achieve, Marx and Engels's work remained incomplete. Only three of *Capital*'s many planned volumes were completed and published and Marx and Engels only managed to present some of the core essentials of their larger ground-breaking approach to the evolution of human society and its latest and most problematic form, capitalism. Many other analytical results were often published in journalistic writings or even remained unpublished notes. This problem can only be dealt with by careful and contextual reading of this corpus.

Second, as European working classes became more organised, the objective need for immediate gains through reforms that would cement workers' loyalty led to the rise of reformist currents in the working-class movement (Joll 1974). Reinforced by the structures of imperialism that permitted greater material concessions in the homelands of capitalism, this tendency also assimilated imperialist thinking into the culture of the Second International (Eley 2002) and narrowed Marxism (Colletti 1972). Only after the Russian Revolution did the Third International rectify this capitulation politically, if not theoretically, and absorbed the energetic input of the anti-colonial movement (Riddell 1993) into the consistently anti-imperialist legacy of Marxism–Leninism. However, despite considerable Soviet ideological influence in the West, the Second International's brand of socialism was consolidated as a pro-capitalist, anti-Communist and, crucially, pro-imperialist social democracy. This problem can only be rectified through political action. The narrowing of the possibilities of reform under neoliberalism and the sharpening of class conflict in the wake of pandemic and war make this rectification more urgent.

However, a key part of this rectification must be the undoing of the intellectual paths taken by the narrowing of Marxism towards reformism and compromise with imperialism. They are the third problem. The split in the international working-class movement and the narrowing of Marxism were accompanied by the 'Marxist economics' that has been so influential in Western Marxism and beyond. It buried under multiple layers of misinterpretation Marx and Engels's original understanding of capitalism as contradictory value production that ensnarls host societies and their international relations. Separating left forces from the most powerful and sophisticated understanding of capitalism we have the good fortune to inherit and must develop, these misinterpretations prevent us from understanding how capitalism's contradictions have driven its history forward through multiple crises to its present debility and how its initially vigorous imperialist expansion was stalled and, from the early twentieth century onwards, even rolled back by socialist and nationalist challenges. In short, the misinterpretations prevent us from understanding how the struggles of nations as well as classes have shaped capitalism's historical political and geopolitical economy, and how, for over a century, socialist nations have played a prominent part in it. This can be rectified through intellectual critique.

That is what this chapter provides. Given the central role Marxist economics has played in these misinterpretations, we focus our critique on it. Marxist economics emerged from the unexpected turn taken by the encounter between Marxism and neoclassical economics. The latter had emerged to displace classical political economy because it was providing an increasingly assertive working class with powerful intellectual weapons, a tendency that was poised to strengthen as Marx and Engels brought that tradition of classical political economy to a critical culmination and the first volume of *Capital* was published in 1867. As if on cue, neoclassical economics emerged circa 1870 to displace and dismiss these bodies of thought.

Instead of resisting and contesting neoclassical economics, as one might have expected, most Marxists followed what Bukharin called a 'policy of theoretical reconciliation' (1914/1972, 163) with it, seeking to fit Marxism into its alien and opposed framework. The result was 'Marxist economics' and today it leads most Western Marxist scholarship to reject Marx's value analysis, deny the contradictions that have today led to capitalism's productive debility, question the 'necessity' of imperialism to capitalism, dismiss actually existing socialisms as premature attempts that have led to 'authoritarianism' and discount the objective force of reformism in capitalism's homelands. Today, it is more urgent than ever to recognise this and recover Marx and Engels's original analysis of capitalism. Doing this also enables us to put Marx and Engels in their rightful place as the link between classical political economy and later critics of neoclassical economics as well as capitalism, such as Keynes or Polanyi, strengthening our ability to understand how the critique of capitalism has developed since Marx and Engels and how well their analysis has stood the test of time.

We begin by outlining how Marx and Engels resolved classical political economy's major conundrums to produce their penetrating analysis, and indictment, of capitalism as the contradictory, and thus crisis-prone, production of value at the intersection of the vertical, inter-class, axis of exploitation and the horizontal intra-class axis of competition. We go on to show how the neoclassical economics emerged, how fundamentally it was opposed to Marxism and how later Marxists who sought reconciliation with it produced 'Marxist economics'. After outlining its chief distortions, we return to Marx and Engels's real understanding of capitalism as contradictory value production to understand it as constituting not an 'economy', separate from state and society, harmonious and eternal, but as a contradictory dynamic that must deform society, impose contradictory demands on it in all the realms it must modify to secure its existence. We must also understnad, how the state must manage these contradictions to ensure capitalism's continued existence and how that management makes capitalism as value production itself historical. The chapter concludes with a discussion of the variety of capitalism's contradictions, which take horizontal and vertical forms in the core realms of value production, the production of commodities embodying value and the realisation of that value in money through sale in the market, and in the wider realms that must be adapted to secure capitalism's unnatural existence: money, finance, environment, state and international. We outline the first three in this chapter, leaving the discussion of contradictions plaguing the all-important state and inter-state realms for the next chapter so it may provide the theoretical basis for the understanding of geopolitical economy of capitalism and socialism.

We do note here that, given their responsibility for managing the myriad contradictions of capitalism, within and beyond value production, and the limits of their ability to do so, no state has been able to reduce society to pure value production: not only do other social structures and even forms of production—state, voluntary, family (Elson 2000)—necessarily co-exist with capitalist accumulation, they are often critical resources for managing the contradictions of value production. So, individuals, society or the entire world is never fully adapted to capitalism and can never be (Rosa Luxemburg had a point). Moreover, states' means and options for managing crises are limited. So, in the end, while capitalism's actual history is driven forward by states managing capitalism's contradictions by acting domestically to mediate among classes and internationally, to impose or oppose imperialism, each phase can only be temporary and compound capitalism's contradictions. This understanding provides the theoretical ground for the historical account of capitalism in the next two chapters.

Marx's critical political economy

Marxism emerged from a critique of classical political economy, which is best understood as the effort to understand the emerging capitalism as a novel social form, drawing attention to promises of rising prosperity as well as to threats like the misery it created alongside wealth, the regular crisis-inducing gluts of goods and the tendency of falling profit rates. At least up to Ricardo in the early nineteenth century, the enterprise remained an honest one despite its bourgeois bearings as Marx emphasised (Marx 1867/1977, 95–6, 174–5n), making honest observations and posing honest questions, even if it did not answer many cogently.

Armed with the Hegelian ability to think dialectically—of the totality and its contradictions—Marx resolved key questions classical political economy correctly raised but proved unable to answer. What was value? Where did surplus value originate from? And if, as political economists since Adam Smith if not earlier believed, only labour produced value, why, as production progressed to more efficient forms, did it not only employ ever more capital than labour but also permitted capitalists that employed proportionately more capital to make a higher rate of profit, that is, accumulate value at a higher rate even with the same absolute investment outlay? How did values correspond to prices in this case? Smith simply abandoned the effort to untangle these interrelated knots and Ricardo's unrelenting efforts proved fruitless (Desai 2018; Dobb 1963; Meek 1956).

Marx resolved these questions by understanding capitalism in its contradictory totality as a drive to produce not the variety of products and services human societies needed, but value and, moreover, to accumulate it, rather than to satisfy society's needs. Value was capitalism's defining abstraction, not a 'mental' but a 'real' one (Colletti 1972, 82–92). Just as the objective force of gravity regulated the physical world, the value that capitalists sought to accumulate was the unseen regulator of capitalism, the set of contradictory social structures the production of value required. The essence of value was socially necessary labour, the minimum of labour that *must* be expended on producing a given commodity at current levels of technology, skill and socially acceptable pace and pattern of work in quantities corresponding to levels of effective demand. It had to be distilled into money through the sale of such commodities and money was also the form in which it was accumulated. Structured thus, capitalism vastly raised surplus, appropriated and accumulated, compared to any previous society.

Value production and its two axes

Value is produced at the intersection of two axes as depicted in Figure 2.1. The vertical one involving the employment and exploitation of labour by capital and the class struggle between them is the one along which capital extracts surplus value from labour. The horizontal one involves competitive relations among capitalists works to depress prices to their value, that is, to the socially necessary labour commodities emnody. Together they enable value production and appropriation.

On the vertical axis, capitalism requires human labour power itself to become abstract—abstracted from any connection to its livelihood and rendered interchangeable with the labour of others. This is achieved through political processes such as its eviction from the land to 'free it', through legislation that enables its purchase and sale and through its degradation through deskilling to make the great diversity of the labour capacity of individuals mutually replaceable, distinguishable only by labour's duration at least at each skill level. Ultimately impossible, such abstraction of labour must succeed sufficiently to give abstract labour a semblance of reality.

Abstract labour forms the foundation of the second abstraction: If labour under capitalism is *ideally* distinguished only by its duration, the products of labour under capitalism are *ideally* distinguished not through the infinite variety of their physical or useful attributes but by the amount of socially necessary labour they embody. Along the horizontal axis, competition among capitalists in markets pushes the prices of the products of abstract labour they sell towards their value, the price below which even the most cost-effective producer cannot afford to sell. A tendency, not a law, it is rare for prices to reach the end-state where they match the relevant values.

Under the whip of competition, which gives capitalist production its anarchic character, capitalists must organise production, and make investments, to keep costs down to the socially necessary level. Those who fail to do so take losses by making less profit and potentially even facing bankruptcy, since other producers bring goods to market at lower prices, thanks to their investment and resulting efficiency gains. Competition therefore also acts to direct capital from less to more profitable activities producing tendencies towards equalisation of profit rates.

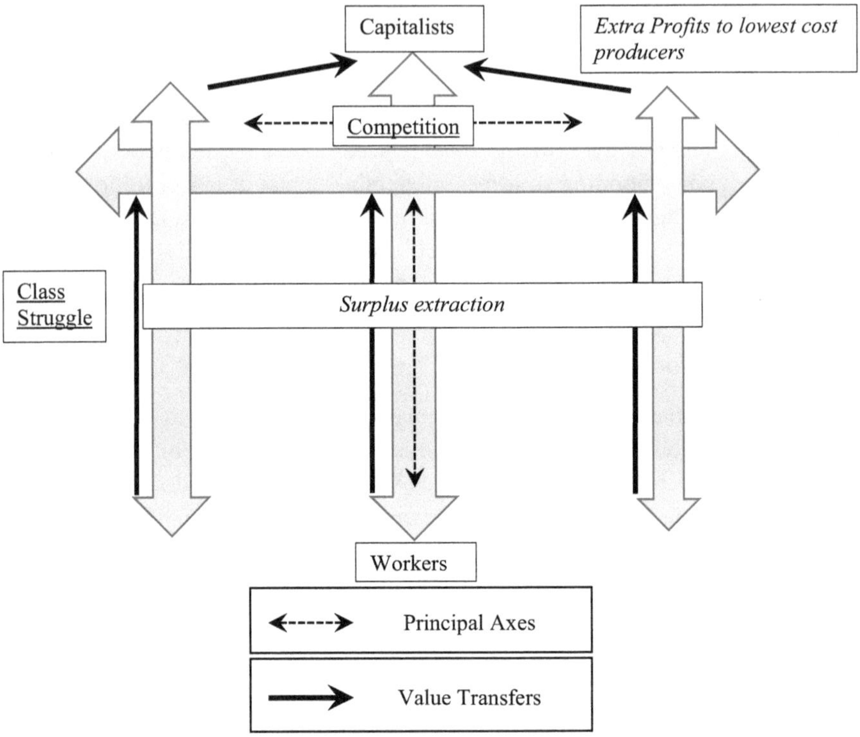

FIGURE 2.1 Value production and its two axes.

Source: Created by author.

So much for value. What about surplus value? Capitalists accumulate abstract value, that is, they get more value than they invested, simply because commodified labour power produces more value than its own worth or price. Even when capitalists purchase labour power at its value (rather than below it, as they would prefer), when they put it to work, it produces an excess that capitalists appropriate. To put it another way, capitalists would not purchase labour unless this was true. This appropriation gives value production its unjust and exploitative character. It also contains a contradiction, possibly the most fundamental one.

Since, unlike working people who tend to spend all they earn, capitalists cannot be relied on to spend all they earn whether on their lavish lifestyles or on investment, capitalism is always haunted by the ever-present possibility of gluts, crises of overproduction or underconsumption, where goods brought to market remain unsold because there is not enough demand for it. For Marx, the 'poverty and restricted consumption of the masses' in which this problem of insufficient demand is rooted is also the 'ultimate reason for all real crises' (Marx 1894/1981, 615).

Finally, the surplus thus accumulated by capitalists is distributed among them through two distinct processes. First, competition ensures that the most efficient producers, usually those with proportionately higher investment in capital than labour, tend to make a higher rate of profit as long as their costs are lower than the ones still prevailing in the market and thus take a disproportionate share of total profits at the expense of less efficient producers. While this same competition creates incentives, even imperatives, for the less efficient capitalists to up their game by making similar efficiency-enhancing investments and leads, in the long run, to a tendency towards the equalisation of profit rates, it was only a tendency. At any given time, profits are unequally distributed among capitalists. Second, financial capitalists and landowners struggle with productive capitalists for a share of the latter's profits as interest and rent.

Socialising labour and developing the productive forces

The drive to raise efficiency and cut costs leads to the increasing socialisation of labour, involving more and more workers and machines into ever more intricate organisation of production. Marx, relying on Adam Smith's early insights on the productivity enhancing character of increasing division of labour, considered the socialisation of labour to be the foundation on which capitalism led to the development of humanity's productive powers, in the words of the famous 1859 Preface (Marx 1859/1977), to the development of the forces of production. Marx saw this as occurring in two forms (Marx 1867/1977, 492–639), which were also two phases. In the early period of capitalism, labour is socialised *between* firms and producers, as each specialises in the production of a product or a segment of the production process of another product. As capitalism develops and the processes of competition, aided by the efficiency gains of increasing scale and scope of production, lead to monopoly, production comes to be socialised *within* firms, whose size grows to often gigantic proportions, turning into vast apparatuses of planned production that form the pinnacle of the development of the 'productive forces [that] slumbered in the lap of social labour' (Marx and Engels 1848/1967, 85).

These processes of competition along the horizontal axis of value production also contain a critical contradiction: the imperative to accumulate ever more capital, and thus to invest ever more capital to increase efficiency—whether to enjoy the temporary advantage of higher profit rates or to stave off losses and bankruptcy—leads to a long-term tendency, counteracted to be sure by a range of countertendencies (Marx 1894/1981, 339–48), for the rate of profit to fall (TRPF) even as it increases the productive capacities of socialised labour. Over time the TRPF can reduce capitalists' motivation to invest, reducing growth and the expansion of capitalism. More generally, it implies a '*memento mori* [sign of mortality] . . . for capitalism in a secular perspective' (Mandel 1981, 51) and, we might add, a sign also of the natality of socialism. Keynes had his own version of the TRPF: the diminishing marginal efficiency of capital, which was also similarly progressive, leading away from capitalism towards a more rational society unburdened by punishing levels of labour (Keynes 1930/1963).

In Marx's view, this contradictory capitalism was historically progressive because it developed the forces of production by advancing the socialisation of labour, even if it did so on the basis of exploitation and competition, brutally and chaotically, unjustly and anarchically. How this laid the foundation for socialism we glimpse most clearly in chapter 27 of *Capital* Vol. III. Marx had seen in the ever-greater concentration of capital in large monopoly firms, facilitated by the emergence of joint-stock companies, as a huge advance in the socialisation of production. In this new type of firm, what was once individual, capital

> now receives the form of social capital (capital of directly associated individuals) in contrast to private capital, and its enterprises appear as social enterprises as opposed to private ones. This is the *abolition of capital and private property within the confines of the capitalist mode of production itself.*
>
> *(Marx 1894/1981, 567, emphasis added)*

The transition to monopoly, aided by state intervention and credit is, Marx continues, 'a self-abolishing contradiction, which presents itself *prima facie* as a mere point of transition to a new form of production' (Marx 1894/1981, 569), namely socialism.

As production is thus amalgamated and massified, its profoundly social character is on full display. The owner-operator capitalist of early capitalism is split functionally into two: the manager, paid for his/her labour of oversight of a complex organisation, and the 'mere money capitalist' who no longer makes profit but only interest, 'a mere reward for capital ownership which is now completely separated from its function in the actual production process' (Marx 1894/1981, 567–8). The result is a historical, rather than merely conceptual, clarification: profit reduced to interest is exposed as

> simply the appropriation of other people's surplus labour, arising from the transformation of means of production into capital; i.e. from their estrangement vis-à-vis the actual producer; from their opposition, as the property of another, vis-à-vis all individuals really active in production from the manager down to the lowest day-labourer.
>
> *(Marx 1894/1981, 568)*

Such 'capitalist production in its highest development' is a

> necessary point of transition towards the transformation of capital back into the property of the producers, though no longer as the private property of individual producers but rather as *their property as associated producers*, as directly social property. It is furthermore a point of transition towards the *transformation of all functions formerly bound up with capital ownership* in the reproduction process into simple functions of the associated producers, *into social functions.*
>
> *(Marx 1894/1981, 568, emphasis added)*

Engels observes editorially at this point that tendencies towards cartelisation and towards concentrating 'the entire production of the branch of industry in question into *one* big joint-stock company with a unified management' prepares 'in the most pleasing fashion its future expropriation by society as a whole, by the nation' (Engels's note in Marx 1894/1981, 569), a development likely to be aided by the fact that this transformation also 'gives rise to monopoly in certain spheres and hence provokes state intervention' (Marx 1894/1981, 569).

The credit system, which is everywhere a creature of state regulation, greatly aids these processes.

> It reproduces a new financial aristocracy, a new kind of parasite in the guise of company promoters, speculators and merely nominal directors; an entire system of swindling and cheating with respect to the promotion of companies, issue of shares and share dealings. It is private production unchecked by private ownership.
>
> *(Marx 1894/1981, 569)*

The realities of capitalism are exposed: saving can no longer pose as the origin of capitalism when the speculator demands that '*others* should save for him'; abstinence goes by the wayside when luxury 'becomes a means of credit' (Marx 1894/1981, 570). Capitalism, which begins in expropriation, comes full circle when expropriation of small and medium and even some large enterprises by the giant ones, greatly aided by the credit system, lays the foundation of the expropriation of the few remaining owners.

The credit system not only accelerates capitalist development, but it also accelerates crises and the dissolution of capitalism itself. In doing so, it moves capitalism closer to socialism:

> The credit system has a dual character immanent in it: on the one hand it develops the motive of capitalist production, enrichment by the exploitation of others' labour, into the purest and most colossal system of gambling and swindling, and restricts ever more the already small number of exploiters of social wealth; on the other hand however, *it constitutes the form of transition towards a new mode of production.* It is this dual character that gives the principal spokesmen for credit, from Law through Isaac Péreire, *their nicely mixed character of swindler and prophet.*
>
> *(Marx 1894/1981, 572–3, emphasis added)*

This is how capitalism—value production that is unjust and anarchical, exploitative and competitive and prone to crises on both its principal axes - lays down, as surely as it does so inadvertently, the foundation for socialism. This emerges from Marx's resolution of the problems of classical political economy in *Capital.*

Enter neoclassical economics

The first of *Capital's* many planned volumes was published in 1867. If such a radical understanding was not already dangerous in itself, the expansion and increasing organisation of working classes in late nineteenth-century Europe made it more so. Indeed, even before Marx and Engels's intervention, the honest investigations of classical political economy already provided these movements with much intellectual ammunition: though stockbroker, MP and political economist, David Ricardo, celebrated capitalism, his conviction that only labour produced value inspired Ricardian socialism (Hunt 1980), such as Hodgkin's, which John Stuart Mill warned was 'subversive of civilised society' (Dobb 1973, 98).

Indeed, alongside classical political economy, capitalism had always needed the supplement of what Marx called 'vulgar economy'. Concerned less with truth than with whether a statement was 'useful to capital or harmful', it was the work not of 'disinterested inquirers' but 'hired prize-fighters'. Its Panglossian thinking aimed to legitimise capitalism. With the publication of *Capital*, this never-very-satisfactory arrangement became positively dangerous. The justification of capitalism could no longer be left to these flimsy efforts. New discourses legitimising capitalism as fulsomely and one-sidedly but with greater authority were needed and they appeared. Around 1870, the work of three unconnected scholars—the English Stanley Jevons, the Swiss Leon Walras and the Austrian Carl Menger—founded neoclassical economics. Little more than vulgar economy given pretentious theoretical elaboration—nearly every criticism Marx aimed at vulgar economy, particularly in his section on 'the fetish character of commodities' and in his critique of Proudhon, applies to them (Marx 1867/1977, 163–77, 1847), neoclassical economics constituted a momentous break.

Just how momentous is seldom understood. On the rare occasions that departments of economics teach their discipline's history, they elide and erase just how radically neoclassical economics broke from classical political economy and Marx's resolution of its conundrums. Instead, they present the history of economics as if it were a single tradition going back to the eighteenth century and earlier.

Most fundamentally, neoclassical economics simply repudiated classical political economy's conviction that capitalism was defined by contradictory value production, erasing its historical specificity. Instead, it conceived capitalism as a 'system of provision for human needs' (Clarke 1991, 9) through commodity production, which, or the funactional equivalent of which, had always existed. Naturalising markets and commodity production as spontaneous and eternal forms of human social organisation, distorted only by political intervention, it provided ideological cover for capitalism, the one form of social production that was the farthest thing in human history from a system for provisioning human needs. Ironically, the same quality made neoclassical economics better suited to designing welfare systems and planned economies (Meek 1977; Blackburn 1991). Indeed, it was through its brushes with the socialist calculation debate that Austrian economics, the neoclassical school most resolutely committed to capitalism, dispensed with any claims about equilibrium, fearing that

> on the one hand, the postulate of perfect competition could well lead to reflection on the gap between ideal and reality, with critical consequences for actual market processes; on the other, the assumption of perfect knowledge

> might on the same grounds prompt an interest in central planning, as a more logical embodiment of it than in decentralized markets.
>
> *(Anderson 1992b, 275–6)*

Neoclassical economics naturalised markets. By assuming that everything that was bought and sold, including land, labour and money, was a commodity, it spurned the attention classical political economy had given to the political processes that commodified the latter three and, given that they were not produced for sale, the special laws that governed their prices. By naturalising the commodification of labour in particular, they erased exploitation and therefore also demand deficits and gluts, overproduction and underconsumption. Indeed, their assumption that markets miraculously coordinated the actions of millions of individuals harmoniously despite lacking central coordination brushed aside any notion of capitalism's contradictions arising from anarchic competition.

While classical political economy analysed capitalist society as a historically evolving social whole composed of antagonistic classes, neoclassical economics detached the system for provisioning human needs as a separate self-regulating sphere, 'the economy' composed of individuals (or households) and firms. Max Weber would soon justify this separation, arguing that modernity itself separated different spheres of social action from one another and each needed separate study, giving rise to a wider social scientific division of labour between various disciplines studying separate spheres of society around the core of neoclassical economics. This was not politically innocent. Weber, originally trained as an economist who had sided with neoclassical economics against German historicism in the *Methodenstreit*, was concerned above all with the autonomy of the economy. It had an 'especially privileged position'. Its structures were 'the supra-historical manifestations of reason and so the universal foundations of a society characterised by its formal rationality, capitalism' (Clarke 1991, 267). The workings of this privileged sphere were to be left alone, protected from political interference, particularly any working classes clamouring for its reform.

The intellectual cost of this politically motivated separation of the social sciences is noted, if at all, only in laments about separation of the social sciences that conjure with 'inter-' and 'multi-disciplinarity'. However, the far greater blow neoclassical economics dealt—its negation of the value of history and the history of value (Desai 2016)—is rarely commented on.

If neoclassical economics erased capitalism's historical specificity as a mode of production, it also erased the historical character of capitalism in a second sense, by erasing the contradictions that made it volatile and unstable, drove its historical dynamic, hurtling it to its doom. Blind to the very notion of contradictions, neo classical economics subscribed to assumptions of equilibrium or market perfection. Denying historical change, as neoclassical economics and with it the social sciences generally do (as betrayed in the pervasive use of the simple present tense in them—parties do this, or unemployment does that, as if things never change), they can understand neither capitalism nor its historical dynamic towards socialism.

Rejecting the classical focus on production, neoclassical economics focused primarily on exchange. In it, the 'utility' of commodities, a fictional measure of the subjective satisfaction individuals drew from commodities, determined demand while the disutility of work and production constrained supply. Prices were formed by their interaction. The theoretical showpiece of neoclassical economics, this theory of prices is presented as a vast improvement over the classical and Marxist focus on costs of production. However, not only did Marx never neglect exchange, which was central to his conception of value, he provided a superior analysis of supply and demand (Lysandrou 2000; Kristjansen-Gural 2017a; Kristjansen-Gural 2017b). Moreover, in his understanding, the price fluctuations they cause aid in the operation of the law of value, with rising demand and prices, for instance, calling forth a supply response that put pressure on prices to return to values, while rarely reaching them. If neoclassical price theory was already not adequate for competitive markets, it was even less so for the monopoly phase capital had already entered when neoclassical economics arose and developed. Its administered prices had, if anything, rendered their conception of exclusively market determined prices even less relevant, as the institutionalists pointed out at the time. (See Jo 2016 for a comprehensive discussion on the theoretical ramifications of this fundamental mistake.)

Neoclassical economics reached over Marx to Ricardo—not the Ricardo who insisted on the labour origin of value but the Ricardo who accepted Say's Law that there was no demand deficit in markets (Desai 2016) and conjured up his theory of comparative advantage. Accepting Say's Law meant that neoclassical economics denied capitalism's most fundamental contradiction and tendency towards crises, whether in Walrasian notions of equilibrium or in the sterner Austrian insistence that capitalism's outcomes, however bad one may consider them, could not be bettered. Equally importantly, as both Marx and Keynes pointed out, neoclassical economics conceived exchange as barter, leaving out any consideration of the independent role of money in capitalist society (Sardoni 1997).

With Say's Law went comparative advantage. Ricardo may have devised it only 'to support his *theory of value* or to demonstrate that his views on foreign trade are not foreign to it' (Marx 1972, 253), but it became very influential. In claiming that free trade benefitted all nations, it justified colonial patterns of trade (Patnaik 2005), papering over international tensions caused by powerful capitalist countries seeking to externalise the consequences of capitalist contradictions, for example by exporting their excess production to colonial or otherwise unprotected markets and undermining prospects for industrial development there. Between them, Say's Law and comparative advantage denied the essential link between capitalism's contradictions and its expansionism or imperialism. (For an alternative interpretation of Marx, see Desai 2013, 2012, 2021; and for Karl Polanyi's astonishingly similar ideas, see Polanyi 1944, 201–13; Desai 2020a.) The result was a Schumpeterian rather than a Marxist conception of capitalism, capable of 'innovatively' expanding the forces of production incessantly.

Neoclassical economics justified capitalism in the name of free markets and competition precisely when capitalism was coming to the end of its early competitive phase and entering the age of monopoly. This forced neoclassical economists into intellectual contortions. Take Friedrich Hayek: on the one hand, his *The Road to Serfdom* had to shift the argument away from the principle of 'laissez faire' to that of 'planning for competition' on the model of early twentieth-century US Anti-Trust Law, which sought to preserve a modicum of competition in an age of monopoly by breaking up monopolies. On the other, Hayek intuited (rightly as we shall see later) that this was already conceding too much if the justification of capitalism was the aim. So, he also argued that monopoly was not inevitable, hanging on to shreds of evidence produced by the Temporary National Economic Committee of the US Congress when monopoly was robustly in evidence all around and claimed that competition made markets produce the right price signals in a complex economy when monopoly was doing the opposite. He also had to concede that, in the short run at least, optimal use of technology may require the suppression of competition (Hayek 1944, 32–9).

Policy of theoretical reconciliation produces 'Marxist economics'

If this was all, Marxism would have provided those oppressed by capitalism with their theoretical weapons, including a thoroughgoing critique of neoclassical economics, which would have armed their oppressors. However, it wasn't. As more and more intellectuals came to Marxism already schooled in neoclassical economics, rather than fighting their intellectual formation, most of them followed 'a policy of theoretical reconciliation', as Nikolai Bukharin, one of the few who opposed this tendency quite consistently, called it (Bukharin 1914/1972, see also Hilferding 1949). The result was the establishment of a 'Marxist economics' (Desai 2010, 2016, 2017, 2020b).

To be sure, Marxist economics is critical of many aspects of neoclassical economics—for instance, its exclusive focus on exchange at the expense of production or its neglect of exploitation. However, its (vain) effort to fit Marxism into the methodologically and theoretically antithetical neoclassical economics is the source of enormous problems. Most fundamentally, as strangers to Marx and Engels's philosophical frame of totality and contradiction, their social and historical approach and to the very notion of value as a real, objective abstraction (as opposed to a mental one, see Colletti 1972, 82–92), it never appreciated just how opposed the two traditions were.

Most fundamentally, Marxist economics accepted the separation of 'the economy' from the rest of society and of 'economics' from the study of other social spheres (Colletti 1972, 64–6, 76–82). Unable to understand value, able to operate only in the realm of neoclassical prices or some pre-Marxist, chiefly Ricardian, conception of 'labour values' distinct from prices, they ended up accusing Marx's analysis of suffering from a 'transformation problem', of being unable to 'transform' values into prices in a way that was consistent with both the labour origin of value and what they wrongly assumed to be a law of equal profit rates. Concretely, they asked, when two capitals of equal value were divided between outlays in labour and capital in unequal proportions, with one spending proportionately more on labour than the other, they would necessarily yield commodities that sold for more or less than the value they embodied and led to unequal rates of profit. In reality, this problem was Ricardo's and Marx resolved it (Desai 2019).

Instead of assuming a uniform rate of profit, Ricardo should have asked 'how far its existence is in any way consistent with the determination of value by labour time' (Marx 1951, 212). Had he done so, 'he would have found that instead of being consistent with it, *prima facie*, it contradicts it, and its existence has therefore to be explained through a number of intermediary stages' (Marx 1951, 212). The first of those was that value and price are not always identical in magnitude—'The possibility . . . of a quantitative incongruity between price and magnitude of value . . . is inherent in the price-form itself' (Marx 1867/1977, 196)—though they consist of the same substance, socially necessary labour. Second, Ricardo did not grasp that the equalisation of profit rates was rarely, if ever, an accomplished fact but a dynamic and chaotic *process* in which profit rates tended to be, but rarely were, equalised. It was a process of 'the leveling out of different rates of surplus value in different commodities produced by equal capitals' (Marx 1968, 198–9) as capital left sectors yielding low surplus value for those yielding higher surplus value. The latter, once capitalist development has reached a certain stage, are those with higher levels of investment in the means of production relative to labour. Such processes take time; over this time, the values of various commodities routinely diverge from their prices as the most competitive producers are able to produce at lower values but are still able to charge the prevailing higher prices. These higher prices yielded the higher profit rates Marx termed surplus profit (Mandel 1974). It becomes the operational mechanism driving investment and hence rising productivity.

Surplus profit ensures that rates of profit diverge from each other until enough capital enters the sector with higher profits to sharpen competition there and depress prices of products to their values and profits to their average rates. Marx would argue that Ricardo almost understood all this (Marx 1968, 197–8) but not well enough to proceed further in his analysis. That it is Marxist economists' training in neoclassical economics that is the principal obstacle to their understanding all this is underlined by Ferdinand Tönnies' brief and perfectly lucid defence of Marx against these accusations of his own followers (1887/1957, 101).

Thanks to the neoclassical assumption of a separate economic sphere capable of functioning harmoniously, Marxist economics was also deeply resistant to the idea of contradiction and crises, insisting on the one hand that that Marx did not believe capitalism suffered from deficits of demand and that that he was wrong to think that the rate of profit tended to fall in the long run (for further elaboration and refutation of these claims, see Desai 2010, 2016, 2017, 2020b).

Most of what passes for Marxist economics is preoccupied with mostly fruitless debates over these essentially false claims. They also limit the contribution Marxist economics can make in understanding the current condition of capitalism and informing the struggle for socialism.

Of course, not all Marxists in the West accepted this conception of capitalism. Ernest Mandel, a rare Western Marxist linked to the revolutionary working class, used the label of Marxist economics to describe his work but did not make the mistakes delineated here. As his introductions to the three volumes of *Capital* attest (Mandel 1977, 1987, 1981), he rejected and contested all the main claims at issue—the 'transformation problem', the dismissal of demand problems and the TRPF. Along with Alan Freeman, he particularly contributed to the effort to expose the nullity of the so-called transformation problem (Mandel and Freeman 1984). One major result was the Temporal Single System Interpretation (TSSI) of Marx's analysis (Freeman and Carchedi 1996, Kliman 2007), which demonstrates that, provided prices and values are seen to constitute a single system and input and output prices as being determined not simultaneously but separated in time, there is no transformation problem. Long ignored, TSSI began gathering momentum, helping all those who were captured in the maze of confusion created by Marxist economics. However, it is even more important to insist that Marx can and should be read without its distortions.

The damage to be undone is wider still. Various 'Marxist' social sciences have proliferated around Marxist economics—whether Marxist sociology or Marxist geography or Marxist international relations and their utility is limited by their acceptance of Marxist economics' distorting claims about the capitalist 'economy', which seeps into their treatment of their respective subjects separated from the rest of society and devoid of history (Desai 2016, 2017), blithely ignoring Marx's holistic and historical approach centered on the totality of capitalist society and its multiple contradictions.

Not only do most Western Marxists thus misunderstand capitalism's core mechanisms of value production, realisation, accumulation and distribution, they hardly give any thought to its imbrication in society and history.

Capitalism in society and history

Even if *Capital* may be seen to have focused on the core mechanisms of value production, realisation, accumulation and distribution, it did so primarily but not exclusively. There is no indication anywhere in Marx and Engels's corpus either that they reduced capitalism to these mechanisms or that they assumed that they could exist independently, without supporting social structures. Bourgeois revolutions have been necessary to transform pre-capitalist state and social structures so they may support these mechanisms. However, not only is no revolution, no matter how thoroughgoing, capable of reducing social structures to those of value production, the advance of capitalism also fails to create such a society, if only because its contradictions mount, requiring ever more social and political adjustment and management, particularly if capitalism's human costs are to be kept sufficiently low to prevent revolution, this time socialist.

Not only did Marx and Engels call, in the 1848 *Communist Manifesto* (1848/1967), on the nascent working classes to smother capitalism in its European cradle, well before it could dominate more societies and generations, but in 1895 Engels also explained to Conrad Schmidt (Engels 1890/1968) that there was no purely capitalist society and it was the duty of revolutionaries to ensure it did not get to that. For her part, Rosa Luxemburg (1913/1951; see also Patnaik and Patnaik 2017) intuited, in a different context, that if it did, it would have nothing more to stabilise it. Finally, Karl Polanyi understood and expressed this in terms of the greater or lesser 'embedding' of markets in society (Polanyi 1944/1985; Thomasberger 2020). In capitalist societies, while much material production is dominated by the mechanisms of value production, a great deal—state, family or voluntary (Elson 2000)—remains outside them, as does a vast array of its institutions, even if the contradictions of value production ensnarl them into a tumultuous history and an equally turbulent imperialist geography.

The historical specificity of capital

A major obstacle in the way of a wider appreciation of this is the general assumption that Marx had a 'stagist' and 'economistic' view of history. A closer look at the record yields surprising results. The idea of economic stages of history is one that Marx *inherited* from classical political economy and transformed into a far richer and nuanced view.

The development of capitalism in Europe, combined with its encounter with other, less developed societies (particularly the native American), led many Enlightenment thinkers to propose theories of distinct stages of history. Smith's Hunting, Pastoral, Agricultural and Commercial stages were typical and, as Ronald Meek argued, political economy '*arose out of*' such stagist views as these thinkers then turned to 'making a sustained economic analysis' of the highest stage (Meek 1976, 219). This stagism was, moreover, resolutely materialist. The stages were defined in terms of productive systems and some, like John Millar, not only proposed that they determined the form of the rest of society and were 'productive of suitable variations in taste and sentiments', he considered such material determination the 'master-principle' that penetrated 'beneath that common surface of events which occupies the details of the vulgar historian' (quoted in Meek 1976, 164). This was a materialist stagism pure and simple.

Marx and Engels' understanding of this matter was vastly more nuanced, accurate and sophisticated. Bringing his knowledge of antiquity, his training in jurisprudence and his penetrating analysis of capitalism to bear on what was known about variety of human social forms hitherto, a knowledge expanding fast thanks to the burgeoning corpus of historical and ethnographic knowledge made available by a spreading imperialism, Marx linked them more intricately to their legal and property structures. This dispatched any neat succession of stages in favour of various routes—antiquity, feudalism, the Asiatic and Germanic—out of 'the original unity of a specific form of (tribal) community and the property in nature connected with it' (Hobsbawm 1964, 36 quoting Marx, 94).

Moreover, their purpose was to bring out the true historical novelty of capitalism. It consisted in

> the separation of free labour from the objective conditions of its realization [,] . . . from the soil as his natural workshop . . . hence dissolution of small, free landed property as well as of communal landownership resting on the oriental commune [where] the worker relates to the objective conditions of his labour as to his property [and] individuals relate not as workers but as proprietors—and members of a community, who at the same time work. The aim of this work is not the creation of value . . . rather, its aim is sustenance of the individual proprietor and of his family, as well as of the total community. *The positing of the individual as a worker, in this nakedness, is itself a product of history.*
>
> (Marx 1858/1973, 417–2)

Rather than proposing any crude materialism or stagism, Marx and Engels' extensive writings on historical social forms were geared to a single question: what had to happen in human history before human beings were reduced to the status of mere workers, of abstract labour, bereft of access to means of production and the dignity of being a working member of a community, valued only for their ability to produce *value*?

It is not widely appreciated that this way of conceiving capitalism overturns the Enlightenment portrayal of capitalism as a natural form, opposed to the artifices of feudalism. For Marx, capitalism was the most unnatural form of production, severing humans from their original unity with the earth, the instruments of production and the means of consumption they produced out of it, severing them also from one another, self and society. A long historical path led from the original historical unity, through various more and less oppressive social forms in which workers 'still belong among the objective conditions of production and are appropriated as such', to capitalism. What has to happen, Marx and Engels were asking in their writings on the social forms that preceded capitalism, before such an unnatural mode of production establishes itself?

The history and geography of contradictory value production

To this sophisticated sense of capitalism's historical specificity as a social form, we must add a second complex sense in which capitalism was historical for Marx, a sense that helps us understand its tumultuous history and violent, imperialist geography (Desai 2013, 2016, 2017).

If capitalism is distinguished from previous forms of social production by the production of abstract value at the intersection of two contradictory axes, if value production needs to be established and secured by further contradictory demands on a range of other social realms, value production must necessarily lurch from crisis to crisis and experience increasing legitimacy deficits thanks to its anarchy and injustice, all of which the state must manage.

Not only is state power critical to bringing capitalism into being, giving bourgeois revolutions—whether they were sudden and dramatic or long drawn out (Anderson 1992a)—their centrality to the story, capitalist states must remain engaged in and shape capitalism on an ongoing basis as they manage capitalisms' contradictions domestically and internationally, making and remaking the social foundation and international position of their capitalisms in the dialectic of uneven and combined development that drives its international relations.

Of course, even the most savvy and competent states cannot prolong capitalisms' lives indefinitely. Their efforts come up against many obstacles. Capitalism's contradictions compound and multiply, inducing not only systemic incoherence but also incoherence and disunity among the political forces that govern them. The overriding priority of keeping societies capitalist severely restricts the range of capitalist states' actions. Not only do their actions fail to resolve the underlying contradictions in any lasting manner, their attempts to manage them temporarily add new layers of contradictions and give them new forms. Such management, whether it succeeds (temporarily) or fails, has determined the historical trajectory that has brought capitalist societies where they are today.

Since the capitalist state can only manage contradictions without eliminating them, this management itself becomes an element in that history. This is the central plot that makes capitalism's tumultuous history intelligible. If its manifold contradictions constitute a set of disjointed and uncoordinated motors of capital's history and geography, pulling this way and that, the state forms its harassed driver. Without state actions, left to the mercy of its multiple contradictions, capitalism would hurtle so blindly and waywardly along, pulled and pushed this way and that, as to meet an early end. Only states managing capitalisms' contradictions have given them the longevity they have.

'Marxist political scientists' who wonder if capitalism, conceived as an 'economic' form, needs the 'political' form of the nation state (Wood 1999) or ask whether capitalism needs a plurality of states and whether states' international actions do not have an irreducible 'realist' of 'political' moment, separated from the 'economic logic' of capitalism (Callinicos 2007) are relying on Marxist economics' unwarranted separation of the economy from society, polity and other realms of society.

Contradictions

The full range of contradictions that implicate states in their management and thus in capitalisms' history has not been analysed systematically. As Mandel pointed out (Mandel 1981, 42–53) though Marxist economists embroil themselves in a fruitless search for the single, most fundamental cause of crises, usually more than one of the many Marx identified—overproduction (or underconsumption), disproportionality, and the Tendency of the Rate of Profit to Fall

(TRPF)—is at work in any given historical crisis, interacting in complex ways with one another. Paul Sweezy identified crises associated with falling rates of profits and realisation. On the basis of our analysis so far, we can, however, take a wider, more systematic, view.

While crises certainly occur in production and realisation, the core realms of value production, capitalism relies on the right conditions in at least five other realms. First, value is expressed and, critically for capitalists, preserved, in money and states must furnish money of stable value. Second, money is inseparable from credit and states must ensure that financial systems function as capitalist classes require. Third, like all other modes of production, capitalism relies on the free resources nature provides and must organise reliable access to them. Fourth, states must have the resources to perform their core functions—to create and maintain the legal and political framework of private property, secure capitalist accumulation and manage its legitimacy crises domestically. There is, finally, the international plane where capitalist states must secure and expand opportunities for accumulation and the management of capitalism's contradictions.

In each of these seven spheres, crises may take two forms: intra-class horizontal forms arising from competition and struggles among capitalists and property-owning classes and inter-class vertical forms, arising from class struggle. These seven sources and two forms give us at least 14 different readily identifiable mechanisms of crises, as in Table 2.1.

Contradictions of value production

By contradictions of value production we meas those that occur in the core the realms of production and realization. To take the horizontal axis first, competition tends to push the prices of the commodified products of labour down to wards their value expressing the 'socially necessary' labour they embody. It also makes investment in labour-saving technology imperative, spurring technological development and developing the forces of production. Once one capitalist has lowered costs significantly through investment in more advanced technology, others must follow suit or suffer lowered sales and/or lower prices, reducing profits or even inflicting losses. While all this is socially progressive in that it develops the forces of production, it is tortuous for capitalists: with increasing investment, the rate of profit, the ratio of profit made to capital invested, tends to decline in the long run. This is the Tendency of the Rate of Profit to Fall (TRPF), though in the short run it may be counteracted by many factors. Marx enumerated the following: more intense exploitation of labour, reduction of wages below their value, cheapening of elements of constant capital, relative surplus population (which reduces wages), selling goods above their value in foreign trade and increase in share capital or expansion of the share of capital that must be satisfied with the (lower) rate of interest rather than (higher) rate of profit (Marx 1894/1981, 339–48). In the long run, however, the TRPF is inexorable and bound to affect capitalists' willingness to invest in production.

TABLE 2.1 Crises by source and form

Source / *Form*	*Production*	*Realisation*	*Money*	*Finance*	*Ecological*	*Domestic*	*International*
Intra-class	Tendency of the Rate of Profit to Fall	Disproportion	Deflation	Credit crunch/ Speculative bubble	Corporate ecological destruction	Fiscal crisis	Uneven vs. capitalist combined development
Inter-class	Profit Squeeze	Overproduction/ Underconsumption	Inflation	Mortgage crisis	Ecological destruction from human desperation	Legitimation crisis	Uneven vs. popular or socialist combined development

Source: Created by the author.

Competition also implies anarchy; there is no overall organisation of production. The unplanned anarchy of capitalist production may lead to disproportionate production: excesses of some goods and dearth of others, too many capital goods and too few consumption goods, for instance.

On the vertical axis, capitalists produce goods and services by employing the labour of workers who, without direct access to the means of production, must work for capitalists whom the long historical process of separating people from their original access to the means of production has left in possession of those means of production. Capitalists employ workers only because they are capable of producing far more value than their labour is worth as expressed in prevailing wage rates. This allows capitalists to appropriate the difference, provided the goods are sold. This is exploitation and is organised through markets, markets for labour and for the products of labour. Union activity can modify these basic structures of exploitation, for instance by increasing wages or bettering working conditions, but not erase them.

The chickens of this exploitation in production come home to roost in realisation. In order to realise the value embodied in goods so produced, to convert them into pure value, expressed in money, the goods and services must be sold. To realise their value fully, all of them must be sold. While workers will usually spend pretty well all their income, creating demand to its full extent, the same does not apply to capitalists' income, their profits. The surpluses they appropriate can far exceed the total of their most ostentatious consumption and spending on investment. If demand conditions and profit expectations do not appear good to capitalists, they may hoard their incomes—usually in the form of financial or other assets—rather than invest them productively, meaning that a growing proportion of accumulated capital simply does not re-enter production (Freeman 2012). Therefore, there is never any guarantee that all the goods and services produced will be sold and capitalism tends to suffer from periodic demand deficits, gluts of unsold inventory, which can lead further to lowered utilisation of productive capacity and shedding of jobs. This is overproduction or underconsumption (Desai 2010 salvages the unduly despised latter term).

While capitalist accumulation needs exploitation, while capitalist societies are managed by capitalist classes and states to enable this and while the structural difficulties of organising workers also permit it, the vertical contradiction can, and sometimes has, worked the other way and well-organised workers have pushed wages up to levels where they squeeze profits.

Contradictions beyond value production

These contradictions of the core processes of value prodution do not exhaust the contradictions of capitalism. Establishing and maintaining capitalism also requires that wider social realms must be transformed in quite unnatural ways generating more contradictions. This is why bourgeois revolutions are necessary. Capitalist production must transform these realms to suit its purposes, imposing its conditions of existence on them. The resulting contradictions endanger not only individuals and societies but, as Karl Polanyi acutely observed (Polanyi

1944/1985), capitalist businesses themselves. As he argued in the case of the need to maintain a stable money, when this failed,

> The danger was to the single enterprise—industrial, agricultural, or commercial—in so far as it was affected by changes in the price-level. For under a market system, if prices fell, business was impaired; unless all elements of cost fell proportionately, 'going concerns' were forced to liquidate, while the fall in prices might have been due not to a general fall in costs, but merely to the manner in which the monetary system was organized.
>
> *(Polanyi 1944/1985, 131)*

Capitalist states must also manage the resistance and difficulties they face in transforming these realms and be able to manage contradictions generally. The contradictions that emerge in realms other than the core realms of value production may be briefly outlined.

Value is expressed, carried and, critically for capitalists, hoarded, in money. Capitalist states must impose on money, in itself an ancient social institution for accounting social and political obligations, including debts (Hudson 2018; Graeber 2011) as well as exchanging products, the requirements of facilitating capitalist production by stably expressing the value of commodities. This is never reliably accomplished (Desai 2020a). As classical political economy understood, and Karl Polanyi explicitly argued, land, labour and money are not commodities. They are not produced, not produced for sale and their prices are set by 'laws' quite distinct from those of actual commodities, goods and services produced for sale with a determinable 'socially necessary' cost of production. Not only does money have no value, there being 'no "natural" rate of interest' (Marx 1894/1981, 478), the prices of land and its products (Marx 1894/1981, 213–16) and of labour fluctuate, since their production cannot be planned or predictable, and can cause inflation, as can the mismanagement of money creation. When that happens, monetary authorities, since the late nineteenth century, central banks, have only the blunt instrument of recessionary monetary restriction to dampen it. In general, the principal monetary policy means they have to keep the value of money stable is to restrict its issue. That, however, along with the relentless downward pressure of competition on prices (Vilar 1976, 11), tends to be deflationary. Historically, inflation has also involved keeping the prices of labour and primary commodities low through politically organised repression and restriction of labour organisation and through imperialism over agricultural and primary commodity producing countries (Patnaik and Patnaik 2016).

Since, in a capitalist economy, money is, in good part, credit, money is inseparable from finance, credit and debt, and states must ensure that financial systems function to facilitate accumulation. There are two critical dangers here. First, the financial system must be prevented from generating speculative bubbles in which the competition for speculative gain among holders of capital and recipients of credit drive asset values far beyond any rational calculation of worth to prevent destructive crashes and the diversion of capital from productive investment. As Keynes famously said,

> Speculators may do no harm as bubbles on a steady stream of enterprise. But the position is serious when enterprise becomes the bubble on a whirlpool of speculation. When the capital development of a country becomes a by-product of the activities of a casino, the job is likely to be ill-done.
>
> *(Keynes 1936/1967, Ch. 12, part VI, para 1.)*

On the other hand, financial systems must also be prevented form overextension of credit. Unsustainable debt leads to debt and mortgage crises, which can be very deflationary as they restrict spending and investment.

Ecological crises occur when capitalist firms compete to appropriate and plunder the free resources of nature and when this very appropriation and plunder forces working people to overexploit their ever-shrinking share of these resources leading to climate change, pollution and biodiversity loss.

Finally, capitalist states must also control territories and populations, domestically and internationally, to advance the interests of their capitalists. Since their doing so implicates them centrally in capitalism's history, we leave that to the next chapter.

References

Anderson, Perry. 1992a. 'The Notion of Bourgeois Revolution', in *English Questions*. London: Verso.

Anderson, Perry. 1992b. 'Components of the National Culture', in *English Questions*. London: Verso.

Blackburn, Robin. 1991. 'Fin de Siècle: Socialism After the Crash', *New Left Review*, 185(January–February), pp. 5–66. https://newleftreview.org/issues/i185/articles/robin-blackburn-fin-de-siecle-socialism-after-the-crash

Bukharin, Nicolai. 1914/1972. *The Economic Theory of the Leisure Class*. New York: Monthly Review Press.

Callinicos, Alex. 2007. 'Does Capitalism Need the State System?', *Cambridge Review of International Affairs*, 20(4), pp. 533–49. https://doi.org/10.1080/09557570701680464

Clarke, Simon. 1991. *Marx, Marginalism and Modern Sociology: From Adam Smith to Max Weber*. 2nd ed. Basingstoke: Macmillan Academic and Professional.

Cohen, Gerald A. 1983. 'Forces and Relations of Production', in Matthews, Betty (ed), *Marx: 100 Years on Paperback*. London. Lawrence & Wishart.

Colletti, Lucio. 1972. 'Bernstein and the Marxism of the Second International', in *From Rousseau to Lenin: Studies in Ideology and Society*, pp. 45–108. London: New Left Books.

Desai, Radhika. 2010. 'Consumption Demand in Marx and in the Current Crisis', *Research in Political Economy*, (26), pp. 101–41. https://doi.org/10.1108/s0161-7230(2010)0000026005

Desai, Radhika. 2012. 'Marx, List and the Materiality of Nations', *Rethinking Marxism*, 24(1), January, pp. 47–67.

Desai, Radhika. 2013. *Geopolitical Economy: After US Hegemony, Globalization and Empire*. London: Pluto.

Desai, Radhika. 2016. 'The Value of History and the History of Value', in Subasat, Turan (ed) *The Great Meltdown of 2008: Systemic, Conjunctural or Policy-Created?*, pp. 136–58. Northampton, MA: Edward Elgar Publishing. https://doi.org/10.4337/9781784716493.00017

Desai, Radhika. 2017. 'Capital at 150', *Red Pepper*, pp. 48–9.
Desai, Radhika. 2018. 'Political Economy', in Pendakis, Andrew; Szeman, Imre; and Diamanti, Jeff (eds), *The Bloomsbury Companion to Marx*, pp. 199–218. London: Bloomsbury Publishing.
Desai, Radhika. 2020a. 'Commodified Money and Crustacean Nations', in Desai, Radhika and Polanyi-Levitt, Kari (eds), *Karl Polanyi and Twenty-First-Century Capitalism*, pp.78–101. Manchester: Manchester University Press. https://doi.org/10.7765/9781526127891.00011
Desai, Radhika. 2020b. 'Marx's Critical Political Economy, "Marxist Economics" and Actually Occurring Revolutions against Capitalism', *Third World Quarterly*, 41(8), pp. 1353–70. https://doi.org/10.1080/01436597.2020.1741346
Desai, Radhika. 2021. 'Marx's Geopolitical Economy: "The Relations of Producing Nations"', *Capital & Class*, pp. 3–10. https://doi.org/10.1177%2F03098168211017433
Dobb, Maurice. 1963. *Studies in the Development of Capitalism*. London: Routledge and Kegan Paul.
Dobb, Maurice. 1973. *Theories of Value and Distribution Since Adam Smith*. Cambridge: Cambridge University Press.
Eley, Geoff. 2002. *Forging Democracy: The History of the Left in Europe*. Oxford: Oxford University Press.
Elson, Diane. 2000. 'Socializing Markets, Not Market Socialism', *Socialist Register*, (36), pp. 67–85.
Engels, Friedrich. 1890/1968. 'Engels to Conrad Schmidt in Berlin', in *Marx and Engels Correspondence*. New York: International Publishers.
Freeman, Alan. 2012. 'The Profit Rate in the Presence of Financial Markets: A Necessary Correction', *Journal of Australian Political Economy*, 70, pp. 167–92.
Freeman, Alan; and Carchedi, Guglielmo (eds). 1996. *Marx and Non-Equilibrium Economics*. Cheltenham: Edward Elgar.
Graeber, David. 2011. *Debt: The First 5000 Years*. New York: Melville House.
Hayek, Friedrich A. von. 1944. *The Road to Serfdom*. London: George Routledge and Sons.
Hilferding, Rudolf. 1949. 'Bohm-Bawerk's Criticism of Marx', in Sweezy, Paul (ed), *Karl Marx and the Close of His System by Eugen von Böhm-Bawerk and Bohm-Bawerk's Criticism of Marx by Rudolf Hilferding*. London: The Merlin Press.
Hobsbawm, Eric J. 1964. 'Introduction' to Karl Marx, *Pre-Capitalist Economic Formations*. London: Lawrence and Wishart.
Hudson, Michael. 2018. *. . . and Forgive Them Their Debts*. New York: Islet.
Hunt, E.K. 1980. 'The Relation of the Ricardian Socialists to Ricardo and Marx', *Science & Society*, Summer, 44(2), pp. 177–98. www.jstor.org/stable/40402242
Jo, Tae-Hee. 2016. 'What If There Are No Conventional Price Mechanisms?', *Journal of Economic Issues*, 50(2), pp. 327–44. https://doi.org/10.1080/00213624.2016.1176474
Joll, James. 1974. *The Second International, 1889–1914*. London: Routledge & K. Paul.
Keynes, John Maynard. 1930/1963. 'Economic Possibilities for Our Grandchildren', in *Essays in Persuasion*, pp. 358–73. New York: W. W. Norton & Co.
Keynes, John Maynard. 1936/1967. *General Theory of Employment, Interest and Money*. London: Macmillan.
Kliman, Andrew. 2007. *Reclaiming Marx's Capital: A Refutation of the Myth of Inconsistency*. Lanham: Lexington Books.
Kristjansen-Gural, David. 2017a. 'Demand, Values and Prices in Marx: Contrasting Simultaneous and Temporal Approaches', *Rethinking Marxism*, 29(4), pp. 538–55. https://doi.org/10.1080/08935696.2017.1417082
Kristjansen-Gural, David. 2017b. 'Demand and Socially Necessary Labor-Time', in Brennan, David M.; Kristjanson-Gural, David; and Mulder, Catherine P. (eds), *Routledge Handbook of Marxian Economics*, pp. 155–67. Abingdon, UK: Routledge.

Luxemburg, Rosa. 1913/1951. *The Accumulation of Capital*. New Haven: Yale University Press.
Lysandrou, Photis. 2000. 'The Market and Exploitation in Marx's Economic Theory: A Reinterpretation', *Cambridge Journal of Economics*, 24(3), pp. 325–47. https://doi.org/10.1093/cje/24.3.325
Mandel, Ernest. 1974. *Late Capitalism*. London: New Left Books.
Mandel, Ernest. 1977. 'Introduction', in Marx, Karl (ed), *Capital* (Vol. 1), pp. 11–86. London: Penguin.
Mandel, Ernest. 1987. 'Introduction', in Marx, Karl (ed), *Capital* (Vol. 2), pp. 11–79. London: Penguin.
Mandel, Ernest. 1981. 'Introduction', in Marx, Karl (ed), *Capital*, (Vol. 3), pp. 9–90. London: Penguin.
Mandel, Ernest; and Freeman, Alan (eds). 1984. *Ricardo, Marx, Sraffa: The Langston Memorial Volume*. London: Verso.
Marx, Karl. 1847. *The Poverty of Philosophy*. London: Martin Lawrence.
Marx, Karl. 1858/1973. *Grundrisse*. London: Penguin.
Marx, Karl. 1859/1977. *A Contribution to the Critique of Political Economy*. Moscow: Progress Publishers.
Marx, Karl. 1867/1977. *Capital* (Vol. 1). London: Penguin.
Marx. Karl. 1894/1981. *Capital* (Vol. 3). London: Penguin.
Marx, Karl. 1951. *Theories of Surplus Value* (Selections). London: Lawrence and Wishart.
Marx, Karl. 1968. *Theories of Surplus Value* (Vol. 2). London: Lawrence and Wishart.
Marx, Karl. 1972. *Theories of Surplus Value* (Vol. 3). London: Lawrence and Wishart.
Marx, Karl; and Engels, Fredrick. 1848/1967. *The Communist Manifesto*. Translated by Samuel Moore. With an Introduction by A.J.P. Taylor. London: Penguin.
Meek, Ronald L. 1956. *Studies in the Labour Theory of Value*. London: Lawrence and Wishart.
Meek, Ronald L. 1976. *Social Science and the Ignoble Savage*. Cambridge: Cambridge University Press.
Meek, Ronald L. 1977. 'Marginalism and Marxism', in *Smith, Marx, & After*, pp. 165–75. Boston, MA: Springer. https://doi.org/10.1007/978-1-4899-7303-0_9
Patnaik, Utsa. 2005. 'Ricardo's Fallacy: Mutual Benefit From Trade Based on Comparative Costs and Specialization?', in Jomo, Kwame Sundaram (ed), *The Pioneers of Development Economics*, pp. 31–41. London: Zed.
Patnaik, Utsa; and Patnaik, Prabhat. 2016. *A Theory of Imperialism*. New York: Columbia University Press.
Polanyi, Karl. 1944/1985. *The Great Transformation*. Boston: Beacon Press.
Riddell, John (ed). 1993. *To See the Dawn: Baku 1920, First Congress of the Peoples of the East*. New York: Pathfinder Press.
Sardoni, Claudio. 1997. 'Keynes and Marx', in Harcourt, Geoffrey C. and Riach, Peter (eds), *A 'Second Edition' of the General Theory*, pp. 261–83. London: Routledge.
Thomasberger, Claus. 2020. 'Fictitious Ideas, Social Facts and the Double Movement: Polanyi's Framework in the Age of Neoliberalism', in Desai, Radhika and Polanyi-Levitt, Kari (eds), *Karl Polanyi and Twenty-First-Century Capitalism*, pp. 135–63. Manchester: Manchester University Press.
Tönnies, Ferdinand. 1887/1957. *Gemeinschaft und Gesellschaft [Community and Society]*. Oxford: Michigan University Press.
Vilar, Pierre. 1976. 'A History of Gold and Money, 1450–1920', *Science and Society*, 41(3), pp. 355–8. https://doi.org/10.1177/003981687700300106
Wood, Ellen Meiksins. 1999. 'Unhappy Families: Global Capitalism in a World of Nation-States', *Monthly Review*, 51(3), pp. 1–12. https://doi.org/10.14452/mr-051-03-1999-07_1

3

THE GEOPOLITICAL ECONOMY OF CAPITALISM AND SOCIALISM

Capitalist states, that is to say states that represent and promote the interests of primarily capitalist ruling classes, must act on the domestic and international planes to do so, including to manage the contradictions of their capitalisms. Moreover, capitalisms' history, including their international expansion, is driven forward precisely by capitalist states' domestic and international management of their contradictions, producing new mutations in its political and geopolitical economy. In this chapter, we finish the discussion of the contradictions of capitalism begun in the last by taking up the contradictions relating to the realms of the state and the international. This discussion forms the basis for the outline of its history up to the end of capitalism's post-war Long Boom that follows. Several key aspects stand out.

First, it has been a history neither of ever-greater development of the productive forces domestically nor of ever-expanding markets or 'hegemony' internationally. Rather, capitalism entered its monopoly phase relatively early and did so not chiefly in England, where industrial capitalism had its longest roots, but, thanks to the dialectic of uneven and combined development (UCD), in the countries that industrialised to challenge her supremacy, giving the world capitalist economy a contradictory structure of different and even antagonistic national capitalisms.

Second, the most momentous difference among them, one that would be given a significance lasting down to our times of neoliberal financialised capitalisms, was in the bank–industry relations that characterised Britain on the one hand and the successful industrialisers that challenged her dominance on the other. Britain's archaic financial structures, which accounted for Britain's persistent industrial decline, were also the foundation of Britain's gold-sterling standard. The pursuit of its desire to replace it with a dollar system led the US to resurrect such financial structures on an even grander scale in the form of a dollar creditocracy run out of New York and London, complete with US deindustrialization. This is also

DOI: 10.4324/9781003200000-3

what gives the United States and the United Kingdom their central roles in the argument of this book.

(That, after 1971, the dollar system was unanchored from gold only meant that the value of money could fluctuate more, though it still has to be maintained with some stability as Patnaik and Patnaik (2016) argue. To their correct argument that it is maintained chiefly by deflating the incomes of working people and the Third World, we add that financialisations are the other major instrument.)

Third, there is the story of socialism. Not only did the dialectic of UCD lead directly to the competition among the major capitalist powers that erupted in the First World War and capitalism's greatest crisis to date, the Thirty Years' Crisis of 1914–1945, it was accompanied by waves of Communist and nationalist unrest and bookended by two of the greatest Communist revolutions so far, the Russian and the Chinese. While contemporary anticipations that the world would take a turn towards socialism after 1945 were not entirely fulfilled, these energies would ensure capitalism in its homelands would survive and even thrive thereafter only thanks to extensive socialistic reforms while in the developing world projects of autonomous national development would also lean toward socialism.

If, three decades after the end of the Cold War, a new confrontation between capitalism and socialism has re-emerged, it is simply because the Cold War was a chapter in the unfolding geopolitical economy of capitalism, of its history of UCD, of imperialism and anti-imperialist resistance. The end of the Cold War did not and could not end that (Desai and Heller 2019). To do so, capitalism would have had to change its spots, to offer the lands outside its core of powerful capitalist countries a better relation than imperialism, a better position than that of a subordinated 'outside' (Luxemburg 1913/2003; Patnaik and Patnaik 2016, 2021) made to bear costs of its contradictions. Or it would also have had to be better at preventing their autonomous development. Given the consequences of subordination, all but the most authoritarian governments outside capitalism's core must, to retain a modicum of legitimacy, resist it to some extent and engage in some sort of combined development. Historically, socialism has just been the strongest form of combined development, possible where popular power was best organised.

The demise of the first socialist state, the Soviet Union, was not due to inherent limitations of the organisation of its economy, society or politics but due to a counter-revolution by its own leadership. It demonstrated that class contradictions do not disappear in the process of building socialism, that reverses are possible, but no more (Kotz 1997/2005; Lane 2017). In any case, as if to demonstrate the possibilities of socialism, the People's Republic of China not only survived but is prospering just when the productive decrepitude of capitalism is more apparent than ever, its imperial offer unable to obtain submission and its military power unable to compel it, only to rain destruction on societies that are the targets—such as Afghanistan, Iraq or Syria—or proxies—such as Ukraine today—in vain efforts to do so. Against this background, Chinese and other persisting socialisms demonstrate to increasingly interested publics worldwide, particularly amid the pandemic and the war, that there are saner ways to organise society, material production, politics and culture as well as a society's relations with nature and other societies.

The current productive malaise in the historic homelands of capitalism forces us to put it too in a longer historical perspective. When we do, we are increasingly forced to the conclusion that early twentieth-century Marxist writers, and the others, such as Keynes or Polanyi, whose judgements overlapped with them, were onto something when they suggested that capitalism had fulfilled what historic mission it may have had and that the time for socialism had arrived. Though these views were easily dismissed after the Second World War by simply pointing to capitalism's Long Boom, four decades of neoliberalism have thrown into relief how that period of growth depended on the socialistic measures taken at the time, and how the freedoms returned to capital by neoliberalism only prolonged the slump of the 1970s into the Long Downturn of financialisaton and productive decline even as socialism was putting in a far superior performance.

This chapter elaborates on the intertwined trajectories of capitalism and socialism. In what follows, after brief reflections on capitalism and the revolutions that make and break capitalist states, we outline our understanding of the contractions of capitalism in the realms of the state and the international before tracing the political and geopolitical economy of capitalism and socialism up to the end of capitalism's post-war Long Boom.

Capitalism and revolutions

More than any other form of society, capitalism has an intimacy with revolutions because it is neither natural nor in possession of Promethean capabilities of developing the forces of production and creating prosperity everywhere and for all time. Violent revolutions were necessary to usher capitalism into history and appeared surprisingly early in its comparatively short life, to usher it out.

Bourgeois revolutions established capitalist states that set about forcibly separating producers from the means of production (Marx 1867/1977, part 8), securing the many other conditions for capitalism and its expansion and managing its many and interacting contradictions. It faced opposition from the start, first from those, such as pre-capitalist ruling classes, invested in previous forms of class exploitation. Although, against them, it was often able to secure the support of nascent working classes in the struggles that birthed capitalist states, opposition from working people it exploited at home and abroad as well as peoples threatened with subordination through its imperialist expansionism soon occupied çentre stage.

Capitalism's class and national exploitation and oppression have ensured that revolutions have threatened it from the start, not just since 1917, when popular revolutions, at once socialist and anti-imperialist, began the long, still ongoing process of ushering it out of the history of one country after another Such revolutionary threats early on made counter-revolution a major preoccupation of capitalist states (van der Pijl 2020). From its beginnings, capitalism has faced populations resisting proletarianisation in its homelands and imperial subordination outside them. Many relatively egalitarian communities that capitalist imperialism encountered have opposed it and to this day Indigenous peoples that have survived its onslaught continue resisting it in the name of ancient rights, land, the environment and community (Kulchyski 2020; Barkin and Sánchez 2020). The image of capitalism as a fount of prosperity has not rung true for the vast majority of humanity.

Humanity's path to socialism will have to articulate all such varieties of resistance to capitalism. That of wageworkers in capitalism's homelands is an important one, but far from the whole and getting farther as capitalism deindustrialises them. In this endeavour, the articulations that actually occurring revolutions, and resistances, against capitalism and imperialism, have devised among themselves under the force of historical necessity will surely prove useful guides.

The matrix of political and geopolitical struggle

With Second International Marxism narrowed (Colletti 1972), it fell to the Bolshevik leaders of the Russian Revolution to recover the key elements of Marx and Engels's understanding that imperialism and national resistance to it were as important as class struggles against capitalist exploitation in the struggle for socialism, that capitalisms have a political as well as a geopolitical economy, that they are products of the relations of classes as well as what Marx called 'the relations of producing nations'. Inevitably, as revolutionaries in struggle, their recovery was oriented to political understandings and decisions, leaving theory prey to Marxist economics and associated distortions in many ways (see, for instance, Zarembka 2002). Impelled by the historical necessity of allying with peasants, the oppressed peoples of the Tsarist empire and with anti-colonial movements (Petersson 2014) more widely, Bolsheviks founded the alternative Communist tradition to which anti-imperialism has remained central even if they were unable to reconcile it entirely with their understanding of Marx's critical political economy of capitalism as contradictory value production (Desai 2020).

However, knowing that consistency can be the hobgoblin of little minds, they did not let their theoretical confusions prevent them from seeing clearly that capitalism was imperialist, exploiting colonial and semi-colonial nations as well as working classes, and that both also resist. For them, both class and international struggles were usually very complex. Domestic class struggles are rarely neat confrontations between capitalists and workers, international struggles also feature a combination of competition and conflict among capitalist nations, struggles between their imperialisms and national struggles, of varying social character, capable of resisting imperialism with greater or lesser radicalism and success.

Class competition and struggle

Domestically, capitalist states must establish territorial control and the legal structures that commodify labour, including those that deprive people of their historic rights to given territories through force. They must create and maintain institutions of private property and police them as well as support capitalist accumulation generally while retaining a modicum of legitimacy and stability, including through welfarist concessions.

On the vertical axis of class struggle, the fundamental illegitimacy of capitalist states' core functions in the eyes of working people leads to regular legitimacy crises (Habermas 1975). However, these erupt on a very complex domestic terrain, which offers both resources and challenges. While, undoubtedly, there are tendencies in capitalist society towards simplifying the class structure to a confrontation between a tiny capitalist and a vast working class facing one another in deadly combat, these tendencies work very slowly and never quite arrive at full simplification. Therefore, the idea that socialism can develop only after capitalism developed the productive forces to the fullest and its class structure is simplified was always absurd. Not only did Marx and Engels call on revolutionaries of 1848 to overthrow capitalism without waiting for it to lay the entire planet to waste and proletarianise the vast mass of humanity, Engels clarified that the capitalism of *Capital* never referred to any real system of 'pure' capitalism of capitalists and workers alone. Such a system existed nowhere: While the law of value and the other laws of capitalism

> only attain their most complete approximate realisation on the presupposition that capitalist production has been everywhere completely established, society reduced to the modern classes of landowners, capitalists (industrialists and merchants) and workers. . . . This does not exist even in England

where proletarianisation had been 'accomplished in a radical fashion'. And, Engels confidently predicted, such a society 'never will exist—we [revolutionaries] shall not let it get so far as that' (Engels 1895, see also Mandel 1978, 68). He might have added, as we saw in the last chapter, that capitalism's impossible demands on the various social realms it must modify to exist, the multiple contradictions they give rise to and the need to manage them through state action that modifies capitalism, also make that impossible.

Even where the process of proletarianisation is considerably advanced, employed workers co-exist with peasants, small proprietors and family labour. Moreover, capitalist ruling classes not only use inherited divisions—those of gender, race, ethnicity or nationality, religion or region—to segment the working class, they also create new ones, such as those of wage or skill. Ironically, it was only under the 'socialistic' organisation of Western capitalist societies after the Second World War, aided by Fordist industrial organisation (Aglietta 1976), that the working classes of the major capitalist countries acquired the unprecedented uniformity that formed the foundation of historically unprecedented union densities in the various capitalist countries. Under neoliberalism, by contrast, the waged working class began being returned to what may appear its 'natural' state of being riven by inequality of pay, working conditions, contracts and 'skill' and by gender, race and other 'diverse' oppressions.

In light of these complexities, for the purposes of political organisation for socialism, the working class is best thought of not as the waged working class, much less the waged industrial working class, but as all those who must work for a living, whether they are employed or not, whether they are paid for their work or not. This way, they include all those who have been substantially separated from their means of production, whether they are left with none or not enough for more than a precarious living in perilous markets as small producers. They also include that vast majority of women who must perform the reproductive labour that working people's existence requires.

The struggles of the working class thus conceived not only include the struggle of waged workers, from the shop floor to the political arena, but also of many others, of women, peasants and farmers, the small and precariously propertied, unemployed, students, oppressed nationalities and groups and others. Successful struggle requires that they be composed into what Antonio Gramsci called historic blocs (Gramsci 1971, 366) depending on the history and social structures of different societies. They must force concessions on capital in the form of pay, farm and petty production prices, protection for small property, unionisation, working conditions, welfare, regulation of land, labour and money and taxation on capital to protect labour, the land and society. Such gains are critically important because they humanise working people's lives. They also form stepping stones to socialism: 'such measures stiffen the will of the people to resist, help the process of changing them from objects to subjects, and hence contribute to the process of sharpening of class struggle' (Patnaik 2009). At the same time, socialists must recognise that while workers' struggles have nearly everywhere blunted the edge of the commodification of labour and its exploitation to some extent, as the sheer size and scale of post-war welfare states in the major capitalist countries show, they have been particularly successful in the imperial countries where capital has greater capacity (and need, if only for the resulting political stability in lands where it concentrates its directive functions in head offices) for concessions. There the balance between repression and material concessions tilts more to the latter than elsewhere, making more reform possible. It has also historically made reformism a viable strategy in the imperialist countries, though with the narrowing of room for concessions, it is arguably less viable in these late neoliberal times.

In addition to struggles between capitalists and working people, there is competition among capitals and factions thereof. On this horizontal axis, capitalist states are threatened by competition among capitalists to evade taxes and to place demands on the state, leading to regular fiscal crises (on the US case, see O'Connor 1973). Moreover, competition among capitalists co-exists with their struggles with other propertied classes—such as landlords and rentiers—over the distribution of the surplus. As competition produces winners and losers, monopoly advances across major sectors of capitalist production. As it does so, tendencies towards stagnation set in. Productively dynamic periods, when productive investment grows at a fast clip and industrial capital dominates, grow rarer and shorter. Periods of stagnation, when profits are not invested productively, but in financial assets, and financial and rentier fractions dominate, grow longer. Stagnation signals the dwindling historical utility of capital, while also dividing big corporate capital from small capital ever more sharply and opening up the possibility of the latter forming some part of a socialist 'historic bloc' in many countries.

International competition and struggle

Finally, there is the international realm. Not only does the centrality of the state in the management of capitalism's contradictions rule out the 'free trade' and 'globalisation' assumption that capitalism can operate with minimal state intervention or none, contrary to quite widespread belief—not least among advocates and theorists of 'US hegemony'—that capitalism can or should have a world state, that is precisely the jurisdictional form that is impossible under capitalism and possible, if at all, only under an advanced form of socialism. This is thanks to capitalism's UCD.

Though the *locus classicus* of UCD is generally held to be Trotsky's *History of the Russian Revolution* (1934), the idea was widely shared among Bolsheviks and underlay their understanding of their revolution's historical character (Desai 2013, 51–3). It was also ultimately rooted in Marx and Engels' writings (Desai 2013, 36–43 and 51–3, 2012, 2021) and also transplanted from its Marxist and Bolshevik sources into Western mainstream scholarship by the Russian émigré intellectual, Alexander Gerschenkron (1962), in the form of ideas about 'late development' and the 'advantages of backwardness'. Since most extant interpretations of UCD have been vitiated by the distortions of Marxist economics, my own interpretation may be briefly outlined.

Inherently uneven, capitalist development is concentrated in particular countries and regions, creating inequality in productive capacity and material prosperity between nations. Just as class inequality leads to class struggle *within* societies, such international inequality leads to struggle *between* them. If the content of class struggles is the distribution of surplus, income and control over social production, that of international struggle is the international division of labour and the position of various nations in its hierarchy. The more advanced capitalist nations seek to maintain and extend the uneven distribution of productivity and productive power, and the resulting control over the sources of surplus profit, that privilege them and permit them to impose the costs of their capitalism's contradictions on other societies.

Historically, the need to deal with surpluses of commodities and capital and deficits of inputs, including labour, lead to formal and informal imperialism to secure markets, investment outlets, labour and raw materials. Resolving them domestically would have empowered working people in the major capitalist countries beyond levels tolerable to capital. So imperialism became a matter of encouraging where possible and imposing where necessary an economic openness to the capital, commodities and input needs of major capitalist countries, on other countries inevitably preventing their own industrialisation (Semmel

1970; Kindleberger 1978; Chang 2002). However, this is not always easy. While weak-state or stateless territories are easy prey to imperialism, stronger states can resist such subjugation (as, eventually, did the colonies) and mount challenges to the productive, political and military powers of stronger states through state-directed protectionist industrialisation of the sort advocated by Alexander Hamilton or Friedrich List in the nineteenth century and today by scholarship on developmental states (List 1841/1856; Wade 1990; Amsden 1992). This is combined or contender development—hothousing industrial development through protection and planning. In short, while dominant states seek *complementarity* between their economies and those they dominate, contender nations reject this status and seek *similarity*, in terms of levels of industrial and technological development. The effort to achieve the latter aim, to pursue combined development, rather than free markets, has been responsible for the spread of productive capacity in the capitalist era.

As within class societies, so in the iniquitous international order of capitalism, there is a considerable distance between ideas and realities. Just as the dominant ideas in a society are the ideas of the ruling classes in which their special interests are tricked out in the garb of general social interests, so at the international level, the dominant ideas are the ideas of the ruling classes of the dominant nations in which their special interests are articulated as those of the countries they dominate. Cosmopolitan ideas about free markets and free trade historically articulated British dominance in the mid-nineteenth-century era. Later, when the world was being divided up into a number of empires, regional ideas circulated, whether the United States' Monroe Doctrine or Japan's Greater East Asian Co-prosperity sphere. In the twentieth century, US efforts to dominate the world were articulated as the leadership of the 'free world' when it was locked in struggle with the Communist Bloc, ideas of 'US hegemony' emerged in the 1970s while 'globalisation' and US 'empire' articulated the same efforts in the 1990s and 2000s.

Such ideas dissimulate the critical role all states have played in the economic advance of the dominant nations. Other nations, to the extent they accept such ideas, are kept open to accepting the commodities and capital and supplying the input needs of the dominant nations, discouraging the only type of effective challenge to their dominance, namely state-led industrialisation. However, such challenges are inevitable simply because other nations do not suffer subjugation and relegation gladly.

So, given capitalism's uneven development and formative reliance on states, the capitalist world is necessarily composed of many nations and, equally necessarily, they either compete with one another as nationally organised blocks of capital, particularly in its monopoly phase, or are locked in struggles of domination and subordination. In earlier phases of this dialectic of UCD, such resistance was capitalist and Germany, the United States or Japan industrialised in the late nineteenth century through state-led protectionist efforts to challenge Britain's dominance of the world market. Their combined development needed to overcome far smaller gaps in productive and technological capacities than would be faced by countries engaged in combined development later and they succeeded not only in matching but surpassing the dominant power of the time, Britain, and in becoming imperial powers in their own right. In their case, struggles for markets and investment outlets transformed into a competition of national capitals for colonies, leading to the First World War.

The next phase of combined development was very different from this first. Combined development was now attempted by countries with far lower technological and productive capacities, thanks largely to imperialism, and it included socialist countries—pre-eminently the Soviet Union and the People's Republic of China—and newly independent states pursuing national autonomous development often inspired by the former. All were pitted against what now appeared to be the established structures of imperialism.

The unfolding of uneven and combined development

As we have seen, capitalism developed neither 'globally' through markets nor under the 'hegemony' of a single country, but through UCD. Once capitalism developed in one country, it posed stark choices for others: accept inevitable subordination to it or undertake combined development, state-directed industrialisation behind protectionist walls. Not all countries were equally capable of this, not all could produce that combination of political will and administrative capacity to accomplish this.

The United Kingdom's original industrial and imperial dominance thus came to be challenged by a bevy of successful industrialisers—Germany, the United States and Japan—though weaker efforts elsewhere were not without their successes. As the dialectic of UCD unfolded, by the early twentieth century, it had produced a number of major capitalist states and made the capitalist world multipolar and, given the nationally distinct capitalisms that emerged, each marked by historically and nationally distinct institutional structures—whether Germany's *landesbanken* or Japan's *Zaibatsu* or the United States's Morganised monopolies—pluripolar. Not only did this combined development spread productive capacity beyond the homeland of the first industrial revolution, this geographical spread was also the bearer of capitalism's historical advance from its competitive to its monopoly phase, and from the first industrial revolution of light consumer industries characterised by small firms operating in competitive markets to the second industrial revolution of heavy industry, fostered by huge corporations monopolising markets.

The 'leapfrogging' character of combined development meant that it was not in the erstwhile industrial leader, Britain, that the new capitalism of the second industrial revolution appeared. It appeared in its rivals enjoying the 'advantages of backwardness', leaving Britain suffering the disadvantages of being the first mover (Trotsky 1934), laden down not only with technologically obsolete plant but also a historically obsolete industrial structure. While such lags could be overcome, there was one particular aspect of the lag that ensured that such rectification would not even be attempted and Britain's relative industrial decline would become a long-running show that continues to this day.

This fateful element of British backwardness was noted and discussed, *inter alia,* by Hilferding in his *Finance Capital* (1910/1981). Marx had anticipated that finance would be transformed from its archaic short-term, speculative and predatory medieval form inherited by capitalism to a mature capitalist form capable of supporting large-scale investment. Capitalism's maturation would lead to the 'subordination of interest-bearing capital to the conditions and requirements of modern industry', principally through the 'transformed figure of the borrower': no longer a supplicant in financial straits but a capitalist to whom money is lent 'in the expectation that he . . . will use [it] to appropriate unpaid labour' (Marx 1894/1981, 735, see also Hudson 2010).

The new form, which Hilferding termed finance capital, revealed itself as at once an historical and geographical development. Where it developed, in Britain's industrial challengers, Germany and the United States, it dominated over industrial capital and did so to expand industry, instead of squeezing it. Earlier banks supplied only short-term commercial credit, as City of London banks still did in England. The continental bank (as Hilferding called it, given his focus on Europe, specifically Germany), however, financed long-term production. As such, it had to 'necessarily concern itself with the long-range prospects of the enterprise and the future state of the market'. The earlier 'momentary interest' in its borrowers became the 'enduring one' of the continental bank: 'the larger the amount of credit supplied and, above all, the larger the proportion of the loan capital turned into fixed capital, the stronger and more abiding will that interest be' (Hilferding 1910/1981, 95). Such a bank may remain 'the more powerful party' with access to 'capital in its liquid, readily available, form', but it focuses on long-term productive investment (Hilferding 1910/1981, 95).

By contrast with such finance capital of the 'protectionist countries', free trade England had a less elastic monetary system, very different banking structures, different, less monopolised and cartelised industrial structure in which individual capitalists played a greater role and, of course, its far larger empire (see particularly, Hilferding 1910/1981, 301–10). That empire was formatively constitutive of this structure of English capitalism: 'the large sums flowing in from the colonies, especially India, and from the exploitation of England's trade monopoly, were also accumulated in the hands of individual capitalists' (Hilferding 1910/1981, 306). When these individual investors did expand out of the commercial credit in which they had hitherto specialised into 'capital investment', they did so only by extending credit in the form of interest-bearing capital, by investing in US railway bonds for instance, and not as profit-making capital. This type of investment had 'a negligible influence on the American railway barons' (Hilferding 1910/1981, 325) or any industrial capitalists and obtained 'no more than interest, because the entrepreneurial profit' went to 'American banks' (Hilferding 1910/1981, 428n).

Not only did the protectionist countries follow the logic of finance capital that so contrasted with the British focus on commercial profit and interest, but the two logics developed a complementary relationship. The protectionist countries not only exported profit-making industrial capital of their own, they

> *also import[ed] a part of the capital required for their own economies from abroad . . .* in the *form of loan capital from countries with a slower rate of industrial development but greater accumulated capital wealth.* In this way they not only gain from the difference between the industrial profit which they make in foreign markets and the much lower rate of interest which they have to pay on the capital borrowed in England or France, but also ensure, through this kind of capital export, the more rapid growth of their own industry.
>
> *(Hilferding 1910/1981, 326, emphasis added)*

Here, rentier England (and France) served the protectionist and productive finance capital countries. While the former earned a lower rate of interest, the latter earned a higher rate of profit.

Though Hilferding detected some movement in England towards a more protectionist model, in the main, England remained set in its old ways, supplying chiefly commercial credit or interest-bearing investment credit. From our point of view, two things are important about this.

First, while the unfolding of UCD explains why decline set in, the question remains, why did it persist? Why did England not emulate her competitors and adopt similar strategies of combined development when its decline became manifest? Some initially attributed this persistence to Britain's lack of a developmental state, of the sort sported by her challengers, capable of combined development (Hobsbawm 1968). However, a closer examination refutes that. Early British industrial development had been as mercantilist as elsewhere, and free trade became the United Kingdom's dominant ideology only after it had achieved industrial supremacy (Chang 2002) as a way of maintaining that supremacy. And during the Second World War, the British government proved entirely capable, not only of planning for 'fair shares and equal sacrifices', but also of a massive import-substitution operation in agriculture.

The real reason why similar efforts were not made more broadly acorss the economy and more persistently lay in the peculiarities of Britain's class structure. While the capitalist transformation of the relations of production had advanced furthest in Britain, that country's early capitalist and industrial revolutions and its long imperial lead and reach had left it with a capitalist class dominated not by industrial but first by an agricultural and then 'gentlemanly' financial and commercial activity, carefully avoiding 'coarse' manufacturing (Ingham 1984; Anderson 1968; Leys 1990; Weiner 1981).

It was the political dominance of this class that prevented Britain from undertaking its own form of combined development and reversing, if not its relative decline (which was inevitable as other countries industrialised) at least its persistent problems of low productivity and manufacturing competitiveness. However, this would have required, most fundamentally, transforming its forms of finance, unacceptable to its primarily commercial and financial capitalist class.

Moreover, early in the process, the British Empire rendered this less urgent. First, it counteracted pressures of industrial competition with the colonies' massive export surpluses with the rest of the world, permitting Britain to tolerate declining industrial competitiveness for decades. Britain's relative industrial decline became more of a problem as Britain lost her empire and concern mounted in the post-war decades, the Long Boom notwithstanding (Gamble 1994, see also Grant 2014), prompting a sprawling literature on the problem. In the neoliberal era, however, particularly as the Thatcher government facilitated its participation in the new structures of the dollar creditocracy with its Big Bang reforms of the late 1980s, concern about it was deflected into other debates (as in English and Kenny 2000) while Britain became an ever more financialised and rentier economy (Hutton 1995; Christophers 2020).

The second way in which the Empire rendered British combined development less urgent the gold-sterling standard. It had very little to do with gold, which only provided an anchor to sterling's value. Aa Kwynwa explained in his *Indin Currency and Finance* (1913), a book widely regarded as the primer on the workings of the gold-steling standard, 'less gold than the central bank of any other first-class power—far less than even the Caja of the Argentine', the Bank of England still met 'its international engagements' with 'promptness and certainty' (Keynes 1913, 126) thanks to the efficient working of Britain's front line of defence: her *short-term* international creditor position. It permitted Britain to counter 'gold claims . . . for immediate payment' with 'counter-balancing claims . . . for equally immediate payment' (Keynes 1913, 12) by simply raising the bank rate, which prompted the London money market to reduce international lending below claims falling due (Keynes 1913, 12–13). A financial system geared to longer-term investment would not have been capable of this.

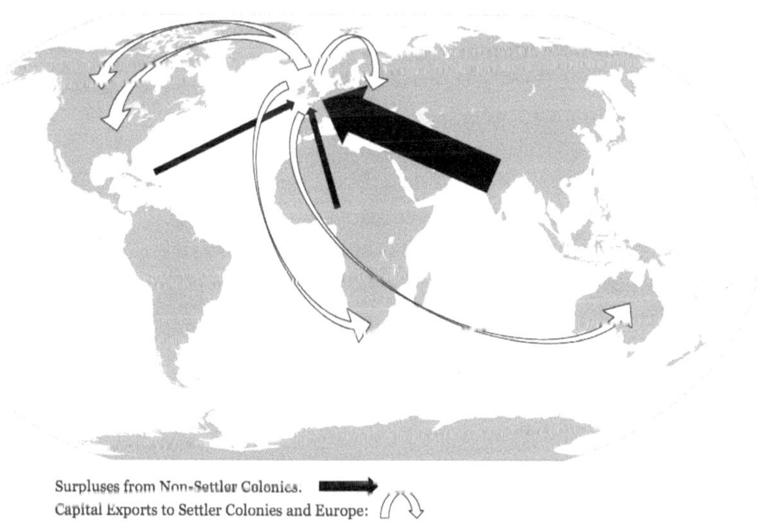

FIGURE 3.1 How the gold-sterling standard provided world liquidity.

Source: Map from https://commons.wikimedia.org/wiki/File:WorldMap-Blank-Noborders.svg (CC0 1.0).

Created by Natalie Braun and the author, used with permission.

Nor was gold the foundation of its functioning, empire was. Britain was able to supply the world, including, as we have noted, the protectionist countries of finance capital, with sterling liquidity chiefly because its financial system functioned to suck out surpluses from its non-settler colonies, chiefly British India—the key reason why a book on 'Indian currency and finance' has served as a primer on the functioning of the gold standard (Desai 2018b)—but also sub-Saharan Africa and the Caribbean and export them as capital chiefly to her former and extant settler colonies and to Europe. These surpluses also eased balance of payments concerns.

Given the United States' attempt to emulate the sterling standard, a couple of other things are worth noting. The first is that the idea that the currency of a particular country can be the world's currency in a stable or lasting fashion is a figment of the economically cosmopolitan imagination of free traders, hegemony theorists and globalists. It does not work in the real world of UCD and rising pluripolarity. Even with an empire as vast as the British, the gold-sterling standard was never as pervasive, permanent or pure as nostalgic accounts assume. Though more and more countries pegged their currencies to gold after 1870, their motives were varied and telling. While gold appreciated, some countries, such as the landed oligarchies that exported primary commodities, Austria-Hungary and Russia, remained with depreciating silver (De Cecco 1984, 51–2). Other countries adopted the gold standard for various reasons: to escape the depreciation of silver, to obtain credit, or, in the case of contender industrialisers such as Germany, to gain international acceptability for their own currency as part of a drive to expand market share and challenge the dominance of sterling (De Cecco 1984, Chapter 3).

As industrial and imperial competition mounted, the result was international monetary instability. After all, 'a stable gold exchange standard could exist only so long as the political sovereignty of the centre countries vis-a-vis the periphery remained unchallenged' (De Cecco 1984, 57). So,

> the system was stable while it remained a Sterling Standard, and . . . it began to oscillate more and more dangerously, till its final collapse in July 1914, as Britain declined and other large industrial countries rose to greater prominence, and adopted the Gold Standard [i.e. sought to become key currency countries] as a form of monetary nationalism, in order to deprive Britain of her last power, that of control over international financial flows.
>
> *(De Cecco 1984, vii–viii)*

If, internationally, the geopolitical economy of capitalism made it impossible for a national currency to function as the world currency even with gold backing and even with a vast empire, domestically, the political economy of capitalism also posed obstacles. While Eichengreen's (1992) account of the role of organised labour in undermining the gold standard by refusing to tolerate the periodic bouts of recession and unemployment it necessitated (see also Polanyi 1944/1985, 192–200) is confined to the inter-war years, Britain's legendary commitment to the gold standard was weakening well before 1914, inducing it to avoid its 'discipline' and 'adjustment' 'rather than continuing to accept the sacrifice of domestic unemployment' (Block 1977, 14; Lindert 1969, 74–5). Cosmopolitan legends—particularly theories of 'US hegemony'—that kept the image of the gold-sterling standard as stable and pervasive, even natural so the dollar's role might appear so despite much evidence to the contrary (Desai 2013, 124–51 for a fuller critique on these lines) were greatly helped by a critical historical turn in which the gold-sterling standard did not die a natural death brought on by its international and domestic contradictions but at the hands of an even greater contradiction of capitalism.

As we have seen, competition among capitalist countries as nationally organised blocs of capital for markets and 'economic territory'—the horizontal or competitive element of struggle between capitalist nations—also led to imperial competition for colonies. These forms of competition culminated in a profound and violent crisis of imperialism as well as capitalism, the Thirty Years' Crisis. It buried the gold-sterling standard and would have done the same to the idea that a single country's currency could pose as the world's—certainly Keynes went to Bretton Woods in 1944 with proposals originally intended to do precisely that (Desai 2009)—but for the United States' vain desire to emulate Britain's dominance by making the dollar the world's money.

It is often claimed, erroneously, that Keynes was defeated at Bretton Woods by the United States's Harry Dexter White. In reality, both were defeated by the US drive to foist the dollar on the world (Tily 2007; Block 1977; Hudson 1972/2003). Critically from our point of view, though it appeared to triumph, it was a vain, indeed, impossible project relying on a capitalist cosmopolitanism that would fail to prevail over the political economy that pointed towards socialism and the geopolitical economy of pluripolarity that was poised to aid it (Desai 2009). After the first attempt at forcing the dollar on the world failed thanks to this political and geopolitical economy, the United States' finance capital would be transformed into something resembling the United Kingdom's archaic and unproductive one, with very similar consequences for the United States' productive economy. But this is to run ahead. First, we must deal with the crisis in which the gold-sterling standard met its demise.

The Thirty Years' Crisis

Dominant understandings of the Thirty Years' Crisis see it as a merely temporary breakdown of the liberal world order of free trade and financial flows in two World Wars and Great Depression, an entirely contingent break between two 'waves of globalisation' or an 'interregnum' between British and US 'hegemonies'. After it, the onward march of capitalism through history and over the world is assumed to have continued.

However, it was a profoundly transformative crisis of both imperialism and capitalism. its class and national struggles intertwining to make it 'an 'international civil war' (Mayer 1967, 10). An authoritarian capitalist and imperial world had entered the crisis in 1914. Capitalism plumbed the nadir of its reputation thanks to its widely recognised implication in all the catastrophes of the period, including the world wars and the Great Depression. Working classes in the major capitalist countries demonstrated unprecedented combativeness, Communist revolutions inaugurated and concluded the crisis and, along with struggles for national liberation which crested in this period, the colonial world began rolling imperialism back. What emerged from the crisis was a world of unprecedented popular empowerment that was not easily amenable to either capitalism or imperialism.

Crisis of imperialism

In 1887, Engels, whose knowledge of matters military led Marx to nickname him 'the General', had foreseen a world war emerging out of the industrial and imperial competition of the major capitalist powers with uncanny accuracy. He spoke of 'a world war . . . of an extent and violence hitherto unimagined' with '[e]ight to ten million soldiers . . . strip[ping] Europe barer than a swarm of locusts'. Its dislocations, he warned, would bring about the 'irretrievable dislocation of our artificial system of trade, industry and credit, ending in universal bankruptcy; collapse of the old states and their conventional political wisdom to the point where crowns will roll into the gutters by the dozen, and no one will be around to pick them up'. It was not clear who the victor would be, '[o]nly one consequence is absolutely certain: universal exhaustion and the creation of the conditions for the ultimate victory of the working class' (Engels 1887, 451).

Although, given the Russian Revolution, not to mention the revolutionary waves throughout central Europe after the First World War, Engels was remarkably prescient, his prediction about the 'ultimate victory of the working class' was not realised. However, the extent of the transformation of the capitalist world order should not be underestimated. While a combination of objective pressures towards reformism, an acceptance of aspects of imperialism and the narrowing of Marxism as represented by the emergence of 'Marxist economics' prevented European social democracy from stopping the war in August 1914, and while a restoration of capitalism in its homelands, where it experienced a historically unprecedented Long Boom was a major outcome, much else underlay this surface appearance.

It was a crisis of imperialism, first and foremost, in that its causes lay in the contradictions of capitalism and the inevitable rivalry of capitalist imperialisms to which they gave rise. This was clear in the early twentieth-century starburst of Marxist writings on imperialism: Hilferding's *Finance Capital* (1910), Luxemburg's *The Accumulation of Capital* (1913), Lenin's *Imperialism, the Highest Stage of Capitalism* (1916) and Bukharin's *Imperialism and World Economy* (1917, but written in 1915). We add John Hobson, whose 1902 work, *Imperialism: A Study* (1902/1965) undoubtedly influenced by Marx's work, was much discussed in Marxist social circles, though we exclude Schumpeter's contemporaneous work (1919), which attributed imperialism not to capitalism but the persisting feudal influences.

Some, like Hobson and Luxemburg, established the formative and enduring relationship between capitalism and imperialism, rooted in the former's demand deficit. Others traced the intensified and competitive imperialism of their age to the new stage in the development of capitalism represented by the second industrial revolution and associated industrial, financial and political developments, naming it variously finance, monopoly or nationalised capital (Desai 2013, 43–53). Whatever their differences, however, these works were the first to understand the international relations of the capitalist world in relation to capitalism's structure and contradictions. As the first works to study the international relations of the capitalist world systematically, they are far more deserving of being considered the founding works of the discipline than the insipid, compromised and derivative 'idealism' of Woodrow Wilson that E. H. Carr named to that status instead (Carr 1939/1989).

Though dominant Western discourses long rejected this view of the causes of the First World War, accepting instead versions of the theory of German guilt that underlay the deeply faulty Versailles treaty that only ensured the Second World War, foremost Marxist historian, Eric Hobsbawm, had long refused this intellectually retrograde step (Hobsbawm 1987) and the Marxist view has recently been supported by Christopher Clarke's recent work (2012; see also Desai 2018a).

The Second World War was umbilically linked to the inter-imperialist First World War as a result of the punitive nature of the Versailles treaty, which settled little. Many of the dislocations of the inter-war period, including the shift to the right of which the rise of fascism and Nazism were the most extreme manifestations (Hobsbawm 1994, 112), were rooted in it. This is the key reason the entire period spanning the two World Wars must be considered a single crisis. The difference between the two wars can be better accounted for by the fact that the crisis of imperialism also led to the Russian Revolution and, as Lenin had foreseen in 1916, it began the 'most difficult but most important task[,] . . . to merge the class struggle of the workers in the oppressing nations with the class struggle of the workers in the oppressed nations.' Without Communist influence among the working-class combatants and partisans in Europe, the critical contributions of the Soviet Union itself, those of Communist forces in China and elsewhere in Asia, and those of colonial armies raised on promises of decolonisation, the victory of liberal capitalism against over capitalism's own distinctive evil, Nazism and fascism, would not have been possible.

Communism was working on fertile ground worldwide. The Thirty Years' Crisis occurred in the age of mass politics that began in the late nineteenth century and advanced it explosively. The First World War brought mass conscription involving arming ordinary working people and industrialised warfare to authoritarian capitalisms, making for an 'inseparability of strain of defeat in war and reform or revolution' (Mayer 1967, 7). The dislocations of the First World War coincided with a revolutionary wave that swept Europe and reverberated much farther. The three pre-capitalist empires that had survived thus far into the capitalist world fell, giving rise to new nations. Throughout Europe, revolutions—Germany's November Revolution, Italy's Biennio Rosso, Austria's social democratic governments and Red Vienna, to name the most prominent—threatened both defeated and victorious powers. Reaction, including fascism, rising in their wake, imparted to these decades their civil war-like character.

The Bolshevik Revolution of 1917 was the only one in this revolutionary wave to survive largely because, as is widely understood, Tsarist Russia was the 'weak link' in the imperial chain, though the Bolsheviks' deft incorporation of the peasantry and the various non-Russian peoples of the Tsarist empire into the revolution were critically important too. Moreover, after the Bolshevik Revolution. capitalist powers did everything in their power to destroy it and to prevent further revolutions. That included the decisions made at the Versailles peace conference 'all of which, in varying degrees, were designed to check Bolshevism' and generally set back the revolutionary wave. These measures included making territorial concessions to bordering nations, aiding them and the White counter-revolution, direct military action and blockade against the revolution, economic assistance and the establishment of the International Labour Organization and the League of Nations to 'immunize . . . the non-Bolshevik Left against the ideological bacillus of the Bolshevik Revolution' (Mayer 1967, 9).

In these unpropitious international circumstances, and even less favourable domestic ones given the economic backwardness of most of Russia, the Russian Revolution began humanity's long march towards socialism. Doing so from outside the homelands of capitalism, it had combined achieving social justice critically important to its legitimacy with developing the productive forces not only from a very low point, further lowered by war, but also against unremitting imperialist hostility. If this was hard enough, the revolutionary authorities had to experiment in their attempts to build socialism for lack of guidelines, particularly relating to a backward economy. Against these odds, the Soviet Union was created in 1922 and survived, stabilised, and industrialised rapidly just when the West was in the throes of the Great Depression. By the end of the First Five Year Plan, the Russia had become the second industrial power, massively increased literacy, life expectancy and access to medical care.

Thanks to the far from ideal conditions in which the transition to socialism had to be attempted, there were, of course, major distortions. They included the great famine, the consequence of the need to transfer resources from agriculture to industry without which industrialisation was impossible in non-imperialist countries, combined with ideological limitations and those of state capacity. The bureaucratised and 'institutionally paranoid' state apparatus was another result of the difficult conditions as were the problems of forced collectivisation and the inconsistency of Soviet Policy towards revolution elsewhere, whether in Europe or in the Third World. All these distortions were usually associated with Stalin but had deeper historical roots (Lewin 1995).

While these blots in the Soviet Union's socialist copybook provided the Western left with so many weapons to wield in dismissing actually occurring socialist revolutions, at least one major chronicler of the Third World was in no doubt that any historical balance sheet on the Soviet Union will have to accept that

> the Russian Revolution and the Five-Year Plans have affected fundamentally the course of contemporary history. They made possible, for example, the decisive

> Soviet contribution to the defeat of Nazi Germany. And for the Third World, the Soviet system represents the first break-away from the international market economy and the first viable alternative model to traditional Western capitalism.
>
> *(Stavrianos 1981, 510)*

Moreover, in the context of the Great Depression, the attractions of Soviet Communism spread around the industrialised world too, with the Webbs hailing a new civilisation and Keynes seriously considering its 'experiment' (Webb and Webb 1935; Keynes 1933).

Though the Russian Revolution represented the strongest challenge to it, imperialism was also drastically set back elsewhere. Beyond Europe, popular movements were transforming the political landscape: in Turkey, Japan, China and India, 'an old order was being jostled by a new one' (Mayer 1967, 7). Resistance to imperialism in the colonies and semi-colonies before 1914 had remained largely confined to ineffectual 'conservative traditionalists and . . . conformist Westernizers' (Stavrianos 1981, 425). Those attuned to Marxism's critique of capitalism, its contradictions and imperialism, had remained few, thanks to the Second International's weaknesses on matters of imperialism and anti-imperialist resistance.

However, even before 1914, there had been ferment in Mexico, Turkey, China and Ireland and during the First World War, mass politics spread in the colonies. The First World War had already seen sufficiently strong nationalist mobilisations to prevent the victorious powers from simply taking over all the colonies of the defeated powers and force upon them the pretence that was the mandates system. As the Thirty Years' Crisis wore on, the Great Depression intensified pressures on colonial peasantries through low prices and high debt (Rothermund 1996, 11–12) radically undermining the already thread-bare legitimacy of colonial orders and boosting nationalist movements in important colonies such as India. However, the Second World War was decisive:

> Though it was far more than this, it was unquestionably an inter-imperialist war and, until 1943, the great colonial empires were on the losing side. France collapsed ignominiously. . . . The Japanese overran . . . British, Dutch and other Western colonies in South-east Asia and the Western Pacific. Even in North Africa, the Germans occupied what they chose to control up to a few score miles West of Alexandria. At one point the British seriously considered withdrawing from Egypt. . . . What fatally damaged the old colonialists was the proof that white men and their states could be defeated, shamefully and dishonourably, and that the old colonial powers were patently too weak, even after a victorious war, to restore their old positions.
>
> *(Hobsbawm 1994, 216)*

With the wars necessitating colonial levies of troops and rising wartime taxes, as the war wore on it was clear that decolonisation was imminent in British India, the largest colony, and could only be briefly postponed elsewhere.

At the same time, the Soviet Union supported self-determination for the colonies, aided the establishment of Communist parties in them, consolidated an international Communist movement by creating the Comintern in 1919 and engaged in anti-imperialist cooperation with nationalist movements. As decolonisation began after the end of the Second World War, the Soviet model for developing economies and societies resonated far more among them than Western ones.

The Chinese model would resonate even more. Indeed, the Soviet Union and the nascent Chinese revolution became as two eyes of the storm of progressive forces assailing capitalism and imperialism worldwide during the Thirty Years' Crisis. If the Russian Revolution was the only surviving rump of the revolutionary wave in Europe, the Chinese revolution was the leading edge of the anti-colonial movement. With the countries liberated by the Red Army in the Second World War having turned to socialism after 1945, and the Chinese revolution of 1949, very large swaths of the world's territories and populations came under Communist leadership and were subtracted from the capitalist world.

While Soviet and Comintern aid and advice were not always consistent or correct, the Communist International contributed to the 'birth, development, consolidation and maturation' of the Communist Party of China and 'advanced its theoretical self-consciousness' at a time when it 'was itself conducting theoretical exploration', which required it to 'adjust its own theories and change its strategies'. Of course, in the end, it was 'the ability of Chinese communists to Sinicise Marxism–Leninism in what amounted to a theoretical revolution under Mao Zedong's leadership that accounts for the revolution's ultimate victory' (Cheng and Yang 2020, 1338).

The two Communist revolutions had important differences. Unlike the Bolshevik Revolution that took power amid the sudden collapse of the Tsarist order, the Chinese revolution gestated over decades, beginning well before the Thirty Years' Crisis, and transforming itself in its course from a movement for national liberation into one for Communism. This may explain the contrast between the Soviet Union's demise and the People's Republic of China's continuing advance towards socialism:

> perhaps the most decisive of all the differences between Russia and China lay in the character of their political leadership. In command of the PRC was not an isolated, inexperienced functionary, surrounded by aides and publicists infused with a naive *Schwärmerei* for all that was Western, but battle-hardened veterans of the original Revolution, leaders who had been Mao's colleagues, and had suffered under him, but had lost none of their strategic skills or self-confidence.
>
> *(Anderson 2010)*

Moreover, China under Mao achieved 'developmental and socialist goals which defied most post-colonial and developing nations' including 'self-sufficient and self-reliant economy free from . . . foreign control', an end to capitalist exploitation, a 'highly egalitarian and participatory society', increases in nutrition and welfare, rapid industrialisation and a 'solution to the peasant question: equity via land reform cooperation and communisation for the peasant majority and avoidance of a host of problems from unemployment to marginality associated with the rush to cities elsewhere' (Selden 1988).

As such, China became and remains an experience from which the Third World has more to learn that the Soviet Union, let alone the West.

Crisis of capitalism

Thanks to post-war decolonisation, the Thirty Years' Crisis is readily recognised as a crisis of imperialism but much less as a crisis of capitalism. The Great Depression is certainly not ignored. The contrast between the capitalist West suffering in its throes and the Soviet Union industrialising at an astonishing pace led some to wonder if it was 'new civilization' (Webb and Webb 1935) and others to wonder if capitalism had not entered 'secular stagnation' (Hansen 1939). At the end of the Second World War most in the West feared a return to the Depression conditions. However, the post-war 'golden age' or Long Boom of capitalism appeared to shrug off this history. Historical realities do not support such nonchalance and, as should become clear with the progress of our argument, they have acquired a heightened relevance today. It is important, therefore, to outline them.

When Lenin and the other Marxists argued that capitalism had reached its 'highest stage' already in the early twentieth century, they were only developing Marx's quite accurate insights about capitalism's trajectory. Insofar as capitalism had a progressive historical role of developing the productive forces by socialising labour and production, once it transited from its competitive to its monopoly phase, from socialising productive labour between productive units to socialising it within them, once it had transformed finance from its archaic predatory and speculative form to one that assisted the productive expansion of capital, it had completed its historic mission, brought capitalism to the point where it was: incapable of spontaneous productive dynamism, however disruptive and destructive. Once it had taken the further socialisation of labour out of the governance of the market and put it under that of the authoritative (and authoritarian) planning of production and finance in capitalist firms and financial institutions, monopoly capitalism inevitably forsook the virtues of competition.

Capitalism was now ripe for transition to socialism, for a popular takeover of the vast apparatuses of planned production that were its corporations and the even vaster apparatuses of planned financial allocation that were its banks. It was time to replace capitalist authoritative planning in giant firms with democratic socialist planning of them, and replace such economic coordination as provided by monopolistic or oligopolistic markets with democratic central planning of entire economies. Keynes proposed to keep national capitalisms (Keynes 1933), bending them to the fulfilment of popular needs and designed his original proposals at Bretton to support such policy priorities (Desai 2009). In the United States, a National Survey of Potential Product Capacity revealed the gap between productive capacity and unfulfilled need and advocated closing it by increasing purchasing power

(Loeb et al. 1935). Polanyi looked forward to 'crustacean nations' transforming the 'universal capitalism' of the nineteenth century (Polanyi 1945) into a 'new pattern of international life', which Polanyi argued, 'greatly improved' the 'chances of democratic socialism' (Polanyi 1945). For his part, Paul Sweezy was convinced in 1942 that after the war, 'the socialist sector of the world would quickly stabilize itself and push forward to higher standards of living while the imperialist sector would flounder in the difficulties with which we are already sufficiently familiar'. He rejected the idea that there would be a clash between the two, hoping that

> the gravitational pull . . . of the fundamentally stronger and more stable socialist system would exercise a progressively disintegrating effect on the structure of the imperialist system, first paralysing its capacity for aggression and then chipping out bit by bit the cement which holds it together as a cohesive social structure.
>
> *(Sweezy 1942, 361)*

If, despite these hopes and expectations, the world's major capitalisms were not transformed into socialisms, it was thanks to the confluence of several factors.

The first was imperialism. Certainly, at the start of the Thirty Years' Crisis, not only did it nurture strong reformist currents among the working classes of imperial countries, capitalist countries' command over vast colonial economies gave them the political and geopolitical strength to resist what revolutionary currents existed and it is not surprising that fascisms, the other available means for opposing socialism, were strongest in countries with smaller or, in the case of Germany, lost, empires. Empires also contributed considerable blood and treasure to ensure the victory of the Allied powers. Having remained in possession of considerable territories over the course of the crisis, major colonial powers put up serious rear-guard action to preserve or restore their empires such the French in Vietnam, the Dutch in Indonesia and the British in Malaya.

The second was, paradoxically, anti-imperialism and Communism: Communist and other anti-imperialist forces saved capitalism from its own progeny, fascism. The Soviet Union, the coalition of nationalist and Communist forces of China and colonial armies had, as we have seen, made the difference between victory and defeat against fascism. At the same time, having won the war against fascism with the aid of Communist and anti-imperialist forces, the liberal capitalist powers did not hesitate to harness fascist personnel and even organisations to secure capitalism in its historic homelands and elsewhere.

Finally, the structures of imperialism underwent a shift, an unexpected one. On the eve of the Thirty Years' Crisis, they had been formed by Britain's early industrial and imperial lead, which left it in possession of the greatest empire in history even as it lost industrial competitiveness and the Empire, along with the gold-sterling system that rested on it, allowed Britain to remain the most powerful capitalist nation. Had competition among major industrial powers not led to the First World War, pressures generated by the dialectic of UCD, including competition between nationally organised blocks of capital, would have likely resulted in the consolidation of rival capitalist empires.

This was certainly the drift of events. As we have already seen, with the rise of challengers, Britain faced historical choices: to abandon the commitment to free trade that was undermining her industry and join the rest of the capitalist world by creating a protectionist bloc out of her empire or to stick to that commitment and try to expand the liberal free-trading world. Even as the historical undertow pulled in the latter direction, its ruling classes, their historically formed character, their Empire and their archaic financial system committed Britain to the second option. This was why Britain made the second fateful choice to 'fight Germany rather than the United States' in the coming war with the result that, over the Thirty Years' Crisis, 'while the British helped to defeat Germany, it also lost its power to the US' (Gamble 1994, 59)

Nothing could have been more agreeable to US business and policymakers. Since the early twentieth century, they had sought to replace the United Kingdom as 'the managing segment of the world economy'. Knowing they could never acquire an empire the size of Britain's, they settled on trying to make the dollar the world's money run from New York, as sterling had been run from London. The fly in this ointment was, as we shall see, that sterling's role had rested on empire and was, even then, being destabilised. Without an empire, the dollar's career as world money could only be rocky (Desai 2013, 2018b).

The story of the phase of imperialism dominated by the United States is that of its relentless attempts to realise its unrealisable ambition. During the Thirty Years' Crisis, in pursuit of this ambition the United States timed its late entry in both wars so as to maximise the benefit to its economy by acting as the unscathed supplier of war materiel (Lens 2003, 252–3). As Figure 3.2 shows, the wager succeeded: the two wars constitute the two greatest periods of growth in the US economy in modern times.

However, its efforts to become the world's financial power by demanding repayment of its loans to its First World War allies only led them to demand reparations from Germany, forming that umbilical cord that tied the First World War to the Second (Hudson 1972/2003, 50, 112). The financial merry-go-round it created between German reputations, Allied repayments and US loans to Germany also contributed to the 1929 stock market crash (Desai 2013, 82–3). After the Second World War, US attempts to restore capitalist imperialism of the pre-1914 variety, this time under its leadership, was up against the inexorable unfolding of UCD towards multi- and pluripolarity. As we shall see, they prevented the United States from succeeding in its mimetic ambition.

The socialistic golden age

Theories of US hegemony emerged in the 1970s to proclaim that in the post-war decades 'US hegemony' had engineered the conditions of prosperity. The truth is, however, near the opposite (Desai 2013, 124–37).

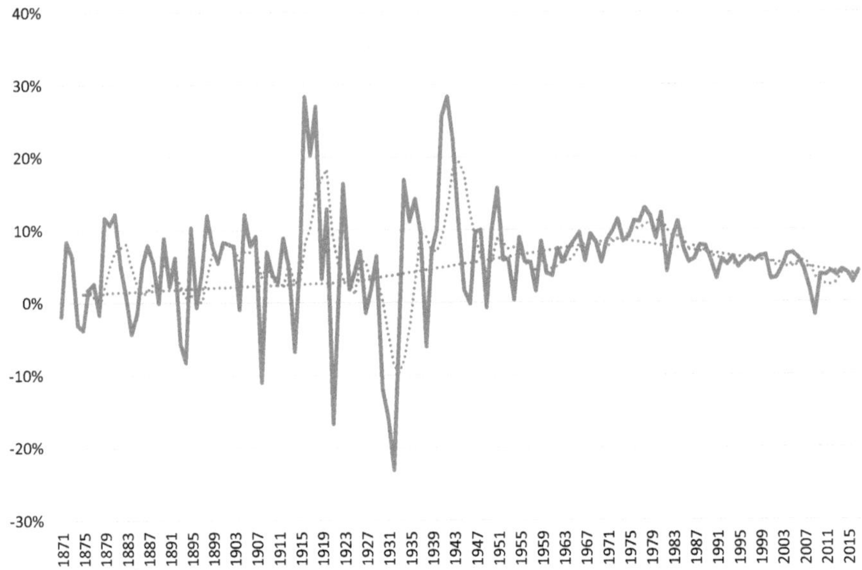

FIGURE 3.2 US annual GDP growth 1871–2015 and five-year moving average.

Source: Data from Jordà, Òscar; Schularick, Moritz; and Taylor Alan M. 2017. 'Macrofinancial History and the New Business Cycle Facts', in Eichenbaum, Martin and Parker, Jonathan A. (eds), *NBER Macroeconomics Annual*, 31(1), pp. 213–263. Chicago: University of Chicago Press.

Created by Alan Freeman, used with permission.

Neither the overwhelming productive dominance the war gave the United States nor the devastation of the rest of the world's major economies in war could overcome the powerful undertow of pluripolarity. Pressures emanating from the United States' capitalist rivals, the Communist world and the Third World constrained its effort to create an open world economy under its dominance.

Rival capitalist powers were jealous of their remaining privileges—including the empires the United States wanted to loosen from their grips—and needed to pursue state-led combined development for recovery from war. The United States may have managed to ensure that Keynes's proposal for 'bancor' as the world's currency for international settlements, managed by an International Clearing Union designed to run the world economy in such a way as to permit all countries to pursue maximum and relatively egalitarian growth and full employment and thus to advance pluripolarity, was rejected, and the dollar forced on an unwilling world. However, it had to promise its rivals dollar–gold convertibility, a burden it would soon fail to bear, and concede a critically important element of Keynes' scheme, capital controls, for fear that economically destabilising capital movements would increase the attractions of Communism among highly mobilised working classes in war-ravaged capitalist countries (Block 1977; Desai 2009). With trade subject to multilateral negotiation, Europe and Japan also managed trade heavily.

With the Communist world simply subtracting vast territories and populations from the sphere of capitalism and the Third World pursuing national autonomous, that is, combined development, the world economy was far from an open free market and free trade utopia US elites desired. United States' power over even its capitalist parts was uncertain at best.

Political economy

The lineaments of the resulting post-war order underlined the veracity of Marxist anticipations that, in its monopoly phase, capitalism was ripe for socialism, and Keynes's and Polanyi's anticipations of a world of planning. After 1945, capitalist economies could stabilise and even enjoy a three-decade-long 'golden age' only by ringing their monopoly capitalist corporations around with socialistic structures, committing to running economies for full, or at least very high, employment with 'Keynesian' demand management and borrowing social welfare, public ownership and planning from the policy toolkits of the Communist countries, essentially complementing the planning within monopolistic corporations that dominated the economy with state planning. 'Politicians, officials and even many of the businessmen of the post-war West' understood that

> a return to *laissez-faire* and the unreconstructed free market were out of the question. Certain policy objectives—full employment, the containment of communism, the modernization of lagging or declining or ruined economies—had absolute priority and justified the strongest government presence. Even regimes dedicated to economic and political liberalism now could, and had to, run their economies in ways which would once have been rejected as 'socialist'.
>
> *(Hobsbawm 1994, 272–3)*

If this was true of Western Europe, Eastern Asia, the other side of the Communist world, had its own counterpart: land reform formed the basis of Japan's economic renaissance and of the rise of the other two major capitalisms of the region, South Korea and Taiwan.

The resulting Keynesian welfare states and developmental states were supported by the immensely more productive Fordist production organisation, the assembly line production of standardised goods for mass markets (Aglietta 1976) and they also enabled its adoption beyond the United States, hitherto stalled by the Great Depression, throughout the world. *Inter alia*, the focus on fuller employment, higher wages and the welfare state expanded working-class consumption to compensate major capitalist countries for their loss of colonial markets (Desai 2015), contributing critically to alleviating the demand problem (Desai 2015) while also preventing Western working classes and Eastern peasants from yielding to the attractions of communism. The United States was, therefore, forced to tolerate and even aid the very statist 'miracle' recoveries of rivals while also employing many of the same measures. Indeed, inter-capitalist rivalries ensured that all major capitalist countries used newly minted tools of 'Keynesian' macroeconomic management to the fullest to promote national economic growth, including by sponsoring research and development for productivity growth (Freeman and Soete 1997). Planning, state ownership, economic and trade management, public funding for research and development in 'national system of innovation' (Freeman 1987) and fiscal and monetary policy geared towards full employment and development were normal and pervasive among post-war capitalist economies while capital controls confined capital in national cages, orienting it to productive investment.

It was no wonder then that many imagined that the advanced countries were already advancing towards socialism, peacefully and gradually rather than through violent revolutions (Crosland 1956), and many others argued that the Soviet Union and the planned economies of the West were converging (Galbraith and Men'shikov 1988; Tsagolov 2017).

Geopolitical economy

To this political economy post-war capitalisms' golden age and Long Boom of capitalism corresponded a distinct geopolitical economy. With its war-swollen economy having attained overwhelming dominance over its capitalist rivals, the United States not only sought to impose the dollar on the world, it led the campaign against Communism by dropping atomic bombs on Japan (their purpose had little to do with ensuring Japanese surrender. IT was to demonstrate to the Soviet Union that the US now wielded this horrific weapon, as Desai 2022 argues), continuing with its wars in Korea and Vietnam and engaging in other interventions to compel the allegiance of the emerging Third World.

One major implication of this self-assigned role was the US need to maintain a relatively open economy to model the behaviour it was urging on other countries or at least appear to do so. This meant that, while domestic demand expanded under socialistic Keynesian welfarist arrangements in all major capitalist countries and 'must have helped endow these economies with greater stability than in the past' (Brenner 1998, 91), the Long Boom was more robust outside the United States and the United Kingdom, particularly in the 'miracle economies' of Germany and Japan, while the United States, and the traditionally more open United Kingdom, stagnated in the 1950s and enjoyed only a brief and highly inflationary boom in the 1960s.

> Where the autonomous growth of demand did operate powerfully to augment investment and growth, it appears to have done so, paradoxically, less within national boundaries than across them. German and Japanese manufacturers derived much of their dynamism by means of appropriating large segments of the fast-growing world market from the US and the UK. This redistribution of market share . . . gave a powerful boost to their investment and output, while detracting somewhat from the growth prospects of the US and the UK. The resulting pattern of development was extremely uneven, but it made for a boom of historic proportions.
>
> *(Brenner 1998, 91)*

From 1950 to 1973, the US annual average growth rate as 3.6% while that of Germany and Japan was 5.9 and 9.3% (Brenner 1998, 39).

Not only did the United Kingdom continue its decades-long industrial decline, the United States too began experiencing a similar decline. While the war had turbocharged its economy, the United States entered the post-war war era laden down with industrial plant of older technological provenance while the recovering economies could invest in the latest technologies. At the same time, its desire to dominate a world economy open to itself constrained it to model free market and free trade policies, or at least feign to do so and this prevented the United States from taking recourse to the sort of developmental state industrial policies that its strongest capitalist competitors, Germany and Japan, were pursuing.

Reduced to no more than demand management over an economy losing competitiveness, the United States was unable to generate growth without inflation, even though its attack on labour from the 1960s onwards prompted 'a fundamental shift in the balance of class power and in the character of management–labour relations', which persisted into the neoliberal era (Brenner 1998, 58) wherein the traditionally high-wage US economy would be transformed an increasingly low-wage one. While it increased profitability, it did little to expand markets, which were, in any case, prone to import penetration thanks to the United States' comparative trade openness. Thus, already during the Long Boom, large parts of the US economy came to rely not on technological advancement but on depressing wages and exchange rate devaluation to increase competitiveness. And of these, the latter could not be a normal one given US project of enthroning the dollar as the world's currency.

Even so, the gold-backed dollar's career as world money during the Long Boom was a troubled one and ended in 1971. Without an empire, in competition with its capitalist rivals to maintain high growth rates, the United States could not export capital to provide liquidity and ran current account deficits instead, particularly to finance its wars in Korea and Vietnam. This method was subject to the Triffin dilemma (Triffin 1961): deficits lowered the dollar's value. After 1958, when major European currencies became convertible, the United States' vast gold hoard was drained down so quickly by countries that ran trade surpluses with it, particularly European countries, that, by 1961, there was not enough gold to back dollars in circulation given that US law required 20% of the paper currency in circulation to be backed by gold. The United States has to persuade its allies to pool their gold to retain the dollar's gold peg.

Over the next decade, the dollar lurched from crisis to crisis and exhausted all expedients for dealing with the drain of gold (detailed in Desai 2013, 111–23). They ranged from claiming that there was no objective problem, only one of confidence under Kennedy to ending domestic gold convertibility to trying to deal with the deficit through 'special transactions tax' and persuading allies to repay war and Marshall Plan debts early, buy more US military supplies, make advance payments on them, hold their surplus dollars in non-convertible US Treasury bills and, not least, agree to a de facto embargo on US gold sales under Johnson. Having exhausted them all, knowing that restoring the dollar's gold value would require punishing economic measures at home, Nixon abandoned convertibility in August 1971. Just over a quarter century after the United States scuttled Keynes' plan at Bretton Woods to install the dollar as world money, it had failed and all it had to show for it was the loss of its enviable gold reserves. Given this tumultuous history, it is ironic, to say the least, that theories of 'US hegemony', in which the dollar's world role is usually the leading element, consider the post-war period to be that of US hegemony *par excellence* (Desai 2013, 124–37).

Outside the imperial heartlands, meanwhile, Communist-led countries enjoyed robust and enviably sustained growth, reinforced by technological innovation. Economic growth until the mid-1970s was higher in the USSR than in the West largely because of its greater investment, its freedom from cyclical downturns, fuller employment and its skilled and productive workforce (Kotz 1997/2005, 37–8). In the 1960s and 1970s, the USSR and the Communist bloc entered a relatively high-level stasis where productivity was high and more and more consumer goods were widely available, though agricultural productivity remained a problem, particularly as Soviet diets began to include more meat, generating secondary demand for grain, which was higher than could be produced domestically. The Soviet Union produced deterrent nuclear weapons by 1949, launched the Sputnik satellite in 1957 and put Yuri Gagarin into orbit in 1961, forcing the United States into the envious stunt of landing 'Man' on the moon.

While Communists struggled for power in many Third World countries, and succeeded in some, nearly all Third World countries engaged in some form of autonomous national development and, considering that they did not enjoy the luxury of imperial surpluses to aid their development, they inclined towards Soviet or Chinese models rather than Western 'development' recommendations.

Though it disappointed the high hopes of the early years, the development record of the Third World represented a vast improvement over the colonial period. Indian growth and per capita growth, for instance, were estimated at 0.8% and 0.04% annually between 1900 and 1947 and at 4.2% and 2.1% between 1950 and 2005. During these decades, Third World growth often surpassed that of the fast, even miraculously recovering capitalist world, as Figure 3.3 shows.

While, undoubtedly, the limits, political and administrative, of the Third World development efforts largely accounted for their limited success, the West's Long Boom also contributed by making industrialisation less urgent by increasing demand for Third World primary commodities. Though there were some significant successes in developing industry, too much of the growth of Third World economies in the 1950s and 1960s was due to expanding primary production. Both First and Third World dominant classes had vested interests in the continuation of these relationships and were able to keep them in place.

Overall, the post-war world's political centre of gravity shifted decisively to the advantage of the world's working and popular classes. While there were blockages in this broad sweep of progressive advance, pre-eminently the Sino-Soviet split, most expected the world's leftward inclination to continue into socialism.

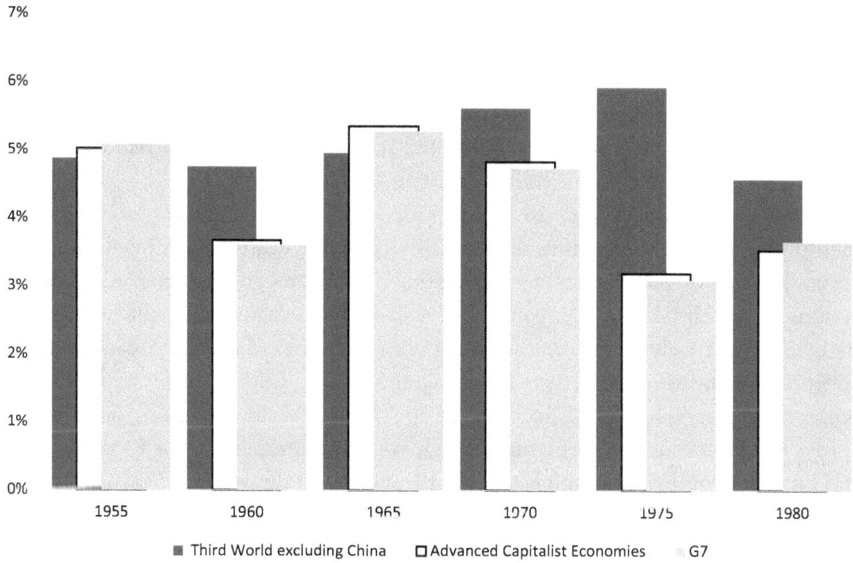

FIGURE 3.3 Five-year annual average real growth of the G7, the advanced capitalist economies and the Third World, 1950–1980.

Source: Data from World Development Indicators, World Bank https://databank.worldbank.org/source/world-development-indicators.

Created by Alan Freeman, used with permission.

If there was one problem in the world's broad leftward tilt, it was that capital remained in command in major capitalist economies, no matter how much they were reformed. Inevitably, it expanded productive capacity, with the support of states, and while increased working class consumption and socialist and developmental advances vastly expanded demand of the post-war era, inevitably production outstripped demand. Productivity growth also peaked, despite considerable state support and, as highly organised Western working classes and Third World countries demanded higher wages and prices, they also squeezed imperialist capital's profits. Inevitably, investment and growth slowed, and imperialist economies entered a crisis: the Second Slump of the 1970s, 'a classic overproduction crisis' rooted in a 'general overabundance of capital relative to the possibilities of valorisation', that is, demand (Mandel 1982, 22, 30).

Descent into crisis

Going beyond impressionistic accounts blaming the crisis on Organization of Petroleum Exporting Countries (OPEC) or the unions, Marxist and Marxisant writers analysed it in various ways. While all emphasised its multifaceted character, they tended to emphasise a particular element. The regulation school, for example, which attributed the golden age to the massive productivity increases that came with the Fordist organisation of production, ascribed its end to Fordism's inability to yield further productivity increases thanks to its separation of intellectual from manual labour (Lipietz 1992, a point that is, empirically at least, supported by Robert Gordon's analysis of the history of productivity increases in the US economy (Gordon 2012). Andrew Glyn attributed it to increased labour militancy eroding profits (Glyn 2006).

However, these accounts, like most, focused on the domestic level, at best identifying common elements across major capitalist countries. However, while certainly both of these were factors. we need a proper political and geopolitical economy, which takes account of the role of states in managing capitalism's contradictions not only domestically but also in their international engagement in competition and struggle between 'producing nations', both capitalist and socialist. Robert Brenner's historical account of the Long Boom and Long Downturn comes closest to our requirements, though we must compensate for its theoretical and analytical quirks and limitations—for instance, its dismissal of Marx's account of the TRPF or its elision of imperialism.

In this account, the slump of the 1970s was the inevitable result of the Long Boom, thanks to capitalism's contradictions. During it, the recovery of Western Europe and Japan, and the United States' ability to maintain fairly robust growth, added far more capacity than demand, leading to overcapacity and overproduction. Though he does not discuss the problem of demand deficits theoretically and in the opening pages even relies on the Marxist economics' dismissal of the problem of the Tendency of the Rate of Profit to Fall (TRPF), Brenner's explanation is located squarely at the intersection of the two. Overcapacity and overproduction could be said to exist, he remarkes, 'in the sense that—*there is insufficient demand* to allow the higher cost firms to maintain their former rates of profit; they have been obliged to cease using some of their means of production and can make use of the rest only by lowering their price and thus their profitability' (Brenner 1998, 25–6, emphasis added). Internationally competing producers face falling profits, therefore, thanks to

> the tendency of producers to develop the productive forces and increase economic productiveness by means of the installation of increasingly cheap and effective methods of production, without regard for existing investments and their requirements for realization, with the result that aggregate profitability is squeezed by reduced prices in the face of downwardly inflexible costs.
>
> *(Brenner 1998, 23–4)*

That is to say, competition leaves 'the cost-cutters' rates of profit . . . the same as before [while] . . . the higher cost firms' rates of profit are reduced', resulting in an aggregate reduction in profit rates. Moreover, such overcapacity and overproduction are premised on paucity of demand: they exist 'in the sense that—there is insufficient demand to allow the higher cost firms to maintain their former rates of profit' (Brenner 1998, 25–6). Once the capitalist world entered the slump, the United States and the United Kingdom, which had already had a considerably less Golden Age than their capitalist rivals, also suffered deeper slumps.

By 1970s, moreover, post-war dollar system was in crisis. During the Long Boom, the dollar's fortunes remined tied to those of the US productive economy and its trade performance and, as it lost competitiveness while incurring expanding current account deficits to its wars in Korea and then Vietnam, its troubles mounted until the dollar's gold link had to be broken.

With two comparatively liberal economies losing out, with the post-war dollar system in tatters thanks to the United States' peculiar combination of productive decline and imperial overreach, the slump of the 1970s should have been the moment for a deepening of capitalist regulation and for the liberal economies to follow the productive lead of their more regulated and developmentalist rivals, particularly Germany and Japan. What followed the onset of the Long Downturn is little more than the story of how capitalist world, led by the United States and the United Kingdom, has resisted this option and led the world down the path that could only weaken productive economies and expand predatory and speculative finance and lead to the disasters of the pandemic and the current war.

References

Aglietta, Michel. 1976. *A Theory of Capitalist Regulation: The US Experience*. London: New Left Books.

Amsden, Alice H. 1992. *Asia's Next Giant: South Korea and Late Industrialization*. New York: Oxford University Press.

Anderson, Perry. 1968. 'Components of the National Culture', *New Left Review*, I/50, July–August, pp. 3–57.

Anderson, Perry. 2010. 'Two Revolutions', *New Left Review*, 61, pp. 59–96. https://newleftreview.org/issues/ii61/articles/perry-anderson-two-revolutions

Barkin, David; and Sánchez, Alejandra. 2020. 'The Communitarian Revolutionary Subject: New Forms of Social Transformation', in Desai, Radhika and Heller, Henry (eds), *Revolutions*, pp. 1421–1441. London: Routledge.

Block, Fred. 1977. *The Origins of International Economic Disorder: A Study of United States International Monetary Policy From World War II to the Present*. Berkeley: University of California Press.

Brenner, Robert. 1998. 'The Looming Crisis of World Capitalism: From Neoliberalism to Depression?', *Against the Current*, 13(5), p. 22.

Bukharin, Nicolai. 1917. *Imperialism and World Economy*. New York: Monthly Review Press.

Carr, Edward Hallett. 1939/1989. *The Twenty Years' Crisis, 1919–1939*. London: Macmillan.

Chang, Ha-Joon. 2002. *Kicking Away the Ladder: Development Strategy in Historical Perspective*. London: Anthem.

Cheng, Enfu; and Yang, Jun. 2020. 'The Chinese Revolution and the Communist International', *Third World Quarterly*, 41(8), pp. 1338–52. https://doi.org/10.4324/9781003178323-6

Christophers, Brett. 2020. *Rentier Capitalism: Who Owns the Economy, and Who Pays for It?* New York: Verso.

Clarke, Christopher. 2012. *The Sleepwalkers: How Europe Went to War in 1914*. New York: HarperCollins.

Colletti, Lucio. 1972. 'Bernstein and the Marxism of the Second International', in *From Rouseau to Lenin: Studies in Ideology and Society*. New York: Monthly Review Press.

Crosland, Anthony. 1956. *The Future of Socialism*. London: Jonathan Cape.

De Cecco, Marcello. 1984. *The International Gold Standard: Money and Empire*. 2nd ed. London: Pinter.

Desai, Radhika. 2009. 'Keynes Redux: From World Money to International Money at Last?', in Anthony, Wayne and Guard, Julie (eds), *Bailouts and Bankruptcies*, pp. 123–43. Halifax: Fernwood Books.

Desai, Radhika. 2012. 'Marx, List and the Materiality of Nations', *Rethinking Marxism*, 24(1), January, pp. 47–67.

Desai, Radhika. 2013. *Geopolitical Economy: After US Hegemony, Globalization and Empire*. London: Pluto.

Desai, Radhika. 2015. 'Look Back in Hope? Reassessing Fordism Today', in Van der Pijl, Kees (ed), *The International Political Economy of Production*, pp. 192–210. Cheltenham: Edward Elgar. https://doi.org/10.4337/9781783470211.00023

Desai, Radhika. 2018a. 'The First World War: Climax and Crisis of Imperialism', in Bromber, Katrin; Lange, Katharina; Liebau, Heike; and Wetzel, Anorthe (eds), *The Long End of the First World War: Ruptures, Continuities and Memories*, pp. 17–44. New York and Frankfurt: Campus Verlag.

Desai, Radhika. 2018b. 'John Maynard Pangloss: Indian Currency and Finance in Imperial Context', in *The General Theory and Keynes for the 21st Century*, pp. 116–31. Cheltenham: Edward Elgar Publishing. https://doi.org/10.4337/9781786439888.00016

Desai, Radhika. 2020. 'Marx's Critical Political Economy, "Marxist Economics" and Actually Occurring Revolutions Against Capitalism', *Third World Quarterly*, 41(8), pp. 1353–70. https://doi.org/10.1080/01436597.2020.1741346

Desai, Radhika. 2021. 'Marx's Geopolitical Economy: "The Relations of Producing Nations"', *Capital & Class*, pp. 3–10. https://doi.org/10.1177%2F03098168211017433

Desai, Radhika; and Heller, Henry. 2019. 'Cold War', in Ness, I. and Cope, Z. (eds), *The Palgrave Encyclopedia of Imperialism and Anti-Imperialism*, pp. 1–22. London: Palgrave Macmillan. https://doi.org/10.1007/978-3-319-91206-6_16-1

Desai, Radhika. 2022. 'The Long Shadow of Hiroshima: Capitalism and Nuclear Weapons', *International Critical Thought*, 8 April, pp. 1–21. https://doi.org/10.1080/215982 82.2022.2051582 Eichengreen, Barry. 1992. *Golden Fetters: The Gold Standard and the Great Depression, 1919–1939*. Oxford: Oxford University Press.

Engels, Friedrich. 1887. 'Introduction to Sigismund Borkheim's Pamphlet *In Memory of the German Blood-and-Thunder Patriots, 1806–1807*', in *Marx and Engels Collected Works*, 26.

Engels, Friedrich. 1895. 'Engels to Conrad Schmidt', *SW Ryazanskaya*, 12 March, pp. 456–60.

English, Richard; and Kenny, Michael. 2000. *Rethinking British Decline*. London: Palgrave Macmillan.

Freeman, Chris. 1987. 'National Systems of Innovation: The Case of Japan', in Freeman, C. (ed), *Technology Policy and Economic Performance: Lessons From Japan*. London and New York: Pinter Publishers.

Freeman, Chris; and Soete, Luc. 1997. *The Economics of Industrial Innovation*. Cambridge, MA: MIT Press.

Galbraith, John Kenneth; and Men'shikov, Stanislav. 1988. *Capitalism, Communism and Coexistence: From the Bitter Past to a Better Prospect*. London: Hamish Hamilton.
Gamble, Andrew. 1994. *Britain in Decline: Economic Policy, Political Strategy and the British State*. London: Macmillan International Higher Education.
Gerschenkron, Alexander. 1962. *Economic Backwardness in Historical Perspective: A Book of Essays*. Cambridge, MA: Harvard University Press.
Glyn, Andrew. 2006. *Capitalism Unleashed: Finance Globalization and Welfare*. Oxford: Oxford University Press.
Gordon, Robert. 2012. *Is US Economic Growth Over? Faltering Innovation Confronts Six Headwinds*. Washington, DC: Center for Economic Policy Research.
Gramsci, Antonio. 1971. *Selections From the Prison Notebooks*. Edited and translated by Quintin Hoare and Geoffrey N. Smith. London: Lawrence and Wishart.
Grant, Wyn. 2014. 'What Happened to British Decline?', *Speri*, 15 October. http://speri.dept.shef.ac.uk/2014/10/15/happened-british-decline/
Habermas, Jürgen. 1975. *Legitimation Crisis*. New York: Beacon Press.
Hansen, Alvin H. 1939. 'Economic Progress and Declining Population Growth', *The American Economic Review*, 29(1), pp. 1–15. https://doi.org/10.4324/9781351291521-24
Hilferding, Rudolf. 1910/1981. *Finance Capital: A Study of the Latest Phase of Capitalist Development*. London: Routledge & Kegan Paul.
Hobsbawm, Eric. 1968. *Industry and Empire, an Economic History of Britain Since 1750*. London: Weidenfeld & Nicolson.
Hobsbawm, Eric. 1987. *The Age of Empire: 1875–1914*. London: Weidenfeld & Nicolson.
Hobsbawm, Eric J. 1994. *Age of Extremes: The Short Twentieth Century, 1914–1991*. London: Michael Joseph.
Hobson, John A. 1902/1965. *Imperialism, a Study*. Ann Arbor: University of Michigan Press.
Hudson, Michael. 1972/2003. *Super Imperialism: The Origin and Fundamentals of U.S. World Dominance*. 2nd ed. London: Pluto Press.
Hudson, Michael. 2010. 'From Marx to Goldman Sachs: The Fictions of Fictitious Capital, and the Financialization of Industry', *Critique*, 38(3), pp. 419–444.
Hutton, Will. 1995. *The State We're In*. London: Random House.
Ingham, Geoffrey K. 1984. *Capitalism Divided?: The City and Industry in British Social Development*. Basingstoke: Macmillan.
Keynes, John M. 1913. *Indian Currency and Finance*. London: Macmillan and Company.
Keynes, John M. 1933. 'National Self Sufficiency', *Yale Review, New Statesman and Nation*.
Kindleberger, Charles Poor. 1978. 'Germany's Overtaking of England, 1806–1914', in *Economic Response: Comparative Studies in Trade, Finance and Growth*. Cambridge, MA: Harvard University Press.
Kotz, David. 1997/2005. *Revolution From Above: The Demise of the Soviet System*. London: Routledge.
Kulchyski, Peter. 2020. 'Bush/Revolution: Theses on the Challenges That Gatherers and Hunters Pose to Dominant Structures', in Desai, Radhika and Heller, Henry (eds), *Revolutions*, pp. 1406–20. London: Routledge.
Lane, David. 2017. *Elites and Classes in the Transformation of State Socialism*. London: Routledge.
Lenin, Vladimir. 1916/1970. *Imperialism, the Highest Stage of Capitalism, a Popular Outline*. Moscow: Progress Publishers.
Lens, Sidney. 2003. *The Forging of the American Empire*. London: Pluto Press.
Lewin, Moshe. 1995. *Russia-USSR-Russia: The Drive and Drift of a Superstate*. New York: New Press: Distributed by W.W. Norton & Co.
Leys, Colin. 1990. 'Still a Question of Hegemony', *New Left Review*, I/181. pp. 119-128

Lindert, Peter H. 1969. *Key Currencies and Gold, 1900–1913* (No. 24). International Finance Section. Princeton, NJ: Princeton University.

Lipietz, Alain. 1992. *Towards a New Economic Order: Postfordism, Ecology, and Democracy*. Europe and the International Order. New York: Oxford University Press.

List, Fredrick. 1841/1856. *National System of Political Economy*. Philadelphia: J.B. Lippincott and Co.

Loeb, Harold, et al. 1935. *The Chart of Plenty*. New York: Viking Press.

Luxemburg, Rosa. 1913/2003. *The Accumulation of Capital*. Routledge Classics. London: Routledge.

Mandel, Ernest. 1978. 'Introduction', in Karl Marx (ed), *Capital* (Vol. 2). London: Penguin.

Mandel, Ernest. 1982. 'The Second Slump: A Marxist Analysis of Recession in the Seventies', *Science and Society*, 46(3).

Marx, Karl. 1867/1977. *Capital* (Vol. 1). London: Penguin.

Marx, Karl. 1894/1981. *Capital* (Vol. 3). London: Penguin.

Mayer, Arno J. 1967. *Politics and Diplomacy of Peacemaking: Containment and Counterrevolution at Versailles, 1918–1919*. New York: Alfred A Knopf.

O'Connor, James. 1973. *The Fiscal Crisis of the State*. London: New Left Books.

Patnaik, Prabhat. 2009. 'Socialism and Welfarism', *International Development Economics Associates*. www.networkideas.org/news/aug2009/print/prnt250809_Socialism.htm

Patnaik, Utsa; and Patnaik, Prabhat. 2016. *A Theory of Imperialism*. New York: Columbia University Press.

Patnaik, Utsa; and Patnaik, Prabhat. 2021. *Capital and Imperialism: Theory, History, and the Present*. New York: Monthly Review Press.

Petersson, Fredrik. 2014. 'Hub of the Anti-Imperialist Movement: The League against Imperialism and Berlin', *Interventions*, 16(1), pp. 49–71. https://doi.org/10.1080/1369801x.2013.776222

Polanyi, Karl. 1944/1985. *The Great Transformation*. Boston: Beacon Press.

Polanyi, Karl. 1945. 'Universal Capitalism or Regional Planning?', *The London Quarterly of World Affairs*, 10(3), pp. 86–91.

Rothermund, Dietmar. 1996. *The Global Impact of the Great Depression: 1929–39*. London: Routledge.

Selden, Mark. 1988. 'Mao Zedong the Political Economy of Chinese Development', *China Report*, 24(2), pp. 125–39. https://doi.org/10.1177/000944558802400202

Semmel, Bernard. 1970. *The Rise of Free Trade Imperialism*. Cambridge: Cambridge University Press.

Stavrianos, Leften S. 1981. *Global Rift: The Third World Comes of Age*. New York: William Morrow and Co.

Sweezy, Paul. 1942. *The Theory of Capitalist Development*. London: Dennis Dobson.

Tily, Geoff. 2007. *Keynes's General Theory, the Rate of Interest and "Keynesian" Economics: Keynes Betrayed*. Basingstoke: Palgrave Macmillan.

Triffin, Robert. 1961. *Gold and the Dollar Crisis; the Future of Convertibility*. Rev. ed. A Yale paperbound Y-39. New Haven: Yale University Press.

Trotsky, Leon. 1934. *The History of the Russian Revolution*. London: Gollancz.

Tsagolov, Grigoriy. 2017. 'Galbraith's Revolution and Convergence Theory Development', in Bodrunov, Sergey (ed), *Galbriath Restored*. St. Petersburg: S.Y. Witte Institute for New Industrial Development.

Van der Pijl, Kees. 2020. 'The Russian Revolution at 100: The Soviet Experience in the Mirror of Permanent Counterrevolution', in Desai, Radhika and Heller, Henry (eds), *Revolutions*, pp. 1272–88. London: Routledge.

Wade, Robert. 1990. *Governing the Market: Economic Theory and the Role of Government in East Asian Industrialization*. Princeton, NJ: Princeton University Press.
Webb, Sidney; and Webb, Beatrice. 1935. *Soviet Communism: A New Civilization?* (2 Vols). London: Longmans Green & Co. Ltd.
Weiner, Martin J. 1981. *English Culture and the Decline of the Industrial Sprit, 1850–1980*. Cambridge: Cambridge University Press.
Zarembka, Paul. 2002. 'Rosa Luxemburg's Accumulation of Capital: Critics Try to Bury the Message', *Bringing Capitalism Back for Critique by Social Theory*, 21, pp. 3–45. https://doi.org/10.1016/s0278-1204(02)80004-4

4

NEOLIBERALISM AND ITS FINANCIALISATIONS

The onset of the slump made the 1970s a decade of crisis, a Gramscian 'organic crisis' in which economic crisis reverberated through society, politics and culture. It consisted 'precisely in the fact that the old is dying and the new cannot be born', an 'interregnum' in which 'a great variety of morbid symptoms appear' (Gramsci 1971, 276). As growth slowed and inflation and unemployment rose together, giving rise to the then new portmanteau, 'stagflation', political contestation over capitalism erupted. In the major capitalist economies, strikes, mass movements, protests and even terrorism entered the political battlefield, shaking the hold of capitalist ruling classes so hard as to prompt their intellectual representatives to complain openly of an 'excess of democracy' (Crozier et al. 1975). Political alignments shifted as new left and right movements appeared.

Abroad, these countries' grip on the rest of the world was also slipping dangerously. The United States had to close the gold window in 1971 and faced impending defeat in Vietnam. OPEC countries quadrupled and then doubled the price of oil in 1973 and 1978. US manoeuvring to have them deposit their surpluses in Western banks had the perverse effect of sending these banks on a lending spree among Third World and even some Communist countries and many deepened their industrialisation by investing in heavier and higher technology industry with practically free money, further undermining the United States' already declining relative productive power. The Third World, increasingly organised in the form of the Non-Aligned Movement and the Group of 77 complete with its own development policy think tank, the United Nations Conference on Trade and Development (UNCTAD), even had the gall to demand a New International Economic Order at the United Nations (Murphy 1984; Hudson 1977/2003; Desai 2020), one better suited to its development needs. If US power to dominate a capitalist world was constrained during the Long Boom, it now faced threat of rollback.

DOI: 10.4324/9781003200000-4

The major capitalist countries faced a stark choice: deepen socialistic reform, public ownership and initiative, and invest in the still growing Third World to expand demand so as to keep growth going or, as the neoliberals in their think tanks bankrolled by capital and some politicians already converted to the new creed recommended (Desai 1994; Slobodian 2018; Cockett 1995), lift postwar restrictions on capital, now blamed for the growth slowdown, at home and campaign to lift them abroad. The former favoured working people the world over while the latter favoured capital and its comprador allies in the Third World. Capital won. Though union density and the political strength of the historic parties of labour and the left were at historic highs, the left was intellectually too weak to present viable alternatives. Over the post-war decades, non-Communist working class parties and organisations in the major capitalist countries 'had no economic policy of their own' and had focused only on 'improving the conditions of their working-class constituencies' through reliance 'on a strong wealth-creating capitalist economy to finance their aims' (Hobsbawm 1994, 272).

Against this backdrop of left intellectual and political weakness, the triumph of neoliberalism is frequently portrayed as an intellectual victory. Certainly, the long intellectual surrender of the left, whose roots we have traced to the triumph of reformism and imperialism along intellectual paths determined by the Marxism's surrender to neoclassical economics, played its part in creating this impression. However, notwithstanding that, neoliberalism's political victory was simply a case of the moment of neoclassical economics finally arriving as the capitalist world scraped the bottom of its barrel of ideas.

Until the 1970s, for all the damage it did to Marxism, neoclassical economics and the free market wisdom of its Austrian wing in particular, had failed to become politically influential. Having been born in the late nineteenth-century era of heightening protectionism, monopoly and industrial policy, for a generation or more, it had to struggle, if not with Marxism then with an epigone of classical political economy, the historical school, and in policy terms, with ideas inclined to industrial policy, protection and reform. And soon thereafter, critics appeared, with the greatest of them, John Maynard Keynes, consigning it, if not to the dustbin of history, at least to an unfrequented waiting chamber for decades as his ideas, in suitably deradicalised form (Robinson 1974), dominated economics and economic policy during the post-war Long Boom. Though the shift in the United States began with post-war McCarthyism (Morgan and Rutherford 1998), even there it remained challenged thanks to the political utility of the suitably defanged Keynes. Only when the Long Boom ended, provoking intense economic policy discussion, did ruling capitalist elites reach for what they could to steer capitalism away from the progressive alternatives towards which the world was being drawn, more thanks to the force of objective circumstance than to left conviction and advocacy. What they found at hand was neoclassical economics, particularly in its virulently free market and free trade Austrian form. Along with its emphasis on individualist microeconomics, it now displaced most other traditions in university economics departments and its 'rational choice' models invaded other social science disciplines. Presidents and prime ministers, not to mention military dictators, as well as major international economic governance institutions, such as the IMF and the World Bank, would begin following its free market nostrums beginning in the 1970s.

However, even with all the political influence in the world, neoliberal policies could not revive capitalism. In the form of neoclassical economics, it had emerged to *deny* capitalism's transition to monopoly, its prescriptions of freeing capital from the shackles that states, workers and societies placed on it in the post-war era could only compound the vices of monopoly rather than restore the virtues or vigour of competition. As neoliberal governments freed capital from national and social obligation, regulation and taxation, expanded its domain by privatising valuable state assets and making them new arenas for private profit and rolled back union and workers' rights, it only exacerbated the underlying demand problem that caused the downturn of the 1970s. Even the slow technical progress of the neoliberal era (Gordon 2012), in so far as it made production more efficient amid stagnant demand, reduced employment and therefore demand, further reducing incentives for productive investment. The place of productive investment at home was taken by three distinct phenomena: a small amount, surprisingly small given the hype surrounding world-girding multinational corporations, of foreign direct investment (FDI) in lower wage locations; a great deal of outsourcing to independent producers there as well as smaller capital at home; and by financial investment.

The last was all the easier given that the basic building blocks of the soon-to-emerge dollar creditocracy had already been laid in the 1970s, when the United States lifted capital controls to permit the expansion of dollar-denominated international financial activity and the followed it up with the Volcker Shock that tilted the balance of power in finance decisively towards creditors. The result was the neoliberal financialised economy, most fully developed in the United States and the United Kingdom, where capital increasingly refused to produce anything with well-compensated and well-treated labour, outsourced more and more production, indulged in speculation and predation in the burgeoning financial sector, and avoided taxation and social obligation. In the homelands of capitalism, high value goods and services continued to be produced with comparatively well-paid and often highly skilled labour. The rest of the productive economy was increasingly restructured into the sort of 'frills economy', serving the wealthy and such relatively privileged labour in a growing service economy reliant on the labour of women and immigrants, that was already ailing by the late 2010s and proved so vulnerable to the pandemic-triggered economic crisis. This sort of economy also began losing ground to the BRICS in the new century, most consistently to China's socialist market economy.

The pandemic and then the war have precipitated an overdue reckoning with these realities. They represent a turning point for capitalism not because the pandemic is more lethal than previous ones (history has seen worse), or because the war is more lethal (it is definitely not), or even because of the havoc they have caused in financial markets (as most crises of neoliberal era have), but because they have exposed the weaknesses, distortions and imbalances of the *productive* apparatus, shrunken and distorted by neoliberalism and its financialisations over four decades.

In this chapter, we review how things came to such a pass before going on to examine how this sort of capitalism responded to the pandemic and waged war in the next two. Here we begin with how the financial foundations of the dollar creditocracy, the form in which the dollar system would now operate, were laid after the closing of the gold window in 1971. We then examine the chief mechanisms of the Long Downturn and the pace and pattern of economic activity it produced, undermining production and expanding financial activity, exacerbating the demand problem and increasing inequality astronomically in the process. We also outline how the volatile dollar system operated, requiring ever larger financialisations to keep going even as US authorities' abilities to deal with the consequences of crashes manifestly failed to keep up with them.

We pay particular attention to how long-standing historic differences among the major capitalist economies already apparent to Hilferding in the early twentieth century re-emerged, with one key difference. Now, it was not only the United Kingdom's economy with its archaic financial system that contrasted with the rest of the major capitalist economies, particularly the industrial powerhouses of Germany and Japan, but also the United States's. Since the 1970s, it had started 'deregulating' (or perhaps it would be more accurate to say re-regulating, given that the state and the Federal Reserve remained its chief shapers) its financial system away from its historically productive orientation, reinforced by Depression-era banking regulation, and towards more predatory and speculative short-termist activity in ways that contrasted with the more productive economies of Japan and Germany. The chapter concludes with reflections on the contradictions of both neoliberalism and the dollar system and on the declining ability of the US state in particular to manage their contradictions.

The financial foundations

There must be a classical story somewhere, in some culture, which tells of how, in a period of progress and growth, it is the strongest that take the lead and in one of decline, the weakest, most corrupt and most desperate. Be that as it may, that is certainly been the story of the capitalist world as Margaret Thatcher took office in 1979 and Ronald Reagan in 1981 to lead the neoliberal way. Their leadership would be founded on the new structures of finance that became the dollar creditocracy, the second and last foundation of the United States' vain attempt to enthrone the dollar as world money. Two major parts of its foundation were laid in the 1970s.

The first came in 1974 when Nixon lifted the capital controls imposed in the late 1960s to deal with the dollar's increasing difficulties. Amid generalised economic, monetary and financial dislocations of the 1970s, including a falling dollar, which the OPEC countries sent down further by quadrupling the price of oil. The dollar stabilised only after the Kissinger's Machiavellian diplomacy persuaded OPEC countries to deposit their oil surpluses as dollar deposits in US and other Western financial institutions and lifted capital controls to facilitate this, in the process scuttling alternative plans for recycling oil surpluses. A proposed IMF 'oil facility' was kept deliberately small (Kanburi and Mansur 1994; Hudson 1977/2003, 100), European plans to provide OPEC countries inflation-protected bonds in payment for oil were sidelined and the prospect of OPEC countries buying productive assets in advanced countries met with hostility (Hudson 1977/2003, 108–20).

With capital controls out of the way, the stage was set for the expansion of dollar-denominated financial activity that formed the foundation of the dollar's world role after 1971, variously named the Dollar Wall Street Regime (Gowan 1999), or the world dollar creditocracy (Desai and Hudson 2021). It inaugurated a new era of explosive growth in dollar-denominated financial transactions. Given their sheer volume, downward pressures on the dollar were now counteracted by expanding financial demand for the dollar. From here on, on the one hand, dollar-denominated international capital flows would expand in leaps and bounds to ever greater orders of magnitude, reaching a peak in 2008.

However, initial results were mixed at best. Though US financial institutions, awash with petrodollars, did go on a lending spree, the great expansion of dollar-denominated financial flows was not enough stabilise the dollar and, after tottering through most of the 1970s, it began a new slide late in the decade, reaching levels so low that the price of gold, usually an inverse indication of the value of the dollar, reached $800 per oz (just under $3,000 in 2022 prices when, after considerable rises, the price of gold stood at about $1,840.00 per oz at the time of writing). This plunge forced the second measure, the Volcker Shock. It would seal the terms on which booming dollar-denominated finance would now operate.

The Volcker Shock dealt a severe blow to domestically oriented industrial capital in the United States, which, during the previous decades, had been the chief beneficiary of expansionary post-war fiscal and monetary policies. As their inflationary consequences put downward pressure on the dollar, US multinational and financial capital, reliant on the dollar's world role, opposed 'fiscal irresponsibility' (Brenner 1998, 180). Post-war US governments had not neglected to protect their interests despite their focus on industrial expansion at home to maintain the relative dominance of the United States in the world economy. For instance, restrictions on capital movements in the late 1960s were matched by permitting a deregulated Eurodollar market. And, after 1974, financial capital had benefitted from recycling oil surpluses and the elimination of capital controls that it necessitated.

As their interests became more frontally opposed, manufacturing capital was the weaker of the two 'with profitability failing to recover and wages stagnating in the face of rising inflation, enthusiasm for traditional demand-side policies was waning, while the political clout of its most fervent advocates, namely the labour movement, was rapidly evaporating' (Brenner 1998, 180–1). Moreover, demand management, while incapable on its own, without proper industrial policy and other elements of a productivist developmental state, of delivering non-inflationary growth or reviving manufacturing competitiveness, was becoming unbearable for capital itself: what was the point of accumulating capital in dollars that were losing value?

To these domestic developments, we can add an international one that also contributed to the Volcker Shock. The direction financialisation had taken since the recycling of OPEC oil surpluses in tio dollars began was proving counterproductive to US imperial ambitions and had to be corrected. With rampant inflation, prevailing real interest rates, net of inflation, were very low or often even negative. So virtually free capital was being lent in torrents to developing and Communist countries, financing their industrialisation and robust growth in that decade (see Figures 3.2 and 4.1), freeing them of the foreign exchange constraint and supporting their international assertion.

Contrary to the myth that most of the borrowed money was lost to corrupt Third World governments, in many countries, this borrowing was aiding industrialisation efforts, boosting the developing world's share of world manufacturing from 7.6% in 1970 to 10.2% in 1980, that of the socialist countries from 21.3% to 26.6% while that of the developed world declined correspondingly from 71.1% to 63.2% (Singh 1989, 105),

> With liquidity apparently capable of infinite expansion, countries deemed credit-worthy no longer had any external check on foreign spending. Several countries, in fact, while running large current-account deficits, nevertheless greatly increased their official monetary reserves by borrowing from the Eurodollar market. Under such circumstances, a balance-of-payments deficit no longer provided, in itself, an automatic check to domestic inflation. Countries in deficit could borrow indefinitely from the magic liquidity machine.
>
> *(Calleo 1982, 138)*

Rampant liquidity expansion had increased competition between lender banks and tilted the balance of power in favour of borrowers who were moreover, beginning to eat into what remained of US productive dominance. It was now time to tilt the balance back to favour lenders and secure the dollar's value.

With the US government unable to constrain external sources of inflation, such as oil and commodity price rises and unwilling to deal with the domestic sources of inflation with an adequate developmental policy since it would threaten to take the reins of the economy out of the hands of capitalists and make it blindingly clear that they have been so taken, incoming Federal Reserve Chairman took the only other alternative: the 'nuclear option' of sacrificing the productive economy to save the value of money. Paul Volcker, a 'sound money' man if there was one, restricted money supply and let interest rates rise as far as they would, and they rose to the upper teens, even hitting 20% at one point.

The Volcker Shock not only caused severe recession in the United States, sending unemployment rates to levels not witnessed in the post-war period, thanks to the overextension of Western financial institutions to the Communist and developing worlds, it also caused major debt crises both domestically and internationally as higher interest rates inflated debt burdens. The domestic debt crisis witnessed the destruction of the US savings and loans (S&L) sector of the economy (Lowy 1991). Internationally, too, these crises proved serious for the creditors. The default of three of the biggest debtor countries, Mexico, Brazil and Argentina, dealt a considerable shock to creditor financial institutions whose assets were suddenly at risk.

US banks gravely exposed to Third World lending received help from two quarters. Applying the 'too big to fail' principle for the first time (Ugarteche 2020), some banks, like Continental Illinois, were effectively nationalised and bailed out. US banks were also aided by the settlement of the Third World debt crisis in favour of creditors by the International Monetary Fund and the World Bank. Created at the Bretton Woods conference of 1944, their roles had remained quite limited until they were brought in to act as bailiffs for Western creditors. Their rescheduling of the international debt with only symbolic write-offs or 'forgiveness' erased long-established practices of creditor co-responsibility with debtors for debt and imposed all responsibility on debtors. Draconian Structural Adjustment Programmes that imposed austerity also ensured that austerity, rather than any developmentalist attempt to increase capacity to pay, would be normalised as the way out of debt. Inflicted on the vast majority of Third World countries, many of whom were not, in fact, big debtors, these programmes accounted for the unprecedented economic retardation of one or more 'lost decades' of development that the Third World suffered in the 1980s and 1990s.

Having narrowly avoided catastrophe, Western financial institutions changed their lending practices to securitised lending. Banks would not lend directly because keeping the loans on their books exposed them to default risks. Instead, they floated bonds, thus spreading the risk around and also giving bond-holders the option to sell bonds if problems were suspected. Securitisation transformed debt from a relationship—long term in financial systems of the 'finance capital' sort, geared to long-term lending for big capital investments with long gestation periods—into a tradeable asset, usually held short-term. Markets for these new assets, up to and including the infamous 'toxic securities' that swelled the housing and credit bubbles of the 2000s, would only provide new arenas for speculation. Moreover, as bondholders often discovered, the risk reduction in securitisation was largely notional. In practice, the exposure of problems led all holders to seek to sell and hardly anyone to buy, turning markets illiquid.

The 1970s also witnessed the beginnings of financial deregulation. As rising inflation rendered the regulatory structures of US finance, constructed by Depression-era banking legislation that had made the US financial sector among the most heavily regulated in the world, obsolete, no attempt was made to update them so as to preserve the original aims of preventing excessive build-up of risk and shaping the financial sector to mobilise savings and finance productive investment. Instead, government action became biased towards deregulation. As the Long Downturn dragged on, this bias only became more pronounced. It would also increase competition and narrow profit margins, forcing banks into increasingly risky practices (for a brief history see Desai 2013a, 239–41).

With the Third World on its knees, hitherto empowered domestic working classes being disciplined at home, popular misery under the notorious 'Shock Therapy' impending for the former Soviet Union and European socialist countries with capitalist restoration by the early 1990s, and the foundations for financialisation laid, neoliberalism was ready to do its work for metropolitan capital.

The long downturn

Neoliberalism was supposed to reinvigorate capitalism, restore the 'animal spirits' allegedly dampened hitherto by the 'dead hand of the state' and by overpowerful unions. It never did. In reality, it was less about reviving productive growth than it was about tilting the political balance of power in favour of capital, monopoly capital at that, and against working people in the major capitalist countries and the rest of the world generally. In achieving this, neoliberalism prolonged the slump of the 1970s into a Long Downturn out of which the major capitalist economies have yet to recover. As is clear from Figure 4.1, growth rates for the world as a whole and for its major parts with the major exception of China, have consistently remained below those of the 'statist' 'socialistic' postwar 'Golden Age' or Long Boom of capitalism (Freeman 2019).

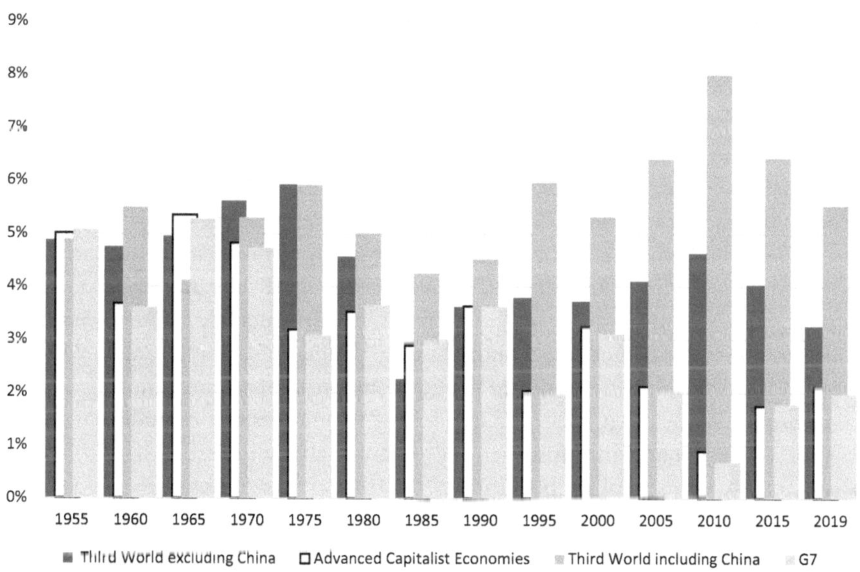

FIGURE 4.1 Five-year annual average real growth of the G7, the advanced capitalist economies and the Third World, 1950–2019.

Source: Data from World Development Indicators, World Bank https://databank.worldbank.org/source/world-development-indicators.

Created by Alan Freeman, used with permission.

If the slump was caused by the recovery of the United States' capitalist rivals from war, it persisted, according to Brenner, thanks to the unwillingness of firms and governments to permit 'what Marx called a "slaughtering of capital values"' (Brenner 1998, 157). Specifically, 'the decline in profitability, precipitated by the overcapacity and overproduction that resulted from the intensification of international competition from around 1965', failed 'to set off the standard processes of adjustment' (Brenner 1998, 147), in effect, eliminating enough excess productive capacity to permit a resumption of investment, accumulation and growth.

Instead, 'the *further* strategies individual capitalists found it best to adopt to restore their own profits, like the initial ones, continued to bring about an insufficiency of exit and too much entry, exacerbating the initial problem of manufacturing over-capacity and over-production' (Brenner 1998, 147) in relation to existing demand. Such 'insufficient exit' was caused by the '*intangible* assets' firms built up 'in their own line but not others—information about markets, relationships with suppliers and customers, and above all technical knowledge' (Brenner 1998, 147) and by 'barriers against their entering new lines', particularly when the new lines were outside manufacturing (Brenner 1998, 148). To unrelieved overcapacity and overproduction, neoliberalism added a new problem: 'With the growth of profits—and thus of investment and wages—suppressed, *aggregate demand grew more slowly*' (Brenner 1998, 148, emphasis added).

If the governments of the advanced industrial world contributed to the problem of insufficient exit, those of the Newly Industrialising Countries and later the emerging economies, which directed their domestic capitalist (and in the case of China, market socialist) development and entered the world market for manufactures, contributed to 'too much entry.'

It is worth reflecting on Brenner's explanation. What it indicates is that though the socialistic structures erected around the major capitalist economies after the Second World War expanded demand and enabled their historic Long Boom, their underlying capitalist character eventually caught up with them, inducing a crisis of overproduction, with critical international dimensions. That crisis was prolonged into a Long Downturn, according to Brenner, because, neither the firms nor the governments of the competing economies were willing to permit a 'slaughtering of capital values' on the necessary scale for the resumption of accumulation.

Brenner assumes that such a 'slaughtering' would restore capitalism's mojo, its productive dynamism. However, it is questionable whether in its monopoly phase and given expanding possibilities for financial as opposed to productive investment, capital was capable of such a revival spontaneously, without pretty massive state intervention. Without it, might not monopoly capital simply stabilise at low levels of production and employment?

Second, while such 'slaughter of capital values' may well be necessary to restore investment and growth in competitive capitalism, it is interesting to note that Marx did not use the term 'slaughter of capital values' anywhere (though he discusses cognate pressures, Marx 1894/1981, 357–9) and it is highly doubtful he would have in the sense Brenner does, as a resolution to the contradictions of capitalism.

As we have seen, Marx recognised that even societies where the capitalist mode of production prevails are societies. They will resist what is involved in such 'slaughter' for the simple reason that, capitalist or otherwise, it is their economy, their form of material production. Both capitalists and workers will resist any real loss of productive capacity, and capitalists will resist even any write-downs of the value of capital assets. Surely, the point where capitalist economies lose their productive dynamism in their monopoly phase, the question of socialism arises.

We know that even Herbert Hoover did not accept Andrew Mellon's advice to 'liquidate labor, liquidate stocks, liquidate the farmers, liquidate real estate', which would have amounted to the 'slaughter of capital values' to which Brenner refers and undertook such steps as his free market ideology would permit to mitigate the Great Depression. The political power of capital over its home government as well as considerations of political and economic stability have tended to preclude permitting such 'slaughtering'. Hoover's successor as US president, Roosevelt, famously went further with the most massive government stimulus known hitherto. Though it was not enough to lift the United States out of the Great Depression (the Second World War did that), the direction of travel was clear already then.

Among major capitalist economies, the economically masochistic Thatcher government in the United Kingdom did impose a 25% contraction on British manufacturing in the early 1980s as an acceptable price to set back militant unions (Tomlinson 2021) and the United States too would suffer greater deindustrialisation than countries, such as Germany or Japan, with more industrially focused economies and policies. Indeed, as Brenner points out, these economies found it particularly difficult to sacrifice industry: 'to the degree that this entailed transferring means of production into the service sector'. This was particularly difficult for them given that their 'levels and rates of productivity growth in manufacturing lines were significantly higher than in services' so preserving profitability would have required cuts in wages (Brenner 1998, 148–9).

For the capitalist world as a whole, if the growth of the productive economy was thus caught in pincer between expanded productive capacity and suppressed growth of demand, the expansion of demand, including through expansion of productive investment, would have to be undertaken at the initiative of governments, given the private sector was unable or unwilling. *Inevitably such measures would be considered, and would likely objectively be, socialistic, if not socialist. Neoliberalism has been about keeping this option closed by whatever means necessary.*

Pace and pattern

The standard set of neoliberal policy prescriptions—regressive taxation, privatisation of public enterprises, contracting out in publicly provided services, deregulation, cuts in social services and social protection, freer trade, end to capital controls and attacks on wages, working conditions and unions—have remained remarkably unchanged, not least since they are all tailored to benefit capital at the expense of working people. Originally, these measures were applied to societies still plump with the socialistic measures of the Long Boom. Over time, particularly in societies that applied neoliberalism most zealously and fully, pre-eminently the United States and the United Kingdom, their effects on working people have intensified with leaner government, social services and productive structures, decreasing union density and strength, low investment, high levels of unemployment, stagnant real wages, fewer benefits, smaller welfare states, rising inequality, more powerful employers and greater exposure to international competition and associated downward pressure on wages. While most of the major capitalist countries retained inherited structures of welfare states and social services, they were restructured as arenas for private profiteering.

In this context, downward pressure on profitability was at least partly counteracted by key neoliberal measures such as taking previously state-owned production into private hands, lowering taxes on capital and the wealthy, and putting downward pressure on wages and supply prices both at home and abroad. Neoliberalism also indulged capital's miserly refusal to pay decent taxes, wages or supply prices, which only exacerbated the problem of stagnant demand and inequality, as did its offshoring of manufacturing to lower wage locations.

Over the neoliberal period, with demand remaining constrained and inequality rising, markets in neoliberal financialised economies were transformed from mass markets for standardised goods that most could afford into markets polarised into those for the rich offering them an ever greater variety of high-priced products and services they might be persuaded to buy, including an explosion of personal services from domestic cleaning to nail bars, and dollar stores and open air markets increasingly catered to working class consumption. As Third World primary producers, straining to raise exports under the yoke of debt crises and structural adjustment, supplied everything from cotton and silk to coffee and strawberries at historically low prices, they kept inflation and working people's dissatisfaction low.

Contrasts and complementarities

Long Boom socialistic measures had made most major capitalist economies fairly uniformly statist and interventionist. As the United States and the United Kingdom led the capitalist world down the neoliberal path, however, and the more productively oriented German and Japanese economies followed only slowly, adopting neoliberalism more selectively and drawing back from some of their excesses with considerably less damage to their productive structures, their formative differences, originally with the United Kingdom but now also with the rapidly deregulating US economy, re-emerged.

New generations of scholars invented new terms for these contrasts. Today, as Table 4.1 shows, they have entered public discourse in the forms of contrasts between 'Wall Street' and 'main street', 'stock market capitalism' and 'welfare capitalism', 'liberal market economies' and 'coordinated market economies'. They pervade political economy, particularly the literature on 'varieties' and 'models' of capitalism.

The fates of Germany and Japan are particularly instructive. After their 'miraculous' growth during the Long Boom, enabled by the ability of their heavily

TABLE 4.1 Capitalist contrasts

Elements	*(Neo)liberal model*	*Regulated model*
State role	Aiding capital	Regulating capital
Inter-firm relations	Market governed	Relationship based
Focus	Finance	Production
Type of financial sector	Speculative	Productive
Type of capital	Short-term fickle capital	Long-term patient capital
Social character	Limited welfare state	Generous welfare state
Labels		
In popular parlance	Wall Street capitalism	Main Street capitalism
In mainstream scholarship	Liberal market economy	Coordinated market economy
Alexander Gerschenkron's terms	First developer(s)	Late developers
Ronald Dore's term	Stock market capitalism	Welfare capitalism
Kees van der Pijl's term	Lockean heartland	Contender capitalism
Hilferding's term	Free trade England model	Protectionist country finance capital
Cultural distinction	Anglo-Saxon capitalism	Rhineland and Nordic capitalism

Source: Created by the author.

regulated and state-directed capitalisms to take disproportionate shares of the world market, they entered the neoliberal era reluctantly, applying neoliberal policies sufficiently selectively to preserve their productive advantages and their productive successes continued to be admired well into the early 1990s. Though now largely forgotten, UK and US deindustrialisation in the 1980s and even the 1990s continued to be unfavourably contrasted with Germany's 'Rhineland' model and in the United States, the businessman, Ross Perot, ran for US president, campaigning on the platform that the United States had to beat the Japanese challenge by emulating Japan and breaking 'publicly with the free trade orthodoxy that had dominated American public policy since the New Deal' (Ferguson 1995, 307).

Indeed, in the 1980s, Japan's legendary growth once threatened the United States in much the way that China's even more spectacular growth does today with many believing that Japan was poised to take over from the United States as the world's dominant economy and that it showed the way for the future in terms of its productive structure and economic organisation. Ezra Vogel's *Japan as Number One* sounded the tocsin as early as 1979 and as late as 1994, world systems analyst, Giovanni Arrighi, concluded his extensive and erudite account of the United States' efforts at world dominance by noting that Japan's economic 'catch up' was not only 'sustained and spectacular', but had displaced the United States as 'the dynamic center of processes of capital accumulation on a world scale' (Arrighi 1994, 332). The following year, Chalmers Johnson, after discussing the Cold War subordination of Japan to the United States, announced that 'the Cold War is over and Japan won' (1995, 9).

Germany too was able to keep its industrial economy largely intact, benefitting as it did from the European Union (EU) enlargement, particularly after 1989 and the launch of the Euro, both of which expanded its markets and the labour force available to German capital (Serfati 2016). However, with Germany also prioritising the stability of the mark and the euro above all else (Streeck 2014) and Japan unable to exercise even limited regional influence (Wade 1996; Wade and Veneroso 1998), both were bound to come up against the demand barriers that caused the slump and that neoliberalism exacerbated.

The contrasts were also complementarities, however. On the one hand, with demand remaining constrained and neoliberalism only exacerbating overcapacity, currency devaluation could direct demand powerfully. By the 1990s, it was clear that each major part of the world economy, centred respectively around the United States, Germany and Japan, could grow only at the expense of the others in a zero-sum game of export-led growth.

> [L]ocal expansions typically occurred by way of a kind of hydraulic dynamic, in which one leading economy or group of them took advantage of reduced exchange rates to undertake manufacturing-led, export oriented expansions, but heavily at the expense of others with correspondingly increased exchange rates.
>
> *(Brenner 2009, 13)*

The United States, as we have seen, could rely on such devaluations only to a limited extent if the dollar's world role was not to be endangered.

The two industrial powerhouses also had their own encounters with the expanding dollar creditocracy. Japan deregulated first, transforming its financial system from one that expanded productive investment to one that became, partially at least, oriented to speculation in asset markets, lending to the United States at high interest rates and blowing up a vast property bubble in Japan in the course of the 1980s. When the Bank of Japan burst it by raising interest rates in 1990, it cast Japan into its 'secular stagnation' from which it still struggles to emerge, though its damage can be exaggerated in a comparative perspective in neoliberal times. As *The Economist* recently noted, 'Overall growth has remained sluggish, but growth per head has recently been comparable with others in the G7. Unemployment has been minimal, longevity has increased and inequality has stayed relatively low.' (*The Economist* 2021).

Germany's encounter came with the housing and credit bubbles of the 2000s. Much was made after 2008 about how the surpluses of the export engines—preeminently Japan, South Korea, Taiwan, and China—were mirrored by US deficits. The former economies' dollar reserves are usually held to explain the dollar's continuing world role after 1971 in that their lending covered the United States' twin deficits, budget and current account. Indeed, major figures from George W. Bush to Ben Bernanke (2005) were part of the chorus that blamed the US housing and credit bubbles on the 'Global Savings Glut', specifically Chinese reserves.

While these reserves did cover US deficits, they were dwarfed by the flows that actually held up the dollar creditocracy by counteracting the Triffin dilemma's downward pressure on the dollar and made trade surplus countries minimally willing to hold dollars. Those flows had an altogether different source.

A focus on trade and reserves is narrow, confined to net flows, as Claudio Borio and Piti Disyatat (2011) pointed out. The real story lay in the gross capital flows. When these were examined, it was clear that China had only a bit part in the larger drama whose principal *dramatis personae* were investors and financial institutions in other advanced economies, chiefly European, which had followed up the lifting of capital controls in the 1980s with financial deregulation.

European financial deregulation only came with the launching of the Euro. Soon after the euro's launch, US and UK banks introduced European financial institutions, used to providing long-term industrial credit, to Anglo-American trading in securities. Swollen with cash and recently deregulated, they invested heavily in US 'toxic securities' (Nesvetailova and Palan 2008). No wonder, outside the United States and the United Kingdom, the Eurozone suffered the most in 2008, making that crisis a North Atlantic Financial Crisis, not a global one. In the Eurozone, it also laid the basis of the Eurozone crisis that erupted two years later. The rest of the world suffered a short, sharp trade shock and resumed growth thereafter.

With the 2008 crisis, the dollar creditocracy took a beating as international capital flows crashed and, despite some recovery, remained less than half of their 2007 peak a decade later as investors, particularly European and Japanese, disengaged (Lund et al. 2017). Hereafter, Federal Reserve intervention would be necessary to hold up the asset markets on which the dollar's value relied.

So, while through their respective dalliances with neoliberalism, particularly financial deregulation, the Europeans, particularly the Germans, and the Japanese, got badly burned, both retained vast productive systems and the regulatory apparatuses that kept them focused on production and with them the option to turn away from neoliberalism and deepen economic relations with the China-centred part of the world economy. There is plenty of evidence that Europe and Japan were beginning to exercise these options when the war over Ukraine brought them up short.

Neoliberalism beyond the capitalist core

If the spread of neoliberalism within the imperial heartlands was uneven, it was even more so in the rest of the world. After all, it was imposed forcibly on much of the Third World in the form of IMF- and World Bank-imposed Structural Adjustment Programmes after the debt crises of the 1980s and in the form of 'shock therapy' on the Eastern Europe and the former Soviet countries in the 1990s. The well-known consequences—economic retardation, deindustrialisation, low prices for exports, burdensome debt service, enforced privatisation, loss of subsidies and social welfare programmes, to name a few—imposed severe human misery, including widespread hunger and even, in the USSR, reductions in longevity. This had already resulted in resentment and critique when

IMF and World Bank interventions the 1997–98 East Asian Financial Crisis exposed the pro-West and pro-US biases more blatantly than ever and the IMF in particular,

> emerged from the East Asian crisis a greatly weakened institution in regards to its credibility around the world. . . . Critics on both the left and the right railed against the institutions' mission creep, heavy handedness, ideological capture, domination by the US government and private financial interests, its myriad failures in East Asia prior to and following the crisis, and its excessively harsh and intrusive conditionality.
>
> *(Grabel 2011, 808; See also Sachs 1998; Khatkhate 1998)*

In the new century, not only did the roles, and loan portfolios, of these institutions shrink, developing countries, while not returning to projects of national autonomous development that the debt crises of the 1980s had so rudely interrupted, began to be more adventuresome in their developmental policies. In doing so, they enjoyed two other particularly favourable circumstances arising from different ends of the emerging new confrontation between capitalism and socialism. On the one hand, the United States turned to a new regime of historic low interest rates after the dot-com bubble burst, prompting a new burst of lending to the rest of the world, this time securitised. Though much of this was used to support the import-dependent cosmopolitan lifestyles of rising middle classes in these countries, it was not without developmental consequences. On the other hand, China increased its presence in the rest of the world, offering aid, investment and trade partnerships, vastly expanding the options for developmentally minded governments.

The overstretched productive economy

Given the limitations of neoliberalism as a prescription for reviving productive economies, it is no surprise that investment in the West did not revive. It was not that investment in the homelands of capitalism was replaced by investment abroad. While the US-led West, aided by the IMF and the World Bank, wreaked economic havoc on numerous Third World countries, chiefly in Latin America and Africa, in the name of opening them up to receive productive investment, in reality, after a brief dalliance with investment in low-wage, low-skill production in some poor countries in the early 1970s and again in the early 1980s, foreign direct investment (FDI), passed by these countries almost entirely. As Figure 4.2 shows, though most of the twentieth century, FDI was a 'triad affair', going from one rich country of the 'triad' of North America, Western Europe and Eastern Asia to another. The FDI that went elsewhere was concentrated in a few favoured countries. While, starting in the new century, the share of the developing world did grow, this growth went hand in hand with a growth in outward investment from that category of countries. And, from the 1990s onwards, China took a disproportionate share of inward FDI going to developing countries.

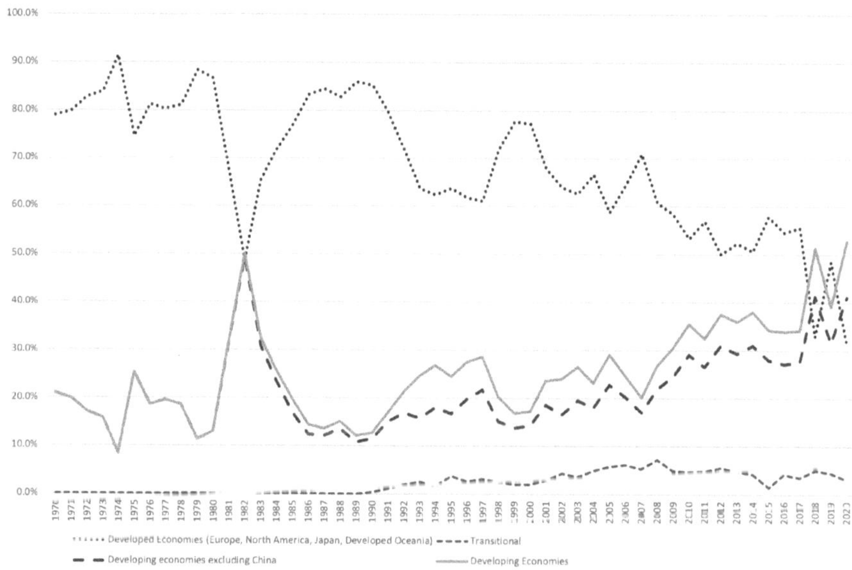

FIGURE 4.2 Inward FDI as a proportion of the world total, 1970–2020.

Source: Data from UNCTAD, https://unctadstat.unctad.org/wds/TableViewer/tableView.aspx?ReportId=102

Created by Natalie Braun and Alan Freeman, used with permission.

Moreover, as is clear from Figure 4.3, as a proportion of total investment or gross fixed capital formation in any category of countries, with the exception of a wave of intra-EU FDI and the rush of capital into Eastern Europe and the former Soviet Union, in the 1990s and 2000s respectively, inward FDI never averaged more than about 10% of gross fixed capital investment, meaning that about 90% of investment remained domestic.

As we shall see later, East and South-East Asian countries that lifted capital controls found that, rather than long-term productive investment, fickle short-term 'hot' money entered in torrents, temporarily swelling asset markets before exiting equally capriciously, causing the East Asian Financial Crisis of 1997–98 that devastated the region.

For all the hype about Western multinationals bestriding the world with their investment, what really expanded was outsourcing, with Western corporations contracting locally owned and operated firms in certain lower wage jurisdictions, which also boasted the relevant pools of labour, skills, infrastructure and inputs and networks of strong relations among firms—above all China followed by Mexico in the case of the United States, and Eastern Europe in that of Western Europe. Since outsourcing is notoriously difficult to measure, and since the trade in intermediate goods to which it gives rise is a high proportion of world trade, world trade becomes a proxy for outsourcing. Interestingly, as indicated by

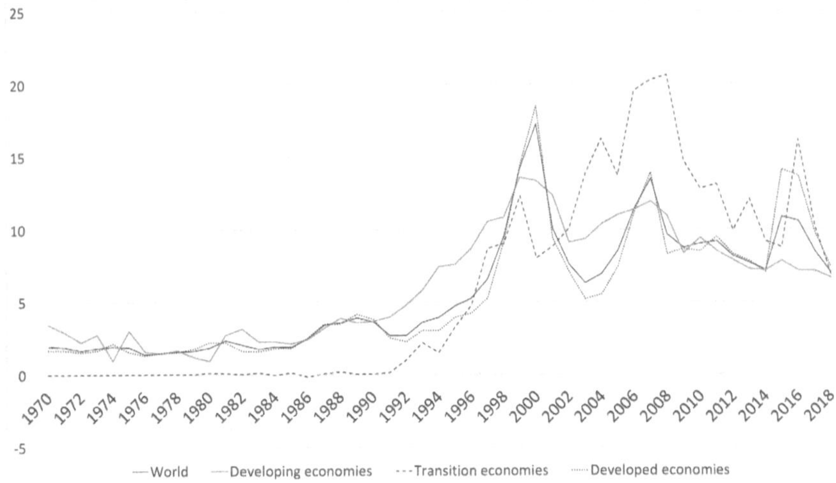

FIGURE 4.3 FDI as a proportion of gross fixed capital formation 1970–2019.

Source: Data from UNCTAD, https://unctadstat.unctad.org/wds/TableViewer/tableView.aspx?ReportId=102.

Created by Natalie Braun, used with permission.

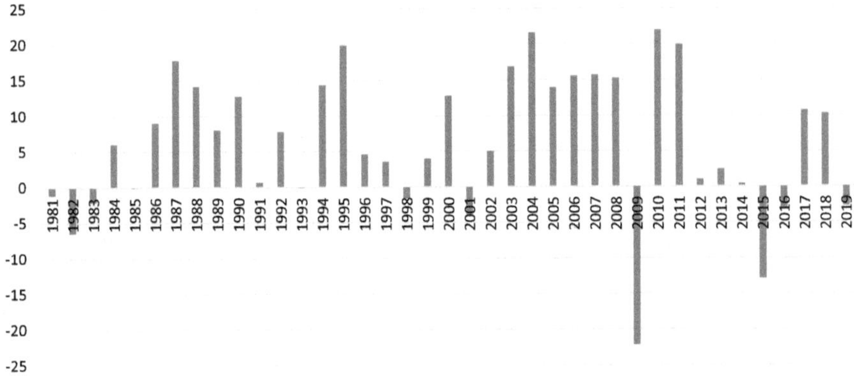

FIGURE 4.4 World exports, annual growth rate, 1981–2019.

Source: Data from UNCTAD, https://unctadstat.unctad.org/wds/TableViewer/tableView.aspx?ReportId=102.

Created by Alan Freeman, used with permission.

this proxy, after showing a broadly rising trend through the neoliberal decades, it was also reaching its limits in the 2010s.

While for about a decade after 1995, Western supply chains expanded into China, in particular, their growth was already slowing well before the 2008 crisis, thanks to a complex array of factors including the saturation of Western markets strangulated by neoliberalism and rising wages in China (Constantinescu et al. 2014). Moreover, as the decade of the 2010s wore on, not only was trade intensity in goods declining for the developing economies and China, there was more regional trade and production was, more generally, more oriented to domestic or regional markets (Lund et al. 2019). In effect, while major capitalist economies, particularly the leaders of deindustrialisation, the United States and the United Kingdom, remained dependent on producers aboard, particularly in China, China and other developing economies become less dependent on the major capitalist economies, whether as sources of intermediate goods or as final markets.

However, in the UK case, the boom in financial activity after the 'Big Bang' reforms of the financial sector shunted decades-long concerns about UK industrial decline onto a lonely siding by the late 1990s. It stayed there until the 2010s when, particularly with UK financial activities no longer as robust, the many ills of neoliberalism began to get attention and became politically consequential in the form of Brexit and the interminable political crises that followed.

In the US case, such concern over industrial decline peaked in the 1980s and vanished in the late 1990s amid talk of an information and communications technology boom reviving productivity and investment, creating a 'new economy' and even launching, according to Alan Greenspan, a veritable fourth industrial revolution (Woodward 2000). However, apart from the dot-com bubble, much encouraged by Greenspan's own hype (Fleckenstein and Sheehan 2008; Brenner 2009, for a fuller discussion, see Desai 2013a), and a massive and mis-directed increase in investment in information technology, driven by the dot-com bubble rather than any objective assessment of conditions and only adding to overcapacity problems, there were there were few signs of any such thing.

Overall, US investment remained at historic lows, productivity grew far slower than during the Long Boom (Gordon 2012) even after factoring in the 'hedonic adjustments' to US national income statistics that began to inflate the value of many goods, particularly electronic. Statistics indicated some productivity revival of the 1990s. However, not only was it largely confined to the production of computers, leaving the rest of the economy dry (Gordon 2000, 50) even here, productivity measures were inflated by hedonic adjustments (Henwood 2005, 52). Worse, most 'computer-using industries like finance, insurance, and real estate (FIRE) and services . . . continued to lag in productivity growth' (Jorgenson and Stiroh 2000, 6), except 'mundane wholesale and retail trade'. This sector registered the most significant increases in productivity outside information and communication technology (ICT) equipment manufacturing (Glyn 2006, 133–4, citing Nordhaus 2002). In the wholesale and retail trade sectors, it was not ICT (McKinsey 2001, 4) that increased productivity but 'organizational improvements, the advantages of large-scale Big Box stores, and the shift to higher value goods associated with the growth in the number of high-income consumers' (Glyn 2006, 135–6). That is to say, the 'productivity increases' came from shifting much of the work onto consumers by turning warehouses into retail stores and from inequality. Worse, since such productivity increases in retailing were distinctive to the US economy, they were, Gordon cautioned, likely to have been inflated by hedonic adjustments too. The retail sector relied heavily on selling ICT products whose value was inflated and its productivity was measured by the value of goods sold per employee (Gordon 2004, 12). Finally, statistics about increasing productivity tended to assume that measures of hours worked were reliable at a time when employees up and down the pay scales were putting in more unrecorded hours than ever before (Henwood 2005, 67).

For all the hype about ICT in the 1990s, there was probably little point expecting it to yield productivity increases. It was more likely to lead to 'a high-technology version of a crafts economy, based on worker skills, thinking, and inventiveness, rather than on the muscle of large-scale factories and distribution networks'. With the contemporary economy being unable to 'remove human beings from the production process as rapidly as the old standardized economy of the mass production age', productivity increases were inherently more difficult (Madrick 1998).

The genius of ICT lay in aiding central control in productive enterprises and across supply chains. Soviet-era research had explored its enormous potential for socialist economic management and planning (Spufford 2010). In the neoliberal era, designed as it is to avoid socialism, rather than exploiting its enormous potential for creating planned socialist economies aimed at addressing human and social need, large monopolistic capitalist corporations used ICT instead to aid the concentration and centralization of capital, creating vast corporate monopolies and far-flung supply chains. It also aided capital in financial plunder and speculation, in appropriating land and resources and increasing control over employees. Corporations also used ICT to manipulate customers, short-circuiting rather than addressing the demand problem and proliferating false needs in oceans of unfulfilled real need. Such capitalisms diminish human well-being, the quality and quantity of jobs and social services.

By the end of the 2010s, critical observers were expecting a major recession if not a depression, this time originating in the weakened productive system, not the still over-bloated financial system. Nouriel Roubini, for instance, foresaw in August 2019 (Roubini 2019) that some combination of the deterioration of US–China relations into trade and technology wars and potential oil supply shocks emerging, once again, from US foreign policy initiatives, could increase prices of imports and inputs and disrupt established supply chains.

> Worse, the Sino-American conflict is already fuelling a broader process of deglobalization, because countries and firms can no longer count on the long-term stability of these integrated value chains. As trade in goods, services, capital, labour, information, data, and technology become increasingly balkanized, global production costs will rise across all industries.
>
> *(Roubini 2019)*

If such supply shocks hit an already weakened and over stretched productive structure with low investment rates, they could also affect still-strong consumption by raising prices and delivering a demand shock. Moreover, these supply shocks were likely to be permanent and monetary accommodation would only lead, eventually, to inflation. The monetary policy and (very weak) fiscal stimuli may have sufficed (just) after 2008. They were unlikely to now.

Financialisations: profits, demand and the dollar

Unable to revive profitability in productive activity, constrained by the limits of demand, which it only further exacerbated, neoliberal capitalism could only expand financial activity. It was a fix for both the profit and the demand problems, at least from the point of view of big capital, though even as such, it was inadequate one, capable only, as Streeck (2014) put it, of 'buying time' or kicking the proverbial can down the road, not fixing the underlying problem.

For most economists, the shift towards financial activity was entirely natural, a shift from one branch of activity to another, while that towards the internationalisation of finance, inevitable, the result of the infinite fungibility of money and the difficulty of controlling its flows. However, the first assumption ignores long traditions of thought preceding and succeeding neoclassical economics that regarded finance as an unproductive if necessary cost, to be kept to the minimum necessary to aid the expansion of production. The second ignores the US, the IMF and the World Bank's strenuous efforts at convincing governments to lift capital controls and deregulate finance. They would not bother if finance were naturally impossible to control.

In reality, the expansion and internationalisation of financial activity is the result of government (de)regulation at the behest of capital beginning by lifting capital controls, in the United States in 1974 and in the United Kingdom in 1979, the first act of the incoming Thatcher government. Deregulation played a central role in transforming the capitalist world's financial structures. After the Second World War, financial sectors in major capitalist countries had acquired a strong productive orientation. Levels of financial activity were modest and financial crises rare if not non-existent. The Long Boom was greatly facilitated by this dispensation. In the neoliberal era, with US actions taking the lead and the United Kingdom following closely behind, financial sectors of major capitalist economies shifted to a greater orientation to speculation and predation, moving away from the finance capital model and towards the archaic British model, choking rather than expanding production.

While the first works to study this change began to appear in the 1980s and 1990s (Lipietz 1985, Hutton 1995), the literature on 'financialisation' really proliferated in the new century. That was when, as Figure 4.5 shows, financial activity, markets and their internationalisation, for which we take international capital inflows depicted in it as a proxy, had made several leaps of orders of magnitude upward from the initial increase in financial activity as capital controls were lifted in the 1970s and 1980s. Only in the 1990s and 2000s did they reach the levels witnessed in the bubbles in East Asia followed by the dot-com and housing bubbles of the 1990s and 2000s.

In understanding these, the generic term 'financialisation', used in the singular, can be misleading, implying a uniform phenomenon across space and time. With deregulation proceeding to differing extents and speeds, national financial systems remain distinct, with national savings and investment largely correlating, thanks

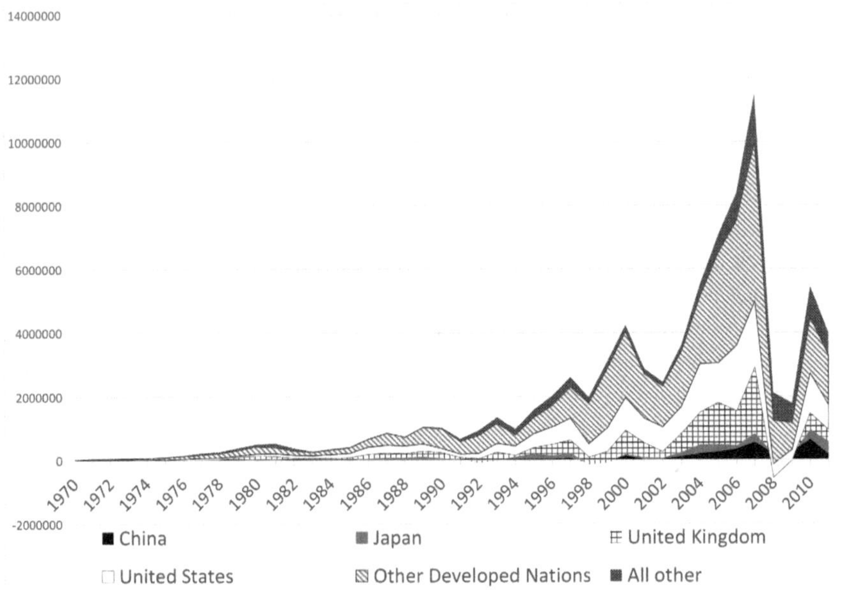

FIGURE 4.5 Capital inflows by country and category, 1970–2012.

Source: Data from International Monetary Fund (IMF), International Financial Statistics July 2012 [CD-ROM].

Created by author and Natalie Braun, used with permission.

to differences of inherited structures, of location in the asymmetrical and hierarchical world economy and of politics (Hay 2020, 305–6). Increases in financial activity, the inflation of financial bubbles and their bursting and even patterns of financial flows, domestic and international, remain national and nationally distinct and contagion travels along distinct paths rather than over-spilling uniformly onto the rest of the world. Moreover, financial activity also changes over time, involving different patterns of debt and speculation. So, examining nationally and historically discrete financialisations, expansions in financial activity, linked if at all, in specific ways, is a more rewarding approach.

Of these financialisations, those in the dollar-denominated international financial system have been the weightiest. After 1971, the US dollar's world role became reliant on expansion of dollar-denominated financial activity, so that financial demand for the dollar could counteract the downward pressure on the dollar that US budget and current account deficits place and make the dollar a safe currency to hold. This expansion has taken the form of a series of financialisations, each larger and more volatile than the one before, at least until 2008. These dollar-denominated financialisations have been the biggest and a variety of national financialisations have tapped into them: for example, the financialisation of the Eurozone that occurred with the launch of the Euro tapped into the housing and credit bubbles of the 2000s (Nesvetailova and Palan 2008).

In that sense, the neoliberal era is coincides with, and deeply implicated in, the dollar's second, post-1971, career as the world's money.

On the supply side, it required enough countries to lift capital controls, and opt for 'financial openness', which permitted capital to escape national regulation into foreign financialisations and constrained governments' developmental role. In the 1980s, governments of the major capitalist countries lifted capital controls and in the 1990s, the Clinton administration's priority was to get developing countries, particularly the 'big emerging markets' in East Asia, to lift capital controls. The success of this enterprise not only led directly with the series of financial crises of that decade but also to the greatest known until then, the East Asian Financial Crisis of 1997–98.

In the debate around capital controls that it set off (Wade and Veneroso 1998), the constraints on governments' room for policy manoeuvre came to be expressed in terms of the so-called impossible trinity: that it is possible to achieve only two of three key aims—a stable exchange rate, an independent monetary policy and free capital flows—at once. The fallacy here is that free capital flows have never been an unmitigated good and if capital controls in some form—as sophisticated as they need be to manage an economy's external linkage for expansion—are accepted as a 'good' instead, there is no impossible trinity to worry about. Of course, this was the one option that was never discussed except by critical economists (Rodrik 2006).

On the demand side, US financial authorities had to organise expansions of financial activity involving dollars. After the disasters of the first expansion—that of lending to Third World and Communist countries in the 1970s—and after Japanese lending to the United States at high rates of interest prevailing in the early 1980s, these expansions have taken the form of asset bubbles, beginning with the stock market bubble that burst in 1987. They were aided by the shift towards securitised lending in the 1980s. These asset bubbles have been encouraged by the Federal Reserve in two further critical ways: by its sponsorship of financial deregulation and by converting the 'Greenspan put' the supply of liquidity with which incoming Federal Reserve Chairman, Alan Greenspan, supported crashing markets into a 'Federal Reserve put', essentially the standing promise of bailouts for the major investors and financial institutions through injections of liquidity and lax monetary policy at every financial crash.

We are now ready to examine the role of financialisations vis-à-vis profits, demand and the dollar.

Financialisations and profits

Capital has long taken recourse to financial investment, often blowing up asset bubbles, when conditions for productive investment are unpropitious. However, that recourse has historically been limited by regulation and risk. It was only when deregulation, beginning in the 1970s in the United States continued and spread, and when, beginning with Alan Greenspan's tenure as the Chairman of the Federal Reserve, the 'Federal Reserve put' effectively eliminated risk (and introduced 'moral hazard') at least for the systemically important financial institutions and richest investors, that financialisations could acquire the dimensions they did in the neoliberal era.

Government and central bank rescues of financial interests after financial and asset market busts became the entrenched pattern, at the greatest scale in the United States. There deregulation reached had a peak in the repeal of the Depression-era Glass–Steagall Act. It had separated speculation and commercial banking by offering protection at the price of heavy regulation to the latter while leaving small speculative investment banks to take risks on their own dime and at their own peril. With its repeal, the large commercial banks, now enjoying both protection and the freedom to speculate, inflated the greatest financial bubbles yet seen, the US housing and credit bubbles that burst in 2008. Meanwhile, in the same crisis, the 'Federal Reserve put' also crossed a Rubicon of sorts when support for asset markets after crashes became permanent in the form of quantitative easing (QE), swelling the Federal Reserve's balance sheet to an extent where its 'unwinding' could threaten asset markets now dependent on it, as the 2013 'taper tantrum' showed.

As financial markets took leave of any comprehensible relation to the productive economy, new discourses emerged to naturalise them. One was to consider financial activity no different from productive activity, despite centuries of argument to the contrary leading, in the United States at least, to financial intermediation no longer being considered 'a drain on national income' or an 'unproductive transfer' but as 'productive' in national income accounts (Assa 2015, see also Assa 2019), significantly inflating the GDP of the very country where financial activity was exploding and productive activity languishing.

A second discourse, naturalised asset bubbles. There was, of course, a vast increase in attention to the work of Hyman Minsky and his 'financial instability hypothesis', much of it stripped of its original critical intent. More telling was the great popularity of Charles Kindleberger's *Manias, Panics and Crashes* (1978, now in its seventh edition), which analysed financial crises going back to the early seventeenth century Tulip mania. Long habituated to putting his impressive erudition, not to mention his intellectual influence, at the service of the US state—he was, after all, the originator of what is called hegemony stability theory (Kindleberger 1973) with its core idea that the United States was no ordinary state but the world's banker (Despres et al. 1966, for a discussion see Hudson 1972 and Desai 2013a)—his purpose in *Manias* was to lull his readers into a sense that financial bubbles are inevitable and natural. Paying no attention to what financial regulation had achieved in the post-war era of 'financial repression' or by productively oriented financial systems, he stressed the 'difficulty of managing the monetary mechanisms to avoid manias and bubbles' (Kindleberger 1978, 17), while pointing to the importance of central banks as lenders of last resort who could 'reduce the likelihood that a shortage of liquidity would cascade into a solvency crisis' (Kindleberger 1978, 15), essentially as janitors who clean up after capitalism's wild parties of speculation.

Increased financial investment compensated at least the upper echelons of investors for the disappointing profitability of productive investment, chiefly because of the absurdly high profits they were able to make there thanks to a combination of insider information (and action) privileges and the Federal Reserve's support for both large financial institutions and asset markets. This only made productive investment less attractive, leading most major corporations that were hitherto part of the productive economy to join the financialisation bandwagon by acquiring or developing financial arms (Krippner 2005) even as financial investment relied parasitically on productive activity, skimming of the profits and wages made therefrom.

In addition to deregulation and what has become the Federal Reserve put, this structure of speculation relied on a vast expansion of debt. Households became more indebted to compensate for stagnant or declining wages, and governments to compensate for declining revenues, while firms were saddled with all the debt their emaciated productive assets could bear to enable their own financialisation, often leading to the stripping of their productive assets. This debt, now taking the form of securitised assets owned and traded by creditors rather than loans on the books of the lending institution, joined traditional objects of speculation—stocks and bonds, currencies and commodities—as objects of speculation, vastly expanding its possibilities.

The process began with government debt. Given the neoliberal penchant for cutting taxes for the rich on the grounds that this would free them to make efficient productive investment in response to market signals and for increasing military spending (military Keynesianism) as a major outlet for compensating for reduced demand, neoliberal governments increased borrowing and did so in a new form. They borrowed not from their central banks but from newly emerging bond markets. (For the US case, for instance, see Garbade 2014.) This had at least four effects. It allowed government to continue spending, now more in the interests of capital than labour or society, even as they cut taxes for the rich Second, such government borrowing only put more interest-bearing assets in the hands of the wealthy ('don't tax us, borrow from us', having been the rallying cry of the propertied going back to the founding of the Bank of England, see Ingham 1984, 48–9, 99–100). Third, it created a set of very safe assets, government bonds, havens of safety to which speculators routinely retreated every time roller coaster financial markets got too hair-raising.

Finally, it made bond-holders arbiters of the range of government actions. Though they benefit from government spending by acquiring income generating assets and capital gains from trading them, rather than paying taxes, though government expenditures made from their borrowing can benefit the economy and thus prospects for investment, bond-holders nevertheless seek to limit government borrowing. The reasons are political. As Kalecki pointed out, capitalists oppose full employment even though 'profits would be higher under a regime of full employment than they are on the average under *laissez-faire*'. However, '"discipline in the factories" and "political stability" are more appreciated than profits by business leaders' (Kalecki 1943, 351) and this can only be ensured by preserving a certain level of unemployment. Similarly, as Patnaik has argued, more than any economic benefit they may derive from the expansion of state borrowing and state activity in the economy, capitalist classes prefer to sustain the myth that 'the unfettered functioning of the system gives rise to a state of full employment where the resources are efficiently allocated' even it goes against the evidence. This also has the advantage that 'if a capitalist economy is doing poorly then the remedy for it lies in providing greater support and concessions to the capitalists so that their "confidence" will revive, and with it the economy' (Patnaik 2009).

All four effects of increased government borrowing from capital markets in the neoliberal era contributed to increasing inequality and further exacerbat the demand problem. With the exception of a brief period in the 1990s, government debt continued expanding throughout the neoliberal period, though never without loudly voiced concern over government deficits. They typically led to further cuts in social spending, even more (regressive) taxes, privatisation to increase revenues and contracting out to provide what remained of social services.

By 2008, however, issuance of government debt seemed to exhaust the capacity of markets to sorb it and central banks had to step in to support these markets through the asset purchases that went under the label of quantitative easing (QE).

Financialisations, demand, wages and inequality

At the same time, there was a great increase in household debt. Starting in the 1990s, when interest rates were still high and chiefly higher income households borrowed to increase their already high spending, it became systemically important to expanding demand. The trend then reached lower down the social scale after 2000 when on the one hand, interest rates hit bottom and on the other, real estate prices began to rise, enmeshing the 'credit-worthy' layers of the working population into the financialisation net as financial institutions touted credit, justifying it in the name of 'financial inclusion' and house prices began the ascent they have continued apart from the dip in the years immediately following 2008. Though, in the runup to 2008, some credit did reach the much-maligned 'sub-prime' borrowers, contrary to popular impression, sub-prime borrowing was only the last and slimmest part of the borrowing that formed the foundation of that financial disaster.

Not only were working people encouraged (though not always permitted) to compensate for the inadequacy of wages with credit, their pensions were increasingly financialised. While this was encouraged with promises of worry-free, prosperous retirement, several things became clear as financialisations proceeded. While workers paid more and more into 'defined contribution' plans that would provide uncertain benefit, while these contributions created vast pools of funds that served the financial institutions, which ran pensions funds, as hefty additions to the throw-weight they could muster as they speculated on ever-thinner margins, pervasive insider trading and the pecking order of finance ensured that workers and pensioners always gained less when markets rose and lost more when they fell or crashed. Over the past decade and more, pension plan insolvency has become increasingly common.

Thus, rather than ending the slump of the 1970s, neoliberalism and its financialisations not only exacerbated the fundamental underlying problem of lack of demand in relation to existing capacity, let alone address it, they made matters worse by increasing inequality. Practically every facet of neoliberal economic policy—from macroeconomic policy focused on low inflation rather than low unemployment, regressive taxation, attacks on labour, outsourcing to smaller less regulated business at home or aboard to tax cuts for the rich—were bad enough, but financialisations took the matter to a whole new level.

Central banks, above all the Federal Reserve, made their contribution by regularly resolving increasingly frequent financial crises to favour creditors against debtors, generally concentrating investable funds into the hands of every narrower unproductive elite. In the 1980s and 1990s, high interest rates benefitted creditors directly. Thereafter, lax , monetary policy—zero interest rate policy (ZIRP), quantitative easing, 'forward guidance'—justified in the name of keeping up growth and employment, instead chiefly benefitted rentier incomes by encouraging asset bubbles. Moreover, over the neoliberal decades, three things happened to place the reins of the economy more or less exclusively in the hands of central bankers. First and most fundamentally, governments simply gave up any serious ambition of bettering economic performance beyond providing favourable conditions for investment, which usually translated into tax cuts, subsidies, deregulation and public provision of infrastructure for private capital. Central banks became the chief managers of the economy, the 'only game in town' (El-Erian 2017). Second, much was made of the 'independence' of central banks, though such independence was more a case of the regulatory capture of these institutions by private finance. Third, much was also made of their remit to pursue both low inflation and high employment, and central banks' actions were routinely justified in terms of the achievement of such goals. In reality, they supported one financialisation or asset bubble after another (Fleckenstein and Sheehan 2008; Leonard 2022).

Governments changed tax laws to permit greater tax evasion and avoidance by the rich and more capital flight to 'Treasure Islands' (Shaxon 2012) and rentier incomes were given more favourable tax treatment than incomes from productive activity. Financialisations also replaced productive innovation with financial innovation, engineering with financial engineering, again restricting growth and investment. By skimming off profits and wages from productive activity, hey directly reduced both investment and consumption demand. By regularly inflating asset prices, financialisations priced housing out of working people's hands, diverted ever more funds into asset markets and attracted funds into them from abroad.

Firms too become more and more indebted. Not only did financial firms borrow more and more so as to benefit from the spread between the profits of financial speculation and predation and the low rates at which they could borrow, non-financial firms also became financialised, earning an ever-greater proportion of their income from dividend, interest and capital gains (Krippner 2005) and borrowing as much as their productive assets could bear for speculation (Leonard 2022). Firms also borrowed to buy back their shares so as to drive up their value, chiefly because higher share values increased executives' compensation. One result was that more and more publicly traded corporations, which, theoretically at least, had 'democratised' ownership over much of the twentieth century, began going private, restricting the ownership of the most lucrative productive assets to a small 'in' group and evading the regulation and reporting requirements to which publicly traded companies are subject.

Systemically, private and public debt together constituted the 'credit Keynesianism' that 'cut recessions short' (Brenner 1998, 151) without ending the Long Downturn. There were two ways of looking at the resulting situation. According to Brenner, had it not been for the unprecedented expansion of both public and private debt in response to these recessions, the world economy could not easily have avoided a depression. Yet, the same expansion of credit, which ensured a modicum of stability, also held back recovery. By cutting recessions short—and more generally making possible the survival of those high-cost, low-profit firms which perpetuated overcapacity and overproduction and prevented average rate of profit from recovering—the subsidy to demand through Keynesian debt creation prolonged the downturn. Keynesianism made the downturn both milder and longer (Brenner 1998, 150–1). Over the Long Downturn, after each recession, unemployment remained higher and growth rates lower than the previous ones.

As the neoliberal decades wore on, growth became reliant on the 'wealth effects' of asset bubbles, increasing the consumption of an ever narrowing elite. In the years of 'austerity' since 2008, even such growth dried to a trickle and the West recorded the lowest growth rates of any decade of neoliberalism. The neoliberal option was exhausted even as a strategy for merely anaemic growth. Demand conditions over the neoliberal decades remained sluggish, with most new consumer as well as investment demand emerging in China and other non-Western countries. After the dot-com bubble burst in 2000, the US economy's growth slowed further, now powered only by the 'wealth effects' of the housing asset bubbles, and the term 'great moderation' (Bernanke 2004) had to be invented to reassure markets that there was nothing fundamentally wrong with the US economy.

Dollar-denominated financialisations

The asset bubbles were, moreover, connected with the dollar's world role and grew to enormous proportions. Though people witnessing, and marvelling at, the already vast asset bubbles of the 1980s and 1990s would hardly have credited it, they were to grow by orders of magnitude in the new century. The comparatively higher interest rates of the 1980s and 1990s meant that investors could afford to be cautious. The dot-com bubble in the late 1990s was a liminal moment. It added to the steady influx of funds into US treasuries enticed by interest rates that remained historically high, a vast influx of funds into the US stock market, sending it skywards.

The stock market ascent was encouraged by Alan's Greenspan's rhetoric about a fourth industrial revolution being engineered by US stock markets' unique ability to foresee technological change and allocate capital efficiently, creating a veritable, and uniquely American, 'New Economy' (Brenner 2009, 29, see also Greenspan 1998) with its low inflation and unemployment adding up to a low 'misery index'. In reality, given that US industry was already struggling thanks to the strong dollar, the stock market bubble only engendered 'massive over-investment' unjustified by prospects for profits and a 'stunning mis-direction of capital among industrial lines' (Brenner 2009, 30).

> Constituting just 8 per cent of GDP, the information technology sector accounted for no less than *one-third* of the growth of GDP between 1995 and 2000. Within that sector, the growth of telecommunications and the industries that supplied telecommunications components were truly phenomenal. Making up 3 per cent of GDP at most, these lines were by 2000 providing no less than one-quarter of economy-wide growth of investment in equipment and software.
>
> (*Brenner 2009, 30*)

It was this inrush of funds into US technology stocks of dubious value that prompted Paul Volcker to remark in May 1999 that 'The fate of the world economy is now totally dependent on the growth of the U.S. economy, which is dependent on the stock market, whose growth is dependent on about 50 stocks, half of which have never reported earnings' (quoted in Fleckenstein and Sheehan 2008, 67).

Inevitably, the dot-com bubble burst, triggered by rate rises Greenspan initiated to stay ahead of the curve and cool the labour market before it got really hot—essentially a euphemism for keeping unemployment high enough to discipline labour (Desai 2013a, 222). The effect of the bursting of the dot-com bubble on the US economy, riding primarily on its wealth effects, was so great that the 'Greenspan put' had to lower interest rates to historic lows, not seen in nominal terms since the 1950s, inaugurating the era of lax monetary policy (Figure 4.6).

As the Federal Reserve and its sister Western central banks responded by lowering interest rates, they inflated the biggest of asset bubbles so far, credit bubble based on mortgage lending of the 2000s. What inflated those bubbles—the low interest

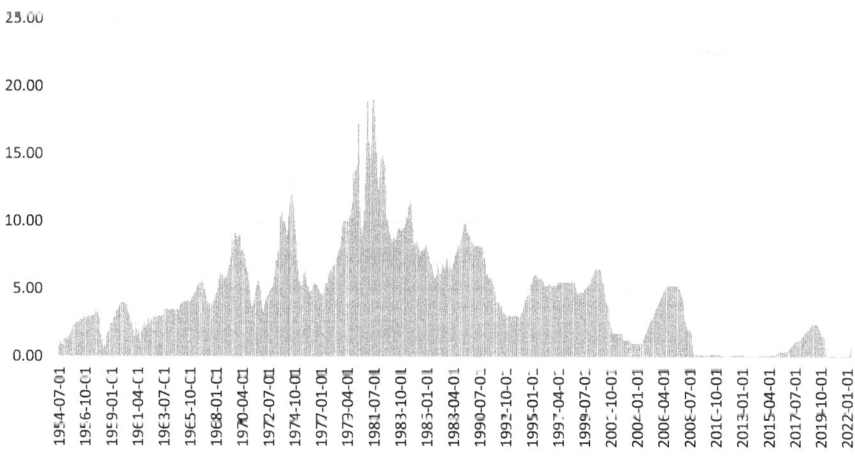

FIGURE 4.6 Effective federal funds rate, 1954–2022.

Source: Data from Board of Governors of the Federal Reserve System (US). 2022. 'Federal Funds Effective Rate' [FEDFUNDS], *FRED, Federal Reserve Bank of St. Louis*, (Accessed 21 June 2022) https://fred.stlouisfed.org/series/FEDFUNDS.

Created by Natalie Braun, used with permission.

rate regime driving up house prices and the vast expansion of mortgage-backed securities fraudulently rated safe and swallowed up by return-hungry investors, including the banks issuing them—is well-enough known, though what pricked the bubble is less so. As demand from China and other fast-growing emerging economies began pushing oil and other commodity prices up, compounded by the failure of the invasion of Iraq to increase the supply of oil under US control (Sarkis 2004; Leonard 2022, 92–3), the Federal Reserve had to react to the downward pressure on the dollar and start raising interest rates, taking them in a long series of increases from 1% in July 2004 to 5.25% in January 2006. These increases pricked the credit bubble. After a couple of years of mounting foreclosures, it burst in 2008.

After 2008 there was much debate over what or who caused the crisis: greedy borrowers or greedy bankers. The sad and shocking truth it was central bankers, above all the Federal Reserve. Since the time when Greenspan first offered markets his Greenspan put, the Federal Reserve's monetary policy had changed from episodic support for markets after crashes into a more permanent lax monetary policy that forced investors to take ever greater risks for what meagre returns they could get (Fleckenstein and Sheehan 2008; Leonard 2022, Brenner 2009; Freeman 2013).

Coping with the bursting of a bubble this size demanded ingenuity. Hitherto, the Federal Reserve had maintained an impartiality towards financial firms and confined its regular open market operations to regulate liquidity and interest rates to purchasing and selling only Treasury securities and those of government-sponsored enterprises such as Fannie Mae and Freddie Mac. After the 2008 crash, its purchases extended to financial institutions deemed 'too big to fail', a principle first invoked to justify the Federal rescue of Continental Illinois from its exposure to the Third World debt crisis in 1984. The rescue inflated the Federal Reserve's balance sheet, which had hitherto remained below $1 trillion to $2 trillion in 2009 (Figure 4.7). Meanwhile, the Federal Reserve left mortgage borrowers out in the cold even though there was the precedent of the Roosevelt administration's Home Owners' Loan Corporation (HOLC) rescuing them in similar circumstances (Mari 2020).

However, while monetary policy has continued replenishing the punch bowl, the party had become distinctly less merry. Since 2008, banks and financial institutions have been weighed down by higher reserve requirements, which the otherwise ineffectual post-crisis Dodd–Frank legislation managed to impose. Given just how much monetary throw-weight is needed to make money in financial markets today—the sheer scale of money seeking returns has thinned margins relentlessly as bubbles got bigger—even this relatively weak imposition has affected financial sector profits. Gross international capital flows, an indicator of the levels of international financial activity, declined, particularly those that had flowed from Europe to the United States as the housing and credit bubbles inflated in the 2000s, remaining less than half their pre-2008 peak (Lund et al. 2018). To compensate, the Federal Reserve's generosity had to extend beyond lowering interest rates to the Federal Reserve's quantitative easing (QE) programme to support asset markets.

Nevertheless, it was a testament to the sheer scale of Federal Reserve's liquidity provision that, notwithstanding the parlous state of the economy, stock markets, along with commodity markets, and even real estate markets, all rose in the 2010s

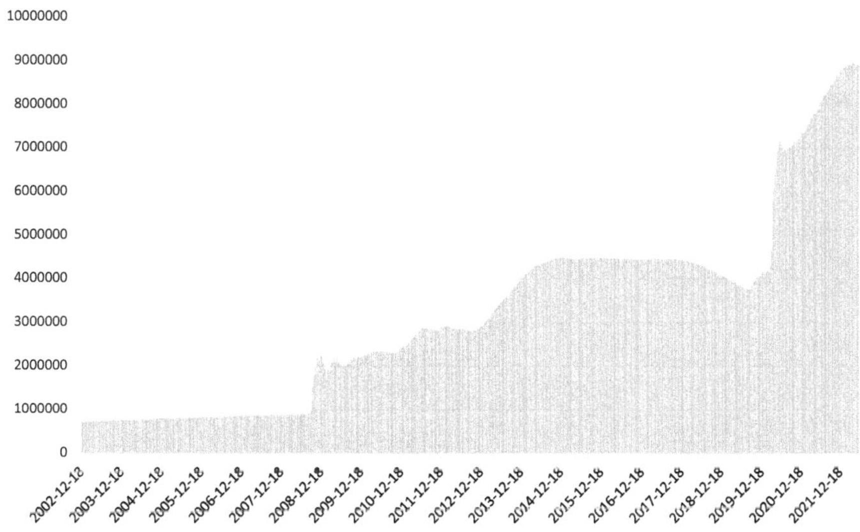

FIGURE 4.7 Federal reserve balance sheet, 2004–2022.

Source: Data from Board of Governors of the Federal Reserve System (US). 2022. 'Assets: Total Assets: Total Assets (Less Eliminations from Consolidation): Wednesday Level' [WALCL], *FRED, Federal Reserve Bank of St. Louis*, (Accessed 21 June 2022). https://fred.stlouisfed.org/series/WALCL.

Created by author.

to unprecedented heights with the S&P 500 (Figure 4.7), for example, rising quickly from its post-2008 lows and approximately doubling over previous peaks by the end of the decade. The Dow Jones Industrial Average and the Nasdaq composite performed similarly.

This had little to do with the attractiveness of these assets. Quantitative easing only made the imperatives created by lax monetary policy that much stronger:

> The Fed was essentially coercing hedge funds, banks, and private equity firms to create debt and do it in riskier ways. The strategy was like a military pincer movement. . . . From one direction there was all this new cash and from the other direction there were the low rates that punished anyone for saving that cash.
>
> *(Leonard 2022, 116)*

Since the 1990s, what passes for economic policy is central bankers making a big show of addressing growth problems through monetary policy alone (2013a). They keep the public mesmerised as they pull ingenious, even bizarre, monetary policy rabbits out of their hats—ever lower interest rates, zero interest rate policy and even negative interest rates, quantitative easing, central bank forward policy guidance and what not—creating the impression that they are straining every grey cell to save the world economy. What all the talk of monetary policy is distracting the public's attention from is fiscal policy, that is, increases in government spending and investment. Sections of the financial press do concede its necessity (Editorial Board of the

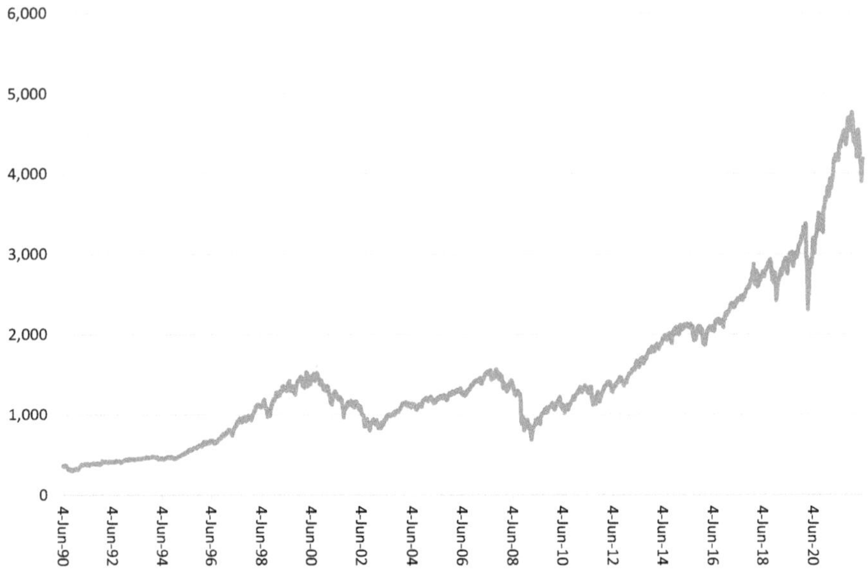

FIGURE 4.8 Standard and Poor 500 Index 4 June 1990–15 May 2022.

Source: Data from Standard and Poor Dow Jones Indices www.spglobal.com/spdji/en/indices/equity/sp-500/#overview, downloaded from Yahoo Finance (https://finance.yahoo.com/quote/%5EGSPC/history?p=%5EGSPC). Accessed 20 June 2022.

Created by Alan Freeman, used with permission.

Financial Times 2020), though they fancifully imagine that a small dose of it will prove sufficient. They forget that Keynes (1936) long ago warned that a time would come when monetary policy would not 'be sufficient by itself to determine an optimum rate of investment' and thus an acceptable rate of growth (Desai 2013b). Its effectiveness would be tantamount to 'pushing on a string'. He had gone on to say, 'I conceive, therefore, that a somewhat comprehensive socialisation of investment will prove the only means of securing an approximation to full employment.' For Keynes, full employment was the overriding economic policy objective, one that, it would not be too much of an exaggeration to say, was the first step beyond capitalism towards a better society (Desai and Freeman 2009; Desai 2009).

For, what Keynes coyly called 'a somewhat comprehensive socialization of investment' would amount to some sort of socialism in which governments step up to make necessary investments for the provision of goods and services, if for no other reason than that the private sector is unable and/or unwilling to make them. To put it another way, already before the pandemic, the scale of fiscal activism that was required to restore an acceptable level of growth, employment and demand was so great as to raise some fundamental questions. If capitalists were unable and unwilling to do the one thing that might make the worst of them tolerable, invest and produce employment, what is the use value of the capitalist class? Why should vowedly democratic states leave them in control of economies? Capitalism has been at this point since at least 2008. What little growth they could muster had to rely on inflating destructive and volatile asset bubbles, as its 'left' and 'right' wing commentators admit (Krugman 2012; Summers 2013). The current crisis, to which we are now ready to turn, has made it impossible to ignore this.

References

Arrighi, Giovanni. 1994. *The Long Twentieth Century: Money, Power, and the Origins of Our Times*. London: Verso.

Assa, Jacob. 2015. 'Gross Domestic Power: Geopolitical Economy and the History of National Accounts', in Desai, Radhika (ed), *Theoretical Engagements in Geopolitical Economy*, pp. 175–203. Research in Political Economy Series. New York: Emerald. https://doi.org/10.1108/s0161-72302015000030a014

Assa, Jacob. 2019. 'Gross Domestic Power: A History of GDP as Numerical Rhetoric', *Annali della Fondazione Luigi Einaudi*, 53, pp. 81–96.

Bernanke, Ben. 2004. 'The Great Moderation', *The Federal Reserve Board*, Eastern Economics Association: Washington, DC, 20 February, (Accessed 20 June 2022) www.federalreserve.gov/boarddocs/speeches/2004/20040220/default.htm

Bernanke, Ben. 2005. 'The Global Savings Glut and the US Current Account Deficit', *The Federal Reserve Board*, at the Homer Jones Lecture, St. Louis, Missouri, 14 April, (Accessed 20 June 2022) www.federalreserve.gov/boarddocs/speeches/2005/20050414/default.htm

Borio, Claudio; and Piti Disyatat. 2011. 'Global Imbalances and the Financial Crisis: Link or No Link?' *Bank for International Settlements Working Paper No. 346*. Basel: Bank of International Settlements, May.

Brenner, Robert. 1998. 'The Looming Crisis of World Capitalism: From Neoliberalism to Depression?', *Against the Current*, 13(5), p. 22.

Brenner, Robert. 2009. 'What Is Good for Goldman Sachs Is Good for America: The Origins of the Current Crisis', Prologue to the Spanish edition of Brenner 2006. www.sscnet.ucla.edu/issr/cstch/papers/BrennerCrisisTodayOctober2009.pdf

Calleo, David P. 1982. *The Imperious Economy*. Cambridge, MA: Harvard University Press.

Cockett, Richard. 1995. *Thinking the Unthinkable: Think-Tanks and the Economic Counter-Revolution, 1931–1983*. London: HarperCollins.

Constantinescu, Cristina; Mattoo, Aaditya; and Ruta, Michele. 2014. 'Slow Trade', *Finance & Development, International Monetary Fund*, 51(4), December, (Accessed 24 May 2022) www.imf.org/external/pubs/ft/fandd/2014/12/constant.htm

Crozier, Michel; Huntington, Samuel; and Watanuki, Joji. 1975. *The Crisis of Democracy: Report on the Governability of Democracies to the Trilateral Commission*. New York: New York University Press.

Desai, Radhika. 1994. 'Second-Hand Dealers in Ideas: Think-Tanks and Thatcherite Hegemony', *New Left Review*, January–February (203), pp. 27–64.

Desai, Radhika. 2009. 'Keynes Redux: From World Money to International Money at Last?', in Anthony, W. and Guard, J. (eds), *Bailouts and Bankruptcies*, pp. 123–45. Halifax: Fernwood Books.

Desai, Radhika. 2013a. *Geopolitical Economy: After US Hegemony, Globalization and Empire*. London: Pluto.

Desai, Radhika. 2013b. 'Has Quantitative Easing Had Its Day?', *The Guardian*, 11 January, (Accessed 24 May 2022) www.theguardian.com/commentisfree/2013/jan/11/quantitative-easing-had-its-day.

Desai, Radhika. 2020. 'South–South Cooperation', in Ness, I. and Cope, Z. (eds.), *The Palgrave Encyclopedia of Imperialism and Anti-Imperialism*. London: Palgrave.

Desai, Radhika; and Freeman, Alan. 2009. 'Keynes and the Crisis: A Case of Mistaken Identity', *Canadian Dimension*, 21 July, (Accessed 24 May 2022) https://canadiandimension.com/articles/view/keynes-and-the-crisis

Desai, Radhika; and Hudson, Michael. 2021. 'Beyond Dollar Creditocracy: A Geopolitical Economy', *Real World Economic Review*, 97(23), September, pp. 20–39. https://rwer.wordpress.com/2021/09/23/rwer-issue-no-97/

Despres, Emile; Kindleberger, Charles P.; and Salant, Walter S. 1966. 'The Dollar and World Liquidity: A Minority View', *The Economist*, 6 (February).

The Economist. 2021. 'Japan's Economy Is Stronger Than Many Realise', 11 December. www.economist.com/special-report/2021/12/07/japans-economy-is-stronger-than-many-realise?gclid=EAIaIQobChMIydKbj8zm9QIVThTUAR0BRw07EAAYASAAEgJ5lfD_BwE&gclsrc=aw.ds

Editorial Board of the Financial Times. 2020. 'Active Fiscal Policy Must Be Part of a New Normal', *Financial Times*, 5 January, (Accessed 24 May 2022) https://www.ft.com/content/7d6ffff0-2255-11ea-b8a1-584213ee7b2b

El-Erian, Mohamed. 2017. *The Only Game in Town: Central Banks, Instability, and Recovering from Another Collapse*. New York: Random House.

Federal Reserve System, Board of Governors. 2022a. 'Assets: Total Assets: Total Assets (Less Eliminations from Consolidation): Wednesday Level' [WALCL], *FRED, Federal Reserve Bank of St. Louis*, (Accessed 21 June 2022) https://fred.stlouisfed.org/series/WALCL

Ferguson, Thomas. 1995. *Golden Rule: The Investment Theory of Party Competition and the Logic of Money-Driven Political Systems*. Chicago: University of Chicago Press.

Fleckenstein, William; and Sheehan, Frederick. 2008. *Greenspan's Bubbles: The Age of Ignorance at the Federal Reserve*. New York: McGraw-Hill Education.

Freeman, Alan. 2013. 'The Profit Rate in the Presence of Financial Markets: A Necessary Correction', *Australian Journal of Political Economy*, 70, pp. 167–92.

Freeman, Alan. 2019. 'The Sixty-Year Downward Trend of Economic Growth in the Industrialised Countries of the World', *GERG Data Group Working Paper*, (1), pp. 1–20. https://copejournal.com/wp-content/uploads/2019/01/Decline-of-the-North-21.01.2019.pdf

Garbade, Kenneth. 2014. 'Direct Purchases of US Treasury Securities by Federal Reserve Banks', *FRB of New York Staff Report*, (684). https://doi.org/10.2139/ssrn.2477858

Glyn, Andrew. 2006. *Capitalism Unleashed: Finance Globalization and Welfare*. Oxford: Oxford University Press.

Gordon, Robert J. 2000. 'Does the "New Economy" Measure Up to the Great Inventions of the Past?', *Journal of Economic Perspectives*, 14(4), pp. 49–74.

Gordon, Robert J. 2004. 'Why Was Europe Left at the Station When America's Productivity Locomotive Departed?', *Northwestern University and CEPR*, 31 March.

Gordon, Robert J. 2012. 'Is US Economic Growth Over? Faltering Innovation Confronts the Six Headwinds', *Centre for Economic Policy Research*, Policy Insight (63), September.

Gowan, Peter. 1999. *The Global Gamble: Washington's Faustian Bid for World Dominance*. New York: Verso.

Grabel, Ilene. 2011. 'Not Your Grandfather's IMF: Global Crisis, "Productive Incoherence" and Developmental Policy Space', *Cambridge Journal of Economics*, 35, pp. 805–30. https://doi.org/10.1093/cje/ber012

Gramsci, Antonio. 1971. *Selections From the Prison Notebooks of Antonio Gramsci*. Edited and translated by Hoare, Quintin and Nowell-Smith, Geoffrey. London: Lawrence & Wishart.

Greenspan, Alan. 1998. 'Testimony of Chairman Alan Greenspan, *The Federal Reserve's Semi-annual Monetary Policy Report*', Committee on Banking, Housing, and Urban Affairs, U.S. Senate, 21 July. www.federalreserve.gov/boarddocs/hh/1998/july/testimony.htm

Hay, Colin. 2020. 'Globalization's Impact on States', in Ravenhill, John (ed), *Global Political Economy*, pp. 287–316. Oxford: Oxford University Press.

Henwood, Doug. 2005. *After the New Economy: The Binge . . . And the Hangover That Won't Go Away*. New York: New Press.
Hobsbawm, Eric J. 1994. *Age of Extremes: The Short Twentieth Century, 1914–1991*. London: Michael Joseph.
Hudson, Michael. 1977. *Global Fracture: The New International Economic Order*. New York: Harper Collins.
Hutton, Will. 1995. *The State We're In*. London: Random House.
Ingham, Geoffrey K. 1984. *Capitalism Divided?: The City and Industry in British Social Development*. Basingstoke: Macmillan.
Johnson, Chalmers. 1995. *Japan: Who Governs?* New York: W.W. Norton & Company.
Jorgenson, Dale W and Kevin J. Stiroh, "Raising the Speed Limit: U.S. Economic Growth in the Information Age". OECD Economics Department Working Papers No. 261, Paris: OECD. https://dx.doi.org/10.1787/561481176503
Kalecki, Michal. 1943. 'Political Aspects of Full Employment', *Political Quarterly*, 14(4), pp. 322–31.
Kanburi, Atif A.; and Mansur, S. 1994. 'The Political Economy of Middle Eastern Oil', in Underhill, G.R. and Stubbs, R. (eds), *Political Economy and the Changing Global Order*, pp. 313–27. Oxford: Oxford University Press.
Keynes, John M. 1936. *General Theory of Employment, Interest and Money*. New York: Harcourt, Brace and Company, viewed 1 March 2021. www.marxists.org/reference/subject/economics/keynes/general-theory/ch24.htm
Khatkhate, Deena. 1998. 'East Asian Financial Crisis and the IMF: Chasing Shadows Economic and Political Weekly', *Economic and Political Weekly*, 33(17), pp. 963–9.
Kindleberger, Charles P. 1973. *The World in Depression, 1929–1939: History of the World Economy in the Twentieth Century* (Vol. 4.). Berkeley: University of California Press.
Kindleberger, Charles P. 1978. *Manias, Panics and Crashes*. London: Macmillan.
Krippner, Greta. 2005. 'The Financialization of the American Economy', *Socio-Economic Review*, 3, pp. 173–208.
Krugman, Paul. 2012. *End This Depression Now!*. New York: W.W. Norton & Company.
Leonard, Christopher. 2022. *The Lords of Easy Money: How the Federal Reserve Broke the American Economy*. New York: Simon & Schuster.
Lipietz, Alain. 1985. 'The World Crisis: The Globalisation of the General Crisis of Fordism', *IDS Bulletin*, 16(2), pp. 6–11.
Lowy, Martin. 1991. *The High Rollers: Inside the Savings and Loans Debacle*. New York: Praeger.
Lund, Susan; Manyika, James; Woetzel, Jonathan; Bughin, Jacques; Krishnan, Mekala; Seong, Jeongmin; and Muir, Mac. 2019. 'Globalization in Transition: The Future of Trade and Value Chains', *McKinsey Global Institute*, 16 January, (Accessed 24 May 2022) www.mckinsey.com/featured-insights/innovation-and-growth/globalization-in-transition-the-future-of-trade-and-value-chains
Lund, Susan; Mehta, Asheet; Manyika, James; and Goldshtein, Diana. 2018. 'A Decade After the Global Financial Crisis: What Has (and Hasn't) Changed?', *McKinsey Global Institute*, 29 August, (Accessed 24 May 2022) www.mckinsey.com/industries/financial-services/our-insights/a-decade-after-the-global-financial-crisis-what-has-and-hasnt-changed
Lund, Susan; Windhagen, Eckart; Manyika, James; Härle, Philipp; Woetzel, Jonathan; and Goldshtein, Diana. 2017. 'The New Dynamics of Financial Globalization', *McKinsey Global Institute*, 22 August, (Accessed 20 June 2022) www.mckinsey.com/industries/financial-services/our-insights/the-new-dynamics-of-financial-globalization#
Madrick, Jeff. 1998. 'Computers: Waiting for the Revolution', *New York Review of Books*, 45(5), pp. 29–33. https://doi.org/10.1080/05775132.1998.11472042
Mari, Francesca. 2020. 'The Housing Vultures', *The New York Review of Books*, 11(June).
Marx, Karl. 1894/1981. *Capital* (Vol. 3). London: Penguin.

McKinsey Global Institute (MGI). 2001. *US Productivity Groth 1995–2000: Understanding the Contribution of Information Technology Relative to Other Factors*. Washington, DC: MGI.

Morgan, Mary S.; and Rutherford, Malcolm. 1998. 'American Economics: The Character of the Transformation', in Morgan and Rutherford (eds), *From Interwar Pluralism to Postwar Neoclassicism*. Druham: Duke University Press.

Murphy, Craig. 1984. *The Emergence of the NIEO Ideology*. Boulder, Colorado: Westview.

Nesvetailova, Anastasia; and Palan, Ronen. 2008. 'A Very North Atlantic Credit Crunch: Geopolitical Implications of the Global Liquidity Crisis', *Journal of International Affairs*, Fall, 62/1, pp. 165–85.

Nordhaus, William D. 2002. 'Productivity Growth and the New Economy', Washington, DC: Brookings Institution Papers on Economic Activity.

Patnaik, Prabhat. 2009. 'Finance Capital and Fiscal Deficits', *Monthly Review Online*, 24 May. https://mronline.org/2009/05/24/finance-capital-and-fiscal-deficits/

Robinson, Joan. 1974. 'What Has Become of the Keynesian Revolution?', *Challenge*, 16(6), pp. 6–11. https://doi.org/10.1080/05775132.1974.11470016

Rodrik, Dani. 2006. 'The Social Cost of Foreign Exchange Reserves', *International Economic Journal*, 20(3), pp. 253–66. https://doi.org/10.1080/10168730600879331

Roubini, Nouriel. 2019. 'The Anatomy of the Coming Recession', *Project Syndicate*, 22 August, (Accessed 26 February 2021) www.project-syndicate.org/commentary/global-recession-us-china-trade-war-by-nouriel-roubini-2019-08?barrier=accesspaylog

Sachs, Jeffrey. 1998. 'The IMF and the Asian Flu', *The American Prospect*, March–April(37).

Sarkis, Nicholas. 2004. "Is there really a rise in oil prices?". Le Monde Diplomatique. July.

Serfati, Claude. 2016. 'EU Integration as Uneven and Combined Development', in Desai, Radhika (ed), *Analytical Gains of Geopolitical Economy*, pp. 255–94. Bingley: Emerald.

Shaxon, Nicholas. 2012. *Treasure Islands: Uncovering the Damage of Offshore Banking and Tax Havens*. London: Palgrave Macmillan.

Singh, Ajit. 1989. 'Third World Competition and De-Industrialisation in Advanced Countries', *Cambridge Journal of Economics*, 13(1), pp. 103–20. https://doi.org/10.1093/oxfordjournals.cje.a035077

Slobodian, Quinn. 2018. *The Globalists: The End of Empire and the Birth of Neoliberalism*. Cambridge, MA: Harvard University Press.

Spufford, Francis. 2010. *Red Plenty: Inside the Fifties Soviet Dream*. London: Faber & Faber.

Streeck, Wolfgang. 2014. *Buying Time: The Delayed Crisis of Democratic Capitalism*. London & New York: Verso.

Summers, Larry. 2013. 'Economic Stagnation Is Not Our Fate: Unless We Let It Be', *Washington Post*, 18 December, (Accessed 4 June 2022) www.washingtonpost.com/opinions/lawrence-summers-stagflation-is-not-our-fate--unless-we-let-it-be/2013/12/15/55a1b84e-65c1–11e3-a0b9–249bbb34602c_story.html

Tomlinson, Jim. 2021. 'Deindustrialisation and "Thatcherism": Moral Economy and Unintended Consequences', *Contemporary British History*, 35(4), pp. 620–42. https://doi.org/10.1080/13619462.2021.1972416

Ugarteche, Oscar. 2020. 'Double Movement, Embeddedness and the Transformation of the Financial System', in Desai, Radhika and Polanyi-Levitt, Kari (eds), *Karl Polanyi and Twenty-First-Century Capitalism*, pp. 189–208. Manchester: Manchester University Press.

Wade, Robert. 1996. 'Japan, the World Bank and the Art of Paradigm Maintenance: The East Asian Miracle in Political Perspective', *New Left Review*, I/217, pp. 3–36.

Wade, Robert; and Veneroso, Frank. 1998. 'The Gathering World Slump and the Battle over Capital Controls', *New Left Review*, p. 231. https://newleftreview.org/issues/i231/articles/robert-wade-frank-veneroso-the-gathering-world-slump-and-the-battle-over-capital-controls.

Woodward, Bob. 2000. *Maestro: Greenspan's Fed and the American Boom*. New York: Simon & Schuster.

5

THE UNEXPECTED RECKONING

It is perhaps fitting that the novel coronavirus triggered crises in neoliberal financialised capitalist economies around the Ides of March, the traditional day of reckoning of outstanding debts in Ancient Rome. After all, if one word summed these capitalisms up as the neoliberal decades wore on, it was debt. Governments, households and firms were laden down by more of it than ever before. Asset bubbles based on it—through leveraged trading as well as trading in debt instruments themselves—have punctuated the neoliberal decades and the 2008 North American Financial Crisis was serious enough to lead many to think it might put an end to the neoliberal policies that had led to them. Nothing doing. Neoliberalism only lived on, intensified as 'austerity'. By the late 2010s, critical observers had been expecting a reckoning, not just for financial markets but for the economy as a whole (Roubini 2019). To be sure, financial markets were bound to make their contribution: the housing and credit bubbles were replaced by an 'everything bubble' (Langlois 2019) that was now 'in search of a pin' (Leonard 2022, 263) and the pandemic provided it. Of course, any reasonably major dislocation would have done the trick and told on neoliberal financialised capitalisms, exposed their increasingly obscene inequities and burdened their already emaciated structures.

Moreover, as many argued, the pandemic was itself a crisis of capitalism. Although, thanks to the politicisation of the search for the origin of SARS-CoV-2, we may never know its origins reliably (Koopmans et al. 2021), and while there is at least some robust evidence that the virus did not first infect humans in China (Wei and Qingqing 2021), we also know that recent epidemics are endogenous to capitalism (Davis 2020), related to its extensive and rapacious exploitation of land. The resulting extreme loss of wildlife habitat brings wild animals closer to human habitation and activities, including concentrations of domesticated animals in factory farms, increasing the possibility that viruses

DOI: 10.4324/9781003200000-5

normally confined to animal populations immune to them will jump to other species including humans. Indeed, the beginning of the neoliberal era coincided with the AIDS epidemic and the frequency of such jumps of zoonotic viruses appears to have increased as neoliberalism deregulated capital and its relations with nature. In addition to the horrors AIDS, severe acute respiratory syndrome (SARS), Middle East respiratory syndrome (MERS), Ebola and Zika hold for humans, zoonotic epidemics of recent times have included outbreaks on farms that have resulted in the mass culling of millions of animals (Uhlig 2002). The latest is the still-raging 2022 outbreak of avian influenza.

As the second week of March 2020 opened and the World Health Organization (WHO) declared the contagion a pandemic, it dominated the news cycle as well as the plethora of mis- and disinformation on social media. Cities and even entire countries shut down and businesses of every sort announced layoffs and production stoppages. Amid all this, however, nothing was clearer than that authorities in the leading neoliberal countries were more concerned about financial markets of every imaginable sort plunging to historic depths than about the saving citizens' lives from the pandemic.

Two years later, it is clear that the response of leading neoliberal financialised capitalisms, dominated by attempt to balance 'saving lives' with 'saving livelihoods' (a euphemism for the neoliberal financialised capitalist economy) ended up losing both as the raging virus necessitated repeated lockdowns, weakening economies further and they registered among the highest rates of cumulative COVID deaths. The poor contrast these death rates made to socialist China's successes on both counts contributed both to President Trump declaring his New Cold War on China and to his election defeat later that year. Though the UK government did not have to face an election, and though by early 2022, the pandemic was shunted off the headlines by the conflict over Ukraine, Johnson eventually had to resign as Prime Minister for breaking his own governments' covid restrictions in the 'party-gate' scandal.

From the start, the pandemic also deepened already deep economic, social, cultural and political divisions in neoliberal societies. It impacted working people they disproportionately. they were both more exposed to it and less able to access the best health care. They became even more socially separated from the well-to-do able to work from home. With knowledge of the virus, its effects and the possibility of immunity through vaccines still developing, an unregulated social media sowing confusion, uncertainty, disinformation and fear, governments appearing to economise on the truth of the pandemic and the rationales for their responses, popular distrust of governments and corporate control of science without a coherent left critique to guide it in progressive directions gave rise to a new generation of conspiracy theories. As publics grew tired and doubtful, political controversies erupted over whether, when and how easing should be implemented and the dangers of exposure to the virus extended beyond essential workers.

By mid-2022, as the pandemic still raged despite much-touted vaccines, not only were urges to 'build back better' than the unacceptable 'old normal' that had emerged early in the pandemic largely forgotten amid concerns about inflation and war, even the disparaged old 'normality' was nowhere in sight. If, over two years into the pandemic, the capitalist world remains vulnerable to it, cannot be sure of protecting its economy from it, continues to lose primacy, particularly to China, and finds itself embroiled in a war that can only make matters worse at home and aboard, the explanation lies in economy, society and polity that neoliberalism has fashioned over the past four decades.

In what follows, we first understand what it was about neoliberalism that made the public health crisis, albeit a serious one, so intractable for the leading neoliberal financialised capitalisms. We then contrast China's easy suppression of the virus to the responses of leading neoliberal financialised capitalist economies, the United States and the United Kingdom, and appreciate the true scale of these neoliberal financialised capitalisms' failures. We conclude the chapter with an outline of the economic response so as to set the stage for the discussion of the nature of the capitalism that emerges from this current crisis in the following chapter.

Pandemics and social contracts

The current pandemic has already taken more US lives than the Spanish flu and, though, as a proportion of the population, the Spanish flu killed one in every 150 Americans while COVID-19 has likely killed about one in 303 people, at the time of writing, the number was still rising at the rate of over 300 deaths per day. Considering the advance in medicine over the last century, this is still a rather sorry record (Gamillo 2021).

The Spanish flu, which could have killed as many as 100 million worldwide, struck a very different world and did so in the middle of a World War. For one thing, viruses were incompletely understood and that limited governments' responsibility to little more than warning. Even that was delayed by the war. During the war, the warring sides found it convenient to claim that the epidemic mainly afflicted neutral Spain when it was, in fact, devastating troops and civilians across Europe and had been brought to Europe by US troops (Barry 2004). The situation today is starkly different.

The Spanish flu occurred at the start of the Thirty Years' Crisis. Over its course, the authoritarian and imperial world that entered it was transformed into one of far greater popular power as populations mobilised for war, revolutions and national liberation. That new world was one of social contracts in which governments took responsibility in nearly all sectors of social life, including material welfare, cultural advancement, relative equality and public health. They also advanced knowledge, including knowledge of viruses, their treatment and even their eradication. In the post-war period, the world succeeded in eradicating at least one major virus that had historically caused untold misery, small pox, thanks to the initiative of a socialist country. Having eradicated it domestically in the 1930s, the Soviet Union proposed its worldwide eradication in the 1960s (RT Documentary Channel 2022) and, with the sort of international cooperation that was still possible during the Cold War (Hotez 2014), the last smallpox case occurred in 1977 and in 1980, the WHO declared it completely eradicated.

The 40 years of neoliberalism that followed the post-war era and its Long Boom have pushed back against these contracts. However, while they are certainly down, they are not out. Neoliberals would have dearly loved to repudiate them outright. However, thanks to popular attachment to the gains of the previous era, neoliberal governments were forced to advance more surreptitiously, undermining the material foundation of the social contracts, while claiming to achieve their goals more effectively and efficiently through market mechanisms. So, notwithstanding neoliberalism's efforts, we expect our governments to protect us from such basic public health challenges such as epidemics or pandemics and even the most right-wing government, the most zealously committed to capitalist interests, would lose considerable legitimacy if they were seen not to do the minimally necessary.

However, in 2020, neoliberal governments must fulfil this expectation with public health infrastructures debilitated by four decades of neoliberal policies and the political will to rectify this, whether on a temporary or permanent basis, conspicuous by its absence. Only their ability to create an appearance of fulfilling popular expectations of dealing with the virus while giving their corporate backers new opportunities to make profit was well developed. Over four decades, leading neoliberal governments have underfunded public health systems, privatised or contracted out key parts, and burdened them with increasing payments to the expanding set of private sector suppliers of drugs, equipment, infrastructure, services and even management. Meanwhile, health care professionals suffer low pay, huge workloads, poor working conditions and sheer exhaustion. Worse, medical systems have reoriented away from a focus on promoting health and preventing and curing disease and towards profit opportunities (Leys 2001; Pollock 2004), creating a veritable corporate medical–industrial complex that prioritised lucrative pharmacological products such as drugs and vaccines rather than prevention, cures and treatments that are services relying on the labour of appropriately skilled staff: 'There's gold in them thar pills' (Klass 1975), as an early, witty critic put it. By the late 2010s, the UK National Health Service, for instance, was so depleted that it was regularly overwhelmed in normal flu seasons.

Neoliberalism also permeated research. The increasingly common occurrence of zoonotic viruses led, for instance, to vast and lucrative research projects, such as the Global Virome Project (Jonas and Seifman 2019). Since its aim is profit for the private sector entities involved, rather than protection of human beings and societies, it seeks to map the entire world of viruses, most of which will never reach humans, rather than focusing on the people working along the 'fault lines' where the leaps to humans that prove so fatal are likely to happen. The latter approach (Yong 2020) is based on the understanding that 'Humans are the best sentinels: A virus discovered in humans very obviously can replicate in that host, which will not be the case for myriad viruses identified through biodiversity surveys of other [animals].' It is, however, far less lucrative for corporations and their allies in universities. Needless to say, the outbreak of COVID-19 has offered a veritable cornucopia of heavily subsidised profit opportunities for dozens of Big Pharma corporations and research institutions as they join the race for vaccines and treatments.

When COVID-19 arrived on Western shores, pandemic preparedness was, despite many warnings about imminent pandemic outbreaks (Davis 2020), more or less non-existent in the neoliberal world. Stocks of necessary medical equipment, drugs and safety gear were woefully inadequate to meet the challenge. Indeed, the United States had even reversed what steps previous administrations had taken (Reuters Staff 2020).

By contrast, in China, where socialism remains the goal, the social contract is considerably more robust.

China's socialism in the pandemic stress text

Faced with the novel coronavirus, the People's Republic of China responded energetically, quarantining Wuhan city and Hubei province, building new hospitals to treat the infected, isolating and treating them, sequencing the genome and launching an efficient operation to deal with smaller and future outbreaks.

There was nothing mysterious about this. The approach recognised that when new pathogens arrive, 'drugs and vaccines will not be immediately available', only the public health measures that have been used for hundreds of years will be.

> These methods include . . . controlling infection sources, blocking transmission routes, and protecting susceptible populations. Their effectiveness has been shown by the fact that infectious disease had been largely controlled by the middle of the 20th century, before antibiotics and vaccines became widely used.
>
> *(Tang and Li 2021)*

In China, therefore, 'old school public health strategies . . . often called non-pharmacological interventions' including 'mask wearing, hand washing, social distancing, . . . restriction of public events and travel [i]dentifying and quarantining people with covid-19 and their close contacts' (Tang and Abbasi 2021) were combined with new technologies. They included rapid nucleic acid testing to 'diagnose patients early, detect asymptomatic infections, and assess the potential risk to the entire population', use of mobile phones 'to trace and manage close contacts' and mathematical modelling to assess the 'effects of prevention strategies and informing policy adjustments' (Tang and Abbasi 2021).

China's party-state had the political, governance, infrastructural and resource capacities and the political motivation to act quickly and methodically, mobilising resources, increasing and scaling up needed critical care capacity, encouraging the communication of experience and emerging practices, managing understandable fear in the face of an unknown and deadly virus and encouraging multidisciplinary research (Du et al. 2021). It was able to do all this and ready China for a cautious but sure reopening of its economy within two months of the initial lockdown, minimising the economic damage. The effectiveness of this approach has been demonstrated time and time again in dealing with local outbreaks that were and remain inevitable as long as the virus rages around the world.

Already in February 2020, the Report of the WHO-China Joint Mission on Coronavirus Disease 2019 (COVID-19) (World Health Organization 2020) concluded that:

> In the face of a previously unknown virus, China has rolled out perhaps the most ambitious, agile and aggressive disease containment effort in history. The strategy that underpinned this containment effort was initially a national approach that promoted universal temperature monitoring, masking, and hand washing. However, as the outbreak evolved, and knowledge was gained, a science and risk-based approach was taken to tailor implementation. Specific containment measures were adjusted to the provincial, county and even community context, the capacity of the setting, and the nature of novel coronavirus transmission there.

It was not just China. Other socialist Third World jurisdictions (*The Economist* 2020) were also successful, at least for a time, as was the Communist-ruled Indian state of Kerala (Spinney 2020). As we have seen in chapter 1 and Table 1.1, socialist countries and East Asian capitalist ones also fared far better than the leading neoliberal financialised economies.

Thanks to this strategy, people in China returned to near-normal mobility and work and China's economy became the steady centre of world growth after early 2020. China also developed several vaccines and integrated them into its broader defence against COVID-19 and, starting in early 2021, began delivering them to the developing world in sharp contrast to the developed world's hoarding of vaccines. In early 2022, local outbreaks in Xian and Tianjin were dealt with, in February, the country achieved the feat of holding a COVID-free Beijing Winter Olympics and later that spring was keeping outbreaks in Shanghai and Beijing under control, if with greater difficulty in the former: recent marketist local governance reforms in this most 'capitalist' of China's cities made implementing effective dynamic zero COVID strategies harder and will likely be re-evaluated (Ping 2022). There was no doubt that China's party-state emerged from this with a greatly enhanced political legitimacy.

The neoliberal choice: herd immunity or herd immunity?

The contrast with the leading neoliberal financialised economies, the United States and the United Kingdom, could not have been greater. When most of the capitalist world announced its first lockdowns in March 2020, shocked citizenries complied, expecting them to last perhaps a few weeks. Two years later, helped by war and inflation that were already distracting public attention, US and UK authorities had declared defeat, telling citizens they had to take personal responsibility for their own health and 'learn to live with the virus' and lifted restrictions despite having little control over the pandemic while also putting out confusing messages about the virus becoming 'endemic' as if this made it harmless when, in fact, not only is the epidemiological meaning of the word disputed, but the future of the novel coronavirus remains wide open, including possibilities of new variants (Stern and Wu 2022). It is worth recalling the rocky road that brought them to this juddering denouement.

Even after Italy was badly hit in early 2020, neoliberal authorities wasted precious weeks in denial. In the United States, with a largely private medical system, insurance, cost and other commercial parameters dictated a haphazard response in which even testing remained spotty, leaving the true scale of the pandemic itself a mystery. Indeed, early in the pandemic both the United States and the United Kingdom considered a strategy they dubbed 'herd immunity' (see Bump 2020; Yong 2020), letting the pandemic rip though the population unimpeded, taking whom it would. Involving the wilful abuse of a term normally used to refer to levels of vaccinations necessary to protect populations, this option would have amounted to nothing but a sanitised declaration of bankruptcy with a strong whiff of genocide. Considering that the pandemic would hit the vulnerable—the elderly, marginalised and poor—hardest, accepting that the virus would spread, dozens of 'loved ones' would die and only the fittest would survive, this was like saying 'let the devil take the hindmost'.

If this plan was eventually dropped, it was thanks to public outcry and to the threat it posed to weak health systems and economies. Applied globally, the 'herd immunity' option would have required, studies estimated, hospitalising about 7% of the global population and result in fatalities at a rate of 0.35–0.7% (Meyerowitz-Katz 2020). Near or at its peak, such a freely developing pandemic would overwhelm shrunken and weakened health systems. Economies would be devastated by ill or self-quarantining workers, lost skills, broken teams and supply chains, collapsed demand and rising debt. Political structures, already creaking, could be brought down by the widespread failure of states to ensure basic security of life, not to mention the inevitable train of lies and cover-ups by politically insecure governments that would surely follow and further undermine public trust. Political disintegration or authoritarianism would be the stark options, especially given the atomisation of neoliberal societies. That last eventuality could well spell the beginning of the end of capitalism in these societies.

Though they thus came to fear the consequences of its uncontrolled spread, neoliberal governments were unable to supplement the weakened health infrastructure in short order and equip it with the resources it needed to root out the virus through testing, tracking, isolating, supporting and treating, as China did in Wuhan and in other much smaller outbreaks in the rest of the country. The only alternative for most neoliberal financialised capitalisms was, therefore, to try mitigation, to 'flatten the curve' of infections by slowing their spread, preventing them from reaching levels that would overwhelm public health systems. Thus, were British people, who had every right to expect that the National Health System (NHS) save them as it was established to do, asked to comply with onerous and indefinite restrictions to 'Save the NHS'. In practice, the difference between strategies adopted by neoliberal governments and the strategy of 'herd immunity' was one of degree, not quality (Costello 2020).

The only really effective strategy would have been one variously labelled maximum suppression or zero COVID, as advocated early on by a prominent group of independent medical experts in the United Kingdom, the Independent SAGE. Uncertain whether the advice of the official Scientific Advisory Group on Emergencies (SAGE) would be heeded by the government, and possibly of some of the advice itself—after all, England's chief medical officer was reported to have advised early in the pandemic that 'Britain would be better able to resist a second wave the following winter if the population had acquired "herd immunity" in the meantime', a course that envisaged 40 million infected people (Parker and Burn-Murdoch 2020)—they came together in May 2020 to 'provide independent scientific advice to the UK government and public on how to minimise deaths and support Britain's recovery from the COVID-19 crisis'. They provided weekly public briefings and came up with regular reports and recommendations.

One of the earliest Independent SAGE reports, published in June 2020, spelled out what a zero COVID or maximum suppression strategy would involve: a Find, Test, Trace, Isolate and Support (FTTIS) system (Independent SAGE 2020b) run by locally based well-trained health professionals with the trust of the communities they served. This is the time-tested strategy that saves both lives and livelihoods and does not leave behind the poor and marginalised. A similar if less active group of Canadian medics also recommended such a strategy in its report 'Building the Canadian Shield' (COVID Strategic Choices Group 2020). While many countries have pursued some version of this strategy—Australia, New Zealand, China, South Korea, Singapore, Vietnam, Uruguay, Finland and Norway—China has pursued it most consistently and against great odds, without, for instance, enjoying the luxury of being a remote island country or having a sparse population.

Each component of FTTIS is critical. Finding cases is best done through targeted, not mass, testing of vulnerable or exposed groups. Mass testing can be a wasteful exercise and often an act of choice by asymptomatic individuals who can afford to isolate or wish to travel. Contacts must be traced forward to locate all those who may have been infected by a given case and backward to the original event that began the chain of infections. Isolation has to be strict, supervised and, critically, supported with adequate income and social and medical supports. When left to unsupported individuals, isolation imposes on many who must work to support themselves and dependents the cruel choice of infecting others or losing income and failing to provide. Maximum suppression cannot succeed without generous and multifaceted supports for isolation.

All this requires a public health structure that is decentralised, local, community-based, staffed with health care professionals possessing a variety of health and public health-related skills, is committed to people and community and operates with a high degree of trust, precisely the sort of system neoliberalism has spent the last many decades destroying. The effective suppression of the virus involves altering human behaviour and that requires not so much the high-cost medicine provided by a top-down medical–industrial complex aiming at profit as a lower cost approach that mobilises communities. This was clear in one of the 18 recommendations of the Independent SAGE report:

> Communities and civil society organisations should have a voice, be informed, engaged and participatory in the exit from lockdown. This pandemic starts and ends within communities. Full participation and engagement of those communities on issues such as childcare and public transport will assist with enabling control measures. Conversely, a top-down approach risks losing their support and trust.

This strategy may necessitate an early and very strict lockdown, but it had to be used to put the infrastructure for a full FTTIS in place as quickly as possible to keep cases and deaths to a minimum and shorten the economic pain, as China did, flying in health workers from all over the county to Wuhan and Hebei province and mobilising

> thousands of community workers to scale up a national testing effort, while mapping infections using case definitions based on symptoms . . . They developed apps to monitor people's symptoms and their compliance with quarantine, and set up 24-hour TV channels in every province to update people on data, progress and prevention.
>
> *(Costello 2020)*

As China's experience showed, this strategy makes restrictions and lockdowns less necessary and enables a fuller economic recovery. Independent SAGE also anticipated precisely this early on. The principal recommendation of one of its earliest reports was to urge the government

> take all necessary measures to control the virus through suppression and not simply managing its spread. Evidence must show that COVID-19 transmission is controlled before measures are relaxed. We detect ambivalence in the government's strategic response, with some advisers promoting the idea of simply 'flattening the curve' or ensuring the NHS is not overwhelmed. We find this attitude counter-productive and potentially dangerous. Without suppression, we shall inevitably see a more rapid return of local epidemics resulting in more deaths and potentially further partial or national lockdowns, with the economic costs that will incur.
>
> *(The Independent SAGE 2020a)*

However, that would have entailed a more or less complete reversal of health policy direction of neoliberal privatisation, contracting out, marketisation, corporatisation and the replacement of services with goods, especially pills, of recent decades. Public health infrastructures would have to be returned to their original public service vocation and health care placed in the hands of well-trained and well-paid professionals providing care, not commodities, and oriented towards public service rather than profit. Such a reversal also had the potential to reverberate throughout society, raising questions about neoliberal policies, first in cognate fields—education, for instance—and then across the policy spectrum. This would prove the unravelling of neoliberalism, the only policy paradigm—one involving not so much free markets as corporate power—under which anything resembling capitalism can reliably continue existing.

Moreover, effective suppression of the virus involved altering human behaviour and that required not so much the high-cost medicine provided by the medical–industrial complex to governments at risk-free, high margin prices as a lower cost approach that is less amenable to being an arena for profit-making, focusing on building public health capacity that requires political legitimacy and participation. Without these capacities, public health infrastructures could only be further undermined by the pandemic while gaps in compliance prolonged the pandemic and anti-mask/vaccine/lockdown protests led to political upheaval. While no coherent left movement challenging the inhumanity of neoliberal government's COVID response emerged, political tussles soon broke out within the neoliberal camp over lifting the controls to get the economy going again, complete with capitalists funding protests (Gabbatt 2020) against lockdowns, and this could only make their public health response more incoherent, make new waves infections more likely and lengthen the economic crisis.

Even the strategy of flattening the curve through lockdowns and related restrictions was further compromised with the alleged need to balance the saving of 'lives and livelihoods'. Since, in neoliberal economies, most people have 'livelihoods' only in so far as they serve, directly or indirectly, the accumulation of profit, saving livelihoods was hard to separate from saving profits. Life-saving but profit-killing lockdowns and restrictions had to be used as sparingly as possible and that only led to their repeated imposition. While socialist China managed to save both lives and livelihoods, neoliberal financialised capitalisms, willing to sacrifice lives at the altar of profits, ultimately saved neither.

Friedrich Engels had long ago termed the structural shortening and degradation of working class lives by capitalism 'social murder'. Capitalism places workers in a position where

> they inevitably meet a too early and an unnatural death, one which is quite as much a death by violence as that by the sword or bullet; when it deprives thousands of the necessaries of life, places them under conditions in which they cannot live—forces them, through the strong arm of the law, to remain in such conditions until that death ensues which is the

inevitable consequence—knows that these thousands of victims must perish, and yet permits these conditions to remain.

(Engels 1845/1987, 127)

While the welfarist capitalism had mitigated these tendencies considerably, neoliberalism was restoring them, and the pandemic ratcheted this murderousness a notch: capitalist ruling classes were intentionally sacrificing large sections of the working class and millions of lives at the altar of capital and profit and justifying it as a hard choice between saving 'lives and livelihoods'. The terrifying truth was that what they really meant by 'livelihoods' was the capitalist organisation of our economies. When societies are reduced to saving their form by sacrificing their members, they must change that form.

How to lose both lives and livelihoods

The neoliberal unwillingness to incur the expense of suppressing the virus combined with the equally neoliberal willingness to sacrifice lives at the altar of capital led neoliberal financialised economies to strategies that would ensure they not only lost lives in spades but would also deepen, widen and prolong the economic crisis.

In the United States, without a public health service, and a president denying the seriousness of the virus, there were no country-wide restrictions, lockdowns or strategy, though individual states often took more strenuous action. In a grim irony, having failed to call for national restrictions, Trump could not call for a nationwide end to the patchwork of restrictions imposed by states even when his right-wing social base clamoured for it (Flynn and Chiu 2020), uncaring of how such premature easing would expose disproportionately female and racialised essential workers to the onslaught of the virus.

Trump's Operation Warp Speed did, however, heavily subsidise vaccine development by Big Pharma and, by the end of 2020, along with other Western efforts, it began showing results. Neoliberal financialised capitalist governments, at once relieved and triumphant, now prioritised vaccinations above all as silver bullets against the pandemic. Things would, however, prove considerably more complicated. Initially constrained by supply, rollouts prioritised the elderly and the inhabitants of care homes in accordance with the strategy of reducing the stress on health care systems. This left out vulnerable frontline workers and communities of the poor and racially and socially marginalised living and working in conditions conducive to the spread of the virus, and the relaxation of restrictions could only lead to new spikes in cases.

The incoming Biden administration, elected to bring the pandemic under control, relied almost exclusively on vaccines, focusing on giving at least one dose to 70% of eligible US citizens by 4 July, US Independence Day. However, though availability was now less of a problem, there were others—the United States' mostly private health care, long-standing distrust between public authorities and marginalised groups and far-right disinformation—and only 55% of those eligible were vaccinated by then. Moreover, it soon became clear that one dose was not enough and second doses were even less widely taken. By mid-2021, the United States was facing a third wave of COVID chiefly among the unvaccinated and the inadequately vaccinated and by the end of that year, the highly infectious Omicron variant emerged. Though, thanks to substantial vaccination, death rates peaked at levels comparable to earlier peaks, it soon became clear that protection against it required a third vaccine dose, and later a fourth and more.

By now it had to be admitted that vaccines were not going to end the pandemic. This should have been clear from the start. While vaccines substantially reduce infections, symptoms, hospitalisations and deaths, they are not silver bullets and breakthrough infections are not rare. The longevity of the vaccine's protection was unknown then and has since proved short. Other than exhortation, there was no strategy to ensure high vaccine uptake and, for many of the most marginalised, access has remained a problem. Stigmatisation, of which there was a plentiful supply and which failed to distinguish between the unvaccinated and the anti-vaxxers, only added to the difficulty. Above all, as long as the disease continues to rage around the world, as it did with much of the world left unvaccinated thanks to the neoliberal financialised capitalisms' vaccine apartheid, the possibility of new variants remains.

Long committed to corporate and commodified medicine, neoliberal financialised capitalist governments not only refused to bolster health systems, but they also appeared to prioritise offering capitalist cronies opportunities for private profiteering in the name of providing health and other public services, be they contracts for testing and tracing or subsidies for drugs and vaccines. Tracing systems, for instance, were often confined to forward tracing, organised in a centralised fashion and staffed with barely trained and ill-paid equivalents of call centre workers. Inevitably they missed all-too-many infections, leaving the virus to spread. The neoliberal bias was also clear when governments subsidised Big Pharma (Jorge 2020) with billions without any conditions for making vaccines free or cheap. They also awarded enormous contracts to dozens of other big corporations curtailing normal competitive bidding on the pretext of the pandemic and the losers did not protest, hoping to gain from new rounds of awards (Seiden 2020). The resulting unnecessarily high level of hospitalisations hit public health facilities already underfunded and ill-prepared thanks to decades of underfunding and contracting out, staffed by ill-paid and overworked health care professionals who, inevitably, also suffer from post-traumatic stress disorder.

Finally, neoliberal societies have performed less well even in high-technology elements of a suppression strategy, as in the use of smartphones for contact tracing. Their successful use in China, Taiwan and South Korea (Law and Choon 2020) is decried as authoritarian and an invasion of privacy. The irony is, of course, that the privacy of Western citizens has long been surrendered to internet companies who glean the most intimate information about them from 'big data' to sell to advertisers. Ever more important in a world where firms must reduce uncertainty of demand by creating it through more and more finely targeted advertising, such practices have trapped Western citizens in the so-called privacy paradox (Naughton 2020):

> Whenever researchers, opinion pollsters and other busybodies ask people if they value their privacy, they invariably respond with a resounding 'yes'. The paradox arises from the fact that they nevertheless continue to use the services [such as Facebook and Google] that undermine their beloved privacy.

Worse still, these internet companies are also colluding with the US military–industrial complex (Levine 2018) in aiding its surveillance objectives. While their privacy is assured neither against the state nor against big capital, Western citizens must wait for effective contact tracing while these internet companies compete to come up with apps they can sell for huge profits to governments.

By early 2022, authorities in neoliberal financialised capitalisms threw up their hands, lifted most restrictions and, relying on questionable claims that the virus was becoming 'endemic' and even more questionable interpretations of what that would mean, declared the necessity to 'live with the virus', allowing it to continue circulating, producing new variants. This leaves open the possibility further lockdowns. Alternatively, the damage of the disease will remain confined to 'communities that are already lowest in the indices of multiple deprivations and have been hit hardest' (Independent SAGE 2021) and it will become another disease of poverty, like tuberculosis and AIDS.

Thriving as it does on overcrowding, co-morbidities, stress, poor nutrition and other such conditions in or with which the poor, uneducated and non-white people disproportionately live, COVID has already affected these groups the worst. Most frontline and essential workers also belong to them. The well-to-do—the wealthy, credentialed, white and male—can retreat into home working, their incomes unaffected or even inflated, vaccinated against the pandemic, sporting vaccine passports that would return their lives back to normal, whatever that may turn out to be. They will also have better access to COVID protections and treatments.

The leading neoliberal financialised capitalisms, the United States and the United Kingdom, thus emerged from the real-world stress test for public health systems, economies and polities that the pandemic represented with the equivalent of an F grade and China with an A. Between them at opposite ends of the international political spectrum of covid performance lie other countries. Available statistics indicate that their pandemic performance broadly reflected the pattern of socialist success and neoliberal capitalist failure. Among the successes are socialist countries, such as Vietnam or Cuba and certain exceptional capitalist countries such as South Korea and Japan. Their prior experience of SARS and the greater preparedness maintained as a result have, of course, helped. Such experience and preparedness also appear to have played a role in the better performance of certain African countries. For the rest, however, poor capitalist countries, with means neither for a proper public health response nor for economic stimuli, face the worst in terms of morbidities and fatalities and economic retardation.

The economic crisis

By early 2022, the parlous state of neoliberal financialised capitalist economies as evidenced in the return of inflation could conveniently be blamed on the conflict over Ukraine and particularly President Putin—his war was causing spikes in inflation, particularly in food and fuel prices—and on China, whose zero COVID policies were causing disruptions in supply. However, the pandemic had exposed and exacerbated key weaknesses of neoliberal financialised capitalist economies and the war, provoked by the US-led West, was tied to them too.

The productive system had been weakened and stretched taut in at least three ways. Spatially, its supply lines extended tenuously around the world. Temporally, they were tensed with 'just-in-time' production, low or no inventories and little financial wiggle room to deal with contingencies. Finally, socially, they squeezed workers, agricultural producers and small business suppliers hard, making them yield work and products for low wages and prices and unloading all sorts of social and financial risks on them. The pandemic and the war would expose all these weaknesses. Tenuous supply chains were easily broken, leading to shortages. Lacking inventories, many firms experienced immediate production stoppages. Finally, as would become very clear after restrictions were eased, labour markets shrank with many people leaving the labour force and business shuttering altogether.

Repeated lockdowns affected the bloated 'non-essential' 'frills economy' of optional consumption for the relatively better off—travel, leisure, hospitality, personal services and the like—that was such a large part of neoliberal financialised capitalist economies and employment worst and in 2020 these economies registered historic declines. For instance, UK GDP declined by nearly 10% in 2020 (Partington 2021), the worst decline in over 300 years, while Canadian GDP declined 5.4% that year (*Global News* Staff 2021), the steepest in available records. The United States, which had no national lockdown and the federal government effectively let the pandemic rip among those least able to protect themselves with only inadequate measures from state and local authorities, limited its losses to a 3.5 % (Cox 2021) reduction in GDP in 2020, a post-war worst. This figure not only includes the considerable financial boom engineered by the Federal Reserve response to the pandemic but also the substantial contribution it makes to skewing US GDP upwards through changes in GDP measurement exaggerating the contributions of sectors that are particularly large in the US economy, including finance and weapons production (Assa and Kvangraven 2021).

By contrast, among countries that had coped better with the pandemic with briefer and more local lockdowns, the more trade-dependent German economy, the centre of the region worst affected by the pandemic in 2020, shrank by 5% (Partington 2021), though the dip was not as deep as that in 2008. A similarly trade-dependent Japan, part of the region most successful at coping with the virus, limited its losses to 1% of GDP in 2020 (Harding 2021), with a sharp rebound in the last quarter.

In the leading neoliberal financialised capitalisms, moreover, it was clear from the start that economic losses were being very unequally borne and recovery promised to be a 'K-shaped' one, transmitting inequalities down the years, if not decades. As the pandemic wore on, the incomes and wealth of the already rich grew while working people and, even more, workers marginalised on the basis of gender and race, lost disproportionately, with more job and income loss, and suffered the impact of COVID—with more hospitalisations and deaths—even more (Institute for Policy Studies 2022). Moreover, in tightly knit communities of solidarity—where, for instance grandparents routinely provided childcare—these deaths brought material as well as emotional loss (Fisher and Bubola 2020).

Massive disruption in retail, travel, tourism, hospitality, personal services and recreation sectors led to loss of employment and incomes among the low-paid women and minorities that were so disproportionately employed in these sectors. Indeed, many identified a 'she-cession' (YWCA-GATE 2020; Elting 2022), a recession affecting women overwhelmingly, a comment on the sort of economic integration neoliberalism has offered them given that the influx of women and migrants into the labour force of the major capitalist economies coincided with the neoliberal era. At the same time, equally low-paid women and minorities continued to work in 'essential services' from poor, often overcrowded neighbourhoods and housing, becoming more exposed to COVID-19 and suffering more morbidity and fatality. With limited time, ability and broadband access to facilitate home schooling among the low-paid, women and minorities as schools shut down, these inequalities also threatened to be passed down the generations, accelerating the undermining of gains of historic struggles for inequality already ongoing under neoliberalism. The well-to-do, meanwhile, already spared the worst, have better access to COVID protections and treatments. Such increases in already high inequality could only worsen the demand problem underlying the Long Downturn.

Contrary to expectations, the monetary and fiscal responses did not reverse the neoliberal direction of previous decades but accelerated the pace of travel in it.

The monetary policy response

Even before the WHO declared the novel coronavirus infection a pandemic on 11 March 2020, the Federal Reserve, true to neoliberal financialisation type, announced an emergency rate cut and promise to inject trillions (yes) into the system. Despite that, the following day, stock markets in the United States suffered their largest one-day percentage decline since the Crash of '87 (Wigglesworth 2020) and the Dow Jones Industrial Average experienced three of its greatest point drops in March 2020. Unusually, riskier stock markets were not alone. Less risky bond markets and even markets in those 'safest' of assets, US treasuries and gold fell as investors demanded hard cash.

As the crisis worsened with the WHO declaring a pandemic, US authorities flooded the financial system with liquidity. They cut interest rates back down to zero, using up all the 'ammunition' they had so carefully collected by raising interest rates gingerly, without inflicting pain on the coddled financial sector, and Federal Reserve Chairman, Jerome Powell, promised to do 'whatever it takes'—words ECB Chairman Mario Draghi had used in 2010 at the height of the Eurozone crisis—to defend asset values.

It soon became clear, however, that, in doing this, the Federal Reserve was fighting the last war. Liquidity issuance proved the solution (for the financial sector) in 2008 because the problem had been one of ensuring liquidity to highly leveraged financial institutions bleeding cash. Now, however, the problem was different. The very companies whose assets formed the basis of the post-2008, post-Basel III reserve requirements were drawing them down and '[l]osing these deposits so quickly threaten[ed] the liquidity profile and regulatory compliance of banks themselves', as Rana Faroohar of the *Financial Times* noted (Foroohar 2020), commenting further that 'central bankers will have to keep the money taps on, and probably increase the variety of assets that they are buying or back-stopping'. She was prescient.

A month into the crisis, when Federal Reserve Chairman Jerome Powell urged that Congress also do 'whatever it takes' to secure the economy against a collapse of economic activity, employment and demand, he was actually asking Congress to expand his capacity to intervene further in asset markets and Congress complied. Now, in order to save this even bigger house of cards precariously holding up the wealth of the United States' tiny elite, Congress permitted the Federal Reserve to cross three other boundaries. By passing the CARES Act, it gave $454 billion to the Federal Reserve, to cover any losses in its market operations in which the central bank could leverage the amount allocated 10-fold. The Act also gave the Federal Reserve 'full charge of making advances to . . . corporations' and protected its actions from public scrutiny. And, thus emboldened, for the first time, the Federal Reserve made loans to non-financial corporations by buying their bonds, effectively supporting the huge corporate bond market bubble, with no strings attached (Brenner 2020, 7–8, 13ff). Protected from public scrutiny, the Federal Reserve did not have to bother with coming up with 'principles' like 'too big to fail' to justify its actions, which was just as well. No amount of ingenuity could have covered such blatantly political favouritism directed less towards the industrial and service corporations being supported as towards the parasitical financial institutions for whom their debts were assets.

This point needs underlining. It was not just that the US political establishment had concluded that

> the only way that they can assure the reproduction of the non-financial and financial corporations . . . is to intervene politically in the asset markets and throughout the whole economy, so as to underwrite the upward re-distribution of wealth to them by directly political means.
>
> *(Brenner 2020, 22)*

It was also that, presiding over an economy debilitated by its parasitical financial sector, this political establishment was only driven to bail out non-financial, productive, corporations insofar as they had become, thanks to Basel III, the source of the best assets of the financial sector. The political establishment remained committed, as before, to the protection, perpetuation and proliferation of that sector unconditionally. Concern for all else, even big non-financial corporations, was conditional on that. Over the following two years, the Federal Reserve's balance sheet, an indication of the scale of its asset purchases to shore up asset values, more than doubled from its already 2008-inflated $4 trillion to over $9 trillion (Figure 4.6).

Over the next several months, the new liquidity wiped out nearly all the asset market losses of March. When the *Financial Times* judged the market recovery was driven 'as much by extraordinary monetary policy and the absence of decent alternatives to stocks as by optimism over the strength of the [economic] recovery' (Editorial Board of the *Financial Times* 2020) it was praising with faint condemnation, given that the economy was headed in the opposite direction. Other asset markets, including the housing market, also preserved their value. Driven by lax monetary policy, this rally in asset prices continued into the new year, not only preserving but expanding the wealth of the financial sector and its tiny elite while the economy malingered. As we shall see, this wealth now posed the greatest threat to any US recovery.

The fiscal policy response

Between them, the Trump and Biden administrations passed four major pieces of economic stimulus legislation. The Trump administration followed up the $ 2.2 trillion CARES Act with a $1.9 trillion pandemic relief package in December 2020. Of the total of the Trump administration's spending on the pandemic estimated at about $4 trillion in the fall of 2020, it was calculated that, in addition to the $454 billion that went to the Federal Reserve to effect its bailout of financial corporations and the non-financial corporations whose solvency they relied on, more than half, about $2.3 trillion in direct funding, another $651 billion in tax breaks and $670 billion in 'paycheck protection', went to businesses without having to demonstrate they were affected or that they were keeping workers employed or that they were going to use the paycheck protection funds for the purpose. Only a fifth, about $884 trillion, went to working people and only 16% to fighting COVID (Whoriskey et al. 2020).

Promising not to repeat the Obama administration's mistake of too little stimulus after 2008, the Biden administration took office with a 'build back better' platform, proposing to spend between $2 trillion and $4 trillion on a recovery stimulus and a long-term plan of investment to remedy and augment US infrastructure and invest in green and other technologies to revive the economy.

Biden's stimulus

Biden had campaigned on these expenditures and his promises evoked two opposing sets of reactions. On the one hand, trendy modern monetary theorists (MMT) claimed that US 'monetary sovereignty' meant that these expenditures could be easily monetised with no consequences for inflation, particularly as there was considerable slack in the economy. All gain, no pain. On the other hand, Wall Street knew better: what MMT called 'monetary sovereignty' was actually the United States' ability to attract money into the dollar creditocracy on which the dollar's international acceptability relied. This system was already failing to attract the scale of funds necessary to support inflated US asset markets and the Federal Reserve was already stepping in on a massive scale to support asset markets, including the US bond market, well before the pandemic. As Figure 4.6 shows, the Federal Reserve balance sheet had expanded from under $1 trillion in August 2008 to over $2.5 trillion in December that year. Over the years of quantitative easing, it expanded to $4.5 trillion before beginning a gradual decline as the Federal Reserve began unwinding it gingerly, carefully avoiding 'taper tantrums'. However, between late February and early June 2020, it jumped to over $7 trillion (Federal Reserve 2022). Wall Street knew well enough that such astronomical liquidity injections may temporarily support the fragile structures of dollar creditocracy, but it also revealed their fragility.

Wall Street was already sending bond yields up when the Biden administration took office and rolled out his first $1.9 trillion American Rescue Plan consisting chiefly of temporary income support for working Americans and small business. By late March, the president had also committed himself to ensuring that China would not 'become the leading country in the world, the wealthiest country in the world, and the most powerful country in the world . . . on my watch because the United States is going to continue to grow' (Renshaw et al. 2021), clearly indicating that foreign policy concerns were displacing the pandemic from the administration's concerns.

With the American Rescue Plan passed and other parts of the Build Back Better programme anticipated, by mid-2021, the IMF forecasted a robust US recovery (International Monetary Fund 2021) contributing to the world's recovery. However, a series of obstacles to recovery remained. With inflation concerns already rising, when Biden followed the American Rescue Plan up with the second part of his build back better plan, the $2.3 trillion American Jobs Plan designed to restore and expand the US infrastructure, create jobs, strengthen unions, increase investment, especially green investment, and check China, he had to lace it with corporate tax increases and spread it over eight years, meaning that the stimulus amounted to little more than 0.8% of GDP annually (Baker 2021). After being gridlocked for months, the legislation passed in a slimmed down $1.2 trillion version, notably without its $15 an hour minimum wage provision. The third part, the American Families Plan, has had to be shelved altogether.

So, the fiscal stimulus has already been much weaker than expected. Moreover, given the already high levels of household debt, even the small parts of the 'stimulus' going to working people, would end up in the financial sector. With about 30% going to debt payments and another 30% to savings, only 40% being spent on consumption (Belsie 2020). The stimulus, moreover, constituted little more than a 'sugar rush' for the economy (Roberts 2021), after which even the Federal Reserve expected a long-term growth rate of 1.8% per annum, hardly above the 1.7% growth rate between 2009 and 2019 despite the depth of the pandemic recession in 2020 (Roberts 2021). Only a significant increase in investment can boost US growth out of the 1–3% trap it has been in the twenty-first century. The private sector's reluctance to step up is already evidenced in the massive financialisation of the US economy while state initiative is precluded by the corporate dominance of its politics.

With an even weaker productive economy, more reliant on 'frills' and even less room for fiscal manoeuvre, the United Kingdom not only experienced the worst drop in GDP in its history, it also faces an even weaker recovery the United States.

The less neoliberal and financialised major capitalist economies

It is instructive to compare the response of the United States and the United Kingdom to other G7 economies, particularly Japan and Germany, with their productively stronger economies. Compared to the United States and the United Kingdom, which along with their anglophone sibling Canada, tended to rely on increased spending and tax cuts to support the economy, Japan and Germany relied on government investment and guarantees to industrial enterprises. This had many important effects, including keeping rising government debt under better control and keeping unemployment lower than in the United States. In addition, whereas the United States focused on '"cessation," or keeping individuals and businesses solvent amid temporary restrictions on economic activity. . . . Japan and Germany . . . approved forward-looking investments to increase sustainability, innovation, and resilience while averting a sustained recession' (Goodman 2020).

Inflation and war

As 2022 opened with heightened inflation concerns and war, it also became increasingly clear that the algorithms of the neoliberal management of the neoliberal economies, particularly the US economy, which created and maintained the dollar creditocracy, will face new challenges. They will either bring these economies to a new low in their record of anaemic growth or force a destructive recession on already very weak economies.

Over the neoliberal decades, central banks took credit for keeping inflation low. In reality, as the productive system was reconfigured through deindustrialisation at home and outsourcing abroad, it was kept low by stagnating wages and

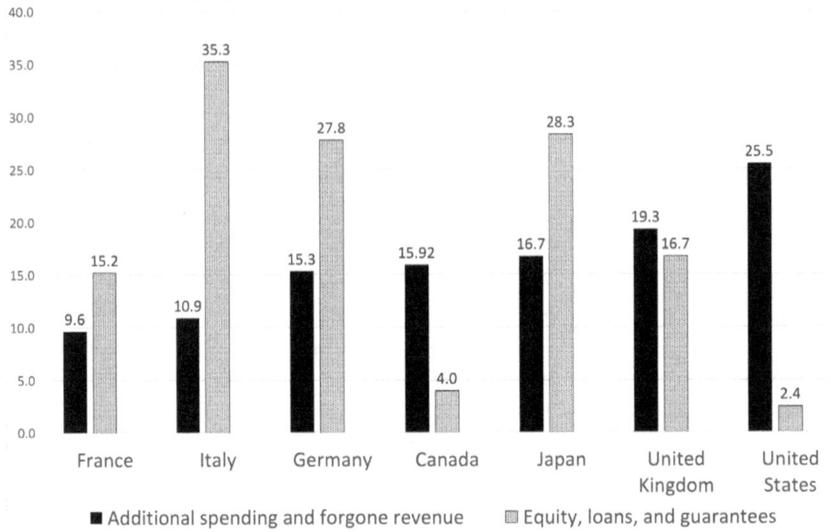

FIGURE 5.1 G7 COVID-19 fiscal responses, January 2020–September 2021 (percentage of gross domestic product).

Source: Data from International Monetary Fund. 2021. 'Fiscal Monitor Database of Country Fiscal Measures in Response to the COVID-19 Pandemic', *Database of Fiscal Responses to COVID-19*, October, (Accessed 22 June 2022) www.imf.org/en/Topics/imf-and-covid19/Fiscal-Policies-Database-in-Response-to-COVID-19.

Created by Natalie Braun, used with permission.

precarity among working classes in the major capitalist countries, cheap goods from the Third World and a dollar overvalued by financial demand for it.

Central banks' success in taking credit for low inflation came back to bite them when inflation rose beginning in 2021. and most blamed it on the excesses of money creation over the neoliberal decades, excesses that became even more excessive in the pandemic. These excesses were not, however, the prime cause of inflation. True, over the neoliberal decades, economic policy had shrunk to monetary policy. True also that it had involved lax monetary policy since about 2000, barring the fateful interest rate increases of 2004–06. However, though monetary policy moves are always justified in terms of their necessity to keep up levels of economic activity and employment, they were never geared to expanding employment, and even geared to keeping it tight enough to act as a barrier to rising wages, only permitting the expansion of predatory and speculative financial activity (Fleckenstein and Sheehan 2008). Neither the monetary laxity since 2000, nor the trillions of dollars created from 2008 onwards, reached consumers and markets for goods and services. They were sucked into the black holes that were the balance sheets of financial institutions, enabling them to return to their speculative games in record time after 2008 and once again after even greater money creation in and after 2020. As we have seen, very little of the fiscal or monetary stimulus ended up in working people's pockets, or if it did, was spent on consumption.

There is the related matter of the decline in the US labour force participation rate, ongoing since 2000 and accelerated by the pandemic. This is bound to make any re-shoring, or 'friend shoring' of production more expensive if and when it takes place. Most of the Third World is increasingly not so 'friendly' or, if it is, it is unlikely to be sufficiently politically stable to permit outsourcing. After all, outsourcing requires a political climate conducive substantial private domestic investment by participating firms in the offshore location. Considering that the structures of Western imperialism, including the IMF, continue prescribing neoliberal or 'austerity' policies for the Third World even as they relax them for Western countries (Oxfam International 2022, for a critique, see Patnaik 2022), they can only further undermine economies and destabilise polities enough to discourage outsourcing-related investment. It is no wonder that bulk of the outsourcing of the world has been concentrated in China, Mexico and Eastern Europe.

However, such friend-shoring has not yet taken place and the inflation of 2021 and 2022 had little to do with rising wages. Wage stagnation and precarity will only be overcome if working people mobilise and union power rises. Although the pandemic and its stresses certainly led to an uptick in working class mobilisation, unionisation and strike activity, in most of the Western world, they have a long way to go before they can begin to undo the wage stagnation of the previous several decades, let alone push inflation up (O'Connor 2022). While it may yet happen, for now, inflation's relation to working people is simply to driveup their cost of living, cutting their real wages even more or, at best with a lot of union effort, keeping them steady.

Inflation, which is worst in its deindustrialised leaders, the United States and the United Kingdom, even though with the start of the war over Ukraine, European economies, including Germany, faced much higher energy costs, has a number of other causes, all of which have to do with the trajectory of neoliberal capitalism. First, given the weakness of the productive structures of leading neoliberal financialised economies, they were unable to make a supply response to shortages and resulting higher prices. This is fundamental. If inflation is too much money chasing too few goods, in any healthy economy, it should be temporary, lasting only as long as firms respond to higher prices with increased production and supply. Persistent inflation must be squarely attributed to blockages in production or supply. Though the formation of inflation expectations plays a role, if the blockages were not persistent, if they became unblocked and supply resumed at 'natural' or 'socially necessary' prices, these inflation expectations would also come unstuck. Given deindustrialisation and outsourcing, the pandemic had already triggered many production and supply blockages including early shortages of personal protective equipment (PPE) and other essentials.

Second, the United States' supply lines, in particular, are still vastly concentrated in China and now vulnerable to the very trade and military tensions that the United States had to ratchet up to in the pandemic context as a last measure against China's challenge, though they also serve to keep its military–industrial complex happy, its allies in line and to justify any investment programme, even one as weak as the jobs plan. Now, the war over Ukraine and its disruptive sanctions, along with the talk of 'friend-shoring', will only add fuel to the fire. Over the past century and more, the US economic policy has not distinguished itself in framing rational industrial policy, only in supporting successive governments' corporate backers.

To this structural reason relating to the productive economy, we may add another relating to the financial sector. In so far as shoring up collapsing asset markets has succeeded, speculation itself is adding to inflation. For example, rising real estate prices also elevate rents, and speculation in commodity markets have led current upswings in primary commodity prices to be exaggerated even more.

Finally, a good part of the food price inflation, which shows little sign of abating, is the result of ecological challenges agriculture faces thanks the ecological emergency created by capitalism. While extreme heat of 2022 affected the crop in India, in many other parts of the world, flooding prevented farmers from sowing. Meanwhile, waves of avian flu are driving up poultry prices. These problems are further compounded by decades of policies that have been squeezing small-holder agriculture between high input prices, low output prices and resulting debt, to favour agribusiness.

As we saw in Chapter 2, capitalist economies of our time have only one rather blunt and destructive weapon against inflation once a certain low threshold for government intervention is passed: very tight monetary policy. This has always had the disadvantage of being deflationary, indeed outright recession-inducing, squeezing production and employment. However, at least in the late 1970s and early 1980s, the United States considered it worthwhile and administered the Volcker interest rate shock. Today, however, this option comes with a new danger. The asset markets and the wealth built on them rely on low interest rates and easy monetary policy in the form of quantitative easing. The higher interest rates and quantitative tightening necessary to fight inflation will not only induce a major recession, it will also crash asset prices, which the Federal Reserve fears even more.

Thus, inflation puts the Federal Reserve in a bind, damned if it does and damned if it doesn't. Raising interest rates beyond a point will crash asset markets and raise the cost of borrowing for the US government at a time when its debt is at an all-time high. This near certainty tempts it to keep interest rates low, confining its battle against inflation to mild rises in the interest rate and a great deal of rhetoric about combatting inflation, which it hopes will affect inflation expectations (Goodhart 2022; Holland et al. 2020; Lachman 2021).

Given that, unlike the capitalist economies of the early 1980s, fresh out of the Long Boom, today's economies are already weakened, exhausted and emaciated by four decades of neoliberalism and a succession of crises, in what form they will survive, either suffering prolonged inflation or suffering the deep recession that will come from the level of monetary tightening necessary to quell it, does not bear thinking of.

A final point before we leave the subject of inflation. While progressives are right to pit themselves against the 'inflation hawks' to prevent the tightening of monetary conditions in principle, they are blind to the fact that confining themselves to that policy recommendation only plays into the hands of the very financialisation that continues to strangle production. The real need is to address the productive limitations of the economy and to dismantle the structures of financialisation. That would also require dismantling the very structures with which the United States has sought, vainly and unsuccessfully, to be sure, to dominate the world economy, those of the dollar creditocracy. Without massive, indeed revolutionary, political change, the likelihood of this happening from within the United States is practically nil. However, the rest of the world may soon be making that effort unnecessary, radically narrowing the options of the US ruling classes. Exactly how, we discuss in Chapter 7.

It should be clear by now that the neoliberal financialised economies are poised, at best, for an anaemic recovery and at worst for continuing public health, economic, social and political deterioration whether under conditions of stagflation or deep recession. This can only accelerate their continuing decline in the world economy vis-à-vis China, though perhaps not against the most of the rest of the Third World given the human and economic cost of the pandemic there. Given that, as we see in the next chapter, the main political engagement presently visible on the pandemic political battlefields of these countries is that between the two types of capital, and given that we cannot expect them to provide any viable solutions, only the wide mobilisation of the left capable of understanding imperialism and the urgency of rebuilding productive economies without the privileges it has hitherto conferred to their countries can provide a historically progressive solution for the people of the core capitalist countries and contribute to moving the world in a broader socialist direction. Barring that, the current will only witness a shift in the nature of capitalism whose lineaments were already clear during the pandemic.

References

Assa, Jacob; and Kvangraven, Ingrid Harvold. 2021. 'Imputing Away the Ladder: Implications of Changes in GDP Measurement for Convergence Debates and the Political Economy of Development', *New Political Economy*, 26(6), pp. 985–1014. https://doi.org/10.1080/13563467.2020.1865899

Baker, Dean. 2021. 'Quick, How Much Is $2 Trillion', *CounterPunch*, 2 April, (Accessed 29 May 2022) https://www.counterpunch.org/2021/04/02/quick-how-much-is-2-trillion/

Barry, John M. 2004. 'The Site of Origin of the 1918 Influenza Pandemic and Its Public Health Implications', *Journal of Translational Medicine*, 2(1), p. 3. https://doi.org/10.1186/1479-5876-2-3

Belsie, Laurent. 2020. 'Most Stimulus Payments Were Saved or Applied to Debt', *National Bureau of Economic Research*, October (10), (Accessed 29 May 2022) https://www.nber.org/digest/oct20/most-stimulus-payments-were-saved-or-applied-debt

Brenner, Robert. 2020. 'Escalating Plunder', *New Left Review*, 123, pp. 5–22.

Bump, Philip. 2020. 'Trump Has Been Publicly Indicating His Openness to Herd Immunity Strategy for Months', *Washington Post*, 29 October, https://www.washingtonpost.com/politics/2020/10/29/trumps-been-publicly-indicating-his-openness-herd-immunity-strategy-months/

Costello, Anthony. 2020. 'Despite What Matt Hancock Says, the Government's Policy Is Still Herd Immunity', *The Guardian*, 3 April, (Accessed 24 May 2022) www.theguardian.com/commentisfree/2020/apr/03/matt-hancock-government-policy-herd-immunity-community-surveillance-covid-19.

The COVID Strategic Choices Group. 2020. 'Building the Canadian Shield: A New Strategy to Protect Canadians From COVID and From the Fight Against COVID', *Global 1 Health Network*, December 30, https://global1hn.ca/wp-content/uploads/2021/01/Building-the-Canadian-Shield_AndrewMorris.pdf

Cox, Jeff. 2021. 'U.S. Economy Closes Out 2020 With Lower Than Expected 4% Gain', *CNBC*, 28 January, (Accessed 29 May 2022) https://www.cnbc.com/2021/01/28/fourth-quarter-gdp-increased-4point0percent-vs-4point3percent-estimate.html

Davis, Mike. 2020. *The Monster Enters: COVID-19, Avian Flu and the Plagues of Capitalism*. New York: OR Books. https://doi.org/10.2307/j.ctv15nbzws

Du, Bin; Wang, Chunting; and Singer, Mervyn. 2021. 'Learning for the Next Pandemic: The Wuhan Experience of Managing Critically Ill People', *BMJ*, 375(e066090), https://doi.org/10.1136/bmj-2021-066090

The Economist. 2020. 'Vietnam and the Indian State of Kerala Curbed Covid-19 on the Cheap', *The Economist*, 9 May, (Accessed 24 May 2022) www.economist.com/asia/2020/05/09/vietnam-and-the-indian-state-of-kerala-curbed-covid-19-on-the-cheap.

Engels, Friedrich. 1845/1987. *The Condition of the Working Class in England*. Victor Kiernan (ed), London: Penguin.

Federal Reserve, Board of Governors. 2022. 'Federal Reserve Balance Sheet', *FRED*, updated 19 May, (Accessed 24 May 2022) https://fred.stlouisfed.org/series/WALCL

Fisher, Max; and Bubola, Emma. 2020. 'As Coronavirus Deepens Inequality, Inequality Worsens Its Spread', *New York Times*, 16 March, (Accessed 24 May 2022) https://www.nytimes.com/2020/03/15/world/europe/coronavirus-inequality.html

Fleckenstein, William; and Sheehan, Frederick. 2008. *Greenspan's Bubbles: The Age of Ignorance at the Federal Reserve*. New York: McGraw-Hill Education.

Flynn, Meagan; and Chiu, Allyson. 2020. 'Trump Says His "Authority Is Total." Constitutional Experts Have "No Idea" Where He Got That', *The Washington Post*, 14 April, (Accessed 24 May 2022) www.washingtonpost.com/nation/2020/04/14/trump-power-constitution-coronavirus/

Foroohar, Rana. 2020. 'How Coronavirus Became a Corporate Credit Run', *Financial Times*, 15 March, (Accessed 24 May 2022) www.ft.com/content/f1ea5096-6531-11ea-a6cd-df28cc3c6a68.

Gabbatt, Adam. 2020. 'Thousands of Americans Backed By Rightwing Donors Gear up for Protests', *The Guardian*, 18 April, (Accessed 24 May 2022) www.theguardian.com/us-news/2020/apr/18/coronavirus-americans-protest-stay-at-home

Gamillo, Elizabeth. 2021. 'Covid-19 Surpasses 1918 Flu to Become Deadliest Pandemic in American History', *Smithsonian Magazine*, 24 September, (Accessed 24 May 2022) www.smithsonianmag.com/smart-news/the-covid-19-pandemic-is-considered-the-deadliest-in-american-history-as-death-toll-surpasses-1918-estimates-180978748/

Global News Staff. 2021. 'Canadian Economy Posts Worst Showing on Record in 2020', *Global News*, 2 March, (Accessed 27 May 2022) https://globalnews.ca/news/7671568/canadian-economy-gdp/

Goodhart, Charles. 2022. 'The Real Cause of Inflation', *The Institute of Art and Ideas (IAI)*, 8 February, (Accessed 4 June 2022) https://iai.tv/articles/the-real-cause-of-inflation-auid-2045

Goodman, Matthew P. 2020. 'Comparing U.S., Japanese, and German Fiscal Responses to Covid-19', *Center for Strategic & International Studies*, 28 October, (Accessed 21 June 2022) www.csis.org/analysis/comparing-us-japanese-and-german-fiscal-responses-covid-19

Harding, Robin. 2021. 'Japan Powers Out of Coronavirus Dip With 3% Fourth-Quarter Growth', *Financial Times*, 14 February, https://www.ft.com/content/6263d776-d1c7-44bf-85d7-2b679c6f3aad

Holland, Ben; Curran, Enda; Chen, Vivien Lou; and *Bloomberg*. 2020. 'After $20 Trillion in Pandemic Relief Spending, There's Still No Sign of Inflation. What Happened?', *Fortune*, 25 August, (Accessed 29 May 2022) https://fortune.com/2020/08/25/trillions-coronavirus-spending-inflation/

Hotez, Peter J. 2014. '"Vaccine Diplomacy": Historical Perspectives and Future Directions', *PLoS Neglected Tropical Diseases*, 8(6), e2808, https://doi.org/10.1371/journal.pntd.0002808

Independent Scientific Advisory Group for Emergencies (SAGE). 2020a. 'COVID-19: What Are the Options for the UK? Recommendations for Government Based on an Open and Transparent Examination of the Scientific Evidence', *The Independent SAGE Report*, 12 May, (Accessed 24 May 2022) https://drive.google.com/file/d/1MD4-8z-yy-lO5ZsfmXAxTUo79iFk1zfy/view

Independent Scientific Advisory Group for Emergencies (SAGE). 2020b. 'Towards an Integrated Find, Test, Trace, Isolate, Support (FTTIS) response to the Pandemic', *The Independent SAGE Report 4*, 9 June, (Accessed 24 May 2022) www.independentsage.org/wp-content/uploads/2020/06/IndependentSAGE-report-4.pdf

Independent Scientific Advisory Group for Emergencies (SAGE). 2021. 'Strategy for COVID-19: Maximum Suppression or Mere Containment?', *The Independent SAGE Report 38*, 26 February, (Accessed 24 May 2022) www.independentsage.org/wp-content/uploads/2021/02/Commentary-on-Strategy-in-UK-Government-Spring-Roadmap-FOR-FINALISING.pdf

Institute for Policy Studies. 2022. 'Covid-19 and Inequality', *Inequality.org*, https://inequality.org/facts/inequality-and-covid-19/

International Monetary Fund. 2021. 'Fault Lines Widen in the Global Recovery', *World Economic Outlook Update*, July, (Accessed 21 June 2022) www.imf.org/en/Publications/WEO/Issues/2021/07/27/world-economic-outlook-update-july-2021

Jonas, Olga; and Seifman, Richard. 2019. 'Do We Need a Global Virome Project?', *The Lancet*, 7(10), E1314–16, (Accessed 24 May 2022) www.thelancet.com/journals/langlo/article/PIIS2214-109X(19)30335-3/fulltext

Jorge, Margarida. 2020. 'Opinion: Big Pharma Is Taking Big Money From U.S. Taxpayers to Find a Coronavirus Vaccine—and Charge Whatever They Want for It', *Market Watch*, 24 June, (Accessed 24 May 2022) www.marketwatch.com/story/big-pharma-is-taking-big-money-from-us-taxpayers-to-find-a-coronavirus-vaccine-and-charge-whatever-they-want-for-it-2020-06-24

Klass, Alan. 1975. *There's Gold in Them Thar Pills: An Enquiry Into the Medical-Industrial Complex*. London: Penguin. www.goodreads.com/book/show/939864.There_s_Gold_in_Them_Thar_Pills

Koopmans, Marion; Daszak, Peter; Dwyer, Dominic E.; Farag, Elmoubasher; Fischer, Thea K.; Hayman, David T.S.; Leendertz, Fabian; Maeda, Ken; Nguyen-Viet, Hung; and Watson, John. 2021. 'Origins of SARS-CoV-2: Window Is Closing for Key Scientific Studies', *Nature*, 25 August, (Accessed 24 May 2022) www.nature.com/articles/d41586-021-02263-6

Lachman, Desmond. 2021. 'The IMF Should Not Support the Biden Stimulus', *The Hill*, 1 March, (Accessed 29 May 2021) https://thehill.com/opinion/finance/540895-imf-should-not-support-the-biden-stimulus/?rl=1

Langlois, Shawn. 2019. 'Here's the Potential Upside When the "Everything Bubble" Finally Pops', *Market Watch*, 26 August, (Accessed 24 May 2022) www.marketwatch.com/story/heres-the-potential-upside-when-the-everything-bubble-finally-pops-2019-08-26

Law, Elizabeth; and Choon, Chang May. 2020. 'How China, South Korea and Taiwan Are Using Tech to Curb Coronavirus Outbreak', *The Straits Times*, 21 March, (Accessed 24 May 2022) www.straitstimes.com/asia/east-asia/how-china-s-korea-and-taiwan-are-using-tech-to-curb-outbreak

Levine, Yasha. 2018. *Surveillance Valley: The Military History of the Internet*. New York: Public Affairs.

Leys, Colin. 2001. *Market-Driven Politics: Neoliberal Democracy and the Public Interest*. London: Verso.

Meyerowitz-Katz, Gideon. 2020. 'Here's Why Herd Immunity Won't Save Us from the COVID-19 Pandemic', *Science Alert*, 30 March, (Accessed 4 June 2022) www.sciencealert.com/why-herd-immunity-will-not-save-us-from-the-covid-19-pandemic

Naughton, John. 2020. 'The Privacy Paradox: Why Do People Keep Using Tech Firms That Abuse Their Data?', *The Guardian*, 5 May, (Accessed 23 May 2022) www.theguardian.com/commentisfree/2019/may/05/privacy-paradox-why-do-people-keep-using-tech-firms-data-facebook-scandal

O'Connor, Sarah. 2022. 'Splintered Labour Market Makes Wage-Price Spiral Unlikely'. *Financial Times*, 30 May, https://www.ft.com/content/14f797c3-910d-4af6-a5e3-49706067d41d

Oxfam International. 2022. 'Behind the Numbers: A Dataset Exploring Key Financing and Fiscal Policies in the IMF's COVID-19 Loans', updated 15 March, (Accessed 24 May 2022) www.oxfam.org/en/international-financial-institutions/imf-covid-19-financing-and-fiscal-tracker

Parker, George; and Burn-Murdoch, John. 2020. 'Cummings Role under Scrutiny over Delay to UK Suppression Policy', *Financial Times*, 22 March, (Accessed 23 May 2022) www.ft.com/content/623a86ec-6c4c-11ea-9bca-bf503995cd6f

Partington, Richard. 2021. 'UK Economy Hit by Record Slump in 2020 but Double-Dip Recession Avoided', *The Guardian*, 12 February, (Accessed 29 May 2022) https://www.theguardian.com/business/2021/feb/12/uk-avoided-double-dip-recession-despite-covid-slump-in-2020-ons-gdp

Patnaik, Prabhat. 2022. 'The Inhumanity of Capitalism', *International Development Economics Associates (Network IDEAs)*, 16 May, (Accessed 24 May 2022) www.networkideas.org/news-analysis/2022/05/the-inhumanity-of-capitalism/

Ping, Yu. 2022. 'In a Lockdown, Hard Lessons for Shanghai's Government Reformers', *Sixth Tone*, 23 May, (Accessed 21 June 2022) www.sixthtone.com/news/1010393/In%20a%20Lockdown,%20Hard%20Lessons%20for%20Shanghai's%20Government%20Reformers/

Pollock, Allyson M. 2004. 'NHS plc: The Privatisation of Our Health Care', *BMJ*, *329*, p. 862. www.researchgate.net/profile/Gary-Schwitzer/publication/24846889_Ten_troublesome_trends_in_TV_health_news/links/004635230b67e2c960000000/Ten-troublesome-trends-in-TV-health-news.pdf

Renshaw, Jarrett; Shalal, Andrea; and Martina, Michael. 2021. 'Biden Says China Won't Surpass U.S. as Global Leader on His Watch', *Reuters*, 25 March, (Accessed 29 May 2022) https://www.reuters.com/article/us-usa-biden-china-idUSKBN2BH2ZE

Reuters Staff. 2020. 'Partly False Claim: Trump Fired Entire Pandemic Response Team in 2018', *Reuters*, 25 March, (Accessed 24 May 2022) www.reuters.com/article/uk-factcheck-trump-fired-pandemic-team-idUSKBN21C32M

Roberts, Michael. 2021. 'The Sugar Rush Economy', *Michael Roberts Blog*, 21 March, (Accessed 29 May 2022) https://thenextrecession.wordpress.com/2021/03/21/the-sugar-rush-economy/

Roubini, Nouriel. 2019. 'The Anatomy of the Coming Recession', *Project Syndicate*, 22 August, (Accessed 24 May 2022) www.project-syndicate.org/commentary/global-recession-us-china-trade-war-by-nouriel-roubini-2019-08?barrier=accesspaylog

RT Documentary Channel. 2022. 'The Forgotten Epidemic: How the USSR Defeated Smallpox', 9 February, (Accessed 24 May 2022) https://rtd.rt.com/stories/how-ussr-defeated-smallpox/

Seiden, Daniel. 2020. 'Billions in Covid-19 Federal Contract Awards Not Facing Protests', *Bloomberg Law*, 22 June, (Accessed 24 May 2022) https://news.bloomberglaw.com/federal-contracting/billions-in-covid-19-federal-contract-awards-not-facing-protests

Spinney, Laura. 2020. 'The Coronavirus Slayer! How Kerala's Rock Star Health Minister Helped Save It From Covid-19', *The Guardian*, 14 May, (Accessed 23 May 2022) www.theguardian.com/world/2020/may/14/the-coronavirus-slayer-how-keralas-rock-star-health-minister-helped-save-it-from-covid-19

Stern, Jacob; and Wu, Katherine J. 2022. 'Endemicity Is Meaningless', *The Atlantic*, 1 February, (Accessed 24 May 2022) www.theatlantic.com/health/archive/2022/02/endemicity-means-nothing/621423/

Tang, Jin-Ling; and Abbasi, Kamran. 2021. 'What Can the World Learn From China's Response to Covid-19?', *BMJ*, 375(2806), (Accessed 22 May 2022) https://doi.org/10.1136/bmj.n2806

Tang, Jin-Ling; and Li, Li-Ming. 2021. 'Importance of Public Health Tools in Emerging Infectious Diseases', *BMJ*, 375(2374), (Accessed 24 May 2022) https://doi.org/10.1136/bmj.n2374

Uhlig, Robert. 2002. '10 Million Animals Were Slaughtered in Foot and Mouth Cull', *The Telegraph*, 23 January, (Accessed 24 May 2022) www.telegraph.co.uk/news/uknews/1382356/10-million-animals-were-slaughtered-in-foot-and-mouth-cull.html

Wei, Liu; and Qingqing, Cao. 2021. 'Coronavirus Found in Multiple Countries Months Earlier Than in Wuhan: Studies', *CGTN*, 22 January, (Accessed 24 May 2022) https://news.cgtn.com/news/2021-01-22/Coronavirus-found-in-multiple-countries-months-earlier-than-in-Wuhan-XfTTs6HacE/index.html

Whoriskey, Peter; MacMillan, Douglas; and O'Connell, Jonathan. 2020. '"Doomed to Fail": Why a $4 Trillion Bailout Couldn't Revive the American Economy', *The Washington Post*, 5 October, (Accessed 24 May 2022) www.washingtonpost.com/graphics/2020/business/coronavirus-bailout-spending/

Wigglesworth, Robin. 2020. 'The Week the World Changed: How a Markets Wobble Turned to Mayhem', *Financial Times*, 13 May, (Accessed 24 May 2022) www.ft.com/content/86f7f914-6536-11ea-b3f3-fe4680ea68b5

World Health Organization. 2020. *Report of the WHO-China Joint Mission on Coronavirus Disease 2019 (COVID 19)*. 16 24 February, viewed 1 March 2021, www.who.int/docs/default-source/coronaviruse/who-china-joint-mission-on-covid-19-final-report.pdf

Yong, Ed. 2020. 'The U.K.'s Coronavirus "Herd Immunity" Debacle', *The Atlantic*, 16 March, (Accessed 24 May 2022) www.theatlantic.com/health/archive/2020/03/coronavirus-pandemic-herd-immunity-uk-boris-johnson/608065/

YWCA-GATE. 2020. *A Feminist Recovery Plan for Canada*, Toronto. www.feministrecovery.ca

6

KNOW YOUR ENEMY

Between pseudo-civic neoliberalism and (neo)fascism?

As the pandemic exposed the inequality and debility of neoliberal financialised capitalisms, talk of 'building back better', of not returning to the discredited 'old normal', was encouraged by monetary and fiscal policy responses that appeared to break major neoliberal taboos and to do so most fulsomely in the leading neoliberal financialised capitalisms, the United States and the United Kingdom. Had neoliberalism ended? Was it giving way to an altogether more progressive form of capitalism?

Unfortunately, as we have seen, the fiscal and monetary responses were entirely within the neoliberal 'wheelhouse' (the baseball term President Biden used to reassure wealthy donors that his proposals were well within the neo-liberal repertoire) (Derysh 2019) and it could not be otherwise. After all, the purpose of neoliberalism was not to realise any free market utopia. Indeed, for reasons we have seen in Chapter 4, that would have bene impossible anyway. The free market mantra was just that: the incantation capital's political representatives mouthed in the major capitalist countries as they tilted the balance of power back in capital's favour and against working people and the rest of the world. That tilt is the essence of neoliberalism. Giving it up would reawaken the alternative—further socialistic reforms, taking capitalist societies even further towards socialism than they had gone during the post-war Long Boom or Golden Age. So long as the tilt is preserved, the mantra, the costume, the props can change. And, indeed, they have. To change metaphors, neoliberalism has had to resort to shifting shape many times in response to its own failures as much as to changing circumstances: from its 'classic' form under Reagan and Thatcher through its 'globalisation form under Third Way politicians such as Clinton or Blair to its 'empire' form under George Bush Jr. and finally its most recent 'austerity' form.

The crisis triggered by the pandemic was certainly leading to another shape shift and its general direction was clear enough by mid-2020 for me to suggest

DOI: 10.4324/9781003200000-6

that it would take a pseudo-philanthropic form (Desai 2020) or what I would now call a pseudo-civic form, one in which the state becomes even more directly involved in resolving metropolitan capital's profitability and demand problems by becoming a more important and extravagant customer than ever. It has long been so for some sectors, such as defence production. Now this relation would be extended to other sectors as the state would pay capital out of tax revenues to produce allegedly essential public goods it would use, or distribute, or feign to distribute, to citizens cheap or free.

While that remains the chief possibility, there have been important developments since that suggest another. The Trump administration gave way, not without a literal fight featuring far-right groups, to the Biden administration. It failed in its public health responses, leaving the pandemic to rage, and its economic response proved too feeble to tackle the accumulated weaknesses of the US economy, leaving it facing either continued stagflation or monetary policy induced recession or both. In this context, the Biden administration changed its agenda, focusing on the threat of China, withdrawing from Afghanistan to do so and seeking to shore up US leadership of 'democratic countries'. None of these seemed to go well until the proxy war against Russia appeared to succeed, initially at least. Soon, however, not only did Russia seem to gain and cracks in allied unity appear, but inflation brought Biden's approval ratings to new lows and the Democrats faced rout in the mid-term election even as Trump kept his hold on the Republicans. These developments, along with the whitewashing of the neo-Nazis integrated into the structures of Ukrainian state and military, bring some darker authoritarian possibilities into play.

In this chapter, we consider how neoliberalism is being re-forged in the crucible of pandemic and war and whether it will take a pseudo-civic form or acquire authoritarian hues in the leading neoliberal financialised capitalisms. To what extent and in what manner might other major capitalist countries follow? What do these options portend for the US attempt to shore up its fast-slipping leadership? In what follows, we begin with a brief review of claims that neoliberalism has ended and highlight the extent to which responses to the pandemic remained recognisably within neoliberal parameters before going on to consider the various avatars of neoliberalism hitherto. We then show how, rather than competitive markets, the preservation of corporate power constitutes the essence of neoliberalism before concluding by considering how pseudo-civic neoliberalism or a more authoritarian version would endeavour to preserve that essence.

The end of neoliberalism?

Though some initial strains were already being heard earlier, debates about the pandemic forcing a turn away from neoliberalism centred on Biden's presidential campaign, his Build Back Better programme and the passage of the American Rescue Plan. Historian Adam Tooze proclaimed that the pandemic had been the 'historic force that finally burst the dykes of the neoliberal order' (Tooze 2021) and opined that '[a]s a sort of ebullient, aggressive ideology, as a doctrine that felt cocky and confident and all-conquering, neoliberalism is clearly dead. . . . There's just not any juice in there, it's a bad brand at this point' (Eaton 2021). Harvard economist Dani Rodrik also underlined the 'a sharp departure from the conventional wisdom in Washington', whether in the White House, Capitol Hill or at the Federal Reserve (Rodrik 2021). 'The economic-policy conversation in the United States', he repeated elsewhere, 'has been thoroughly transformed within the space of just a few years. Neoliberalism, the Washington Consensus, market fundamentalism—call it whatever you want—has been replaced with something very different'. For its part, the *Financial Times* hailed Biden's stimulus bill as 'historic'. While cautious that '[t]alk of the end of neoliberalism, of a new compact between workers and capital, might age badly', it nevertheless could not resist a comparison with the paradigm shift Roosevelt's New Deal represented: 'it is improbable that Americans can lean on government as much as they have over the past year, and emerge unchanged'. As with the New Deal, '[h]aving seen active government at work, voters remained open to it for decades afterwards' (Editorial Board of the *Financial Times* 2021).

However, some, with longer memories could be excused a *déjà vu* feeling. After the 2008 financial crisis, as leading neoliberal states embarked on unconventional monetary policy and talked of coordinated fiscal stimulus, Martin Wolf, leading commentator of the *Financial Times*, declared that 'The State is back' and that 'the age of a hegemonic model of the market economy is past'. Any number of prominent academics were pronouncing neoliberalism dead and hailing a 'post-neoliberal' age though for some (for instance, Altvater 2009; Demirovic 2009) it would remain capitalist while for others, like Kotz, it contained the possibility of a major restructuring entailing *either* a 'corporatist' authoritarian capitalism *or* some sort or reformed socialistic capitalism or even socialism (Kotz 2009). There was even a neo-Proudhonist version, one tailored to the needs and aspirations not of the traditional petty bourgeoisie but of the new petty bourgeoisie of the professional managerial class: an unspecified

> new democratic capitalist system [which] will not be financialised, but the tendencies present in the 30 glorious years toward global and knowledge-based capitalism, where professionals will have more say than rentier capitalists, as well as the tendency to improve democracy by making it more social and participative, will be resumed.
>
> *(Bresser-Pereira 2010)*

However, neoliberalism remained alive (Crouch 2011), if not well. After the crisis, fiscal stimuli turned out to be puny in nearly all G20 countries excepting China, while the lax monetary policy of the Federal Reserve and the European Central Bank, complete with their new quantitative easing, zero interest rate policy and forward guidance bells and whistles, refilled the speculative party punch bowls for financial capital. Monetary authorities also proved unable to impose more than the most minimal of reforms, such as the Dodd–Frank legislation, necessary to re-stabilise the speculative and predatory financial system. So began the 'austerity' phase of neoliberalism, complete with new financialisations. Meanwhile, as private losses were socialised, working people in the major capitalist countries were asked to suffer even lower growth and employment levels, steeply rising inequality and poverty, and creaking social services. While the low-interest regime appeared to provide a bonanza of credit to developing countries, the risk of adverse currency movements remained, as did that of higher interest rate and debt crises, though they appeared remote to most.

So, if the 'state came back', it was only to accomplish all this and to increase its punitive capacities as the 2010s became a decade of rising popular protest (Harbage and Bloch 2019; Younge 2019). It was also the decade in which, thanks to the weakness of the left, the discontents of neoliberalism were mobilised by a harder anti-establishment right pinning the blame for the problems of the working class under austerity on immigrants allegedly coddled by the socially liberal neoliberal establishment. Though the neoliberal establishment prefers to call this right 'populist' so as to be able to tar both its right-wing and all-too-few left-wing opponents with the same brush as right and left populists, the connection of the former with fascistic elements is unmistakable, even if they remain unexplored by mainstream scholarship invested in the 'populism' paradigm (Rodrik 2018; Eatwell and Goodwin 2018).

Plus ça change, plus c'est la même chose

After 2020, it was *déjà vu* all over again. Monetary responses rescued asset markets and, within months, they were booming again, forming a stark contrast with the malaise and uncertainty afflicting the productive economy in which bankruptcies (Tett 2020) multiplied despite the government relief programmes and doubts about the longevity of the 'recovery' (Noonan 2020) turned out to be amply justified. The contrast was great enough to produce absurdities such as the zombie rally, the rally in equities of firms in or close to bankruptcy, by early June 2002: 'Resurrected from . . . bankruptcy filings, these shuffling, groaning and rotting equities have ripped over the past week despite a long line of garlic-lathered creditors waiting to drive a stake through their hearts.' For instance, Hertz, a car rental company that filed for bankruptcy in late May, had returned 521% in early June (Powell 2020). Clearly, monetary policy was performing some speculative miracles, just not that of fixing the productive economy.

Meanwhile fiscal effort necessary to rectify the emaciation of the underlying economy and overburdened medical systems was underwhelming. If, as the pandemic delivered shocks to both supply and demand, the United States and the United Kingdom took the lead in apparently taboo-breaking fiscal support packages, it was because their productive economies were correspondingly more fragile. Over the neoliberal decades, they had hot-housed precisely the sorts of 'non-essential' low-wage, low-skill service sector economic activities—cheap tourism, hospitality, entertainment and personal care, all reliant on cheap labour—that proved most vulnerable to the repeated lockdowns that became necessary in these same economies because their health care systems were also weaker.

Large though they may have been, however, these fiscal efforts conformed to the neoliberal playbook. Predictably, most of the new spending went to bail out businesses directly (Politi and Fedor 2020), from airlines to defence industries. They were overwhelmingly favoured over working people and smaller businesses. The priority these governments placed on saving a tiny elite's private wealth over lives was also evident in how the proportionately modest if absolutely large sums allocated to the public health response were spent. In the United States and the United Kingdom, corporations that had long benefitted from 'privatization by stealth' were at the front of the queue for lucrative contracts handed out with little accountability. For instance, in the United Kingdom, the hurriedly created National Institute for Health Protection under Johnson crony Baroness Diana 'Dido' Harding gave Serco, a company that had already 'mismanaged data at a GP surgery, . . . failed to train staff properly for a breast cancer hotline service [and] . . . claimed money from the government for tracking prisoners who were later found to be dead' a contract for contact tracing (Hobbs 2020). With such contracts, there was little wonder that the £37 billion spent on it, allegedly to create a 'world-beating programme' of testing and tracing, failed to make 'a measurable difference to the progress of the pandemic' in the words of the public accounts committee (Toynbee 2021). Meanwhile, across the Atlantic, US Big Pharma saw a 'once-in-a-lifetime' business opportunity. Long the beneficiary of huge subsidies that they translated into high prices protected by monopolistic intellectual property rights and into big bonusses and dividends, the medical–industrial complex employed lobbyists to thwart efforts to ensure price regulation and limits on intellectual property protection in the legislation to fund the search for treatments, cures and vaccines (Lerner 2020).

This trend in government pandemic spending supporting big financial and non-financial corporations at the expense of everyone else was set early on. Already by April 2020, one British writer noted that while 'virtually no sacrifices have been demanded of banks, landlords or profitable corporations, such as utility companies' and while '[l]andlords have access to mortgage holidays but are not required to pass these on to their tenants' and permitted to 'recoup any missed rent when the crisis is over', little was done to compensate workers for lost income and guaranteed loans for small businesses required people to take on private debt that they will have to pay back when the crisis is over' (Berry 2020). Moreover, much of this was done without adequate oversight while parliamentary scrutiny was disabled by social distancing (Herszenhorn 2020).

Most of the apparently generous measures announced were temporary and economic pain was bound to follow their withdrawal, particularly as it came on top of an unresolved public health crisis and an economy weakened by the damage of repeated lockdowns and restrictions. Unemployment had already skyrocketed (Kretchmer 2020) in nearly all major capitalist countries and threatened to reach Great Depression era levels in the United Kingdom, despite the temporary job retention measures. As the expiration dates of these temporary measures neared, firms laid off more workers and landlords evicted more tenants, given that no real recovery was in sight. Housing advocates predicted a 'tsunami of evictions' in the United States (Legal Services Corporation 2020), United Kingdom (Lovett 2020), Canada (Pablo 2020) and elsewhere after moratoria on debt repayments and evictions ended, predicting social unrest for which the protests of the pandemic years would constitute mere trailers.

Workers and small businesses also faced the usual means-testing, form-filling and complex eligibility criteria that meant that much of the meagre support that was extended to them often did not reach them. In any case, most income support programmes were channelled through employers, giving them the discretion over which jobs to retain. With already heavily indebted governments taking on more debt, the danger remained that, after the crises was, or rather could be declared, over, the burden would be socialised as further austerity in uncertainly recovering economies with low revenues and belligerent bond markets translating into further cuts in social spending and regressive taxation (Plender 2020).

Finally, it is important to remember that neoliberalism has not just been miserly towards ordinary, working and poor people. It has also been punitive, and this aspect was also intensified during the pandemic. Lockdowns effectively incarcerated people in their own homes, often trapping vulnerable women, children and men in situations of domestic abuse. They turned carceral institutions, run for profit in the United States, into nests of infections leading to movements for the release of prisoners otherwise facing death without sentence. Policing of the lockdowns has pushed the boundaries of police power outwards. Police control of the poor and minorities, racism and anti-immigration rhetoric and policy are already in evidence in the West and even more elsewhere, particularly in the Third World (Mander and Verma 2020). As one observer put it, amid material insecurity and uncertainty, police scaled up arrest and imprisonment for minor infractions,

> and curfew violations resulting from homelessness . . . adding corona-related charges to non-corona-related charges. Thus, the criminalization of life and poverty is the only state-sponsored response to a crisis for which there exist no other possible state-sponsored responses.
>
> *(Buchholz 2020)*

While ordinary working people, often living in cramped or overcrowded conditions had to endure repeated lockdowns, losses of loved ones, homes, incomes and society, not only did the wealthy continue a normal if quieter existence in their grand homes in leafy surroundings, many, like Prime Minister Boris Johnson, were violating the rules, largely with impunity (McEvoy 2020).

Despite pandemic lockdowns and restrictions, protests of every variety raged around the world—Black Lives Matter were followed by Indian farmers protests, protests against the police in Nigeria, against racial injustice all over the world and new waves of workers' protests and unionisation drives. Given the ugliness of financialised neoliberal capitalism's underbelly the pandemic revealed, this was hardly coincidence. However, not only did few show signs of coalescing in coherent progressive movements, by early 2022, working people were relegated to taking rear-guard actions against inflation in the forms of unionisation and strikes just to hold up their rapidly declining real incomes while the war over Ukraine found much of the left, if not siding outright with the US-led war, at least disoriented: unable to understand imperialism and anti-imperialism, it was unable to a coherent response in the neoliberal financialised countries.

So, in the pandemic, neoliberalism remains true to form, focusing on keeping the balance of power tilted in favour of capital and an unproductive, predatory and speculative financial capitalist class. Any left that seeks to give effective battle, organise effective and transformative opposition to it, must know itself, its resources and the limitations it must overcome and this we take up in the conclusion. It must also, however, know the resources, strategies and aims of the right and the capitalist classes. 'Know your enemy', said Sun Tzu in *The Art of War*. That, today, also involves knowing the enemy's contradictions. Great as the resources of capitalist and right forces are, and long as their experience in permanent counter-revolution (van der Pijl 2020) is, what they want and need—to launch a new phase of neoliberalism even if of limited staying power—is almost certainly unobtainable. Indeed, the forms neoliberalism has taken so far have proved short-lived and unstable.

Neoliberalism and its avatars

Those who consider neoliberalism to be about 'free markets and free trade' enforced by a minimal 'nightwatchman' state will find that its long record is littered with broken taboos. Even the most zealous neoliberal governments, such as Mrs Thatcher's, remined mindful of competing political and electoral considerations (Marsh and Rhodes 1992; Desai 1994, 59–61). The political limits imposed by the popularity of welfare states and the need to engineer the minimal electoral coalitions necessary to win elections even in first-past-the-post electoral systems that inflated pluralities of the popular vote into big parliamentary majorities were especially important and the resulting compromises alienated the more purist free marketeers. Moreover, even without these considerations coming into play, neoliberalism would have been unable to transform monopoly capitalism back into competitive capitalism.

In reality, from the start, viewed objectively, neoliberalism has been about promoting the interests of large monopoly firms, financial and financialisednon-financial. Within these parameters, neoliberalism has shifted shape about once a decade. These shifts were necessary because of the wide gap between the free market rhetoric and corporate and financialised and monopoly reality of neoliberalism and because of its faulty diagnosis of the growth slowdown of the 1970s. They ensured that neoliberal policies would be unable to do anything other than turn the slump of the 1970s into the Long Downturn, complete with the vast expansion of financial activity and all sorts of non- and even anti-free market strategies, such as 'military' and 'credit' Keynesianism that were deployed generate what little growth enervated capitalist economies were now capable of. One might add that the weakness of the left ensured that these shifts could be executed more easily.

Neoliberal shape shifting was led by the United States and the United Kingdom, its leaders, with the rest of the capitalist world following suit to a greater or lesser degree. It took its first, arguably classical form in the 1980s, with the Thatcher–Reagan mantra of the desirability of free markets. These regimes likely did imagine that they could restore capitalism's productive dynamism by increasing capital's freedoms and assaulting labour. However, all such measures did was to accelerate both the deindustrialisation of the US and UK economies and their financialisation. It was no wonder, therefore, that that decade was one in which this deindustrialisation contrasted with the continuing industrial success of Germany and, above all, Japan. The decade of 'Japan as No. 1' even led directly to Ross Perot's astonishing performance as a third candidate the 1992 US presidential election on a platform advocating protection and industrial policy in the United States to beat the Japanese challenge. By the end of the 1980s, moreover, given the disaster of World Bank- and IMF-sponsored neoliberal structural adjustment in the Third World, not to mention the 'economic miracle' in East Asia that largely escaped such ministrations, the even the World Bank had to concede that a more active government role in the economy was necessary (The World Bank 1993; Wade 1996).

In the following decade, neoliberalism morphed into 'globalisation'. Like all buzzwords, its meanings were at least as many as there were commentators on it. Setting aside discussions that took the opportunity to promote the idea of a naturally seamless capitalist world economy dating back variously to the earliest days of humanity, the early modern 'voyages of discovery', the beginnings of colonialism, the industrial revolution, the post-war era or to the start of the neoliberal era, some historically relevant meanings stood out. One was the feeling that, with the demise of the Soviet Union and East European Communism, capitalism, with or without US 'hegemony' or 'leadership', had become 'global'. Such discourses tended to assume China was well on its way to becoming a suoridnated capitalist economy. Another was that, with the Cold War having ended, and geopolitics having been replaced by what a conservative US pundit called 'geo-economics' (Luttwak 1990), states had to intervene in economies to ensure the 'competitiveness' of their economies, though this was interpreted by social democratic 'Third Way' politicians who had made terms with neoliberalism to mean their ability to attract fickle and footloose multinational capital by lowering corporate taxes, labour and environmental regulation, the strength of organised labour and reforming welfare states to turn them into workfare states (Huws 2020).

Indeed, 'globalisation' can be seen as the way the Clintons and the Blairs of this world set about making social democracy neoliberal (Hay 2020). Since their social base did not permit them to extol the virtues of markets as fulsomely, Third Way politicians like Clinton and Blair found globalisation ideologically handy. They could say to their predominantly working-class constituencies that, while they would dearly love to increase wages, improve working conditions or increase corporate taxation and regulation, their hands were tied. The unstoppable juggernaut of globalisation required welfare and social spending cuts and the transformation of the labour market with weakened unions and workfare. It also required accepting a state role in the economy but only to promote the interests of large corporations in the name of competitiveness (Watson and Hay 2003). This involved pursuing 'free trade', with China entering the World Trade Organization (WTO) and the proliferation of 'free trade' deals that were more 'free investment' deals (Ghosh 2016), aggressively deregulating at home and leaving the economy in charge of central banks representing the interests of big financial houses and promoting free capital flows internationally.

Finally, there was the globalisation rhetoric of the Clinton administration, which aimed at opening up the rest of the world economy to US trade and financial flows with promises of market access and productive investment. Indeed, it was particularly focused on getting developing countries, particularly in East Asia, to open their capital markets. When they did, however, what flowed in was not productive investment but, as prescient financial market observers had warned (Rohatyn 1994), hot money. Chiefly US investors and institutions stampeded into these asset markets making short-term investments without much knowledge of local conditions, only seeking quick easy returns. When this herd stampeded out, just as ignorantly and irrationally as it had stampeded in, it caused the then mammoth East Asian Financial Crisis of 1997–98. As it erupted, economies that, only days before the crisis, were being lauded for their excellent fundamentals, were labelled crony capitalisms (Bagchi 1998). Thereafter, open capital accounts served to expand sources of funds flowing into the now well-advanced US dollar creditocracy (Desai 2013), feeding the massive dot-com bubble whose wealth effects and misdirected investment boom were mistaken for a veritable 'new economy' of technological innovation in the United States, thanks in great part to Greenspan's rhetoric (Fleckenstein 2008).

The globalisation decade ended with the bubble bursting. Though many took the 9/11 attacks to mark the end of the age of globalisation, its characteristic economic process had ended the year before when the dot-com bubble burst and President George Bush Jr., with his distinct aversion to 'globalisation' as too multilateral and preference for the unilateralism of 'empire', was elected president (Desai 2013). This third shape of neoliberalism centred on overt militarism, which, by accepting the outgoing Bush Sr. administration's aggressive post-Cold War 1992 Defence Policy Guidance, the Clinton administration had already accepted and started implementing as part of its wider acceptance of the new

Reagan settlement, thus regaining for the Democratic Party its former position as party of liberal internationalism that it lost in the 1970s under Carter. The unilateralism and militarism of the Bush administration in the 2000s were combined with fiscal largesse towards the rich, breaking the taboo against budget deficits that the Clinton administration had gone to considerable lengths to observe. Finally, as the Bush administration posted the greatest of US budget deficits and left the Federal Reserve to get on with running the economy, it engineered a historic expansion of financial activity with its new low interest rate policy to bail the financial sector out from the bursting of the dot-com bubble and to keep inflating the mortgage and housing bubbles that had started in the late 1990s and now proved the only things powering the United States' meagre growth. This time, the Federal Reserve produced that mother of all financial bubbles (Fleckenstein 2008), the mortgage credit bubble which burst in 2008.

The 2008 crisis inaugurated the fourth phase of neoliberalism, that of 'austerity', with the socialisation of private debt that fiscal and monetary bailouts after 2008 entailed. The world focused on official government bailouts, such as the $700 billion Troubled Asset Relief Programme (TARP), complete with the drama of Treasury Secretary Hank Paulson going down on bended knee before Nancy Pelosi to beg her to get it through a Congress dominated by the Democrats. However, this was peanuts in comparison with the real bailout, organised by the Federal Reserve and involving breaking another taboo, that against 'printing money'. It was estimated to be much higher. One early estimate put it at $7.7 trillion in 'undisclosed loans . . . to struggling financial institutions' (*The Week Staff* 2015) to save institutions that had bankrupted themselves by their own risky behaviour while a later one, carefully accounting for great number and variety of Federal Reserve programmes aimed at saving US institutions at home and abroad, put it at $29 trillion (Felkerson 2011). Austerity was the result as much of the overt socialisation of private debt as it was due to the reduced capacity of markets to finance deficits as indicated in the US case by the extent of Federal Reserve support for the government bond market.

Though austerity was stronger in Europe, thanks to its greater monetary orthodoxy, the Western world in general underwent even slower growth, a more or less complete collapse of productive investment and even greater maldistribution of income as activity was concentrated in finance as opposed to production. The enervated economy was already on its way to a crash when the pandemic hit.

If neoliberalism's career has entailed (at least) these changes, there is absolutely no reason why the recent government responses to the pandemic should not mark just another phase in the history of neoliberalism, one that preserves its essential core, the power of ever-larger private corporations.

Corporate power or competitive markets

At their core, ideologies justifying capitalism must be about preserving the power of private property. The rest is incidental. Capitalist ideologies took a 'free markets and free trade' or 'laissez faire' form in mid-nineteenth-century Britain when the first industrial revolution with its small firms and competitive markets reigned. As we have seen, by the late nineteenth century, capitalism entered a new phase. In the second industrial revolution, led by Germany, the United States, Japan, production units and technology became more massive. Capital requirements were many times greater. Mergers and cartelisation led to monopoly and oligopoly in most sectors. Banks rose to a new prominence in facilitating them in the more advanced capitalisms of Britain's industrial challengers. As expanding working classes organised to demand, and receive, welfarist reforms, as governments responded to populist protests by regulating monopolies and as nationally organised blocs of capital competed aggressively for new markets and economic territory through imperialism, capitalism became encased within 'crustacean nations'.

Some of the most acute analyses of this new capitalism emerged from Marxists who developed Marx's anticipations of the concentration and centralisation of capital and how, as enterprises got larger and larger, the top-down centrally planned authoritarian space of the capitalist firm expanded at the expense of the anarchy of the market. The more social production was planned, the more easily it could be converted into the rational and democratic planning of a socialist economy, inter alia, by making it easy to gain popular and democratic control of the 'commanding heights' of the economy.

These developments formed the context in which neoclassical economics emerged to counter an increasingly organised working class and its increasingly Marxist inspiration. Realising just how close this monopoly-finance-nationalised capital stood to socialism, intellectuals financed by big capital, particularly the Austrian pioneers of neoliberalism, Ludwig von Mises and Friedrich Hayek (Slobodian 2021), organised rear-guard intellectual action in the early twentieth century, combining denial and sophistry.

Against mounting evidence, their theoretical understanding of capitalism assumed that capitalism remained competitive. By the mid-twentieth century, when monopoly was robustly in evidence all around, such pretence became near impossible, Hayek, for instance, relying on shreds of evidence of persisting competition produced by the Temporary National Economic Committee of the US Congress, claimed that competition made markets produce the right price signals in a complex economy. Hanging tight to these shreds, neoliberals elaborately theorised how competitive capitalism promoted freedom and consumer choice and how only competitive markets could process information that millions of competing sellers and buyers had, so supply and demand could produce equilibrium prices and the best possible coordination of their capacities and needs. These arguments rested on theories of price formation that were erroneous even for competitive markets, let alone the new monopolistic or oligopolistic ones (Jo 2016). Despite that, they retain their allure, even for many on the left (Wainwright 1994) who insist that there is much the left must learn from neoliberal market wisdom (Gamble 1996). However, even the most resolute insistence on the persistence of competitive markets could not entirely ignore monopoly and even Hayek had to concede that, in the short run at least, optimal use of technology may require the suppression of competition (Hayek 1944, 32–9).

Against the increasingly insistent demands (Clarke 1991) of highly organised working classes for social reform, neoliberals cautioned against state intervention. If met, these demands would interfere with capitalist accumulation, for instance, by raising wages or regulating capital. Since states were deepening their involvement in the economy—and doing it not only at the behest of capital but, sometimes at least, at that of labour—neoliberals also drew clear lines between what states should and should not do. They must maintain the sphere of private action and accumulation for private capital, at best breaking up monopolies that were unjustified, while conceding as little as possible to the demands of the working class. Keeping up a high-decibel denunciation of socialism as an ill-conceived denial of freedom, Hayek and his ilk reserved a special venom for those who sought to extend the idea of freedom from 'negative' liberal legal and political 'freedoms from' to positive economic 'freedoms to'. Pursuing that would lead, more or less, directly to 'serfdom'.

Finally, the increasing prominence of planning, by states and large corporations, led neoliberals to reject nineteenth-century laissez faire or free markets for 'planning for competition', essentially their theorisation of US anti-trust law, which obliged governments to break up monopolies to ensure competition (Hayek 1944, 13–14). Indeed, as recently elaborated by Slobodian, the neoliberal vision was at some variance from its 'free market' and 'small state' image in at least three ways. First, they argued that 'markets are not natural but are products of the political construction of institutions to encase them'. This was one of the neoliberal state's key tasks. Second, in the age of 'crustacean nations' that was also one of colonialism, they were pitted against both national sovereignty and empowered working classes. Even more than the refusal of concessions to domestic working classes, the openness and subjection of the colonies to metropolitan capital was their lodestar: 'a free, i.e. non-state sphere of economy permeating everything: a global economy' achieved through the abolition of sovereignty and the insulation of government from democratic demands. Finally, it involved establishing this order globally (Slobodian 2018, 7, 10–13, 15–17). It was to be created by self-abnegating states and extended the world over by their multiplication.

Neoliberalism did not win the day immediately. The profound Thirty Years' Crisis of capitalism and imperialism had, as we have seen, threatened to tip the world into socialism, as many contemporary observers hoped as well as feared at the time and, not only did the Russian and Chinse revolutions occur and the vast mass of decolonised humanity embark on more or less socialist projects of autonomous development, the major capitalist countries were also forced to borrow many tools from the socialist toolkit to stabilise capitalism. Indeed, they did much more, enabling capitalism's post-war Long Boom. In terms of economic theory, over the middle third of the twentieth century, Keynesianism, albeit of a deradicalised variety, consigned neoliberalism to a marginal position. It is only when the Long Boom ended in crisis that neoliberalism's moment finally arrived. It did so when capital was, if anything, even more uncompetitive, concentrated, centralised and cartelised. Until now, neoliberalism had remained confined to textbook utopias, particularly to microeconomics textbooks so beloved of the network of neoliberal think tanks that had kept the faith alive through the decades of Keynesian domination (Desai 1994, 46–9).

Finally called on to inform and justify policy, neoliberalism was forced to confront monopoly realities such as imperfect information, barriers to entry and externalities. This forced considerable modification, bringing neoliberalism down from the heaven of competitive markets to the earth of monopoly capitalism, modifying its policies. One major contributor to this was the Chicago school of neoliberal economists and legal theorists. Along with 'corporate lawyers defending anti-trust suits for large corporations', they modified anti-trust law to develop

> a new set of principles that abandoned earlier insistence on the need for actual competition and large number of competitors if the liberal capitalist model was to work. A new theory of the economy emerged, which tended to favour large, market-dominant firms.
>
> *(Crouch 2011, 54)*

So, while anti-trust remained a centre piece, neoliberals sought to modify their stance in three ways but succeeded only in two. First, consumer welfare rather than consumer choice became the justification of a given monopoly position, along with 'the essentially collectivist doctrine that provided that as long as wealth has been created somewhere in the system it does not matter who enjoys it'. Second, they 'made courts, as well as legal and economic analysts' rethink 'the opportunity costs of trying to preserve the neoclassical ideas of an economy dominated by masses of small and medium-sized enterprises . . . in terms of both economic efficiency losses as well as increased government intervention' necessary to enforce such competition. Third, they should have but failed to deal with the critically important question of the interpenetration of economic and political power wherein large 'organizational hierarchies' of economic power are able 'to pursue political purposes and become political actors' (Crouch 2011, 69–70).

In short, neoliberalism had to admit that, as Marx could have easily told them, in terms of technology and efficiency, any return to competition would be regressive. They also had to admit, as Marx knew well, that the rise of monopoly made for a form of authoritarian collectivism. Of course, while Marx concluded from this that this authoritarian collectivism of monopoly capitalism was ripe for conversion into the egalitarian and solidaristic collectivism that was socialism, neoliberals stopped at disingenuous justifications of monopoly as promoting consumer welfare. Without a left to effect this transformation, capitalism remained dominant while the working people everywhere continue to pay the price of an authoritarian collectivism, which, moreover, is less and less capable of producing wealth productively, becoming more and more focused on plundering incomes from production financially and through other rentier means.

Keeping it thus remains the purpose of neoliberalism. However, it is increasingly difficult in the political conditions it has created.

The emergence of pseudo-civic neoliberalism?

Neoliberal capitalism has long tested working people. However, there were clear signs that, by the end of the 2010s, it was sorely testing its owners and managers too. Well before the pandemic, there were strong signs that swaths of the capitalist class were no longer confident about the future. One indication was the unprecedented spate of corporate CEO resignations in the United States. The first 10 months of 2019 witnessed, according to NBC news (Atkinson 2019), a record 1,332 resignations of CEOs, despite the stock markets continuing their historic upward trend. The trend continued into 2020 when a record 219 CEOs resigned in January alone and *Fortune* magazine dubbed 25 February 2020 'the Great CEO exodus of 2020' when a record four CEOs of major companies, Disney, Salesforce, MasterCard and Uber, all resigned on the same day (Marinova 2020). The captains of industry were not only abandoning their ships in huge numbers, they were, unusually, doing so while stock markets were still soaring. They clearly knew something. After declining during the pandemic in 2020, the trend resumed in 2021 (White 2022; Kelly 2021; Colvin 2022; Foremski 2021; DiNapoli 2021; Foroohar 2021), indicating both routine burn-out, pandemic-related revaluation of life goals among the well-off and the stresses created by the unending economic crisis. Rising political hostility towards some corporations, such as the big tech companies like Twitter or Google, also appear to have played a role.

While the owners and managers of productive corporations were thus discouraged, the owners of financial wealth were, it would seem, manoeuvring for gain. The *Financial Times* reported on the extensive insider stock selling (Henderson 2019) that took place throughout 2019, estimating that it would reach a 20-year high, just surpassing that in 2007, while *Bloomberg* (Wang 2020) reported the trend continuing into 2020. This reversed the trend of stock buybacks (Wohlner 2021) that has been particularly strong since 2009 (Vaughan 2021, Kurov and Tattersall 2022). Of course, the usual cosy relationships between the state and corporations were also evident. In March 2020, it was reported that

> a number of [US] senators sold their stock holdings after being briefed about the coronavirus and the massive impact it will have upon the economy, jobs and the stock market. While telling the American public that there wasn't much to worry about, they bailed out of their stock holdings to avoid large losses.
>
> (*Kelly 2020*)

Jeff Bezos went one better, selling $3.4 billion worth of his own stock in Amazon just before markets fell, presumably knowing he could further profit from buying them back at bargain prices before the Federal Reserve's intervention sent stock prices back up. Clearly, those in the know were expecting a major sell-off, which would be followed by the predictable restorative elixir of the requisite levels of liquidity from the Federal Reserve.

If what remained of capitalism's productive economy was already at a sorry pass, the pandemic and war have only made things worse. At the same time, they also resulted in a closer embrace of state and capital to deal with problems of profitability and demand in the face of stiff competition, whether in the form of the crony capitalism of the pandemic and war-related contracts or of the shutting out of key competitors through the declaration of New Cold Wars and the imposition of sanctions of proxy wars. These moves provided clues about how neoliberal capitalism might now shift shape. Capitalist states in the neoliberal era have gone from deregulating capital, reducing taxation on it, providing it with new productive assets through privatisation, risk-free super profits through contracting out and cheap labour by attacking labour on its behalf to public–private partnerships and a range of forms of crony capitalism.

With stiff competition in nearly all markets, whether for energy or high technology, capital in the leading neoliberal financialised countries may logically seek to advance towards an even tighter embrace with the state. Legitimised by a discourse about how states must provide certain civic or public goods and services to many if not all cheaply or free in the face of proliferating threats—whether emanating from viruses or wars—states would act as customers-in-chief for corporations still deemed the most efficient and reliable producers. Inevitably, since corporations will pour millions into the political determination of what these goods will be, they will, not very miraculously, turn out to be what these corporations produce, rather than what the public needs. This has already been ongoing for decades with corporations providing more and more of the goods and services that have displaced those that used to be produced in-house by states and state-owned entities and reached a new peak in the pandemic in which, while the public needed publicly provided zero-COVID or maximum suppression, it got privately produced vaccines, instead.

Such pseudo-civic neoliberalism will take the interlacing of capital with state and society to a new level. In its earliest stages, this interlacing took the form of philanthropy, often used to justify low corporate taxation. Capitalist and corporate philanthropy is an old game and, in modern times, it threw up famous corporate philanthropists like Andrew Carnegie and continued into the Rockefeller and Ford Foundations. Through it, capitalists have on the one hand sought political legitimacy and the low taxation levels they enjoy and on the other, sought to shape politics, society, culture and foreign policy. Neoliberalism has boosted the power of giant corporations further, bringing corporate philanthropy to its peak—the Bill and Melinda Gates Foundation is its latest and largest iteration.

The neoliberal era has, moreover, added a new form of corporate social and political engagement: corporate social responsibility (CSR). Corporate philanthropy refers to corporate activities that do not concern the primary profit-making activities of a corporation—say an airline sponsoring jazz festivals or banks aiding the search for cancer cures. CSR denotes a promise by corporations to act responsibly with regard to their core business activities, for instance, by recognising the 'externalities'—such as environmental degradation or addictions—they produce and deal with them so as to avoid, government regulation or control. Under CSR, Big Pharma would undertake to ensure the drugs it produced had no harmful side effects, social media enterprises would undertake to eliminate or limit harm to children and mining companies would take responsibility for preventing pollution. It is, effectively, a justification for self-regulation. In short, CSR is the public face of neoliberal trends towards deregulation and regulatory capture.

While, undoubtedly, there are differences between corporate philanthropy and CSR, what unites them is a common drive, since the advent of corporate capitalism in the late nineteenth century, towards extending the political control of private corporations over society, culture and politics (as Gramsci detected in Fordism; Gramsci 1971).

Many have thought of CSR as being about 'good corporate citizenship'. Many others are bolder, moving corporations from the status of citizens to that of states. They argue that corporations, to whom more and more core governmental functions have been contracted out—not only the running of hospitals or garbage collections or road building and maintenance, but also core government functions such as the running of prisons, the fighting of wars, the adjudication of justice, the collection of statistics—are more akin to governments (Crane et al. 2008), that they are already governing citizens alongside elected governments.

Given the hollowing out of democracy in the neoliberal period (Mair 2013), the lack of accountability of governments, this idea does not appear as far-fetched as it should to many. Clearly, arguments supporting the power of private property have come a long way. Having begun with free competitive markets, they went through support for oligopoly and outright monopoly in the name of consumer welfare to arrive at the point where the might—financial and political—of giant corporations is so great as to essentially beg the question whether the vocation of government is not thrust on them (Crouch 2011).

The Bill and Melinda Gates Foundation is precisely such a neoliberal monstrosity. It combines corporate philanthropy and the drive to advance 'socially responsible corporate power' in ways that give it quasi state power. It has long been working to promote the full range of public–private partnerships that have proved lucrative to big corporate capital in the name of addressing human welfare. It has made world hunger a profit opportunity for agribusiness and its patented products such as genetically modified organisms (GMO). It has promoted financial sector interests in the guise of 'financial inclusion' and digitalisation of payments to eliminate cash. Most relevantly, it has promoted Big Pharma and other parts of the medical–industrial complex in the name of protecting humanity from viral diseases. The Foundation works with private capital, universities and friendly governments to advance its causes.

India, where the Gates Foundation has been involved since 2002, is a veritable house of its horrors. GMO seeds have long been sold there, and entire constituencies of scientists mobilised in their favour (Todhunter 2020), allegedly to help Indian farmers and end hunger in the country. However, they have only impoverished farmers and often driven them to suicide, while enriching agribusiness corporations such as Monsanto and Cargill. India's great demonetisation disaster (Ghosh et al. 2017) of late 2016 constituted the brutally sudden and sweeping imposition of the policy of eliminating large cash payments in favour of digitisation urged on governments by Bill Gates for many years (Häring 2017), which it suited the India's fascist government to impose for its own reasons at that time. Bill Gates cheered on the Modi government (*The Times of India* 2016), claiming the (corporate) gains would be worth the (poor's) pain and unmindful of the economic mayhem demonetisation was causing. India was yet to recover from it when the pandemic arrived. The government then imposed another brutal measure, this time a country-wide lockdown within four hours' notice. Everyone has, by now, seen the images of migrant workers crowding bus stations and walking along long hot highways bin human caravans, returning home to villages hundreds of kilometres away from the cities that were never home in the first place.

Event 201, a pandemic simulation held by the Gates Foundation, the Johns Hopkins Center for Health Security and the World Economic Forum on 18 October 2019, provides another glimpse into how corporate leaders are imagining what we call pseudo-civic neoliberalism. It published seven recommendations regarding national, international, public and private, economic and media preparedness and coordination amid pandemics (*Event 201* 2020). The central message was that they would involve 'unprecedented levels of collaboration between governments, international organizations, and the private sector'. While assuming a horrific 65 million deaths (on 21 May 2022, the official worldwide count stood at less than a tenth of that), the Malthusian participants of Event 201 assumed that the world economy, its supply chains and financial system would remain largely intact. Only some sectors, such as travel and tourism, would be badly affected. Amid all this, the interlocutors—business, academic and philanthropic, governmental, international and military—as depicted in the heavily edited videos, the only publicly available record of the simulation, discuss how they are going to save the (remaining) world together, or rather with corporations in the lead. The greed is barely concealed under saccharine humanitarian concern.

In these vignettes, we see the outlines of pseudo-civic neoliberalism. Productive monopoly capital will produce over-priced patented products for governments, transformed from 'consumer of last resort' to consumer-in-chief now that four decades of neoliberalism and its squeeze on working class and petty and peasant producers' incomes has left little in terms of a wider market, at least for Western metropolitan capitalism. Governments will distribute these goods 'free' to their citizens, though they will have actually paid with their steeply regressive taxes. Naturally, these products must be justified as being necessary, often, as in the case of medicines or vaccines, urgently so, when, in reality their value may be dubious, if not positively destructive. In this scenario, financial capital can look forward to profiting from lending to governments to enable them to buy these high-priced products from productive corporations while they earn secure interest paid out of taxes. Those who thought they had seen the peaks of neoliberalism's hypocrisy will witness it scaling new heights.

Powerful as capitalist classes and their political agents are, powerfully motivated as they are to establish something like pseudo-civic neoliberalism, they face headwinds. Western neoliberal governments are already heavily indebted and whether they will be able to bear the new burdens that this new phase of neoliberalism puts on them is open to question. The financial markets, for their part, which would have to buy this debt, are already on Federal Reserve life support. Finally, more and more ordinary people are wise to the disasters capitalists and corporations have engineered in the past. Even if they are not organised in a coherent socialist movement, they can ask a lot of uncomfortable questions. The contradictions can only mount.

Or the start of a new authoritarian capitalism?

However, the key obstacle the pseudo-civic option faces is political and arises from the very transformations neoliberalism wrought in politics. They too are most clearly visible, because most advanced, in the leading neoliberal financialised capitalisms.

By the 1990s, with the historic parties of the working class converting to neoliberalism, a cross-party neoliberal establishment that was also socially liberal on issues of gender, race and immigration and sexual orientation and identity came into being. This establishment waged a relentless campaign against socialism. It has been sufficiently successful to ensure that working people discontented with neoliberalism were left without satisfactory political representation.

This was the terrain on which a new breed of political opportunists went fishing, fashioning a harder 'nativist' right to oppose the 'cosmopolitan' and 'globalist' elite establishment. The main ingredients were continuing support for neoliberalism in the name of individualism and market freedoms, opposition to some of its international aspects—'free trade' agreements in the US case and the EU in the UK case along with immigration—in the name of community and belonging and opposition to social liberalism in the name of traditional values. In addition to petty property, the social mainstay of insurgent right-wing movements, and the upper sections of the working class long converted to neoliberalism, this new formation drew in new working-class segments, those left behind by 'globalisation' (Embery 2020 is a sympathetic account). At the same time, the politics of both Trump and Johnson encompass the mobilisation of far-right mobs capable of violence. Though this was clearest in Trump's case with the attack on Capitol Hill on 6 January 2021, Johnson has never been above it (Mason 2022) and the Trucker's Convoy in Canada heralded similar developments there (Desai 2022). Thus, by the second decade of the twenty-first century, the principal opposition to socially liberal corporate neoliberalism comes not from any left force but from an *enrageée* hard right.

Deindustrialisation has been particularly important in this new formation, taking the form of a 'revolt against globalization' (Davis 2017) amid post-2008 onset of austerity. The fact was that the ubiquitous 'free trade agreements' of previous decades had facilitated less trade than foreign investment and outsourcing, less fettered by labour, environmental and other standards, with key provisions relating less to tariffs and more to things like protecting intellectual property, placing restrictions on regulatory practices and the empowering corporations in investor–state disputes (Ghosh 2016). These 'trade' agreements were defended by reams of literature arguing that Western wage and employment levels had nothing to do with trade (For instance Freund 2017). However, in reality, they were eating into both, particularly for blue collar workers in the West. Such 'globalisation' delivered few benefits in the form of cheaper goods in a world of already very low tariffs even as it deprived lower skill, manufacturing and manual labour of work (Rodrik 2018; Wade 2017).

The resulting political upsets—the election of Trump and the referendum in favour of Brexit—were the visible tip of the iceberg of political rot in the leading neoliberal financialised capitalisms. It went much deeper. In the two leading neoliberal financialised capitalisms, the United States and the United Kingdom, four decades of neoliberalism has reduced state capacity, destroying its critical institutions and losing the best personnel. In both countries, political classes have lost their credibility and political systems have been disarrayed to such an extent that they have permitted outrageous charlatans to occupy their highest public offices, displacing temporarily at least the less interesting or shocking ones that today pass for politicians. This has also been enabled by the domination of information systems by private media and social media, which have led a level of mis- and dis-information, which can only compound these problems.

The new political axis that now governs politics in the leading neoliberal financialised capitalisms also reflects a new division within the capitalist class between the upper reaches of the corporate capitalist class and capital operating a few notches lower down the scale. While the former or 'house-trained' section of the capitalist class would be the natural ally of the neoliberal establishment in effecting the transition to pseudo-civic neoliberalism, the latter, the 'Lumpen' or 'Warlord' section would favour a more authoritarian politics (Monbiot 2020, Farber 2018, Davis 2020, 18). The latter section of the capitalist class has bankrolled politicians who can win elections by mobilising the discontents of neoliberalism by adding protectionism, xenophobia, racism and misogyny to economic neoliberalism, as Trump and Johnson did. Their political strength, estimated in the United States at about a solid 40% of the electorate (Davis 2020, 18), has transformed US electoral politics. Between

> 1920 and 1984 the contest between the two parties resembled World War Two, with a high level of mobility and rapid gains and losses of large swaths of territory. By contrast, the contemporary era resembles World War One, with a single, mostly immobile line of battle and endless trench warfare.
>
> *(Galston 2020)*

One might have thought that the Biden administration, representing the return of the United States' neoliberal elite to power after Trump's rude interruption, might have been ideally placed to affect the transition to pseudo-civic neoliberalism. In many ways, his Build Back Better programme, if implemented, would have initiated the transition. However, the emergence of the new harder right had transformed the political landscape. It was not just that it made Biden's victory that much harder and more expensive—Biden received the highest number of votes for any president not by mobilising people but by outspending Trump by over a third and Clinton's 2016 campaign by a factor of two. It is also that the Trumpist right exercises a gravitational pull on the Biden administration. Though Biden campaigned on being the 'anti-Trump', his presidency increasingly came to resemble his predecessor's, certainly on pandemic policy, economic policy or on waging a New Cold War on China (though whether Trump would have gone as far as the current US proxy war on Russia is questionable).

By mid-2021, Nouriel Roubini was noting that Biden had completed the transformation of the ruling policy paradigm, initiated by Trump, from neoliberal to neopopulist—with 'nationalist, inward-oriented trade policies', a preference for a weaker dollar and routine public debt monetisation and even some redress for income inequality. Any differences, such as Biden's expressed preference for progressive taxation, were (perhaps conveniently) irrelevant given the political logjam in Congress. Biden's shift was, moreover, inevitable: 'Whenever inequality becomes excessive, politicians—of both right and left become more populist. The alternative is to let unchecked inequality become a source of social strife or, in extreme cases, civil war or revolution' (Roubini 2021). Another commentator spoke, in nearly identical terms, of 'a profound shift' towards forms of nationalist Keynesianism: public spending in the service of great national causes. A comparable project has been embraced by the French president, Emmanuel Macron, who increasingly speaks of Europe as a civilisation-state and who championed the EU's €750 billion economic stimulus (Eaton 2021).

With the rise of the hard right as the principal opposition to the right-wing neoliberal establishment, it is not clear that any transition to pseudo-civic neoliberalism can be smoothly affected or that the politics of neoliberal financialised capitalisms cannot take an even more authoritarian turn. It is telling that, in the war against Russia over Ukraine, led by the Biden's United States and fervently supported by the Johnson's United Kingdom, the former a government of the socially liberal neoliberal establishment and the latter one of the insurgent hard right, support neo-Nazis integrated into the Ukrainian state and military, up to and including their encouragement for the creation of an international neo-Nazi fighting force on the model of the various Islamic forces the US government has sponsored abroad. It is also telling to recall that not only did Horkheimer say that 'whoever is not willing to talk about capitalism should also keep quiet about fascism' (Horkheimer 1939)', neoliberalism has long had connections with racism, authoritarianism (Slobodian 2021) and even fascism (Anderson 2005, 13).

With Biden having launched his proxy war on Russia, the political structures of capitalism can only be further distorted, leaving its deep conflicts unresolved, its economy can only further decline, leaving its people bereft and tipping the balance of international power even more steeply in favour of socialism, as we see in the next chapter.

References

Altvater, Elmar. 2009. 'Postneoliberalism or Postcapitalism? The Failure of Neoliberalism in the Financial Market Crisis', *Development Dialogue*, 51, pp. 73–86.

Anderson, Perry. 2005. *Spectrum*. London & New York: Verso.

Atkinson, Claire. 2019. 'Why Have More Than 1,300 CEOs Left Their Post in the Past Year?', *NBC News*, 6 November, (Accessed 30 May 2022) www.nbcnews.com/business/business-news/why-have-more-1-000-ceos-left-their-post-past-n1076201.

Bagchi, Amiya Kumar. 1998. 'Growth Miracle and Its Unravelling in East and South-East Asia: Unregulated Competitiveness and Denouement of Manipulation By International Financial Community', *Economic and Political Weekly*, 33(18), pp. 1025–42.

Berry, Christine. 2020. 'Don't Be Fooled: Britain's Coronavirus Bailout Will Make the Rich Richer Still', *The Guardian*, 13 April, (Accessed 29 May 2022) www.theguardian.com/commentisfree/2020/apr/13/britain-coronavirus-bailout-rich-

Bresser-Pereira, Luiz Carlos. 2010. 'The Global Financial Crisis and a New Capitalism?', *Journal of Post Keynesian Economics*, 32(4), pp. 499–534. https://doi.org/10.2753/pke0160-3477320401

Buchholz, Casey. 2020. 'The Coronavirus and Carceral Capitalism', *Developing Economics*, 11 April, (Accessed 29 May 2022) https://developingeconomics.org/2020/04/11/the-coronavirus-and-carceral-capitalism/

Clarke, Simon. 1991. *Marx, Marginalism and Modern Sociology: From Adam Smith to Max Weber*. London: Palgrave Macmillan.

Colvin, Geoff. 2022. 'CEOs Are Joining the Great Resignation as Experts Predict a Record Number to Quit This Year', *Fortune*, 28 April, (Accessed 30 May 2022) https://fortune.com/2022/04/28/ceos-are-joining-the-great-resignation-as-experts-predict-a-record-number-to-quit-this-year/

Crane, Andrew; Matten, Dirk; and Moon, Jeremy. 2008. *Corporations and Citizenship: Business, Responsibility and Society*. Cambridge: Cambridge University Press.

Crouch, Colin. 2011. *The Strange Non-Death of Neoliberalism*. Cambridge: Polity.

Davis, Mike. 2017. 'Election 2016', *New Left Review*, 1(3), January/February, https://newleftreview.org/issues/ii103/articles/mike-davis-election-2016

Davis, Mike. 2020. 'Trench Warfare', *New Left Review*, 126, pp. 5–32. https://newleftreview.org/issues/ii126/articles/mike-davis-trench-warfare

Demirovic, Alex. 2009. 'Postneoliberalism and Post-Fordism: Is There a New Period in the Capitalist Mode of Production', *Postneoliberalism: A Beginning Debate, Development Dialogue*, 51, pp. 45–58.

Derysh, Igor. 2019. 'Joe Biden to Rich Donors: "Nothing Would Fundamentally Change" If He's Elected', *Salon*, 19 June, (Accessed 22 June 2022) www.salon.com/2019/06/19/joe-biden-to-rich-donors-nothing-would-fundamentally-change-if-hes-elected/

Desai, Radhika. 1994. 'Second Hand Dealers in Ideas: Think-Tanks and Thatcherite Hegemony', *New Left Review*, 1(203), January–February, pp. 27–64. https://newleftreview.org/issues/i203/articles/radhika-desai-second-hand-dealers-in-ideas-think-tanks-and-thatcherite-hegemony

Desai, Radhika. 2013. *Geopolitical Economy: After US Hegemony, Globalization and Empire*. London: Pluto.

Desai, Radhika. 2020. 'Know Your Enemy: The Dangerous Futility of Pseudo-Philanthropic Neoliberalism', *Canadian Dimension*, June 18, (Accessed 26 May 2022) https://canadiandimension.com/articles/%20%20%20view/know-your-enemy-pseudo-philanthropic-neoliberalism

DiNapoli, Jessica. 2021. 'More Chief Executives Join the "Great Resignation"', *Reuters*, 18 November, (Accessed 30 May 2022) www.reuters.com/business/more-chief-executives-join-great-resignation-2021-11-18/

Eaton, George. 2021. 'Is the Neoliberal Era Finally over?', *The New Statesman*, 16 June, (Accessed 29 May 2022) www.newstatesman.com/business/economics/2021/06/neoliberal-era-finally-over

Eatwell, Roger; and Goodwin, Matthew. 2018. *National Populism: The Revolt Against Liberal Democracy*. London: Penguin.

Embery, Paul. 2020. *Despised: Why the Modern Left Loathes the Working Class*. Cambridge: Polity Press.

Event 201. 2020. 'Public-Private Cooperation for Pandemic Preparedness and Response', *Centre for Health Security*, (Accessed 30 May 2022) www.centerforhealthsecurity.org/event201/recommendations.html.

Farber, Samuel. 2018. 'Donald Trump, Lumpen Capitalist', *Jacobin*, 19 October, (Accessed 29 May 2022) www.jacobinmag.com/2018/10/donald-trump-lumpen-capitalist-class-elections

Felkerson, James. 2011. '$29,000,000,000,000: A Detailed Look at the Fed's Bailout by Funding Facility and Recipient', *Levy Economics Institute of Bard College, Working Paper No. 698*, pp. 1–35. https://www.levyinstitute.org/publications/29000000000000-a-detailed-look-at-the-feds-bailout-by-funding-facility-and-recipient

Financial Times, Editorial Board. 2021. 'A Historic Moment in US Stimulus', *Financial Times*, 8 March, (Accessed 29 May 2022) www.ft.com/content/9806c184-5b41-4d73-b59f-5f7f9c88c474

Fleckenstein, William A. 2008. *Greenspan's Bubbles: The Age of Ignorance at the Federal Reserve*. New York: McGraw-Hill.

Foremski, Tom. 2021. 'Why Is the Tech Industry Losing Record Numbers of CEOs?', *ZDNet*, 29 November, (Accessed 30 May 2022) www.zdnet.com/article/industry-is-losing-record-numbers-of-ceos-why/

Foroohar, Rana. 2021. 'CEO Exodus Gathers Pace as Pressures Mount at the Top', *Financial Review*, 7 December, (Accessed 30 May 2022) www.afr.com/work-and-careers/careers/ceo-exodus-gathers-pace-as-pressures-mount-at-the-top-20211207-p59ff1

Freund, Caroline. 2017. 'Three Ways to Reduce a Trade Deficit', *Peterson Institute for International Economics*, 6 November, (Accessed 3 June 2022) https://www.piie.com/blogs/trade-and-investment-policy-watch/three-ways-reduce-trade-deficit

Galston, William A. 2020. 'In the Popular Vote, Why Wasn't Biden's Victory Bigger?', *Brookings*, 12 November, (Accessed 22 June 2022) www.brookings.edu/blog/fixgov/2020/11/12/in-the-popular-vote-why-wasnt-bidens-victory-bigger/

Gamble, Andrew. 1996. *Hayek: The Iron Cage of Liberty*. New York: Routledge.

Ghosh, Jayati. 2016. 'The End of US-Led Economic Globalisation?', *International Development Economics Associates (Network IDEAs)*, 6 September, (Accessed 24 May 2022) www.networkideas.org/news-analysis/2016/09/the-end-of-us-led-economic-globalisation/

Ghosh, Jayati; Chandrasekhar, C.P.; and Patnaik, Prabhat. 2017. *Demonetisation Decoded: A Critique of India's Currency Experiment*. New Delhi: Routledge India.

Gramsci, Antonio. 1971. *Selections From the Prison Notebooks of Antonio Gramsci*, Hoare, Quintin and Nowell-Smith, Geoffrey (ed. and trans.). London: Lawrence & Wishart.

Harbage, Claire; and Bloch, Hannah. 2019. 'The 2010s: A Decade of Protests Around the World', *NPR*, 31 December, (Accessed 29 May 2022) www.npr.org/sections/pictureshow/2019/12/31/790256816/the-2010s-a-decade-of-protests-around-the-world

Häring, Norbert. 2017. 'Money and More', Blog By Norbert Häring, 21 February, (Accessed 30 May 2022) https://norberthaering.de/en/war-on-cash/gates-india-demonetization/

Hay, Colin. 2020. 'Globalization's Impact on States', in Ravenhill, John (ed), *Global Political Economy*, 6th ed., p. 282. Oxford: Oxford University Press. https://doi.org/10.1093/hepl/9780198820642.003.0011

Hayek, Friedrich A. von. 1944. *The Road to Serfdom*. London: George Routledge and Sons.

Henderson, Richard. 2019. 'Insider Stock Sales Rise to Two-Decade High in the US', *Financial Times*, 23 September, (Accessed 30 May 2022) www.ft.com/content/d95e12a6-dbed-11e9-8f9b-77216ebe1f17

Herszenhorn, David M. 2020. 'Democracy in Critical Care as Coronavirus Disrupts Governments', *Politico*, 24 March, (Accessed 29 May 2022) www.politico.eu/article/democracy-in-critical-care-as-coronavirus-disrupts-governments/.

Hobbs, Cat. 2020. 'Outsourcing the Coronavirus Crisis to Business Has Failed—and NHS Staff Know It', *The Guardian*, 7 May, (Accessed 29 May 2022) www.theguardian.com/commentisfree/2020/may/07/outsourcing-coronavirus-crisis-business-failed-nhs-staff.

Horkheimer, Max. 1939. 'The Jews and Europe', *The Charnel-House*, December, (Accessed 22 June 2022) https://thecharnelhouse.org/2015/03/20/the-jews-and-europe/

Huws, Ursula. 2020. *Reinventing the Welfare State: Digital Platforms and Public Policies*. London: Pluto Press.

Jo, Tae-Hee. 2016. 'What If There Are No Conventional Price Mechanisms?', *Journal of Economic Issues*, 50(2), pp. 327–44. https://doi.org/10.1080/00213624.2016.1176474

Kelly, Jack. 2020. 'Senators Accused of Insider Trading, Dumping Stocks After coronavirus Briefing', *Forbes*, 20 March, (Accessed 30 May 2022) www.forbes.com/sites/jackkelly/2020/03/20/senators-accused-of-insider-trading-dumping-stocks-after-coronavirus-briefings/?sh=7a919e5b4a45

Kelly, Makena. 2021. 'As Tech Founders Resign, Congress Loses Its Favorite Targets', *The Verge*, 2 December, (Accessed 30 May 2022) www.theverge.com/2021/12/2/22812641/jack-dorsey-twitter-facebook-amazon-zuckerberg-bezos-congress-resign

Kotz, David M. 2009. 'The Financial and Economic Crisis of 2008: A Systemic Crisis of Neoliberal Capitalism', *Review of Radical Political Economics*, 41(3), pp. 305–17. https://doi.org/10.1177/0486613409335093

Kretchmer, Harry. 2020. 'How Coronavirus Has Hit Employment in G7 Economies', *World Economic Forum*, 13 May, (Accessed 29 May 2022) www.weforum.org/agenda/2020/05/coronavirus-unemployment-jobs-work-impact-g7-pandemic/.

Kurov, Alexander; and Tattersall, Fred T. 2022. 'What's Insider Trading and Why It's a Big Problem', *Yahoo! News*, 18 February, (Accessed 30 May 2022) https://news.yahoo.com/whats-insider-trading-why-big-130737567.html?guccounter=1&guce_referrer=aHR0cHM6Ly93d3cuZ29vZ2xlLmNvbS8&guce_referrer_sig=AQAAA

Legal Services Corporation. 2020. 'US Looking at a "Tsunami of Evictions" as Moratoriums Expire', 1 June, (Accessed 29 May 2022) www.lsc.gov/spotlight-blog/us-looking-tsunami-evictions-moratoriums-expire

Lerner, Sharon. 2020. 'Big Pharma Prepares to Profit From the Coronavirus,' *The Intercept*, 13 March, (Accessed 29 May 2022) https://theintercept.com/2020/03/13/big-pharma-drug-pricing-coronavirus-profits/

Lovett, Samuel. 2020. 'Coronavirus: Private Renters Facing "Tsunami of Evictions" Once Lockdown Ends, Charity Warns', 7 May, (Accessed 29 May 2022) www.independent.co.uk/news/uk/home-news/coronavirus-uk-private-renters-evictions-lockdown-shelter-housing-allowance-a9503151.html

Luttwak, Edward N. 1990. 'From Geopolitics to Geo-Economics: Logic of Conflict, Grammar of Commerce', *The National Interest*, 20, pp. 17–23. https://doi.org/10.4324/9780203444931-27

Mair, Peter. 2013. *Ruling the Void: The Hollowing of Western Democracy*. London & New York: Verso.

Mander, Harsh; and Verma, Amitanshu. 2020. 'Following Authoritarian Regimes Around the World, India Is Using Covid-19 Pandemic to Crush Dissent', *Scroll.in*, 15 May, (Accessed 29 May 2022) https://scroll.in/article/961431/delhi-police-is-making-arbitrary-arrests-and-crushing-dissent-under-the-cloak-of-lockdown

Marinova, Polina. 2020. 'The Great CEO Exodus of2020', *Fortune*, 26 February, (Accessed 30 May 2022) https://fortune.com/2020/02/26/the-great-ceo-exodus-of-2020/.

Marsh, David; and Rhodes, R.A.W. (eds). 1992. *Implementing Thatcherite Policies: Audit of an Era*. Milton Keynes: Open University Press.

Mason, Paul. 2022. 'Boris Johnson Has Repeatedly Incited Far-Right Mobs—We Are Living With the Consequences', *The New Statesman*, 8 February, (Accessed 22 June 2022) www.newstatesman.com/comment/2022/02/boris-johnson-has-repeatedly-incited-far-right-mobs-we-are-living-with-the-consequences

McEvoy, Jemima. 2020. 'Celebrities and Rich Neighborhoods Won't Stop Hosting Massive Mansion Parties', *Forbes*, 4 August, (Accessed 22 June 2022) www.forbes.com/sites/jemimamcevoy/2020/08/04/celebrities-and-rich-neighborhoods-wont-stop-hosting-massive-mansion-parties/?sh=5b3439ad5035

Monbiot, George. 2020. 'Brexit Stems From a Civil War in Capitalism—We Are All Just Collateral Damage', *The Guardian*, 24 November, (Accessed 29 May 2022) www.theguardian.com/commentisfree/2020/nov/24/brexit-capitalism

Noonan, Laura. 2020. 'Citi Warns Markets Are Out of Step With Grim Reality', *Financial Times*, 31 May, (Accessed 29 May 2022) www.ft.com/content/d84dc366-cd2f-422a-b804-3efa24262275

Pablo, Carlito. 2020. 'Tsunami of Evictions Feared Without Relief for Renters, Landlords: B.C. Tenant Advocate Andrew Sakamoto', *The Georgia Straight*, 4 May, (Accessed 29 May 2022) www.straight.com/news/tsunami-of-evictions-feared-without-relief-for-renters-landlords-bc-tenant-advocate-andrew

Plender, John. 2020. 'The Seeds of the Next Debt Crisis', *Financial Times*, 3 March, (Accessed 29 May 2022) www.ft.com/content/27cf0690-5c9d-11ea-b0ab-339c2307bcd4.

Politi, James; and Fedor, Lauren. 2020. 'What's in the Historic $2tn US Stimulus Deal?', *Financial Times*, 25 March, (Accessed 29 May 2022) www.ft.com/content/0925d61e-6eaa-11ea-89df-41bea055720b

Powell, Jamie. 2020. 'The Zombie Rally', *Financial Times*, 9 June, (Accessed 29 May 2022) www.ft.com/content/7977425b-e50d-45d6-8d50-f205ac5fada9

Rodrik, Dani. 2018. 'Populism and the Economics of Globalization', *Journal of International Business Policy*, 1(1), pp. 12–33. https://doi.org/10.1057/s42214-018-0001-4

Rodrik, Dani. 2021. 'Beware Economists Bearing Policy Paradigms', *Project Syndicate*, 11 May, (Accessed 29 May 2022) www.project-syndicate.org/commentary/economic-policy-must-abandon-universal-paradigms-by-dani-rodrik-2021-05?barrier=accesspaylog

Rohatyn, Felix. 1994. 'World Capital: The Needs and the Risks', *New York Review of Books*, 41(13), pp. 48–53.

Roubini, Nouriel. 2021. 'Biden's Neo-Populist Economic Doctrine', *Project Syndicate*, 3 August, (Accessed 30 May 2022) www.project-syndicate.org/commentary/biden-trump-neopopulist-economic-doctrine-by-nouriel-roubini-2021-08

Slobodian, Quinn. 2018. *The Globalists: The End of Empire and the Birth of Neoliberalism*. Cambridge, MA: Harvard University Press.

Slobodian, Quinn. 2021. 'Hayek's Bastards: The Populist Right's Neoliberal Roots', *Tribune*, 16 June, (Accessed 30 May 2022) https://tribunemag.co.uk/2021/06/hayeks-bastards-the-populist-rights-neoliberal-roots

Tett, Gillian. 2020. 'Swamped Bankruptcy Courts Threaten US Recovery', *Financial Times*, 14 May, (Accessed 29 May 2022) www.ft.com/content/14b07c0e-95e3-11ea-af4b-499244625ac4

The Times of India. 2016. 'Bill Gates Backs Demonetisation, Says It's Worth the Pain', 18 November, (Accessed 30 May 2022) https://timesofindia.indiatimes.com/india/Bill-Gates-backs-demonetisation-says-digital-payments-can-transform-lives-of-poor/articleshow/55486066.cms

Todhunter, Colin. 2020. 'Challenging the Flawed Premise Behind Pushing GMOs into Indian Agriculture', *Counterpunch*, 22 January, (Accessed 30 May 2022) www.counterpunch.org/2020/01/22/challenging-the-flawed-premise-behind-pushing-gmos-into-indian-agriculture/.

Tooze, Adam. 2021. 'Has Covid Ended the Neoliberal Era?', *The Guardian*, 2 September, (Accessed 29 May 2022) www.theguardian.com/news/2021/sep/02/covid-and-the-crisis-of-neoliberalism

Toynbee, Polly. 2021. 'Dido Harding to Head the NHS? Her Position Would Be Untenable', *The Guardian*, 7 June, (Accessed 22 June 2022) www.theguardian.com/commentisfree/2021/jun/07/dido-harding-nhs-test-and-trace-boris-johnson

Van der Pijl, Kees. 2020. 'The Russian Revolution at 100: The Soviet Experience in the Mirror of Permanent Counterrevolution', *Third World Quarterly*, 41(8), pp. 1272–88. https://doi.org/10.1080/01436597.2019.1665462

Vaughan, Liam. 2021. 'Most Americans Today Believe the Stock Market Is Rigged, and They're Right', *Bloomberg*, 28 September, (Accessed 30 May 2022) www.bloomberg.com/news/features/2021-09-29/is-stock-market-rigged-insider-trading-by-executives-is-pervasive-critics-say

Wade, Robert. 1996. 'Japan, the World Bank, and the Art of Paradigm Maintenance: "The East Asian Miracle" in Political Perspective', *New Left Review*, 1(217), 1 May, p. 3. https://newleftreview.org/issues/i217/articles/robert-wade-japan-the-world-bank-and-the-art-of-paradigm-maintenance-the-east-asian-miracle-in-political-perspective

Wade, Robert Hunter. 2017. 'Is Trump Wrong on Trade? A Partial Defense Based on Production and Employment', *Real World Economic Review*, pp. 43–63.

Wainwright, Hilary. 1994. *Arguments for a New Left: Answering the Free-Market Right*. London: Wiley-Blackwell.

Wang, Lu. 2020. 'Red Flags Emerge in U.S. Stocks With Insiders Rushing to Sell', *Bloomberg*, 6 February, (Accessed 30 May 2022) www.bloomberg.com/news/articles/2020-02-06/equity-bulls-beware-insiders-are-rushing-to-sell-their-stocks

Watson, Matthew; and Hay, Colin. 2003. 'The Discourse of Globalisation and the Logic of No Alternative: Rendering the Contingent Necessary in the Political Economy of New Labour', *Policy & Politics*, 31(3), pp. 289–305. https://doi.org/10.1332/030557303322034956

The Week Staff. 2015. 'The Federal Reserve's "Breathtaking" $7.7 Trillion Bank Bailout', *The Week*, 11 January, (Accessed 22 June 2022) https://theweek.com/articles/479867/federal-reserves-breathtaking-77-trillion-bank-bailout

White, Martha C. 2022. 'CEOs Are Joining the "Great Resignation," Trading Fatigue for Family Time', *NBC News*, 18 January, (Accessed 30 May 2022) www.nbcnews.com/business/business-news/ceos-are-joining-great-resignation-trading-fatigue-family-time-rcna12223

Wohlner, Roger. 2021. 'Are Stock Buybacks a Good Thing, or Not?', *Investopedia*, updated 31 December, (Accessed 30 May 2022) www.investopedia.com/articles/financial-advisors/121415/stock-buybacks-good-thing-or-not.asp.

The World Bank. 1993. 'The East Asian Miracle: Economic Growth and Public Policy: Main Report (English)', *A World Bank Policy Research Report*. Washington, DC: World Bank Group, 26 September, (Accessed 22 June 2022) https://documents.worldbank.org/en/publication/documents-reports/documentdetail/975081468244550798/main-report

Younge, Gary. 2019. 'Streets on Fire: How a Decade of Protest Shaped the World', *The Guardian*, 23 November, (Accessed 29 May 2022) www.theguardian.com/culture/2019/nov/23/decade-of-protest-occupy-wall-street-extinction-rebellion-gary-younge

7

CAPITALISM IN THE BALANCE OF INTERNATIONAL POWER

At the height of the crisis over Ukraine in mid-May 2022, President Biden hosted the leaders of 10 Association of South-East Asian Nations (ASEAN) countries at the White House to demonstrate that 'Washington remains focused on the Indo-Pacific and the long-term challenge of China'. Actions took leave of words, however: he committed a paltry $150 million to the grouping in total. The contrast with China was glaring. China officially welcomed 'any cooperation that promotes sustainable development and prosperity', underlining that neither it nor ASEAN promoted 'bloc confrontation'. By contrast, the US official position, while 'not asking countries to make a choice between the United States and China', underlined that 'the United States seeks stronger relationships' with countries deemed susceptible to anti-China agenda. Myanmar, moreover, was pointedly left out. China's unifying and generous approach to the region could not contrast more. 'In November alone, China pledged $1.5 billion in development assistance to ASEAN countries over three years to fight COVID and fuel economic recovery', while $60 million of the already meagre US funding announced at the meeting was to go to 'maritime security'—essentially to the United States' belligerent aims in the region. Much of the rest went to uses lucrative for US corporations, including decarbonising power supply and developing 'digital economy and artificial intelligence laws' while concerns about US jobs precluded any increased market access for ASEAN countries (Hunnicutt 2022).

This was just another episode underlining that, whether the major neoliberal capitalisms face class forces organised for socialism domestically or not, their miserly and punitive imperialism can only hasten other countries' drift away from the capitalist world the United States still seeks to lead. The attractiveness of China's developmental offer, and its respect for its partners' sovereignty, contrasts strikingly, making it the pole towards which they will drift and, given its success at development, the example they will seek to learn from.

DOI: 10.4324/9781003200000-7

Essentially, while the balance of class power remains heavily tilted in favour of capital in its homelands, the balance of international power is tilting markedly away from capitalism, driving all outside the charmed circle of the United States, Europe, Japan and the settler colonies bit by bit, with advances and reverses, steadily away from the major capitalist countries and probably, from capitalism. This process began with the Russian Revolution and, after the reverses of the 1990s, resumed in the new century as an alliance of countries seeking to assert their economic and security sovereignty—including Russia, Venezuela, Cuba and Iran—began forming with China as its economic centre. The pandemic and the war have accelerated these processes. This chapter examines how. The United States' proxy war on Russia acts as a prism that refracts the key elements of the underlying unfolding of the geopolitical economy of capitalism and socialism. It constitutes a resumé of the state of the United states'-declining imperial project, of the balance between US capacities and the possibilities and constraints imposed by the world's geopolitical economy.

After an overview of the proxy war on Russia and its position in the wider US strategy ultimately targeting China, we go on to an account of how the United States not only failed to create a capitalist world under its domination but how the attempt, tied up as it was with the turn to neoliberalism, enervated the already weak US capitalism and financialised it. This enables us to appreciate the constraints under which US governments act today. We then trace the origin of the present conflict and assess how US actions are undermining each of its aims—to unify the world behind capitalism and against China's socialism, to strengthen its core alliances, to destroy the Russian economy, to defeat Russia militarily and to consolidate US power, particularly that of the dollar creditocracy, over the world economy. After some reflections on what the West's irresponsible actions are doing to Ukraine itself, the chapter concludes with reflections on whether and how the Western alliance will break up under the unbearable pressure that Washington's vain commitment to lengthen the life of a defunct capitalism is putting on it and how the world might advance towards socialism.

The US war against Russia over Ukraine

The very contrasting domestic and international pandemic performance of the United States and China rankled the Trump administration sufficiently that, by the summer of 2020, after blowing hot and cold on China for years, it declared a New Cold War on China in a set of apparently 'sudden and inexplicable' speeches (Wright 2020). However, they were neither. The speeches came as the first deadly wave of the pandemic began taking more lives every couple of days than China had lost in total and Trump, who had already been banging on about the 'Wuhan virus', sorely needed to blame China for his own hubristic incompetence, particularly in an election year. In any case, he was only deepening the rut in which Obama's 'pivot to Asia' had put US foreign policy when it finally became clear that, despite decades of deepening engagement that included

China's entry into the WTO and a level of economic integration through FDI, outsourcing, trade and capital flows that prompted many to speak of 'Chimerica' (Ferguson and Schularick 2007), the United States had failed to entice China to turn to neoliberal capitalism and that its rapid socialist development was reducing US economic weight and international influence. The pivot signalled that the United States would now seek to compel Chinese compliance (Woodward 2017). US purposes were no secret. Noting that Beijing put the new 'cold war mentality' down to the United States' 'supposed refusal to accept a multipolar world', the *Financial Times*'s Gideon Rachman conceded there was 'a bipartisan determination in Washington to retain America's status as "number one"' (Rachman 2020).

Both major parties, the Democrats and the Republicans, and both major currents of thought on international relations, the liberal internationalist and the realist, agreed that China was the most powerful threat to this ambition. This point was, for instance, conceded by the 'realist' Atlantic Council's anonymously authored piece, *The Longer Telegram,* a detailed treatment of the major challenge the United States faced, China. Published to mark Biden's inauguration, it was subtitled 'Toward a New American China Strategy'. However, there were divisions over exactly how to deal with China and over how Russia fitted into US aims and methods. While realists believed that '[a]llowing Russia to drift fully into China's strategic embrace over the last decade will go down as the single greatest geostrategic error of successive US administrations' (Anonymous 2021, 10), liberal internationalists of the Zbigniew Brzezinski school had long been maximalists, seeking Russia's subordination, if necessary through its territorial break-up as well as China's. Stabilised after 2000 under President Putin following the disastrous decade of Shock Therapy, Russia was not easily subordinated. Though nowhere as economically dynamic as China, with a distinct neoliberal leaning in economic policy to serve its oligarchical capitalism (Dzarasov 2013) and desirous of US and European acceptance, Russia had learned the hard way—through disasters such as 2,500% inflation and steep falls in life expectancy in the 1990s—what resulted from Russia's subordination to the dictates of the US-led West (Sakwa 2020). As NATO advanced eastwards, and Washington fomented colour revolutions all around it, Russia invested in the military technology to ensure its defence. Tensions came to a head after the Obama administration sponsored the 2014 Euromaidan counter-revolution in Ukraine, triggering its civil war and the United States' New Cold War against Russia waged with economic sanctions. By 2022, after the Trump interregnum in which the United States initiated no new wars, the cold war had become a hot one, as the 'war of sanctions' gave way to what was, in effect, a US proxy war against Russia. Waged to tilt the balance of international power back towards the United States and its brand of capitalism and away from China, to subordinate Russia, to secure the interests of US capitalists, for instance by securing new energy markets for them (Klare 2022), to rally or, indeed, to re-subordinate allies and to demonstrate US effectiveness after the debacle the previous summer in Afghanistan, it soon became clear it would have the opposite effect.

The whole world had already beheld the sorry figures major capitalist governments cut in failing so signally to handle the pandemic and manifesting such selfish short-sightedness internationally over vaccines when, as if still unsatisfied at the demeaning spectacle they made of themselves, uncaring that the pandemic still raged, they initiated their proxy war against Russia. It manifestly risked a wider, even a nuclear, conflict. It undermined food security and destabilised long-standing economic relationships. It prevented advance on climate change even as catastrophic weather events took lives and destroyed crops. The rhetoric of democracy and human rights in which these capitalist countries dressed up their assault on world stability and peace rang hollow given the parlous condition of their own democracies. Indeed, the war itself was undemocratic, and incumbent leaders' approval ratings plummeted: as a European Council on Foreign Relations poll showed, in mid-June 2022, early unity over 'justice' for Ukraine was giving way to fatigued support for 'peace' (Krastev and Leonard 2022) as economic pain mounted. If all this was not enough to detract from the West's vaulting self-congratulation about democracy, there was the proxy war's alliance with Neo-Nazis in Ukraine and the glaringly untruthful propaganda in the Western media that not only demonised President Putin while glorifying President Zelensky to the point that precluded any negotiated end to the conflict, it also sanitised neo-Nazi groups in Ukraine's government and army as mere nationalists. Capitalism's already low reputation after decades of post-Cold War militarism and economic decline plumbed new depths.

One of the much-trumpeted gains of the early phase of the proxy war, NATO's newfound unity, could only paper over deep historic rifts between the United States and its Western European allies. Specifically, over Ukraine, not only had France and Germany opposed offering Ukraine and Georgia NATO membership back in 2008 (Taylor and John 2008), European opposition to US-sponsored regime change in Ukraine infamously prompted the United States' diplomat for European and Eurasian affairs, Victoria Nuland's 'fuck the EU' expletive (Pilkington 2014) during the 2015 regime change operation in Kyiv. While it succeeded in ousting the democratically elected Party of Regions President Victor Yanokovich (Kagarlitsky et al. 2019), Europeans continued pursuing their long-standing cooperation with Russia, including Germany's Nord Stream II pipeline, and with China, with the United Kingdom taking founding membership of the Asian Infrastructure Investment Bank and Germany's trade with China surpassing that with the United States.

Clearly, Biden's proxy war against Russia requires US allies to fall in line behind its maximalist liberal internationalist project but at a great economic cost. If extended to a similar war against China, the economic cost will assuredly be vastly greater. Such extension appears, at the time of writing, more or less inevitable. Not only does China remain the United States' main declared enemy, but the military component of the resources mobilised in pursuit of this goal is being ramped up almost daily. At the Quad Summit in Tokyo, as the Ukraine conflict still raged, Biden proclaimed, for the third time, the United States' commitment to defend Taiwan militarily in case of conflict with China, breaking with the long-standing US posture of 'strategic ambiguity' on the Taiwan question. Though White House officials 'walked back' these statements and even normally supportive media spoke of Biden's statement 'really rais[ing] adrenaline levels in that . . . briefing room' (Smith 2022), changes to official US State Department documents moving away from strategic ambiguity and towards support for Taiwanese independence were soon being reported (Fusero 2022) and the United States continued stepping up its military presence in region (Sevastopulo and Hille 2022).

Undoubtedly Biden seeks what the United States has long sought: to extend, economically and diplomatically if possible, militarily if necessary, the ambit of capitalism by subordinating more and more countries to the US-led West. However, even at the height of its power, the United States was unable to secure the domination it sought (Desai 2013). As its economic and diplomatic resources dwindled, military aggression ominously took their place. In the new century, this resulted in a string of military failures capped by the ignominious withdrawal from Afghanistan that exposed the shocking inadequacy of US military and intelligence capabilities. At the time of writing, though questions are being asked at the highest levels, there is no sign that these failures are provoking any kind of strategic rethink though sections of the Republican Party were breaking with the United States' hawkish stance on Russia (*Quincy Institute for Responsible Statecraft* 2022).

Whatever its outcome, the Ukraine conflict promises to constitute a major turning point. It has brought the decline in US influence and effectiveness to a new stage where US actions are no longer merely ineffective but positively counterproductive. Instead of destroying the Russian economy with its sanctions, instead of defeating Russia militarily through its proxy, or unifying the world under US leadership, instead of strengthening alliances and consolidating US power, particularly that of the dollar creditocracy, over the world economy, US actions are achieving the opposite.

Sanctions against Russia have only damaged Russia enough to prompt further successful measures aimed at reorienting its economy away from the West, while inflicting economic pain on the United States, its allies and dozens of poor countries, particularly with rising food and fuel prices. Financial sanctions, moreover, boomeranged on the dollar system itself. Not only did few countries other than the United States' major capitalist allies impose sanctions against Russia and provide lethal aid to Ukraine, more and more countries were engaged in reviving a Non-Aligned Movement style distancing from US objectives. Even the unity of the Western alliance began cracking, along numerous fault lines running through it like crazing on old porcelain.

Finally, at least up to the time of writing, none of the arms or training provided to the Ukrainian army seem able to prevent Russia from making steady, careful and methodical gains. Russia suffered defeats, if anywhere, only in Western propaganda in which Russia is routinely presented as having failed or been forced to withdraw from this or that absurdly maximalist objective—such as occupying all of Ukraine or taking Kyiv—it never had and by celebrating as battle victories, the largely inconsequential, if not war criminal, exploits of the Ukrainian armed forces, composed of reluctant regulars, nefarious neo-Nazis and fickle foreign mercenaries.

The United States' impossible imperial project

The conflict that the West calls Russia's invasion of Ukraine, and Moscow its special military operations for Ukraine's demilitarisation and denazification, is not a conflict between Ukraine and Russia. It is a phase in the hybrid war that the United States, usually but not always followed by other major capitalist countries, has been waging for over a century against any country that chooses an economic path other than subordination to itself or the broader capitalist world. In its current phase, this war takes the form of a US-led NATO war against Russia *over* Ukraine. In this war, Ukraine is the terrain, and a pawn—one that can be and is being sacrificed with the apparent cooperation of its West-oriented leadership. Although, by baselessly portraying President Putin as either mad or hell-bent on recreating the Soviet Union, wall-to-wall Western propaganda seeks to preclude any serious discussion and assessment of the conflict and its progress, its credibility in the world at large and even among Western publics is limited.

In the West's conceits, this conflict is about closing 'the chapter that began at the end of the Cold War, when Western countries tried to integrate Russia into an international rules-based order' (Heusgen 2022). Or it is about making NATO 'a more united and effective defensive force' (Galston 2022) or vastly improving the prospects for European integration. In reality, it is another rear-guard action against the decline of imperialism that began with the onset of the Thirty Years' Crisis and has progressed with fits and starts since. Involving the inevitable relative economic decline of the major capitalist countries in their monopoly phase, this decline could be reversed neither by neoliberalism nor by the United States' associated attempts, as zealous as they were vain, to prolong capitalism's life and extend its reach around the globe.

Indeed, the paradox of US zeal and vanity can be explained if one considers that it emerged as the leading capitalist country nursing an ambition to emulate what it took to be the United Kingdom's nineteenth-century world dominance precisely in this period of capitalism's decline. In the post-war conjuncture of popular empowerment, capitalism enjoyed its Long Boom and associated economic stabilisation and growth precisely because the political power of capital was hemmed in with socialistic measures that empowered labour and regulated capital to a historically unprecedented extent, while also confining it in distinct national cages with capital controls.

Corresponding to this domestic state of capitalist affairs was the international scene in which the imperial bloc the United States led was constrained by the strength of socialist and nationalist challenges, by the Soviet and Chinese nuclear weapons, by the Warsaw Pact and the Non-Aligned Movement. Within its own camp too, the power of capital had to be restrained and regulated in state-led efforts for recovery and reconstruction if they were to be accomplished effectively and if the citizens of these countries were to be prevented from succumbing to the, at the time considerable, charms of Communism, though such economic strategy was amply supplemented by the Central Intelligence Agency's (CIA's) covert operations around the world as a now extensive literature documents (see, for instance, Coleman 1989; Ganser 2004; Bevins 2020).

As they did so, while the United States left its own economy relatively open, it lost the overwhelming productive dominance it had secured during the Second World War. Its first attempt to establish the dollar as the world's trading currency also failed. On the one hand, the United States was forced to back it with gold to persuade reluctant allies to accept the arrangement. On the other hand, having no capital to export, supplying the world with liquidity by running deficits which only devalued the dollar, forced its own allies and trade partners to opt for gold over dollars of doubtful value. After exhausting all avenues for salvaging this fundamentally unsatisfactory arrangement, the United States was forced to delink the dollar from gold in 1971. To the productive and monetary slide, we must add the military. Notwithstanding the astronomical sums spent on the US military, the United States was unable to win any significant war in pursuit of its ambitions except against tiny countries. In its two major wars of the Cold War era, it had to accept the victory of Communism in North Korea and was defeated in Vietnam.

In the profound class and international struggles that ensued when the Long Boom ended, the United States laid new foundations, this time financial, for a second attempt to establish the dollar as the world's money and, from the 1980s onwards, along with the United Kingdom, sought the neoliberal path out of the economic downturn. However, rather than resolve or reverse the slump, neoliberalism only prolonged it, also ensuring the resumption of imperial decline in the long run.

However, this was not immediately apparent, thanks to a combination of factors. Many observers, including critical ones, confused capital's greater political power, exercised against the Communist and Third Worlds abroad and working people at home, with greater economic dynamism (Duménil and Lévy 2004). To be sure, neoliberal policies inflicted mesmerisingly horrifying levels of damage on much of the Third and Communist worlds in the 1980s and the 1990s while China, many assumed, had been put safely on the path to neoliberal capitalism. As the twentieth century closed, the United States appeared, moreover, to be undergoing a major, investment-led economic boom, which many even advertised as a new industrial revolution. These events undoubtedly gave a powerful impression of US power. The words of Benjamin Cohen, leading US scholar of international political economy, resonated widely: after having narrowed in the late twentieth century, in its last years,

> America's lead seemed, if anything, to be widening again, reinforced by the collapse of the Soviet empire, which left the United States as the world's last remaining superpower. Over the course of the 1990s, the U.S. economy enjoyed its longest peacetime expansion in history, avoiding the high unemployment that plagued continental Europe, the stagnation that dragged down Japan after the bursting of its bubble economy, and the financial crisis that devastated emerging markets from East Asia to Latin America. At the dawn of the new millennium, America's economic primacy was once again unquestioned. Now more than one source was predicting more of the same, perhaps even a 'Second American Century'. . . . If no longer Gulliver among the Lilliputians, the United States had clearly reclaimed its position as number one. The ageing hegemon had gained a new lease on life.
>
> *(Cohen 2008, 77)*

Writing just months before the 2008 crash, Cohen was already overlooking the 'quagmire' of the United States' Iraqi operations and the mounting evidence—chiefly in the form of mortgage foreclosures—of the coming crash.

Reality would soon assert itself. As neoliberalism and financialisation undermined the United States' productive economy, they served as the volatile foundation of the US dollar system. Rocked by the refusal of allies to support it before 1971, thereafter, it has been rocked by the series of financialisations—expansions of purely speculative and predatory financial activity that regularly end in financial crises—that it relies on to function. These progressively weakened productive growth. The 2008 crisis was not only a dramatic manifestation of this true underlying weakness but a turning point with the near-vanishing of Western growth combined with steadily increasing growth in a number of developing countries, shifting the world's economic centre of gravity away from the West, as the more astute commentators noted. The latter group, particularly those the Goldman Sachs economist Jim O'Neill dubbed the BRIC countries——Brazil, Russia, India and China (O'Neill 2001)—had either applied neoliberalism selectively, like India, or reversed it in many ways after suffering its worst excesses, like Brazil and Russia, or escaped it altogether, like China. This economic shift coincided with a military one.

While it existed, the Soviet Union was critical in defeating and deterring US military action and confining it to proxy wars. Even Reagan's high-decibel 'evil empire' rhetoric only justified the Strategic Defense Initiative that was more industrial policy than military policy (Ferguson 1995, 248; Block 2008, 181–2; Parboni 1986, 14–15) when US deindustrialisation was becoming an issue. Only in the 1990s, flush with the false triumphalism of its pyrrhic 'victory' in the

Cold War, did the United States shift to ever more unilateral military aggression, beginning with the 1992 Gulf War, continuing with wars in Yugoslavia, Afghanistan, Iraq, Libya, Syria and elsewhere in the hope that 'American military might could effectively police the world and at the same time ensure the continuing centrality of the United States in the global political economy' (Arrighi 2005, 113).

However, not only was US military capability increasingly hemmed in by its material decline, but its ideological (and capitalist) conviction that victory in war could be had with capital-intensive warfare, with superiority in weaponry alone, led it into catastrophic miscalculations. Technologically inferior and far poorer societies defending themselves against its onslaught, driven to levels of determination, heroism and ultimately military competence that the United States could not match, frustrated or defeated it, as in Korea and Vietnam and thereafter the United States' sorry military record only got sorrier.

Successive US administrations failed to undo the humiliation of Vietnam, let alone police the world or ensure continuing US centrality. Reagan invaded tiny Grenada and declared 'Our days of weakness are over. Our military forces are back on their feet and standing tall'. George H. W. Bush invaded Iraq, failed to overthrow Saddam Hussein and declared nevertheless that '[t]he ghosts of Vietnam have been laid to rest beneath the sands of the Arabian desert'. Apart from tiny and weak adversaries, the United States prevailed nowhere. The August 2021 pull-out from Afghanistan only underlined this record humiliatingly. Such a sorry record is only explicable if the lavish funding of the US military is seen less in terms of performance expectations and more in terms of certain other objectives though the dissipation that inevitably accompanies failure must also have contributed to the less than purposive pursuit of military goals. Indeed, what appears as US efforts to retain dominance militarily can be broken down at least into three distinct objectives which are also at work in the Ukraine conflict. Each is getting harder to achieve.

The first objective is the enduring one of trying to prevent any country from escaping subordination to the United States and the West. The United States aims to prevent such nations from running their economies and engaging with other countries—each other, their neighbours, the West and the rest of the world—on terms of their own choosing. Failure to achieve this has never precluded attempts, and, in the twenty-first century, China is chief among the Unites States's failures. Seeking to contain, if not subordinate China, to stall if not reverse its rise, has been the one foreign policy principle commanding agreement, as we have seen, across the US political and foreign policy spectrum, from the liberal internationalists who have been in power continuously in the post-Cold War period with the possible exception of the Trump interregnum, to the realists, who had their heyday back in the 1970s when Henry Kissinger was Secretary of State. The latter are now, as evidenced by John Mearsheimer's ubiquitous lectures and podcasts on the Ukraine conflict, breaking ranks with the consensus on subject, as are the aforementioned Republican currents.

Not only is China, according to Secretary of State Anthony Blinken's 2022 speech at the prestigious Asia Society as the war over Ukraine raged, 'the most serious long-term challenge to the international order' because it has 'both the intent to reshape the international order and, increasingly, the economic, diplomatic, military, and technological power to do it' (Blinken 2022), as noted, realists at the Atlantic Council concur. Its foreign policy recommendations for the incoming Biden administration—styled as *The Longer Telegram* after George Kennan's famous 1946 'Long Telegram'—was all about China too: it is the United States' 'the single most important challenge' thanks to 'the scale of its economy and its military, the speed of its technological advancement, and its radically different worldview' (Anonymous 2021).

The striking unity within the US ruling elite with respect to China is paralleled by an equally striking disunity over how to achieve the aim of subordinating China and over how to treat Russia. Whereas realists have counselled caution over militarily confronting China and keeping the management of the US–China relationship within the bounds of limited US means and of the overall configuration of power (Mearsheimer 2021), liberal internationalists in the Biden administration have clearly upped the ante, particularly militarily. On Russia, whereas for Blinken, 'Russian President Vladimir Putin poses a clear and present threat', for the realist Atlantic Council, 'the United States must rebalance its relationship with Russia' to divide the two giant countries and undo its 'single greatest geostrategic error' of allowing China and Russia to drift together. Moreover, while even the realists are too Eurocentric to acknowledge this, over the decades, China became the centre of a wider anti-imperialist alliance that included not only Russia but also Iran, North Korea, Venezuela and Cuba. In the Ukraine conflict, that alliance is only growing stronger, with increasing closeness between Russia and China and the re-emergence of Non-Aligned Movement type formations. That it is not just a 'strategic' but a systemic challenge is clear from the currency of the label 'Beijing consensus' to refer to the alternative to the neoliberal 'Washington consensus' that China and the alliance centred around it represent.

The second US foreign and military policy objective is to expand opportunities for the four sectors of economic activity in which US corporations retain an edge chiefly thanks to US imperial endeavours. There is, first, the military–industrial complex, which relies on NATO expansion and its interoperability requirements to expand markets and profits. It can definitely look forward to a bonanza of orders as military 'aid' to Ukraine expands and NATO member countries increase military expenditures in their newfound 'unity' and willingness to spend on defence. Second, there is the fossil fuel and mining sector, which has long been the mainstay of this white-settler state. It will be the chief beneficiary of a captive market in Europe if it does follow through with its current promises to cease relying on much cheaper Russian energy. However, given that they are economically near-suicidal, follow through is far from guaranteed. Third, we have the finance, insurance and real estate (FIRE) sector, which forms the critical underpinning of the dollar creditocracy that, along with the US military apparatus, supports its imperial project. With its upper echelons poised to benefit from any market volatility, not only does it gain from ructions in currency or commodity or asset markets, it will also exploit new opportunities, such as Ukrainian war bonds (Kimble 2022). Finally, there are industries that rely on monopoly and intellectual property rights protections such as information and communications technology and Big Pharma. They hope to benefit from any extension of US dominance since compliance with intellectual property rights is a core US demand. A moment's reflection will reveal that all these sectors involve extending US control, something at which the United States has not been very good.

Finally, Washington seeks to secure its dominance against decline by re-subordinating allies—particularly the Europeans and Japan. This has never been as easy as theories of US hegemony have suggested (van der Pijl 2006). West European capitalist classes erected the structures of the EU to compete with the United States (Mandel 1970). Not only did Japan threaten the US status as the world's leading economy well into the 1990s, as we have seen, European assertion against the United States is also long-standing. In the 1960s, at the height of the Cold War, it took the form of France's departure from NATO command structures and Willy Brandt's Ostpolitik. After the collapse of the USSR, the United States feared worse. As Peter Gowan explained,

> First, NATO—the military cornerstone of the Alliance—had lost its rationale and there were moves in Western Europe (and Russia) to build a new security order in Europe that would tend to undermine US leadership. Secondly, newly united Germany seemed to be building a new political bloc with France through the Maastricht Treaty, with its stress on a Common Foreign and Security Policy leading towards 'a common defence'. This seemed to be more than mere words, since Germany and France were in the process of building a joint military corps, the so-called 'Euro-Corps' outside the NATO framework—a move that profoundly disturbed Washington and London. Thirdly, Germany's drive in relation to Yugoslavia seemed to be geared not simply to domestic German constituencies, but *to the construction of a German sphere of influence* in Central Europe, involving Austria, Hungary, Croatia and Slovenia and, perhaps later, drawing in Czechoslovakia and, eventually and most crucially, Poland.
>
> *(Gowan 1999, 93)*

Although, with the US intervention in Yugoslavia, Germany was forced to cede military leadership to the United States and to modify its plan for a sphere of influence to EU expansion while accepting NATO's eastward expansion alongside, in the new century Europeans returned to elements of this vision again in their moves towards a common security policy and greater autonomy in military matters, as well as through initiatives like the Nord Stream II gas pipeline from Russia to Germany. Notwithstanding the unity that NATO has allegedly forged over Ukraine, a unity that already appeared too good to be true given that, not so long ago,

Macron had declared the alliance 'brain dead' and given that events—Washington's failure in Afghanistan, the 6 January 2021 assault on the Capitol, the resurgence of inflation, exposing the United States' puny productive capacities and threatening to choke off an already paltry recovery from the COVID-19 pandemic— continued to further underline multiple aspects of US decline, these impulses can only strengthen. It is not certain that pressures towards compliance with US strategies will overcome these historical tendencies.

In sum, while the United States aims at the violent defence of all aspects of the imperialist system on which its economy depends, its abilities to achieve them are more questionable than ever. Though this has been clear since the Iraq quagmire at the latest, US ruling circles have proved unable to undertake a serious re-evaluation of their foreign policy, to come up with a plan B, one that would accept the role of an 'ordinary' if still important economy. The evolution of the strategy of and legitimacy for such a plan B has to be the aim of any serious left alternative in the United States. As yet, however, it is not yet on the horizon.

Origins of the US hybrid war on Russia

By early 2022, the US quest for maximalist ends with ever less adequate means had stumbled into Biden's 'deliberate yet impulsive' (Parker et al. 2022) proxy war on Russia. Not content with rejoicing over the break-up of the Soviet Union, the US aims, as expressed by liberal internationalist Brzezinski, had long extended explicitly to a 'loosely confederated Russia' (Brzezinski 1997, 202) or its dismembering on the model of Yugoslavia if the overriding cause of its 'free market' opening up to Western subordination demanded it, a vision that has recently been updated to current 'woke' standards of discourse in US policy-making circles with talk of the 'moral and strategic imperative' to 'decolonize Russia' given 'Moscow's dominion over many indigenous non-Russian nations, and the brutal extent to which the Kremlin has taken [sic] to suppress their national self-expression and self-determination' (CSCE 2022).

Most assume that the current war against Russia over Ukraine started on 24 February 2022 when 'Russia attacked Ukraine'. In reality, the launch of Russian operations was the result of years of US provocations, going back at least to 2014, when the United States supported the Maidan counter-revolution, putting Ukraine under a right-wing regime reliant on neo-Nazis (Katchanovski 2019) and instigated a civil war that the United States has since kept festering, leading to over 14,000 casualties even before the launch of Russian operations on 24 February 2022, something entirely erased in the Western media. Over the past eight years, the United States has continued instigating Kyiv to refuse to implement the Minsk accords, shelling Donbass and deepening NATO's involvement in training and supporting Ukraine's military. These provocations reached a crescendo in the 'negotiations' between the United States and Russia in late 2021. Conducted in patent bad faith and amid high-octane publicity, these negotiations with the Kremlin aimed to discredit Russian security concerns and restore the tattered reputation of the US intelligence establishment after recent catastrophic failures in Afghanistan by feigning to 'predict' what the administration was provoking. Undoubtedly, President Zelensky's 19 February reference at the Munich Security Conference to Ukraine acquiring nuclear weapons (*The Kyiv Independent* 2022) made its own contribution given it was hardly far-fetched. After all, not only does Ukraine have that civilian nuclear technology that is the indispensable stepping stone to nuclear weapons, but also the United States has also long played a leading role in the nuclear weapons proliferation (Desai 2022) down to the recent sale of nuclear-powered submarines to Australia (Masterson 2021), a country lacking even civilian nuclear power, and the sale of nuclear-capable fighters to Germany. These provocations included the 2019 insertion, just before an election in which popular dissatisfaction with the post-Euromaidan government of Petro Poroshenko was poised to express itself, of a commitment to seeking NATO membership into Ukraine's constitution.

In the months leading up to the current Russian military operations, Ukrainian attacks on the Donetsk and Luhansk People's Republics were stepped up and even after 24 February 2022, the civil war character of the current conflict remained prominent as fighting in the Donbass region has been done by the military forces of the Donetsk and Luhansk Peoples' Republics with Russian support including logistic, air and hardware support.

Of course, US provocations of Russia date even earlier to when the United States realised that Russia under Putin was not amenable to complete subordination. In 2008, the United States and NATO offered Ukraine, along with Georgia, NATO membership, continuing the eastward expansion of NATO in 1999 and 2004. Though neither Ukraine nor Georgia became NATO members, further eastward expansion took place in 2009, 2017 and 2020. All this expansion has been in explicit violation of promises by the United States and the West not to expand NATO a single inch beyond East Germany (Norton 2022) and NATO has undertaken increasingly threatening military deployments in the new member countries, clearly directed at Russia.

For what it's worth, one may recall the events of December 1991, when Boris Yeltsin, Leonid Kravchuk and Stanislav Shushkevich, the leaders respectively of Russia, Ukraine and Belarus, were encouraged by the United States and the West to dissolve the USSR—even though 80% if the Soviet electorate had voted in a referendum earlier in the year to keep it together, on a turnout of 80%.

Multiple boomerangs

US abilities having long ceased to match its maximalist aims, the gap between ambition and capacity widened in the Ukraine conflict to the point where efforts to realise US ambitions did not just fail; they were counterproductive and boomeranged. Let us take each of the US aims in the current conflict in turn.

Destroying the Russian economy?

On the commencement of Moscow's special military operation, President Biden announced a slew of sanctions to 'impose severe costs on the Russian economy'. They were 'to maximise the long-term impact on Russia and to minimise the impact on the United States and our Allies'. Specifically, Biden said,

> We will limit Russia's ability to do business in Dollars, Euros, Pounds, and Yen to be part of the global economy. . . . We are going to stunt the ability to finance and grow the Russian military. We're going to . . . impair their ability to compete in a high-tech 21st century economy.
>
> *(The White House 2022)*

The aim of US sanctions—illegal under the UN Charter and the United States' post-Cold War weapon of first resort in its wars to impose its will around the world notwithstanding the long-known limits of their effectiveness (Mulder 2022)—was thus no less than the destruction of the Russian economy with the intention of provoking an uprising against Putin.

Their initial effect appeared to be tough. However, within weeks, despite Russia taking over Iran's status as the most sanctioned country in the world, despite the unrelenting propaganda to delegitimise Putin, the Russian economy stood up well and even strengthened, as indeed it had over the previous eight years when agricultural sanctions, for instance, prompted an agricultural revival, making Russia one of the major agricultural exporters in the world. President Putin's approval ratings rose above their already high levels (whereas President Biden's, as we noted earlier, sank).

With most of the rest of the world not joining sanctions, and Europe continuing its energy imports, Russia was able to continue exporting energy and commodities and even enjoy higher prices for them. This strengthened Russia's balance of trade and, after the government made arrangements to ensure payments within the terms of the financial sanctions, the rouble rose.

A herd of corporations stampeded out of Russia, citing ethical concerns, though they were actually fleeing the 'environment of . . . legal and financial hostility' (Beattie 2022): could they unknowingly end up doing business with a sanctioned individual and get prosecuted? Would they get paid? Could they repatriate profits? The closure of Western luxury brand shops got much publicity in the Western press, though that was hardly an unmitigated evil, the MacDonald's franchise in Russia was bought up by a Russian corporation and kept going under a new Russian brand Yet others 'sold' their businesses for a symbolic dollar with rights to buy them back at that price at a future date.

Shortages of essential items, though much predicted in the Western media, remained limited, suggesting that domestic production that diversified the economy and alternative trade relations, particularly with stepped up trade and investment and financial integration with China, had filled the gaps. To cope with such damage as war and sanctions did to the Russian economy, the Russian government also increased transfer payments to shore up demand, and its own legitimacy in a time of war.

Most decisively, sanctions proved to be a double-edged sword. Not only did the resulting rise in oil and gas prices assure Russia a steady stream of income, they hurt the sanctioning countries with inflation and shortages. Given Russia is a major exporter of energy, fertiliser and grain, it was not surprising that the inflation affliciting the West was led by food and fuel prices. The tragedy lay, of course, in inflation hurting ordinary and poor people in the sanctioning countries and in dozens of other food- and energy-dependent countries.

Politically, this only added to the woes of the US leadership, since despite—or perhaps because of—Biden's persistent attempts to blame all economic woes on Putin, the Third World turned resolutely away from the US economic offensive, while even the US public reacted by turning away from Biden to the point where his standing in the polls fell even lower than the worst showing of his reviled predecessor. Moreover, though the recession still unfolding as I write has its primary origin in the economic contradictions of the world order of a decaying capitalism we have already discussed extensively, the general economic chaos created by these unintended results both exacerbated the recessionary tendencies already present in the economy, and, crucially, created the widespread and, for President Biden and his party, politically dangerous impression that the recession was just another consequence of the United States' ill-advised provocation of Russia.

Destroying creditor power or undermining the dollar creditocracy?

The freezing of Russia's central bank's reserves, intended to be the fatal blow to Russia's economy, initially appeared spectacularly effective. It sent the rouble plunging and forced Russia's central bank to jack up interest rates to 20%, Many were convinced that sanctions were achieving their aims. The Council on Foreign Relations' Sebastian Mallaby (2022) announced grandly that freezing a country's reserves was a 'new weapon' able to 'turn a financially sound economy into a basket case'. However, while Russia was indeed unable to access nearly 60% of its $630 billion worth of reserves, it forced its European customers to pay in roubles through its one major non-sanctioned bank and managed to shore up the rouble's value.

Mallaby also suggested that the freezing of Russia's central bank reserves had benefitted the United States by destroying creditor power, freeing the United States from fear of its creditors. However, on the one hand, powerful debtors have never feared creditors—Philip IV of France destroyed his creditors, the Knights Templar, and Edward III of Britain defaulted against Italian banks, bankrupting them. On the other hand, it was not clear that the United States belonged in this company of powerful debtors. Mallaby argued that the United States had undermined any advantages Russia drew from being a creditor—there is no point in having assets if you cannot access—while the United States had what matters, 'a financial system that commands global trust, based on an independent central bank and an independent legal system'. There, however, lay the rub. In freezing Russia's reserves, essentially daylight robbery, the United States had demonstrated to a very attentive world that its financial and legal systems were far from independent and its financial system far from trustworthy. Robbing anyone's assets the behest of your government smacks not of independence either of institutions or the legal system, but of their profound politicisation, not to say criminalisation. It undermines such 'global trust' as the dollar-denominated international financial system, run out of New York and London, enjoys. Indeed, the undermining has been underway for some time. The United States has frozen reserves before, for instance, Venezuela's or Iran's and, most recently, Afghanistan's. Doing it to Russia, a much larger nuclear-armed permanent member of the United Nations Security Council, simply makes this aspect of US conduct more visible and a much larger number of governments and institutions wary. It amounts to the United States saying to the world, 'Put your money in our banks, we can confiscate it; put your assets in our territory, we can steal them; use our money and we can cancel it; put your yacht in our harbour, we can pirate it; put your gold in our vault, we can grab it' (Armstrong 2022).

In fact, sanctions against Russia are part of a long-established pattern of US behaviour, which has come into its own in the post-Cold War era. While the United States imposed illegal sanctions of all sorts during the Cold War, they had limited effect given that the Communist Bloc offered sanctioned countries, such as Cuba, alternative trade, technology and investment relationships. After the Cold War, imposing legal United Nations Security Council (UNSC)-backed sanctions briefly became possible but, after their horrific effects on the people of Iraq (Ali 2000) in the 1990s—they cut Iraq's national income to one-sixth, and led to over half a million child deaths due to malnutrition—became widely known, their use became profoundly illegitimate.

Thereafter, the search for 'smart sanctions', allegedly designed not to affect ordinary people, targeting only elites and their wealth—lighted on the US dollar and the financial system. As the country controlling most of the major structures of the dollar creditocracy (Desai and Hudson 2021), which functions, *faute de mieux*, as the world's monetary system, the United States could simply make it difficult for governments, central banks, financial institutions or individuals to conduct dollar transactions, effectively ejecting them from it. This weapon was first tried, we are told, by the Bush administration in cutting terrorist financing and it was observed that its effectiveness lay not just in compliance but in 'over compliance': governments and financial institutions bent over backwards to stay away from even the whiff of transactions with sanctioned entities.

Thus, in the twenty-first century, the way was open for the use of financial sanctions. However, when used against other countries, they amount to weaponising, and thus undermining, the very dollar system that is a critical part of apparatus of power the United States wields to achieve its goals. After 1971, as we have seen, the dollar's world role has relied on expanding dollar-denominated financial transactions by enticing investors into it. However, such enticement had to take the form of ever more volatile and unstable financialisations or asset bubbles that not only inevitably burst, causing great economic harm, they also threatened the very financial system that inflated them. This quality of the US financial system had already reduced its attractions for those whose participation in it was essential to its functioning as the basis of the dollar's world role. After 2008, not only did inflows fail to resume growing to reach new peaks as they had done for decades, but they remained less than half their 2008 peak a decade later (Lund et al. 2018). Since then, as we have seen, the inability of these dollar-denominated asset markets to attract sufficient funds to hold up asset values has led to the Federal Reserve's massive balance sheet expansion to hold them up. This already introduces a very substantial element of official manipulation in the dollar's value, the value of a wide range of dollar-denominated assets and the functioning of the dollar system and even this is now threatened. Dealing with resurgent inflation may well require, as we have seen, interest rate increases and quantitative tightening—disposing off the assets on the Federal Reserve's balance sheet—at levels that may crash these asset markets, and the dollar creditocracy.

To this core contradiction of the system, we may add its increasing partiality to US interests and aims demonstrated in the freezing of certain countries' reserves. Another prominent example was the case of the New York court's judgement in favour of vulture funds (Wolf 2014) that sought recoup the full value of Argentina's debt even though the established rules of the game entitled them only to a fraction of the debt they had bought at a heavy discount. This only undermines faith in the fairness and predictability of the system. There is also the case of sanctions against Iran, which inconveniences many US allies who wished to continue trading with Iran. Wary of the United States' mounting use of financial sanctions, Russia, the EU and China have been building alternative international payments systems in the form of SPFS, INSTEX and CIPS, respectively, as well as domestic ones such as China's Union Pay, India's RuPay and Brazil's ELO and they are, further, being coordinated internationally. Finally, it is often forgotten how much the gendarmes of the dollar system, the IMF and the World Bank, have shrunk in terms of their activity and reach as the China-centred international financial system, including not only the Asian Infrastructure Investment Bank but also the major banks of China's financial system, has expanded. In effect, what the United States' financial sanctions are only accelerating the decline in US power and influence instead of stalling it, as they were meant to do.

Defeating Russia?

Rising hostilities in the new century, including NATO's relentless eastward expansion and deployment of ever more threatening weapons on Russia's borders, had already motivated Russia to begin developing new weapons systems, while the 2002 US withdrawal from the Anti-Ballistic Missile Treaty, designed to prevent a new arms race for offensive weapons, left it free to do so. Russia developed its hypersonic missiles, capable of undermining the United States' strategic advantage and President Putin was able to announce in 2018 that, testing being complete, they would now enter production (Martyanov 2019), causing many in Washington to speak of a 'sputnik moment' (Giannetti 2019). These missiles have played an important role in Russia's methodical progress in destroying Ukraine's offensive capacities and neo-Nazi units and securing the Donetsk and Luhansk republics with less than half the personnel deployed by Ukraine, including the forces of the Donbass republics.

Though the US-led capitalist world's role is limited to supplying weapons and though one might imagine, not least given the storied military–industrial complexes they have, particularly the gargantuan US one, that they can supply arms, and thus prolong the war, endlessly, it appears they cannot, and that may be tied to their neoliberal capitalist and financialised character. A couple of months into the war, President Zelensky was already complaining that his troops were not getting enough arms even as Russian and Donbass troops were making steady territorial gains. A comment on the authoritative Royal United Services Institute website was revealing. Given the rate at which arms supplied by the West were being used in Ukraine, or destroyed by Russian strikes, it argued, 'The rate of ammunition and equipment consumption in Ukraine can only be sustained by a large-scale industrial base.' That is precisely what was lacking since the major capitalist countries have not only 'scaled down military–industrial capacity' but also 'sacrificed scale and effectiveness for efficiency' (a byword for the profit-making bottom line).

> The winner in a prolonged war between two near-peer powers is still based on which side has the strongest industrial base. A country must either have the manufacturing capacity to build massive quantities of ammunition or have other manufacturing industries that can be rapidly converted to ammunition production. Unfortunately, the West no longer seems to have either.
>
> *(Vershinin 2022)*

Three 'flawed assumptions' accounted for the West's combat unreadiness. First, that 'precision-guided weapons will reduce overall ammunition consumption' by eliminating enemies' capabilities. However, more ordinary weapons are 'achieving a great deal of precision [because the] digitisation of global maps, combined with a massive proliferation of drones, allows geolocation and targeting with increased precision, with video evidence demonstrating the ability to score first strike hits by indirect fires'. This reduces any special advantage of precision-guided weapons. Second is the assumption that 'industry can be turned on and off at will'. It 'was imported from the business sector' and has spread through US government culture. If a plant is shut down given the episodic nature of military demand, or business and production lines closed for lack of orders, re-establishing them is difficult. Finally, there is the assumption that ammunition consumption will remain low (Vershinin 2022). The writer was, of course, issuing a wake-up call for Western governments, though, if they had made such false assumptions in the first place and initiated the war with so little forethought, it is not clear if this call will be heeded, particularly given that the loss of life, cities and territory is concentrated in faraway Ukraine.

By mid-2022, not even the most sophisticated propaganda and psyops could hide Russia's quietly methodical achievement of its objectives on the ground; Western publics were, in any case, more concerned about rising inflation than about the war. With alternative media well-entrenched in recent decades and many non-Western state and private news outlets—Telesur, Al Jazeera, RT, WION, Global Times—reaching them, Western publics also had increasing access very different narratives on the war.

Already in late May 2022, it was clear that the United States would prove unable to snatch even the appearance of a victory, however limited. Just as the world's business and ruling elites were about to gather in Davos once again, a *New York Times* editorial opined that, while the US goal should remain the 'freedom' of Ukraine, 'it is still not in America's best interest to plunge into an all-out war with Russia, even if a negotiated peace may require Ukraine to make some hard decisions' because 'Russia remains too strong' and that the President should make clear to Ukrainian authorities that 'there is a limit to how far the United States and NATO will go to confront Russia, and limits to the arms, money and political support they can muster' (*The New York Times* Editorial Board 2022). Of course, with the United States having steered clear of any direct confrontation with Russia all along, the real message was to stop the funding and arms deliveries that were keeping the conflict festering.

So, not only was the Biden administration unable to rally the world around to his war on Russia, and not only were allies divided and resentful at the economic sacrifices demanded, it is not clear if US ruling circles were behind it anymore.

Strengthening alliances?

When the United States imposed sanctions, the identity and positioning of its allies were critical: 'The United States is not doing this alone', Biden said:

> For months, we've been building a coalition of partners representing well more than half of the global economy. Twenty-seven members of the European Union, including France, Germany, Italy—as well as the United Kingdom, Canada, Japan, Australia, New Zealand, and many others—to [sic] amplify the joint impact of our response.
>
> *(The White House 2022)*

However, the success of these latest of US efforts to rally allies is not assured. This is not least because, serious as the conflict over Ukraine is, it is but a staging post in the wider US wars in which the chief enemy remains China. Given that even the current conflict is demanding a level of subordination and tolerance of economic and political pain that is likely to prove intolerable, it is far from clear that allies are ready for more punishing conflicts to come, particularly given that any rewards to be reaped may go disproportionately to the United States, as appears to be the case with US firms benefitting from energy sales to Europe.

While the United States and the United Kingdom are taking the lead in the propaganda and sanctions war, their economies, compared with their allies, are more deindustrialised and less integrated with the Russian economy, limiting potential damage. Even so, their sanctions are designed to minimise damage. Meanwhile, the more industrial European economies, more closely integrated with the Russian, have also designed their sanctions more elaborately and their core reliance on Russian gas continues and gas still flows to Europe, inter alia, via Ukraine. While various commitments are being made about ending this reliance, they are far enough in the future to leave open the possibility of reconsideration in light of the military outcome, particularly as the infrastructure of pipelines remains intact.

Early developments in the war permitted the United States to boast of reuniting NATO. It got most European countries to agree to participate, in one way or another, in imposing sanctions on Russia and supplying lethal aid to Ukraine. It got Germany to overturn its long-standing refusal to supply weapons to countries in conflict, commit to spending 2% of GDP on defence, and even announce a €100 billion expansion of its defence spending. The United States even managed to pressure the Swiss to drop their centuries-old neutrality to enact sanctions against Russia.

However, there was, from the start, something contrived about brandishing these accomplishments as major victories. Almost all countries imposed sanctions that were largely symbolic and convenient. Countries that imported little or no oil from Russia, for instance, boasted of banning oil imports. Germany only announced plans for reducing its heavy reliance on Russian energy, beginning by phasing out the import of oil, which it relied on the least, by the end of the year, leaving plenty of time to await military outcomes, while the phasing out of other forms of energy from Russia was pushed back into the even more distant future. The provision of lethal aid from so many different countries only ran up a long tab that Ukraine would eventually have to pay in return for often used, obsolete and uncoordinated arms, many of which its soldiers were not trained to use.

Many other historical cleavages were also widening as the crisis unfolded. East European member states have different historically and strategically grounded attitudes about the war. Traditionally Russophobic Eastern European and Baltic countries called out the French and the Germans for continuing discussions with Russia. Turkey objected to Finnish and Swedish membership. Germany and France continued not only talking with President Putin and seeking a negotiated solution, but they even pressed this on President Zelensky during a visit in the runup to the EU summit that was to decide on Ukraine's candidate status for EU membership (Marsden 2022) while the latter was even witnessing the electoral surge of forces clearly opposed to NATO.

By late May 2022, as Russian military gains on the ground could no longer be denied, prominent voices began to oppose Biden's war. Veteran diplomat Henry Kissinger argued that Russia had always been and remains part of the stability of Europe and escalating tensions with it could only be disastrous for that continent. Restraint and compromise, including Ukraine accepting territorial losses, was better. An editorial in the normally hawkish *New York Times* (The Editorial Board of the *New York Times* 2022), while repeating many illusions about Ukrainian military advances, nevertheless argued that it was not in the US interest to 'plunge into an all-out war with Russia' even if it meant that Ukraine faced some 'hard decisions', a reference to territorial concessions. Moreover, it added, 'popular support for a war far from U.S. shores will not continue indefinitely. Inflation is a much bigger issue for American voters than Ukraine, and the disruptions to global food and energy markets are likely to intensify.' Meanwhile, an opinion piece in the *Washington Post* by noted editor of *The Nation*, Katrina van dan Heuvel, declared that it was time to open up debate on war aims and realities on the ground, including neo-Nazis in the Ukraine government and military (Heuvel 2022).

Moreover, by June 2022, the focus was shifting to China. NATO's Madrid Summit was billed as the organisation's most consequential, a 'transformative' gathering of the post-Cold War era with a crammed agenda including demonstrating its much-vaunted unity, admitting Sweden and Finland, supplying more heavy weapons to Ukraine, adopting a new strategic concept and, above all, creating a Pacific presence. To that end, Japan, South Korea, Australia and New Zealand were invited to attend. The strategic concept is expected to focus on the re-emergence of 'great power competition' and include consideration of the question 'how much emphasis should NATO put on Russia's immediate threat to Europe, as opposed to the more systemic challenge represented by China's strategic rise?' (Simón 2022).

This is certain to give rise to major tensions. The inverse relationship between the United States and the United Kingdom's venomous rhetoric about Russia and Putin and their actual contribution and sacrifice already contrasts highly with the hara-kiri they demand of the Europeans, who will also be more immediately affected if the conflict escalates. That has already bred resentment. If the United States attempts a similar proxy war against China over Taiwan, it can only raise these tensions higher. European countries already exhausted by the price they have had to pay for the war on Russia are unlikely to agree to what they will be required against China. Too many of them have been, rightly and beneficially, deepening economic ties with China. If such cleavages widen, it will also become clear that the new arms expenditure commitments undertaken US allies, such as Germany or Japan, can be re-directed to quite independent uses (Leonard 2022).

It is entirely possible that, as this situation unfolds, it will once again open up the possibility that European countries, particularly Germany and France, will resume asserting their autonomy from the United States as they have long sought to do, pursuing their associated inclination to work with Russia and, over recent decades, with China, on areas of mutual interest. This group even included the United Kingdom, which in the early 2010s, joined the Asian Infrastructure Investment Bank, over President Obama's loud objections. For the moment, European capitals seem home to the most pro-US governments. However, with popular protest against the consequences of the war, and perhaps the war itself, widening, they may not remain so for long.

It should now be clear that the United States is pursuing goals that long ago exceeded its dwindling abilities. It is now time to clarify that arguably the ultimate obscenity of the current war over Ukraine—the discourse about which is liberally peppered with Western media accusations of war crimes and genocide not only against Putin but also against Russians in general—is the wanton destruction of a country in such a vain pursuit.

Ukraine as theatre and proxy

While encouraging Ukraine to provoke Russia to the fullest, including refusing to implement the Minsk II accords, the United States refuses to provide Ukraine any real support beyond the verbal and the lucrative—praising Ukrainians' courage and selling them arms. What the United States hides behind its argument that doing more—for example, involving its own armed forces directly in the conflict, as in Iraq—would be very dangerous, an armed confrontation between two of the biggest nuclear powers is that morally and politically unacceptable, it is sacrificing Ukrainians in a vainglorious pursuit of power and profit for its capitalists. It should have counselled restraint and negotiation all along, particularly since any viable outcome that was good for Ukraine, its people, the region and the world, had to involve negotiations to achieve something resembling like the Minsk II accords. The hypocrisy and irresponsibility of encouraging Ukraine to refuse to negotiate and instead persist in a war that cannot be won, prolonging the conflict so the United States can win more propaganda and business advantages is breathtaking. This is the real war crime. The United States has pushed Kiev to indulge in the worst practices, including arming civilians, so as to incite confusion, looting, marauding and killing of Ukrainians by Ukrainians, ensuring that the conflict continues.

In all this, President Biden has played a personally noteworthy role. Early on in his presidency, when questioned in a CNN interview about alleged Russian disinformation efforts involving his son's liaisons with Ukrainian politicians and oligarchs in the 2020 elections, he called President Putin a 'killer' (CNN 2021). After the military conflict began, Biden followed this up by calling the Russian President a 'war criminal', something which stuck in the craw of even his most loyal supporters, such as Britain's *The Guardian*, which had to clarify that 'declaring someone a war criminal is not as simple as just saying the words' (Associated Press in Washington 2022). And only weeks later, Biden lashed out at Putin again, giving the impression that he was calling for regime change in Russia, an impression his officials then had to 'walk back'. While we will know for sure, if at all, only in time, the visceral anger Biden seems to harbour for Putin may well be rooted Hunter Biden's questionable liaisons with Ukrainian politicians and oligarchs, particularly his membership on the board of its energy giant Burisma, controlled by the same oligarch, Igor Kolomoisky, who bankrolled Zelensky's bid for Ukraine's presidency. Those liaisons are under renewed scrutiny after the Democratic Party and a cooperative media put the lid on it for the 2020 elections.

The Western media portrays President Volodymyr Zelensky, somewhat incredibly, as a Churchillian war hero even as it reports on how his image is manufactured by PR agencies. The persona created is most useful to the United States: it demands the forms of aid the United States can either give or wishes to seek from Congress, it berates any European government for backsliding, it aids in the whitewashing of the neo-Nazis on which his regime is ever more reliant even as it bans opposition parties.

Where does all this leave Ukraine itself? Brussels and the EU and Washington and NATO dangle the carrots of EU and NATO membership before Ukraine. Both know full well that either is impossible. After lots of noise about fast-tracking membership, thanks to disagreements among members who must all approve membership, only 'candidate' status was being extended to Ukraine in the run up to the EU summit in late June 2022, effectively confinement in an ante-chamber, requiring it to conform to often punishing pre-conditions with no guarantee of eventual entry. NATO entry is also opposed by many members. As for NATO, its rules stipulate that no country whose borders are in dispute can be inducted into NATO. Yet the war of impossible NATO inclusion continues. Moreover, while Ukraine may never be in NATO, NATO is in Ukraine, and has been for many years, funding, supplying arms and even training the Ukrainian army's notorious neo-Nazi units, such as the Azov battalion, as top Nazi hunters have recently confirmed (Pugliese 2022).

Indeed, in the current situation, it is, from the US point of view in particular, imperative that Ukraine not be in NATO. If it were, fellow members, the United States included, would have had to go to war with Russia and shoulder its costs. Since it is not, the US military–industrial complex, and that of other countries, are profiteering hand over fist. What is billed as 'aid', as with development aid, is simply financing, not funding (Singh 2022). It is lent, not given. Ukraine, or whatever much-diminished successor entity survives this war, will have to pay. Non-payment can be another excuse for intervention in the region. So, we can expect more macabre developments involving the entity that must pay up.

Given the already parlous state of Ukraine's finances, the lending has had to get inventive. This has recently led to the dusting off of 'lend lease' for operationalisation. 'Lend lease', we are told, enabled the United States to be the 'arsenal of democracy' during the Second World War, and critically contributed to defeating Hitler. News stories explaining what it involves, routinely quoted Allied leaders of the time expressing their appreciation for it. Unfortunately, while they had no choice but to do so, the reality was considerably more sordid. Lend lease was devised when the United States ran out of conventional financing arrangements. New means had to be found to supply arms to the allies, or, in reality, keep selling them to customers. That was when lend lease was devised: the United States would lend or lease these weapons to the allies who would 'return' them or pay for them after the war.

For Ukraine, lend lease will, in the words of Senator Shaheen, allow the United States to 'run a tab' on Ukraine's arms purchases (Mitchell 2022). It is already long and growing even as the Ukrainian state was estimated to need $7 billion a month to continue functioning minimally as a state (*BBC News* 2022). News stories about lend lease also remind readers that the United States discounted allied debt owning under it after the Second World War. Be that as it may, not only did the United Kingdom take until 2006 to pay it down, the *quid pro quo* for any discounting included policy compliance through which the United States broke Britain economically as it demanded more liberal economic policies than Britain's economy could bear. What the United States will do to what remains of Ukraine is going to be a horror film coming soon.

Meanwhile, as refugees began pouring out of Ukraine, the racism of reporters, opinion columnists and policymakers, and even many ordinary citizens of Western countries, who favoured refugees from Ukraine over those from non-white parts of the world, along with the racism of some Ukrainians, who kept underlining how 'European' they, their country and their cities are, came in for considerable criticism. Unacceptable as this was, it did not exhaust the racism that is at work in the Ukraine conflict.

The overlooked racism is the consolation prize poor whites receive from white elites, the prize that permits the latter to consolidate support among the former, whose economic subordination continues or even gets worse. What Ukrainians can hope to have in the embrace of the West, if they ever get there from the conflict into which the West has landed them, will be an even lesser version of the fortunes enjoyed, or should we say suffered, by other countries of the former Communist East and the post-Soviet space that have become integrated into the Western European economy.

Promises of NATO membership in 2008, followed by offers of EU membership, have only ever offered Ukrainians the dubious privileges of decreasing their security to enhance the international aggression capabilities of the West and permitting the devastation of their economies by the EU. Given what happened to other former Communist East European countries, we can expect that under the tender mercies of the IMF, World Bank, EU and United States, what remains of Ukraine's industry will be gutted to eliminate competition to Western corporations. They will take over the most lucrative parts of the Ukrainian economy, buy up their land and exploit their natural resources and cheap labour in situ. Bereft of properly functioning economies, the people of these countries will then be offered the dubious privilege of travelling throughout the continent of Europe so that, *ex situ*, they can earn low wages as farm and service sector workers—and yes, consider themselves white and European as a consolation prize. Even that is of dubious value since their economic subordination is sure to breed, and has already bred, new forms of racism directed at Ukrainians in many parts of Europe.

The future of capitalism in the balance

The United States' proxy war against Russia may be only a way-station in its larger confrontation with China, but it is already exposing the limits of US capacities. Since the early twentieth century, the United States has sought to emulate the domination it thought it had seen the UK exercise over the world economy in the nineteenth century, but never succeeded. Its efforts did, however, prolong the life of a capitalism that had exhausted such historical utility as it ever had, giving the US the singular role it has played in the twentieth century, particularly in capitalism's contest with socialism.

In the current war, however, this more than century-long project has reached a tipping point where US actions are not merely failures, they are counterproductive, accelerating the shift in the world's centre of gravity away from itself and the West and towards socialist China.

Habits of their cosmopolitan minds lead many to ask whether China will be the 'successor' to 'US hegemony'. If our analysis is anything to go by, there has never been such a thing. The United Kingdom's dominance, born of its historical priority as an industrial nation, was lost to industrial challengers by the late nineteenth century. The world was already too multi- and pluripolar for US hegemony and is only more so now. By leading world growth, China will certainly overtake the United States as the largest economy in the world, but will still remain one among other weighty economies.

China's world-historic significance will lie not in being a new 'hegemon' but elsewhere, its internal political dynamics permitting. Hitherto, its market reforms notwithstanding, the party-state's control has corrected for their excesses and kept China on the socialist market economy path that has secured many successes so far. It will continue doing so provided the powerful neoliberal and capitalist forces within the party-state pushing for greater internal and external liberalisation do not prevail.

Provided they do not, China's successes will be beacons. While China on the one hand, and the United Kingdom and the United States on the other, represent two extremes on the spectrum of liberal and regulated economies, most countries fall somewhere in between. Policymakers and public opinion in a world witness to the stark opposition between neoliberal failures on public health, the economy and in politics, and the successes among the more regulated societies will feel their respective repulsion and attraction. Neoliberal ruling classes seeking to stay the neoliberal course will face multiplying problems arising from their contradictory systems and popular pressure to resolve them in ever more illiberal ways. The only question is whether these infractions of liberalism will take right-wing, authoritarian or fascist forms or left-wing and socialist forms. The world is once more before that choice, as it was in the 1930s.

Only the development of strong left forces will tip the balance towards the latter in each country. Though few countries are home to such forces today, and though the left bears heavy legacy burdens, politics can change rapidly in crisis conditions, particularly if the historical mistakes of the left in leading capitalist countries are clearly recognised.

Inevitably, this will occur, depending on the depth of the crisis and the ambition and capability of progressive forces, at different times and to different extents in different countries. As this process unfolds, inevitably internationally, it will broaden the front along which socialism will advance by increasing cooperation among countries led by popular forces who are capable of recognising that *the path to socialism winds through nations.*

References

Ali, Tariq. 2000. 'Throttling Iraq', *New Left Review*, 5(Sept/Oct), https://newleftreview.org/issues/ii5/articles/tariq-ali-throttling-iraq

Anonymous. 2021. 'The Longer Telegram: Toward A New American China Strategy', *Atlantic Council Strategy Papers*, (Accessed 5 June 2022) www.atlanticcouncil.org/content-series/atlantic-council-strategy-paper-series/the-longer-telegram/

Armstrong, Patrick. 2022. 'Hiatus', *Russia Observer*, 20 March, (Accessed 5 June 2022) https://patrickarmstrong.ca/author/gparmru/

Arrighi, Giovanni. 2005. 'Hegemony Unravelling II', *New Left Review*, *32*(33), pp. 23–80. https://newleftreview.org/issues/ii32/articles/giovanni-arrighi-hegemony-unravelling-1

Associated Press in Washington. 2022. 'Is Vladimir Putin a War Criminal, and Who Decides?', *The Guardian*, 17 March, (Accessed 31 May 2022) www.theguardian.com/world/2022/mar/17/vladimir-putin-war-criminal-ukraine-russia-president-justice

BBC News. 2022. 'Ukraine War: Country Needs $7bn a Month in Aid, Zelensky Says', 22 April, (Accessed 23 June 2022) www.bbc.com/news/business-61184275

Beattie, Alan. 2022. 'Sanctions More Than Ethics Have Spurred Corporate Flight From Russia', *Financial Times*, 9 March, (Accessed 5 June 2022) www.ft.com/content/fed1ebb5-e97d-424f-a313-2bb0d1cb8181

Bevins, Vincent. 2020. *The Jakarta Method: Washington's Anticommunist Crusade & the Mass Murder Program That Shaped Our World*. New York: PublicAffairs.

Blinken, Anthony J. 2022. 'The Administration's Approach to the People's Republic of China', *Speech, U.S. Department of State*, 26 May, (Accessed 23 June 2022) www.state.gov/the-administrations-approach-to-the-peoples-republic-of-china/

Block, Fred. 2008. 'Swimming Against the Current: The Rise of a Hidden Developmental State in the United States', *Politics & Society*, 36(2) (June), pp. 169–206. https://doi.org/10.1177/0032329208318731

Brzezinski, Zbignew. 1997. *The Grand Chessboard* (Vol. 1). New York: Basic Books.

Cable News Network (CNN). 2021. 'Biden: I Think Putin Is a Killer', *CNN Politics*, 17 March, (Accessed 31 May 2022) www.cnn.com/videos/politics/2021/03/17/president-biden-vladimir-putin-russia-gma-newday-vpx.cnn

Cohen, Benjamin J. 2008. *International Political Economy: An Intellectual History*. Princeton: Princeton University Press.

Coleman, Peter. 1989. *The Liberal Conspiracy: The Congress for Cultural Freedom and the Struggle for the Mind of Postwar Europe*. New York: Free Press.

Commission on Security and Cooperation in Europe (CSCE). 2022. *Decolonising Russia: A Moral and Strategic Imperative*. Washington, DC: CSCE. www.csce.gov/international-impact/press-and-media/press-releases/decolonization-russia-be-discussed-upcoming

Desai, Radhika. 2013. *Geopolitical Economy: After US Hegemony, Globalization and Empire*. London: Pluto.

Desai, Radhika. 2022. 'The Long Shadow of Hiroshima: Capitalism and Nuclear Weapons', *International Critical Thought*, 8 April, pp. 1–21. https://doi.org/10.1080/21598282.2022.2051582

Desai, Radhika; and Hudson, Michael. 2021. 'Beyond Dollar Creditocracy: A Geopolitical Economy', *Real World Economic Review*, 97(23) September 2021, pp. 20–39. https://rwer.wordpress.com/2021/09/23/rwer-issue-no-97/

Duménil, Gérard; and Lévy, Dominique. 2004. *Capital Resurgent: Roots of the Neoliberal Revolution*. Cambridge: Harvard University Press.

Dzarasov, Ruslan. 2013. *The Conundrum of Russian Capitalism: The Post-Soviet Economy in the World System*. London: Pluto Press.

Ferguson, Niall; and Schularick, Moritz. 2007. '"Chimerica" and the Global Asset Market Boom', *International Finance*, 10(3), pp. 215–39. https://doi.org/10.1111/j.1468-2362.2007.00210.x

Ferguson, Thomas. 1995. *Golden Rule: The Investment Theory of Party Competition and the Logic of Money-Driven Political Systems*. Chicago: University of Chicago Press.

Fusero, Stefania. 2022. 'Taiwan: Red Lines and Strategic Ambiguity', *New Cold War*, 8 May, (Accessed 23 June 2022) https://newcoldwar.org/taiwan-red-lines-and-strategic-ambiguity/

Galston, William A. 2022. 'How the Ukraine War Changed History', *Wall Street Journal*, 3 May, (Accessed 30 May 2022) www.wsj.com/articles/ukraine-war-changed-history-defense-spending-allies-nato-baltics-sweden-finland-macron-china-russia-military-spending-11651590975

Ganser, Daniele. 2004. *NATO's Secret Armies: Operation GLADIO and Terrorism in Western Europe*. New York: Frank Cass.

Giannetti, William. 2019. 'Are Russian Hypersonic Weapons Leading to a New "Sputnik" Moment?', *The National Interest*, 8 June, (Accessed 31 May 2022) https://nationalinterest.org/blog/buzz/are-russian-hypersonic-weapons-leading-new-sputnik-moment-61562

Gowan, Peter. 1999. 'The NATO Powers and the Balkan Tragedy', *New Left Review*, pp. 83–105. https://newleftreview.org/issues/i234/articles/peter-gowan-the-nato-powers-and-the-balkan-tragedy

Heusgen, Christoph. 2022. 'The War in Ukraine Will Be a Historic Turning Point', *Foreign Affairs*, 12 May, (Accessed 30 May 2022) www.foreignaffairs.com/articles/germany/2022-05-12/war-ukraine-will-be-historic-turning-point

Heuvel, Katrina vanden. 2022. 'We Need a Real Debate About the Ukraine War', *The Washington Post*, 24 May, (Accessed 31 May 2022) www.washingtonpost.com/opinions/2022/05/24/ukraine-russia-war-biden-strategy-debate/?utm_campaign=wp_post_most&utm_medium=email&utm_source=newsletter&wpisrc=nl_most&carta-url=https%3A%2F%2Fs2.washingtonpost.com%2Fcar-ln-tr%2F36eb1a7%2F628cfec0956121755a8d04fb%2F6259a68099423173ac57cc8c%2F17%2F72%2F628cfec0956121755a8d04fb

Hunnicutt, Trevor. 2022. 'With China in Focus, Biden Makes $150 Million Commitment to ASEAN Leaders', *Reuters*, 12 May, (Accessed 5 June 2022) www.reuters.com/world/asia-pacific/with-china-focus-biden-plans-150-million-commitment-asean-leaders-2022–05–12/

Kagarlitsky, Boris; Desai, Radhika; and Freeman, Alan (eds). 2019. *Russia, Ukraine and Contemporary Imperialism*. New York: Routledge.

Katchanovski, Ivan. 2019. 'The Far Right, the Euromaidan, and the Maidan Massacre in Ukraine', *Journal of Labor and Society*, 23(1), pp. 1–25. https://doi.org/10.1111/wusa.12457

Kimble, James J. 2022. 'Ukrainian War Bonds: The American Roots of a Powerful Financial and Propaganda Tool', *The Conversation*, 8 March, (Accessed 31 May 2022) https://theconversation.com/ukrainian-war-bonds-the-american-roots-of-a-powerful-financial-and-propaganda-tool-178502

Klare, Michael T. 2022. 'United States: Energy as a Strategic Tool', *Le Monde diplomatique*, June, (Accessed 23 June 2022) https://mondediplo.com/2022/06/03us-energy

Krastev, Ivan; and Leonard, Mark. 2022. 'Peace Versus Justice: The Coming European Split over the War in Ukraine', *European Council on Foreign Relations*, 15 June, (Accessed 23 June 2022) https://ecfr.eu/publication/peace-versus-justice-the-coming-european-split-over-the-war-in-ukraine/

The Kyiv Independent. 2022. 'Zelensky's Full Speech at Munich Security Conference', 19 February, (Accessed 31 May 2022) https://kyivindependent.com/national/zelenskys-full-speech-at-munich-security-conference/

Leonard, Mark. 2022. 'The Real End of Pax Americana', *Foreign Affairs*, 13 June, (Accessed 23 June 2022) www.foreignaffairs.com/articles/japan/2022-06-13/real-end-pax-americana?utm_medium=newsletters&utm_source=fatoday&utm_campaign=The%20Real%20End%20of%20Pax%20Americana%20&utm_content=20220613&utm_term=FA%20Today%20-%20112017

Lund, Susan; Mehta, Asheet; Manyika, James; and Goldshtein, Diana. 2018. 'A Decade After the Global Financial Crisis: What Has (and Hasn't) Changed?', *McKinsey Global Institute*, 29 August, (Accessed 24 May 2022) www.mckinsey.com/industries/financial-services/our-insights/a-decade-after-the-global-financial-crisis-what-has-and-hasnt-changed

Mallaby, Sebastian. 2022. 'War in Ukraine Has Created a New Financial Weapon in the West', *The Washington Post*, 1 March, (accessed 5 June 2022) www.washingtonpost.com/opinions/2022/03/01/ukraine-war-sanctions-new-financial-weapon-against-russia/

Mandel, Ernest. 1970. *Europe Versus America? Contradictions of Imperialism*. London: New Left Books.

Marsden, Rachel. 2022. 'As the Bloc Faces a Looming Energy Crisis, Are EU Leaders Using Potential Membership to Rein in Ukraine's Zelensky?', *RT*, 17 June, (Accessed 23 June 2022) www.rt.com/russia/557322-prospect-ukraines-eu-accession/

Martyanov, Andrei. 2019. *The (Real) Revolution in Military Affairs*. Atlanta, GA: Clarity Press.

Masterson, Julia. 2021. 'U.S., UK Pledge Nuclear Submarines for Australia', *Arms Control Association*, October, (Accessed 31 May 2022) www.armscontrol.org/act/2021-10/news/us-uk-pledge-nuclear-submarines-australia

Mearsheimer, John J. 2021. 'The Inevitable Rivalry: America, China, and the Tragedy of Great-Power Politics', *Foreign Affairs*, November/December, (Accessed 23 June 2022) www.foreignaffairs.com/articles/china/2021-10-19/inevitable-rivalry-cold-war

Mitchell, Andrea. 2022. 'Sen. Shaheen: Lend-Lease Bill Will Let U.S. Run a "Tab" for Aid to Ukraine, Speeding Weapons Delivery', *MSNBC*, 7 April, (Accessed 31 May 2022) www.msnbc.com/andrea-mitchell-reports/watch/sen-shaheen-lend-lease-bill-will-let-u-s-run-a-tab-for-aid-to-ukraine-speeding-weapons-delivery-137237573632

Mulder, Nicholas. 2022. *The Economic Weapon: The Rise of Sanctions as a Tool of Modern War*. New Haven: Yale University Press.

The New York Times, The Editorial Board. 2022. 'The War in Ukraine Is Getting Complicated, and America Isn't Ready', *The New York Times*, 19 May, (Accessed 30 May 2022) www.nytimes.com/2022/05/19/opinion/america-ukraine-war-support.html

Norton, Benjamin. 2022. 'US Gov't Knew NATO Expansion to Ukraine Would Force Russia to Intervene', *Multipolarista*, 27 February, (Accessed 31 May 2022) https://multipolarista.com/2022/02/27/us-nato-expansion-ukraine-russia-intervene/

O'Neill, Jim. 2001. 'Building Better Global Economic BRICs', *Global Economics Paper*, November, 66, pp. 1–15.

Parboni, Riccardo. 1986. 'The Dollar Weapon: From Nixon to Reagan', *New Left Review*, 158(5). https://newleftreview.org/issues/i158/articles/riccardo-parboni-the-dollar-weapon-from-nixon-to-reagan

Parker, Ashley; Pager, Tyler; and Sotomayor, Marianna. 2022. 'Biden at War: Inside a Deliberate Yet Impulsive Ukraine Strategy', *The Washington Post*, 7 April (Accessed 23 June 2022) www.washingtonpost.com/politics/2022/04/07/biden-war-ukraine/

Pilkington, Ed. 2014. 'US Official Apologises to EU Counterparts for Undiplomatic Language', *The Guardian*, 6 February, (Accessed 5 June 2022) www.theguardian.com/world/2014/feb/06/us-ukraine-russia-eu-victoria-nuland

Pugliese, David. 2022. 'Canada Failed When It Trained Ukrainian Troops Linked to the Far Right, Says Nazi Hunter', *Ottawa Citizen*, 13 April, (Accessed 31 May 2022) https://ottawacitizen.com/news/national/defence-watch/canada-failed-when-it-trained-ukrainian-troops-linked-to-the-far-right-says-nazi-hunter/wcm/cd79a966–0b2e-4251-83af-50627cdbd699/amp/

Quincy Institute for Responsible Statecraft. 2022. 'The New Right: Ukraine Marks Major Foreign Policy Shift Among Conservatives', *Zoom Webinar*, 22 June, (Accessed 23 June 2022) https://quincyinst.org/event/the-new-right-ukraine-marks-major-foreign-policy-shift-among-conservatives/

Rachman, Gideon. 2020. 'A New Cold War: Trump, Xi and the Escalating US–China Confrontation', *Financial Times*, 4 October, (Accessed 30 May 2022) www.ft.com/content/7b809c6a-f733-46f5-a312-9152aed28172

Sakwa, Richard. 2020. 'Is Putin an Ism?', *Russian Politics*, 5(3), pp. 255–82. https://doi.org/10.30965/24518921-00503001

Sevastopulo, Demetri; and Hille, Kathrin. 2022. 'US Pledges to Maintain Military Capacity to Defend Taiwan', *Financial Times*, 11 June, (Accessed 23 June 2022) www.ft.com/content/a032267d-e047-4490-a8e9-8b2d8bf327c6

Simón, Luis. 2022. 'The Madrid Strategic Concept and the Future of NATO', *NATO Review*, 2 June, (Accessed 23 June 2022) www.nato.int/docu/review/articles/2022/06/02/the-madrid-strategic-concept-and-the-future-of-nato/index.html

Singh, Darpan. 2022. 'No Matter Who Wins Russia-Ukraine War, West's Arms Suppliers Are Already a Winner', *India Today*, 15 April, (Accessed 31 May 2022) www.indiatoday.in/world/russia-ukraine-war/story/russia-ukraine-war-west-arms-supply-1937710-2022-04-15

Smith, David. 2022. 'Biden's Taiwan Vow Creates Confusion Not Clarity—and Raises China Tensions', *The Guardian*, 23 May, (Accessed 30 May 2022) www.theguardian.com/us-news/2022/may/23/biden-taiwan-china-strategic-ambiguity-us-foreign-policy

Taylor, Paul; and John, Mark. 2008. 'Ukraine and Georgia Face Uphill Battle on NATO Bid', *Reuters*, 1 April, (Accessed 23 June 2022) www.reuters.com/article/us-nato-idUSL0179714620080401

Van der Pijl, Kees. 2006. *Global Rivalries From the Cold War to Iraq*. London, UK: Pluto Press.

Vershinin, Alex. 2022. *The Return of Industrial Warfare*. London: Royal United Services Institute. https://rusi.org/explore-our-research/publications/commentary/return-industrial-warfare

The White House. 2022. 'Remarks By President Biden on Russia's Unprovoked and Unjustified Attack on Ukraine', *Briefing Room, Speeches and Remarks*, 24 February, (Accessed 31 May 2022) www.whitehouse.gov/briefing-room/speeches-remarks/2022/02/24/remarks-by-president-biden-on-russias-unprovoked-and-unjustified-attack-on-ukraine/

Wolf, Martin. 2014. 'Holdouts Give Vultures a Bad Name', *Financial Times*, 2 September, (Accessed 31 May 2022) www.ft.com/content/bf3bd3f2-31ef-11e4-b929-00144feabdc0

Woodward, Jude. 2017. *The US vs China: Asia's New Cold War?* Manchester: Manchester University Press.

Wright, Robin. 2020. 'Why Trump Will Never Win His New Cold War With China', *The New Yorker*, 29 July, (Accessed 24 May 2022) www.newyorker.com/news/our-columnists/why-trump-will-never-win-his-new-cold-war-with-china

8

CONCLUSION

What is to be done?

The United States' attempt to prolong the life of capitalism over the last century went through its phase of jeopardy during the Long Boom, where it was endangered by circumstances arising from a world of popular empowerment whose leading edge was Communism. It then entered its phase of futility under neoliberalism, as neoliberal policies failed to revive capitalism's productive economy, financialising it instead and the capitalist world, led by the leading neoliberal countries, lost its centrality to the world economy. With the pandemic followed by the proxy war against Russia and the New Cold War against China, it appears to have entered a phase of perversity, where its efforts to extend capitalism's life and hold on the world are proving counterproductive (with apologies to Albert O. Hirschman 1991).

While the balance of class forces in each country will determine when and how people and peoples outside the homelands of capitalism take the road to socialism, the advance of the left in the core countries of capitalism can play an important role in this effort by limiting or ceasing imperialist efforts, thus creating more benign objective conditions for socialist advance elsewhere and, because so much of the left elsewhere has historically taken intellectual cues from it (for good or ill), better subjective conditions too. We conclude this book by assessing its problems and prospects.

Few words better captured the political hope that rose in the first weeks and months of the pandemic, when capitalism's obscene inequalities and shocking frailty went on full display, than 'build back better'. As neoliberal governments appeared to execute spectacular policy U-turns, even quite mainstream intellectuals competed to propose radical new ideas for change, from a universal basic income (Skidelsky 2016) to deeply negative interest rates (Rogoff 2020) and the monetary policy magic of modern monetary theory (MMT) (Kelton 2020) to reviving anti-trust legislation to break up large monopolies (Reich 2020). While European governments sought to escape sound money orthodoxy with

DOI: 10.4324/9781003200000-8

non-repayable bonds (Soros 2020), organs of the capitalist press (Financial Times Editorial Board 2020) envisaged a reversal of neoliberalism unimaginable only months before:

> Governments will have to accept a more active role in the economy. They must see public services as investments rather than liabilities, and look for ways to make labour markets less insecure. Redistribution will again be on the agenda; the privileges of the elderly and wealthy in question.

Such impulses were only boosted by comparison of the pandemic with the Second World War, which, in folk memory, set the stage for new 'socialistic' post-war consensus that overturned the 'liberal' imperialism and authoritarianism of the world before 1914.

However, in the ensuing discussions the limitations of the left also came to the fore, limitations that became even more glaring as the United States' proxy war broke out and considerable parts of the Western left aligned themselves with the US-led war against Russia while many others condemned the West's and NATO's role but still considered Russia the principal aggressor. These limitations require reflection on the historical trajectory of the Western left. In this concluding chapter, we review how the chief proposals that emerged in left discussions amid the pandemic reflect these limitations before going on to consider what it will take to overcome them if the working people of the West are to put their political shoulders to the wheel of building socialism worldwide.

Building back (pseudo-civic) neoliberalism

The first thing to note about the proposals that captured public attention during the pandemic is their provenance. While many did come from deeply committed grassroots movements and activists—most prominently, defunding the police in favour of greater investment in communities—those from establishment figures—such as former Bank of England governor, Mark Carney or MMT maven Stephanie Kelton or innovation aficionado Mariana Mazzucato—floated to the top. They appeared radical enough to ride and swell the wave of popular hunger for change while also appealing to at least some influential sections of the political and corporate establishment. They were spiritually conservative in the quintessential sense conveyed by Tancredi in Lampedusa's *The Leopard*, 'If we want things to stay as they are, things will have to change.' Rather than reorienting our societies from profits to people, from capitalism towards socialism, they appear set to re-orient them from the last, 'austerity', phase of neoliberalism to its pseudo-civic phase.

'Mission economy': the theory of pseudo-civic neoliberalism

The book that perhaps did so best was Mariana Mazzucato's *Mission Economy* (2021). It extended her advocacy of a leading role for the state in advancing innovation and exposure of the myth that the private sector drove it to advocating a greater state role in 'doing capitalism differently'.

Mazzucato's prose meant to inspire: 'bold' and 'purpose-driven' 'missions' were to solve 'wicked' problems through 'imaginative' and 'inventive' 'reinvention' of social organisation for 'competence', 'confidence' and 'collaboration'. However, one soon realises that this studiedly lofty rhetoric serves capital in its hour of need, not people. Mazzucato proposes that governments should act not as investors of 'last' but 'first' resort in a new 'narrative of government as a source of value creation' and a new model for tackling the 'wicked' problems we face, 'from health challenges such as pandemics, to environmental challenges such as global warming, to educational challenges such as the divide in opportunity and achievement between students partly caused by unequal access to digital technology' (Mazzucato 2021, 5).

The model concerned, it turns out, is the Apollo space mission to put 'man' on the moon in which the US government took the lead while 'working closely with companies—small, medium and large—on hundreds of individual problems' (Mazzucato 2021, 5) and did not worry about the cost in pursuit of its clear goal. It also led to 'spillovers. . . . Technological and organizational innovations that could never have been predicted at the beginning' (Mazzucato 2021, 4).

The first problem is that this mission was a US Cold War stunt. By launching Sputnik, the world's first satellite, in 1957 and putting Yuri Gagarin into orbit in the first human spaceflight in history in 1961, the USSR acquired a space technology lead, which had become an established fact by the early 1960s. So, President John F. Kennedy, never very enthusiastic about space flight (Muir-Harmony 2020), endorsed the Apollo mission only because it 'had the potential to restore America's geopolitical standing in the wake of recent Soviet advances in space technology' and the contemporaneous 'failure of the CIA-backed Bay of Pigs invasion'. As Mazzucato (2021, 7) herself notes, he argued, no other project would be '"more expensive" or "more impressive to mankind"'.

Undertaken only to impress the world, particularly the vast number of newly independent nations that were the real stake in the Cold War, the Apollo mission, with its well-planned publicity, complete with a Frank Sinatra song, had little serious economic or social rationale. It is no wonder that today thousands of satellites clog the lower earth orbit, and the international space station remains a viable economic, scientific and technological enterprise, but though it could conceivably feature as part of larger space exploration projects, no country has bothered to put a human being on the moon again for its own sake.

Mazzucato could have chosen the Manhattan Project, the United States' crash programme to develop nuclear weapons. However, that would have left her ideas vulnerable to the serious questioning that surrounds the story of the United States' development of these weapons despite warnings about their horrors and the imperialist, Cold War and racist motivations behind their use in 1945 (Alperovitz 1998), not to mention the constant threat of their use since (Desai 2022). Indeed, serious examples of the sort of enterprise she has in mind are singularly missing in the history of the capitalist West simply because it is capitalist. Capital does not tolerate any state action other than that which serves it, at home and abroad. Mazzucato recognises that capitalism is in crisis largely because it has become unproductive, unequal, unsustainable and undemocratic and wishes to rectify this. However, in her insistence on merely changing capitalism, she not only rejects the necessary path of creating productive, equal, sustainable and democratic *socialist* society, she assumes it is an impossible goal.

How productive, equal, sustainable and democratic can her transformed capitalism be? Not very. Her 'mission' or 'moonshot' economy is little more than warmed over public–private partnerships, which have a long history of failure and corruption (Hall 2015). This is clear, as Michael Roberts pointed out, from her own consulting experiences, whether with Germany's Energiewende (energy transition to renewables), 'which failed to deliver any better than others in reducing carbon emissions' or Scottish National Investment Bank proposed by the SNP which, in government 'cut its funding from £241m to £205m, a pathetic amount to start with' given that, when first proposed by Labour under Corbyn, 'it was to be capitalised with £20bn! And as for UK PM Johnson's "Operation Moonshot" for mass test and tracing, say no more' (Roberts 2021).

Mazzucato proposes not to take either government or business as they are: 'Changing capitalism means changing both how government is structured and how business is run—and how public and private organization interrelated' (Mazzucato 2021, 9). To realise her 'mission economy',

> governments need to invest in their internal capabilities—building the competence and confidence to think boldly, partner with business and civil society, catalyse new forms of collaboration across sectors and deploy instruments that reward actors willing to engage with the difficulties. The task is neither to pick winners not to give unconditional handouts, subsidies and guarantees, but to *pick the willing*. And missions are about making markets not only fixing them. They're about imagining new areas of exploration. They're about taking risks, not only 'de-risking'. And if this means making mistakes along the way, so be it. Learning through trial and error is critical for any value creation exercise. Ambitious missions have the courage to tilt the playing field.
>
> *(Mazzucato 2021, 206–7)*

In other words, governments must become even better at handing out contracts under public–private partnerships, not worry about quality or reliability, work with willing firms and feel entitled to brush of criticism of failures by claiming to learn by trial and error. Few could write a better script for pseudo-civic neoliberalism.

Modern monetary theory: camouflaging financialisation

It may surprise many to know that MMT, widely touted as the progressive alternative to austerity, was originally proposed by a hedge fund manager, Warren

Moseler, who began promoting it in the mid-1990s. However, MMT became prominent only after massive money creation had become necessary to rescue the financial sector after the North Atlantic Financial Crisis of 2008. In the era of low interest rates that followed, the argument that government could expand spending and borrowing without too much restraint had, in any case, gained traction. Breaking the decades-long neoliberal taboo against expanding government spending, the Canadian Liberal Party, for instance, campaigned successfully in 2014 on a pledge to expand budget deficits and Britain's Johnson government did the same in 2019, promising to expand spending to 'level up' the north. These efforts did, however, retain considerable caution about deficits.

Only in 2020, when money creation was combined with historic increases in government spending, combined with its outright monetisation, did many begin brandishing MMT to support the argument that 'monetarily sovereign' governments faced no fiscal limits to the expansion of employment, investment and welfare. With Stephanie Kelton's blockbuster, *The Deficit Myth*, MMT acquired advocates among progressive politicians, such as Bernie Sanders and Alexandra Occasio Cortes.

MMT's key idea is that a 'monetarily sovereign government'—one that issues a currency, accepts payment of taxes and related obligations in it and issues debt in it (Wray 2020, 9)—can fund its activities by creating money, that is, borrowing from the central bank without causing inflation so long as the economy is operating below full employment. A key implication is that taxes are not necessary to fund government spending, though they can shape the pattern of growth and the distribution of its gains.

During the 2020 US election campaign, MMT was music to the ears of radical activists battling against 'austerity' arguments that government spending, debts and deficits had to be limited to make Biden's 'build back better' programme as ambitious as it could be. The free money spigot would fund all sorts of social programmes to address the glaring need and inequality the pandemic had revealed. As one influential account put it, radicals needed to reject 'the Marxist [sic] image of money as a private, finite, and alienable quantum of value' and realise that 'money is a boundless public center that can be made to support all' (quoted in Henwood 2019). While MMT theorists favoured certain types of social spending, such as a universal job guarantee and green initiatives, others read MMT as a license for government spending expansion without the pain of taxes.

However, a serpent lurks in this monetary Garden of Eden: MMT gives the wrong answer while distracting attention from the right questions. As an answer to the question posed by advocates of austerity—'Who will pay? Where will the money come from?'—MMT's response that there is no need for taxes and no limit on spending is simply wrong and its advocates admit in more learned writings that inflation, which, according to them, can occur when economies are operating at capacity sets the limit on spending. Their misleading wrong response simply distracts from the real questions: Why can't our economy provide what we need at prices we can afford? Why does so much money go not to productive investment but financial 'investment'? Why is our productive system so limited? Why is income so ill distributed? These questions concern the organisation of production, the proper relation between production and finance and the distribution of the rewards of production.

While radicals and progressives are kept distracted by the wrong answer and the wrong question, MMT also serves the interests of the rich. It is no wonder the upstart theory also found favour among sections of the United States' financial elite that has hitherto typically enforced austerity (Carter 2018 ; Henwood 2019). Only this permits MMT relatively favourable treatment in the mainstream press and at worst a respectful dismissal in the business press.

Tracing these political complicities to the idea that MMT 'can make both the poor and the rich, better off' (Stephanie Kelton quoted in Epstein 2020, 8), Gerald Epstein points out that MMT offers a 'free lunch' to both. The poor people's free lunch, the idea that social spending can rise as long as there is slack in the economy, is matched by a far less noticed billionaires' free lunch. To them, MMT says that 'so long as they see that deficits are not harmful', they can 'avoid higher taxes' because for the government can spend more and the Federal Reserve 'just needs to flick its monetary pen'. With money creation broadly legitimised, they not only avoid taxes, but they can also 'speculate and profit from virtually interest free credit' (Epstein 2020, 8). For those who have made speculative profit through leveraged trading in asset markets, their highway to obscene wealth over the neoliberal decades, particularly over the last two during which monetary policy has got more and more lax and 'unconventional', that is to say, designed to support speculation and financialisation, albeit in the name of encouraging grwoth, employment and investment, this can be sweet music.

Such free lunchism kept attention focused on the uses of MMT, rather than on its veracity. The latter is simply taken for granted because MMT is believed to explain why the astronomical money creation (not $7.7 trillion as widely reported but $29 trillion in the United States, as Felkerson 2011 showed) of the past decade did not lead to inflation.

However, MMT does nothing of the sort. The real reason inflation did not ensue is that the money the Federal Reserve created never entered the economy, serving merely to fill the black holes in bank balance sheets left by 2008 and 2020 and to aid continued speculation by the rich and major financial institutions which inflated asset markets thereafter. Two other factors also accounted for the low inflation: the decades-long depression of wages and prices of imports from the Third World did keep prices low while Boskin Commission's statistical skulduggery on inflation measures resulted in low *reported* inflation. (Interestingly, it was the rise in commodity prices that ran from about 2004 to about 2014 and its downward pressure on the dollar that forced the Federal Reserve to raise interest rates, pricking the housing and credit bubbles.)

Moreover, the two free lunches now appear to be very unequal ones. Not only do advocates of MMT confine their qualification that an economy must be operating below capacity for money creation to be non-inflationary to their scholarly writing, leaving it out of their more popular writings, the claim that inflation cannot occur when there is slack in the economy is invalid. High inflation and unemployment occurred together in the 1970s for the simple reason that large monopoly corporations are easily able to pass the increases in input prices onto consumer prices (Patnaik and Patnaik 2021, 24). The current burst of inflation may further confirm this point. Though official unemployment rates are low, there has also been marked downward dip in labour force participation rates, declining since the mid-1990s (Hornstein and Kudlyak 2022). So, under MMT, the billionaires' free lunch remains sumptuous as ever, the poor peoples' free lunch simply vanishes.

As for the validity of MMT, it is a prime candidate for the old putdown: there is much in it that is new and much that is true; however, what is new is not true and what is true is not new. MMT's distinctive new claim, that money creation will not lead to inflation so long as the economy is operating below capacity, is simply false; MMT proposes no strategy for authorities if inflation does occur other than use the cudgel of recessionary interest rate hikes.

On the other, what is true in MMT—that arguments for austerity are wrong—is not new. Arguments against it have always existed and John Maynard Keynes gave them their modern form in his argument about a 'somewhat comprehensive socialisation of investment'. The problem has been that such arguments have been suppressed by the political, rather than intellectual factors chiefly because addressing the productive limitations of capitalism through state initiative requires more than money creation and has profound political consequences for capitalism. It does not involve just money creation that leaves the dilapidated productive apparatus in place. It involves the state playing an active role making socially useful investment in ways and to an extent that would raise questions about capitalism, whether it does or should continue to exist. This is the truth that the political might of neoliberal thinking has suppressed in recent decades (Patnaik 2009).

Moreover, there is a flaw in the very category of 'monetary sovereignty'. Most criticism has focused on the fact that many countries, particularly developing countries, may formally fit MMT's definition of 'monetary sovereignty' but nevertheless face real obstacles to money creation (Bonizzi et al. 2020). These criticisms have forced MMT to concede that there may be a 'spectrum of monetary sovereignty' (Tcherneva 2016). However, even these writers assume that G7 governments, especially the United States, enjoy monetary sovereignty.

Even this more constrained claim is questionable. Since every country faces an external sector, if a country funds its spending by creating money, including by 'borrowing' from the Central Bank, currency markets can and do put downward pressure on the value of the currency concerned, making imports expensive and thus generating inflation. If, on the other hand, government spending is financed by floating bonds in the country's own currency, investors can still press down the value of these bonds and drive up interest rates. That is why neither European nor Japanese governments have ever tested this theory.

The US case is interestingly different in that the dollar's value and wide acceptance rests the great financial demand for it internationally. However, as we have seen, this system has already shrunk and now requires the Federal Reserve to support key asset markets that are to entice inflows. The current bout of inflation, which requires tighter monetary policy, is threatening these highly leveraged asset markets that rely on low interest rates, and through them, the dollar. Perhaps that is why neither the Biden nor the Johnson administrations appeared to heed MMT's siren call to monetise all debt, choosing instead to fund it very substantially through a combination of higher taxes and borrowing from bond markets.

That said, the most important problem with MMT from the point of view of socialistic reform as much as socialism is that it directs attention away from the all-important matter of reversing financialisation, the chief cause as well as symptom of its productive failure and inequality. It side-steps the need to put capital on notice that unless it is capable of maintaining a productive economy capable of creating tolerably broad-based prosperity, it may be a matter of time before working people will be forced to organise to 'wrest, by degree, all capital from the bourgeoisie' (Marx and Engels 1848/1967, 104).

Universal basic income: questionable entitlement

The final big idea to gain traction during the pandemic is Universal Basic Income (UBI), a regular guaranteed payment from the state to citizens that would purchase the basic necessities of a decent life. Its popularity was already growing amid the austerity that followed the 2008 crisis and came to a head amid the unemployment, precarity and uncertainty generated by the pandemic and lockdowns and the demonstration effect of the various income support schemes that were laid out by governments (Macqueen 2020). Opinion makers from the left website *Democracy Now!* to think tanks such as the Institute for New Economic Thinking (INET), fairly prominent political parties such as the Scottish National Party, public figures and politicians across the political spectrum from left to right and even elements in the Silicon Valley (Morozov 2016) have signalled their support.

The idea had emerged from discussions around the welfare state and its crisis and was well developed by the 1990s (van Parjis 1992). It takes many different forms and, inevitably, shades off into other ideas, such as a guaranteed minimum income or other sorts of income supports. However, as the most serious studies (for instance, Coote and Yazici 2019) point out, if the level of the basic income is to be adequate for citizens to live on and not the sort of derisory payment that at least some of its right-wing supporters advocate, it would cost anywhere between 20% and 30% of GDP.

Moreover, even at this level, it would be no substitute for an adequate welfare state—including quality public health care, education and other public services—and could well draw resources away from them. Indeed, on the right, many support it precisely because it would offer them the chance to dismantle the welfare state, which, they say, is too intrusive but which they really dislike because of the extent to which it affords genuine empowerment to the working classes, making them capable of organising society to produce what they need.

Perhaps the most important argument against UBI is that it leaves the current weakened capitalist productive system intact. This is particularly so in proposals, such as Yanis Varoufakis's (2016), that it be funded not from taxation but from a 'dividend' paid out from profits while the question of its economic feasibility (leaving aside its political feasibility) is evaded. Especially if accompanied by a dismantling of the welfare state, which leaves individuals reliant on purchasing critical services from private, typically corporate producers, it would become the foundation for the rampant commodification of every aspect of social life, for converting the production of everything we need—education, health care, housing, transport—into machines for corporate profit. If our experience with corporate provision so far is anything to go by, we will experience simultaneous declines in the quantity and quality of the relevant goods and services and rises in costs. Even more fundamentally, moreover, UBI takes it for granted that a privately organised economy is capable of handling production at the required pace and in the required pattern. In fact, not only can we not rely on the present capitalist system to deliver the social welfare and environmental protection we need, as we have seen, even in the homelands of capitalism, it is not capable of delivering growth on its own.

Proposals for UBI ignore the real elephants in the room. How shall we reorganise production so that it produces for genuine individual and social need, in an environmentally sustainable fashion and without inflicting low wages and undesirable working conditions on any worker, at home or aboard. And how shall we distribute work among those capable of working and its rewards among all, including those who cannot work because they are too young, too ill or too old?

This involves planning for production as well as distribution. It will have to include plans for taking large private firms that are already vast apparatuses for planned production into public ownership and running them as parts of larger, national plans for social production that also plan the national economy's relation to regional economies and the world economy. It would have to recognise that the current economic structure is unable to produce what is needed, including high-quality public services, at acceptable wages, in acceptable working conditions and reversals of global warming, pollution and biodiversity loss. Today's neoliberal economies are increasingly better at producing what is positively harmful to individuals and society if they produce at all, given its inability to invest productively and preference for plunder and speculation.

As we have seen, socialistic reforms after the Second World War were undermined. They were products of the radicalism that arose from a historical moment when populations were highly mobilised, wartime planning and rationing demonstrated how well societies could produce and distribute, and the reputation of capitalism, responsible for all the major catastrophes of the Thirty Years' Crisis, two imperialist world wars and a Great Depression, was at an all-time low. However, the socialistic reforms left the underlying capitalist character of the economy intact, permitting capital to organise the neoliberal counter-revolution, when the system's persisting underlying capitalist character led to economic crisis. Though many pushing this or that reform today invoke the post-Second World War moment, not only are the proposals they make far less ambitious than those that re-made societies of capitalism's homelands in that moment, they fail to question the continued existence of capitalism in a far more advanced state of decay. Moreover, as the US-led proxy war on Russia rages on, requiring a deepening of left radicalism, even these modest proposals have been forgotten and left critique in the homelands of capitalism is frozen.

It is time to dwell on why.

Political hope in search of an agent

As we have seen in Chapter 3, the left in the imperialist heartlands has been missing in action for a very long time. It has squandered the opportunity to mobilise the discontents of neoliberalism over the past four decades, permitting the ideology and the freedoms it dispenses to capital to advance largely unopposed. Worse, neoliberalism's attacks have depleted the Western left's abilities—levels of union organisation and votes for left-of-centre parties, to take only two of the more obvious indicators. Moreover, if one takes a longer historical view, its debility appears even more serious.

In understanding how things have come to such a pass, perhaps the most fundamental thing to recall is that there has never been a successful revolution in the major capitalist societies. This is despite the fact that the Second International of the early twentieth century, the international federation of European parties of social democracy then marching under the banner of Marxism, expected that revolution would first occur there, in the homelands of capitalism where it was most advanced, and reach the rest of the world only through the mediation of such revolutions. This expectation was belied. The first revolution against capitalism and imperialism occurred in Russia, on Europe's periphery, and the second, in an even more impoverished semi-colonial and semi-feudal country, China, and they have since continued to break out only in much poorer countries. Worse, the evolution of the historic parties of the working classes and the left in major capitalist countries over the past century and a half since social democracy appeared on the historical stage has consisted of progressive moves to the right in terms of both domestic and international policy and of political distantiation from if not opposition to, the actual record of socialist revolutions beyond their borders.

Already before the First World War, despite the revolutionary and internationalist views of its leadership, the Second International was racked by debates over revisionism. It was essentially a dialogue of the deaf. On one side were those who emphasised the centrality of immediate reforms and concessions from the national state to cementing the allegiance of working people to social democratic parties. On the other were those who fixed their eyes on the longer-term goal of revolution and assumed that workers remained committed to revolution, which they conceived in abstract internationalist terms. They overlooked the fact that the historical practice of securing working-class allegiance through national reforms did give 'workers . . . a good deal more to lose than their chains' (Joll 1955, 114) and attached them to the national state. These two elements were not factored into their strategies for revolution.

Revolutionary internationalism went, moreover, hand in hand with imperialist attitudes of many in the parties of the Second International:

> European socialists noticed the question of democracy in the colonial world only very exceptionally before 1914: not only were non-Western voices and peoples of color entirely absent from the counsels of the Second International, but its parties also failed to condemn colonial policy and even positively endorsed it. Socialists commonly affirmed the progressive value of the 'civilizing mission' for the underdeveloped world, while accepting the material benefits of jobs, cheaper good and guaranteed markets colonialism brought at home.
>
> *(Eley 2002, 112)*

Lenin was the major exception. Though his famous pamphlet on imperialism (Lenin 1916/1970) was concerned chiefly with inter-imperialist rivalry, which was likely to cause a war and cost working class lives in Europe, he also understood, perhaps even more than Rosa Luxemburg with her focus on the colonial world and its 'natural economy', the centrality of colonial and semi-colonial domination to capitalism and of national liberation to world revolution. He had welcomed Japan's victory over Russia and nationalist ferment in Persia and Turkey in 1905 and hailed European workers' 'Asian comrades' in 1908. By 1916 he had anticipated the idea of the Three Worlds: with the First World War strengthening anti-colonial nationalism, recalling Marx's firm anti-imperialist position and his dictum that 'no nation can be free if it oppresses other nations', Lenin assigned socialists distinct tasks in the three types of countries.

> First, the advanced capitalist countries of Western Europe and the United States of America [where] . . . bourgeois, progressive, national movements came to an end long ago. Every one of these 'great' nations oppresses other nations in the colonies and within its own country. The tasks of the proletariat of these ruling nations are the same as those of the proletariat

> in England in the nineteenth century in relation to Ireland [to support nationalist movements of oppressed nations].
>
> Secondly, Eastern Europe: Austria, the Balkans and particularly Russia . . . [where] the twentieth century . . . particularly developed the bourgeois-democratic national movements and intensified the national struggle. The tasks of the proletariat in these countries—in regard to the consummation of their bourgeois-democratic reformation, as well as in regard to assisting the socialist revolution in other countries—cannot be achieved unless it champions the right of nations to self-determination. In this connection the most difficult but most important task is to merge the class struggle of the workers in the oppressing nations with the class struggle of the workers in the oppressed nations.
>
> Thirdly, the semi-colonial countries, like China, Persia, Turkey, and all the colonies . . . [where] the bourgeois-democratic movements have either hardly begun, or are far from having been completed. Socialists must not only demand the unconditional and immediate liberation of the colonies without compensation . . . but must render determined support to the more revolutionary elements in the bourgeois-democratic movements for national liberation in these countries and assist their rebellion—and if need be, their revolutionary war—against the imperialist powers that oppress them.
>
> *(Lenin 1916/1970)*

In short, working people in the imperial countries could not hope to overthrow their capitalists without defeating their own imperialisms. In countries that were neither imperial nor colonised, such as Russia, they had to work towards national 'bourgeois-democratic reformation' and link imperial and colonial working-class struggles. Finally, in the colonial and semi-colonial countries, they had to champion national liberation, if necessary, alongside revolutionary bourgeois forces.

In the upheavals of the Thirty Years' Crisis that transformed the left, this position became that of the Third International or the Comintern. The Second International was dissolved on the eve of the First World War as its component social democratic parties voted for war credits instead of opposing the war as its revolutionary leaders had hoped. Now, splits among left forces appeared everywhere and those over the Russian Revolution began the division of Marxism into Western and Eastern wings, with the former facing further splits with the failure of the German November Revolution in 1919, the Italian *Biennio Rosso* and other such uprisings in the wake of the First World War, the Great Depression and the successes of fascism. Meanwhile, it was the not Western social democracy but the Third International and actually existing communisms that inherited the ideas and practices that linked, as Lenin did, socialism, anti-imperialism and national liberation, the working class and the peasantry, and capitalism and imperialism.

After the Second World War, moreover, parties of European social democracy became committed to preserving the capitalist system while relying on what growth it produced to extract concessions—higher wages, expansion of the welfare state, etc.—for working people. This strategy worked as long as capitalist growth continued, at least after a fashion, though it relied on women's unpaid labour and institutionalised racism. As the Long Downturn began with the stagflation of the 1970s, this strategy could no longer work. While in all European countries important left currents emerged to support a decisive leftward move, such as the Labour left led by Tony Benn, with very substantial support in the unions, it was not clear they had a viable economic strategy and the 1970s ended with their defeat.

The 1980s and 1990s witnessed these parties making even further compromises with an ascendant neoliberalism; by the time the twentieth century closed, even social democratic redistribution was abandoned in favour of a new 'Third Way'. Any critique of capitalism was jettisoned in favour of promoting national champions, touting the alleged efficiency of private sector provision to justify privatisation and contracting out public services, treating financial activity as productive (Assa 2016; Callaghan 2014) and signing trade agreements to facilitate, rather than remedy, the enervation of domestic productive sectors.

While neoliberalism was unable to abolish welfare states outright, social democracy participated fully in their neoliberal hollowing out under banners such as 'no rights without responsibilities', branding social protection a 'moral hazard' that disincentivised work. The aim, above all, was to expose working people to market discipline (Ryner 2014, 62–4). Taxation became more regressive, with working people shouldering the highest tax burden and large corporations paying little or nothing. Welfare states were re-designed to benefit the latter as they increasingly took over service provision. Poverty reduction was reoriented to ensure people kept working while transfer payments to them actually acted as wage subsidies for large corporations that paid below poverty wages. These changes turned post-war welfare states that, for all their flaws, had constituted one of the most important working-class advances, into 'a twenty-first century workhouse without walls':

> Gone is the idea that unemployed people, having paid contributions into a national insurance scheme, have an unconditional right to their benefits for a specified period. Instead, as 'jobseekers', they are forced by savage sanctions (withdrawals of benefit) regimes into accepting whatever work is available, however, low paid, or, if no such work is available, into unpaid 'work experience' . . . Once sanctioned, many are rendered destitute: forced to sleep on the street or use food banks to survive. Perhaps the main difference is that the Victorian workhouse would at least have provided them with a bowl of gruel, a dry bed and a roof over their heads.
>
> *(Huws 2020, 17)*

To such 'Third Way' politics, left elements that continued to speak of planning, nationalisation and industrial policy, including parts of the trade union movement, were anathema. Even contemporary figures like Tony Benn or Jeremy Corbyn in the United Kingdom have been regularly sabotaged (McDonnell 2020) by the weightier social democratic or 'Third Way' right in their own party.

While this denouement of social democracy is multifaceted, two aspects are rarely discussed and worth highlighting: one related to its personnel and the other to its ideas.

Brains and numbers

Marx and Engels remarked in *The Communist Manifesto* that 'entire sections of the ruling class are, by the advance of industry, precipitated into the proletariat, or are at least threatened in their conditions of existence. These also supply the proletariat with fresh elements of enlightenment and progress.' Certainly, intellectuals—themselves neither numerous nor working class but members of the slim stratum of the educated, credentialled and professional, that would, with the advance of capitalism in the monopoly period, expand into a 'professional managerial class' (PMC) (Brodhead et al. 1977)—have played a major role in working-class parties and movements (Desai 1994). The historically leftward bent of intellectuals was usually put down by the right (Brinton 1952) as well as the left (Mannheim 1954/2018; see also Mirsky 1935) to the general overproduction of intellectuals: Lacking a place in the existing order of things, surplus to its requirements, they joined forces opposed to it. The Fabians, in their quaintly blunt way, called this the alliance of 'brains and numbers'. This class alliance was never easy and the danger of revisionism—the de-radicalisation of the movement, its understanding and goals—always lurked. In the post-war period, it was realised.

As the weight of the intellectual or professional current in social democracy grew, it led social democracy away from socialism and further down the path to compromise with capitalism (Desai 1994), whether this was explicit, as in German social democracy after the 1954 Bad Godesberg conference, or implicit, as was the case with the Labour Party, which retained a commitment to socialism in its constitution into the 1990s. In the neoliberal era, the historic parties of the working class went beyond deradicalisation to outright acceptance of neoliberalism. This went hand in hand with a decisive change in the pattern of intellectual life.

As the post-war expansion of education swelled the ranks of the PMC, they were absorbed into the wide and deep structures of monopoly capital and the post-war state expanded by its welfare and social commitments and now employing vast numbers of the credentialed (Perkin 1989). A new pattern of PMC political involvement emerged. Whereas earlier they tended to side with liberal and left currents (John Stuart Mill had called the Conservative party of his time the 'stupid party'), the vast expansion of education in the postwar period bifurcated intellectual life: 'The main line of cleavage. . . . ran between those employed by the private or profit-oriented sector and the public sector, including the non-profit-making institutions such as universities, churches and charitable foundations' (Perkin 1989, 437–8). The former gave their political loyalties to parties of the right and the latter to those of the left, the historic parties of the working class.

Among parties of the right, the ascendancy of this new social stratum over the old patricians of conservative politics was marked. In the case of the United Kingdom, for instance, professionals like Edward Heath and Margaret Thatcher succeeded aristocrats like the 14th Earl of Home, Alec Douglas-Home, in its leadership. Working through the various corporate-funded think tanks and media (Desai 1994; Cockett 1995), this new professional class engineered the shift of parties away from conservatism, with its vestiges of noblesse oblige, and towards the harder politics of private property and individualism that neoliberalism represented (Desai 2006).

The emergence of social democratic neoliberalism . . .

For a while, their counterparts on the left half of the political spectrum, having participated in the student and youth revolts of the late 1960s, appeared set to take social democracy farther to the left, in a mirror image of developments on the right. Yet, though many of that generation remained true to the left-wing values they expressed in their youth, by the 1990s, a very different reality was visible. As the boomer generation moved into positions of responsibility and power in the private, public and voluntary sectors, rather than polarising the political spectrum, they moved it, in its entirety, to the right. In this they were undoubtedly helped by capitalist and ruling circles who ruthlessly divided the generation, recruiting and promoting the compliant and viciously repressing those who stood true to their radical ideals. In country after major capitalist country, the new social democracy of the Blairs, Schroeders and Clintons was the work of the generation of 1968.

The result was social democratic accommodation with the neoliberal settlement. To the neoliberalism of the right corresponded a new social democratic neoliberalism, retaining nearly all its miserly and punitive politics towards working people except a few loudly trumpeted concessions, and combined them with a social liberalism championing feminism, environmentalism, anti-racism and lesbian, gay, bisexual, transgender, queer (LGBTQ) issues, all with a pronounced middle-class and tokenistic flavour and very little demand on the public purse, leaving the vast majority of those belonging to these groups as marginalised as before, if not more so.

A final element, perhaps the most important, was what Peter Gowan (2001) called 'neoliberal cosmopolitanism', the latter-day avatar of liberal internationalism. Both were versions of imperialism, a smug and settled attitude that the rest of the world needed Western liberal (that is to say, subordinate capitalist) ideals and organisation, rhetorically dressed up as democracy, freedom and human rights. If the rest of the world was not willing to recognise this, it could be forced to so do. Neoliberal cosmopolitanism in this social democratic version distinguished itself from right wing international aggression by its even greater zeal, such as that exemplified by the Tony Blair government's criminal act of prosecuting war in Iraq on falsified evidence, its resonance with the rhetoric and practices of 'globalisation' and its support for neoliberal Europeanism.

. . . and the working class turn to populism

With this accommodation, the historic parties of the working class cut themselves adrift from the concerns of vast swaths of their original constituency to join a new, cross-party national and international neoliberal establishment. The constitution of that establishment went hand in hand with a 'hollowing out of Western democracy' (Mair 2006, 2013) based on a mutual repulsion: the 'withdrawal' of both leaders and masses from all major parties, right and left. This changed political dynamics fundamentally.

> In the first place, the resulting gap has sometimes helped to fuel a populist mobilization usually, but not exclusively, on the right. In other words, partly as a result of this withdrawal, the political class has itself become an issue of contention in a large number of democratic polities. Second, and as noted above, the growing distance between citizens and their political leaders has also helped to fuel elite demands for more 'nonmajoritarian' decision-making, and a greater role for non-partisan and non-political agencies—judges, regulatory bodies, central banks and international organizations.
>
> *(Mair 2006, 49)*

While the more prosperous sections of the working class had been abandoning their historic parties throughout the neoliberal period, now something qualitatively new was happening. The discontents of neoliberalism, whose numbers swelled greatly under 'austerity' after 2008 as working people paid the price of bailing out big banks and the 1%, should have been organised by parties of the left. However, they were abandoned by these parties which had become part of the neoliberal establishment that promoted globalisation and neoliberal European integration—in effect world- and Europe-wide opportunities for themselves and their credentialed children. The result was to push the discontents of such neoliberalism, by no means all but enough, towards the hard right politics of Trump and Brexit.

The support of certain sections of the well-to-do working class for parties of the right is long-standing and part of the electoral strategy of these parties (McKenzie 1968). Now, however, working people further down the social scale and in deindustrialised regions—the now famous 'blue wall' and 'red wall' in the United States and the United Kingdom, respectively—were successfully wooed by right-wing parties with a harder right, racist and authoritarian appeal, albeit combined with appeals to protecting jobs or addressing inequality. Though much of the literature on this phenomenon classes it as 'populism', it is critical to see this as part of a further rightward shift of entire political spectra.

While in some countries, these currents took over parties of the right, as in the United Kingdom and the United States, and came to power, in others, they challenged these parties and transformed the political landscape, as in Germany or Austria. As working-class allegiance to social democracy loosened, even as their grievances deepened, they were ripe for the picking by those who sought to exploit society's deep divisions without having the slightest intention of healing them.

Despite the resulting victories of the Trumps and the Johnsons, there has been little rethinking on the part of the credentialed social democrats. Along with the other members of their class, they now constitute a single cross-party establishment in most Western countries, facing a revolt from the right and, where some sort of left-wing politics has revived—one thinks of Sanders, Corbyn and now Melanchon—from the left. However, this left faces dangers that are perhaps most clearly visible in the fate of Jeremy Corbyn's leadership of the Labour Party. It was clear as day early on in time as leader of the Labour Party that the credentialed professionals of the neoliberal establishment who dominated the Parliamentary Labour Party (PLP) were resolutely opposed to his left-wing leadership. Taking it upon themselves to do what the continued existence of neoliberal capitalism requires—the destruction of any challenge to it—they went, as we now know, so far as to sabotage Labour campaign in the 2017 general election (Stone 2020) in the hopes of replacing him as leader thereafter.

Moreover, the problem that the distance between the credentialed classes and working people poses for left-wing politics does not end there. Corbyn's leadership is famous for having attracted 400,000-odd new members into the Labour Party, making it the largest party in Europe. These new entrants, overwhelmingly the credentialed or soon-to-be-credentialed post-secondary students attracted to Corbyn's left-wing and environmental positions, not least thanks to the generational inequities they suffer, were actually or aspirationally members of the internationally mobile, socially liberal, credentialed classes who are Europeanists and 'globalisers'. On the critical issues of 'globalisation' and European integration, their attitudes and those of most members of Momentum, the left-wing pressure group of the party, align with those of the neoliberal establishment in the PLP. Corbyn was able to transcend this contradiction in the 2017 election by making his vision of Britain, rather than Brexit, the main election platform. However, in the two years that followed, the PLP leadership's unrelenting attacks on Corbyn, particularly for his alleged anti-Semitism, intensified and one major result was that the party had to bow to the PLP establishment and agree to a Second Referendum, something that the rest of the party also agreed to. This could now be portrayed as a betrayal by Johnson and his ruthless advisors to tip the election in their favour in historic Labour constituencies. With the election of Keir Starmer, the Labour Party, albeit much changed, is safely back in the hands of its neoliberal establishment leadership. Meanwhile, the question of what a truly radical critique of neoliberal capitalism in the major capitalist countries remains unresolved.

Class and left politics today

With the conversion of the historic parties of the working class to neoliberalism, all mainstream politics has turned into a politics of neoliberalism. The main parties form a solid cross-party phalanx, a veritable establishment, operating across parties, corporate foundations, think tanks and even countries. Their unified discourse is policed by forms of censorship more effective than any in the most dystopian vision of allegedly totalitarian societies. Operating with the carrots of preferment and pay, and the sticks of being silenced (as Chelsea Manning, Julian Assange and Edward Snowden most famously have been) or shunned, as with so many critical writers branded 'conspiracy theorists' or 'dangerous' or simply loony. The neoliberal establishment also equates the politics of a Johnson or Trump with the class politics of left leaders such as Corbyn or Sanders or Maduro as versions of populism, striking at both major forms of challenge to their power. Many sections of the left also act as freelance vigilantes for this establishment, particularly by attacking those questioning this neoliberal consensus, whether they call radical supporters of the rights of Palestinians ant-Semitic or accuse critics of wars of 'democracy promotion' of dictator-philia

In this context, action on the political battlefield of the major capitalist countries is largely confined to the right. Biden's government of the Democratic neoliberal establishment representing big corporate and financial capital was opposed most strenuously by the Trumpist right representing only slightly smaller and even less scrupulous capital with a lower tolerance for regulation, a higher propensity to squeeze wages and a greater antipathy to taxes.

Energies generated by the Black Lives Matter protests and left elements that gathered around the strongly anti-neoliberal messages of Bernie Sanders and the so-called Squad of non-white Congresswomen critically aided the Biden's victory in the 2020 US presidential election. Thereafter, however, these forces, whose engagement in strikes, unionisation drives, rent strikes, protests against state repression and proposed legislation curbing the right to protest continues to demonstrate the breadth and depth of opposition to the current order, were once again without political representation. Moreover, thanks to the manifest incompetence and bad faith of public authorities handling the pandemic, even these actions competed for attention with protests against lockdowns in which legitimate protest against the mishandling of the pandemic mingled with politically incoherent, if not blatantly right-wing, currents. By late 2021, Sanders and the Squad were hardly heard from as Trump's shenanigans and the resistance of right-wing Republicans and 'moderate' Democrats to elements of Biden's spending programmes dominated the scene. Nevertheless, such protests continue, now also battling the toll inflation is taking on working people, with small minorities even challenging the war. These developments may well herald a growing spate of mass working-class protest. The question is whether there will be coherent critiques of neoliberal governments' pandemic strategies and wars of the sort presented here that are capable of orienting these protests towards a constructive socialist project so that politics does not remain, as it has become, an entrenched confrontation between an ostentatiously 'woke' neoliberal establishment and an *enragée* hard right.

If the analysis of this book is anything to go by, the left in capitalism's homelands needs to refashion itself. Though it may appear, prima facie, rather esoteric, a, if not the, key to the refashioning required is a better understanding of capitalism, its relation to imperialism and the course of world revolution. Only this can deal with key problems that prevent left forces from articulating the already deep and wide discontent with neoliberal, militarist, capitalist and orienting it towards a viable socialist politics. These key problems are the aversion of the left, including the Marxist left, in the major capitalist countries to thinking about organising production through planning and organising politics through parties. Both are connected to its incomprehension of the intimacy between capitalism and imperialism on the one hand and socialism and anti-imperialism on the other.

Planning, capitalism and socialism

As we have seen, the misunderstanding of capitalism that dominates the left, including its Marxist currents, is rooted in the divorce between most Marxist economists and Marx's analysis. The problem, as we have analysed it, is this: domestically, by accepting the contradiction-free notion of capitalism promoted by Marxist economics, the left has entertained a Schumpeterian rather than Marxist conception of capitalism, in which capitalism is productively superior to other social forms, past or future, capable of developing the forces of production forever or at least charged with developing them before the arrival of socialism. Since, per this understanding, a Promethean capitalism cannot be bettered by any sort of planned economy, what counts as the left's economic strategy is focused on redistribution.

Moreover, this breezy insouciance about production and productivity is actually a product of Western Marxism's blind spot on imperialism, one they share with their capitalist 'enemies'. Both assume that the wealth of the West is a manifestation of capitalism's productive superiority when, in fact, it is as much a manifestation of capitalism's imperialism, its superiority in *appropriation* of the fruits of the labour of the four-fifths of the world that lies outside the imperialist heartlands.

Since they attribute the prosperity of the core capitalist countries not to imperialism but to the allegedly Promethean productivity of capitalism, they can ignore or discount the role of imperialism in furnishing investable surpluses, markets, cheap labour, high-profit investment outlets and cheap commodities. Imperialism also plays a critical macroeconomic role, stabilising the value of money by keeping the prices of Third World products and thus inflation in the major capitalist countries low (Patnaik and Patnaik 2017). It is no coincidence that both the major crises of imperialism of recent times, that of the 1970s and today, have featured inflation.

Western Marxists can also leave out the centrality of the increasingly complex socialisation of labour involved in the development of the productive forces so far and, instead of devoting time to thinking about how the resulting form of production can be brought under socialist control, insofar as the Western left has any conception of a socialist productive economy, it is some sort of decentralised world of small, cooperative and/or worker-managed enterprises. This vision has not altered very much since Marx (1847) excoriated its foremost representative, Pierre-Joseph Proudhon. Essentially a petty-bourgeois socialism, it has today acquired hi-tech versions (Desai 2011). It considers the only freedom worth having to be that of not being a wage worker, the ultimate source of petty-bourgeois pride. It fears that any 'general organization of labour in society . . . would turn the whole of society into a [capitalist] factory' (Marx 1867/1977, 477) and so can only think of any general organisation of labour to be the generalisation of the proletarian subordination they fear rather than as a socialised, collective, autonomy of all.

The vision of decentralised but still market-based small, cooperative and worker-managed firms is precisely the sort of economy that is invoked, as Marx argued in criticising Proudhon, to legitimise capitalism. However, such a capitalism, he argued further, if it ever existed, has had to give way to the full-blown capitalism of big, monopolistic and exploitative enterprises and can certainly be guaranteed to do so in contemporary technological conditions, which favour large scale and scope. This is not an alternative to capitalism, it is capitalism. Moreover, the allergy to socialist planning today also involves an acceptance of the capitalist planning without which the authoritarian corporate behemoths that bestride our economies could not function. The allergy to socialist planning also ignores how the possibilities contained in today's information and communication technologies are incompatible (Reich 2020) with capitalism while their full realisation can involve sophisticated democratic planning (van der Pijl 2020).

Parties or network politics?

The illusion that left economic strategy does not need to involve planning corresponds to a political one—that left politics does not need parties. Social movements and non-governmental organisations (NGOs), loosely coordinated with one another, are supposed to suffice. Such network politics underestimates two necessities, both critically important to challenging capitalism and building socialism. The first should be clear from the above: the necessity of a coherent vision of how production will be organised in a socialist economy, which can only emerge from coherently, if also democratically, organised parties, not networks of loosely connected social movements or NGOs. While no one would advocate the sort of dystopian hyper-centralised planning of the anti-Communist imagination, and every effort can and should be made to decentralise and to create the feedback loops (now enabled by information technology) that will make planning more responsive to popular needs, a certain degree of central planning and decision-making in what will remain national economies for a long time will be inevitable.

Second, any revolution or even advance towards socialism will have to take into account the necessity of preparing to take on the inevitable counter-revolution that will be mounted by metropolitan capital in any revolutionary situation, as Russians, Chinese, Vietnamese, Cubans and today Venezuelans have found out. Rather than recognising the necessity of this minimum of centralisation without which socialist societies can neither plan production nor resist imperialism, most of the left condemns actually existing socialisms as authoritarian denials of liberal freedoms. Such a left also forgets that liberal freedoms are freedoms that kill (Brie 2020).

The left, nations and anti-imperialism

Internationally, Marxist economics' contradiction-free understanding of capitalism has prevented the left from understanding theoretically how imperialism is rooted in capitalism's contradictions and historically how it has set back the prospects of revolution in the major capitalist countries and advanced them elsewhere. It has also prevented the left in the major capitalist countries from appreciating that, whether they take place 'prematurely' in the Third World, or in 'mature' capitalisms of the imperialist world, socialist revolutions will necessarily involve both national and class struggles. The division of the world into nation-states is the result of the uneven and combined development of capitalism. It is rooted in that system's contradictions.

In its working, not only have socialist revolutions occurred as part of anti-imperialist struggles, but if working-class struggles were to issue in socialist revolutions in an imperialist country, they too would be faced with the might—economic, political, financial and military—of the rest of the imperial world. It will have to fashion its own anti-imperialist politics. In these struggles, the bonds of solidarity with actually existing socialisms will be critical.

These two failures—to prioritise a genuine international solidarity with anti-imperialist struggles and to construct socialism at home—are intimately connected. As Marx astutely remarks, 'no nation that enslaves another can ever itself be free'. The social democratic fantasy of building socialism in the 'advanced' countries while giving their own ruling classes carte blanche for every kind of barbarism abroad is not only morally repugnant but practically disastrous, as a hundred years of history have taught us.

It follows that the working and popular movements of all countries will have to fashion their own genuinely anti-imperialist politics. In this struggle, the bonds of solidarity with actually existing socialisms will be critical. This leads us to a further aspect of the centrality of anti-imperialism to the worldwide struggle for socialism.

The dialectic of uneven and combined development has ensured that the international relations of capitalism will be those of struggle among imperialist nations, the most powerful capitalist nations, and struggles between them and other nations, socialist or capitalist, resisting their assaults more and less successfully. A major wave of solidarity between socialist and non-socialist countries against imperialism reached a high point in the post-war decades in the creation of the Non-Aligned Movement and the United Nations Conference on Trade and Development (UNCTAD), and in the demand for a new international economic order (Murphy 1984). While the neoliberal decades drummed most capitalist Third World countries into temporary submission, helped by the end of Communism in Eastern Europe and the Soviet Union, in the new century, the rise of the BRIC countries, above all China, has once again brought the possibility of capitalist anti-imperialism and solidarity among socialist and non-socialist anti-imperialist countries.

While the end of the 2002–2012 boom in commodity prices laid Brazil and Russia low, shifts to right-wing governments slowed growth in India and Brazil, and sanctions set Russia back from 2014 onwards, not only did China remain a beacon, the war over Ukraine in 2022 initiated a clear new phase in which even emphatically neoliberal and hitherto pro-Western leaderships in the Third World such as Bolsonaro's in Brazil and Modi's in India restrained their pro-US stance and refused—resolutely despite great pressure in India's case, at least at the time of writing—to implement US–NATO sanctions.

Finally, it is also clear that, for reasons that need further investigation, other non-socialist countries with a more contradictory attitude to neoliberalism, such as Russia, Turkey or Iran, have stood up increasingly to the imperialist West. At a minimum, their interests cannot be accommodated by the West. Such resistance to imperialism, even when it takes non-socialist forms, can contribute to the progress of the world revolution. Capitalist or comprador regimes in the Third World are often forced to take progressive and anti-imperialist postures due to popular pressure, fear of unrest or because fronts of opposition have opened up between their capitalist classes and imperialist capitalism.

Where stronger, socialist forms of resistance to imperialism are possible, socialist forces must not only 'first of all settle matters with its own bourgeoisie' (Marx and Engels 1848/1967, 93), but also hold their ground against the forces of imperialism, which will inevitably seek to crush them. Relations of solidarity with other socialist, progressive nations and others opposed to imperialism are a necessary part of the advance of socialism worldwide.

As noted, historically, the already discussed limitations of the left in the homelands of capitalism have ensured that the record of revolutions so far has taken paths unanticipated by it. All of them have occurred in countries outside the imperial core in resistance to imperialism and have had to be socialist as well as nationalist. They have, moreover, had to face the task of creating prosperous and equal societies capable of commanding the strong forms of legitimacy required in the face of relentless imperial pressure in extremely difficult circumstances. Ground realities and imperial pressures have usually done more to deform these socialisms than the alleged doctrinal deficiencies most on the Western left finger to deny solidarity to these regimes while dismissing their genuine historical achievements.

This tendency and the aversion to planning, party and the state have been mutually reinforcing. They have resulted in the blank cosmopolitanism of the Western left, which leaves them credulous before narratives such as 'globalisation' and 'empire' and open to supporting or at least remaining indifferent to imperialist ventures against alleged 'brutal dictators' in the name of 'human rights' and 'democracy'. Such credulity has also prevented the Western left from appreciating the real significance of the rise of China, let alone the stiffening of resistance to the imperialist West elsewhere.

In pointing the way out, and by way of concluding this chapter and book, I can do no better than to append the programmatic conclusion of 'Through Pluripolarity toward Socialism: A Manifesto'.

People's and peoples' demands for socialism today

Capitalism long ago ceased to be historically progressive. Humanity faces the task of wresting the world-girding socialisation of production from its control right on the verge of a new industrial revolution involving robotics, artificial intelligence, nanotechnology, quantum computing, biotechnology, the Internet of Things, 3D printing and the like. Capitalism cannot develop its full potential while China leads the way, increasingly gaining control over its standards, intellectual property and associated rents from the capitalist world and challenging the cyber supremacy of the US security state.

Today, a number of peoples are already building socialism, but most are left paying the price of keeping declining and extortionate capital in control. It is high time all working people began building socialism by forming themselves into a 'class for itself', overthrowing the capitalist class and taking political power.

Of course, we will reach Communism—a society that produces use values, rather than (exchange) value, and distributes the social product by taking 'from each according to their ability' and giving 'to each according to their need'—only at the end of a long road. We must traverse several stages of socialism—increasingly socialised production, distribution and outlook—before our productive capacities, our societies and our cultures become capable of relating to other individuals, groups and societies in solidarity, while living harmoniously with other species and the planet.

In doing this, the key is seizing control over the state from capital. The role of the public power, the state, is essential and distinctive and control over it should be in the hands of working people. Though capital may rule over considerable private enterprise, particularly during the early socialist stages, a socialist state must progressively subject all production to social ends through planning for the general interest. Whether to socialise given means of production will be a contextual and often pragmatic decision.

Each country, with its historical configuration of productive development, social organisation and culture, will proceed along this path at its own pace and pattern. Some may join the journey late, some may take interesting detours and some, likely a small number, may not join in anytime soon.

The overriding principle of 'people and planet over profits' implies the following major demands of people and peoples struggling for socialism:

1 Physical, economic and emotional suffering during the pandemic makes the full socialisation of health care, with universal access free at the point of use, the lever that opens the gates to socialism. It must include community-based public health systems extended to the remotest districts and villages capable of offering the best prevention and treatment approaches for present and future pandemics. Such health care systems are possible in poor countries as well as rich and have two further advantages. Their need for skilled medical practitioners will expand public education, training and research in prevention and cure, offering high-quality work for many. Their need for an active public authority strongly committed to social welfare is just what is objectively necessary for the transition to a socialist society. If such a public health system proves possible, if not wholly at least substantially, people will clearly see demand and be willing to work towards, extending its model to other cognate spheres, such as education, child and elder care or housing.

2 To chart the onward path of socialist advance, we recall what Marx knew well: the two main elements of production, land and labour, are not commodities and nor is the chief instrument of their social organisation, money. Capitalism, by treating them as such, entangles itself in contradictions—of the private appropriation of the fruits of social labour, environmental devastation and precarity of agricultural and primary commodity producers, and mismanaged money and financial crises. Decommodifying land, labour and money will constitute a major advance towards socialism.

The urgency of resolving the ecological emergency cannot be overstated. We must take land and water bodies into public ownership for a viable and actionable plan to prevent ecological calamity. Such a plan should be based on wide popular participation and large-scale state investment and will necessarily include divesting from fossil fuels, investing in and deploying renewable energy and zero-carbon public transport on an unprecedented scale, restoring biodiversity, afforestation and reorganising the food system. It will also promote the rational and equitable provision of housing and allocation of land for various economic purposes.

Universal access to work and its rewards for all able to work, combined with support for those unable to work and a reduction in work time for all as productivity advances, opens the door to autonomous and creative pursuits capable of advancing individual fulfilment, science and culture to previously unimagined levels.

We must nationalise money and banking to transform them into instruments of socially organised production and distribution.

In recent years, in addition to land, labour and money, imperialist countries have sought to commodify knowledge and technology through intellectual property rights. Like nature, culture, knowledge and technology are the common heritage of humankind, its second nature. We must reverse its commodification too and make education and research public and flows of knowledge free.

3 Further socialist advance lies in the rational principle that monopolies—such as resource extraction, transportation, the digital platforms whose private ownership prevents the full exploitation of their potential to benefit society—and the production of the essentials of life—food, housing, education or health care—be heavily regulated or nationalised. Their private ownership ill serves society.

Progress towards socialism will be smoother where, thanks to class and international struggles, public provision and public ownership are already quite advanced. Of course, we must remove their existing limitations—class, patriarchal and racist biases—and democratise them, not just formally but substantially.

4 All countries, particularly the wealthy ones, must also separate, through debate and discussion, real need and 'need' simulated by capitalism's need for markets through consumerist illusion and planned obsolescence generating, rather than satiety, only permanent dissatisfaction and covetousness, not to mention environmental destruction.

A critical corollary is halting all wasteful activity—for instance, arms production (beyond basic defence) or financial speculation.

These goals will be easier for societies to pursue in the right international environment.

5 We must oppose the US-sponsored imperialist New Cold War and build an ambitious multilateral international governance enabling all countries to develop, create economic, gender, racial and religious equality, and address shared challenges through economic, political, financial, scientific and cultural cooperation for mutual benefit in 'win–win' relations. True development in the Third World requires investment in human capacities and a new

scientific and technological revolution to fulfil human and planetary needs, cooperative integration of economies to enhance industrial, data and human resource chains and sustainable connectivity and green infrastructure to diffuse the gains widely.

6 We must also mount a challenge to the false and hypocritical universalism with which imperialist countries have articulated their domination for centuries. We must replace it with common values and principles to tackle common challenges: insecurity, mistrust, disrespect, war, inequitable development, rising inequalities of all kinds, serious damage to the land, soils, water, seas and air that sustain human life and whose degradation threatens ecological health, deficient health infrastructure, ineffective disaster management and unsustainable debt. International governance needs to reflect the world's objective and developing pluripolarity. The original ideals of the United Nations Charter and the principles of peaceful coexistence advocated by the Non-Aligned Movement are excellent foundations for further constructing alternatives to institutions of US and Western dominance.

The diversity of our world and its civilisations is a great resource and only principles of equality, mutual respect and mutual trust can sustain it. While peace, development, equality, justice, democracy and freedom are common values of humankind, there is no universal political model. Instead, the world must engage in constant exchange, mutual learning and in sharing the benefits of progress.

Workers of all countries, oppressed peoples and nations, Unite!

References

Alperovitz, Gar. 1998. 'Historians Reassess: Did We Need to Drop the Bomb?', in Bird, Kai and Lifschultz, Lawrence (eds), *Hiroshima's Shadow: Writings on the Denial of History and the Smithsonian Controversy*, pp. 5–21. Stony Creek, CT: Pamphleteer's Press.

Assa, Jacob. 2016. *The Financialization of GDP: Implications for Economic Theory and Policy*. Abingdon, UK: Routledge.

Bonizzi, Bruno; Kaltenbrunner, Annina; and Powell, Jeff. 2020. 'Subordinate Financialization in Emerging Capitalist Economies', in Mader, Philip; Mertens, Daniel; and van der Zwan, Natascha (eds), *The Routledge International Handbook of Financialization*, pp. 177–87. London: Routledge. https://doi.org/10.4324/9781315142876-15

Brie, Michael. 2020. 'This freedom kills', in Desai, Radhika and Polanyi-Levitt, Kari (eds) *Karl Polanyi and Twenty-First-Century Capitalism*, pp. 189–208. Manchester: Manchester University Press. https://doi.org/10.7765/9781526127891.00017

Brinton, Crane. 1952. *The Anatomy of Revolution*. New Jersey: Prentice-Hall.

Brodhead, Frank; Davies, Margery; Erlien, Marla; Ewen, Phyllis; Gordon, Linda; Green, Jim; Hunter, Allen; O'Brien, Jim; Thorkelson, Nick; Withorn, Ann (eds). 1977. 'Professional-Managerial Radicalism', *Radical America*, 11(3).

Callaghan, John. 2014. 'Social Democracy in the Light of Capitalist Crises: The Case of British Labour', in Bailey, David; Escalona, Fabien; de Waele, Jean-Michel; and Vieira, Mathieu (eds). *European Social Democracy During the Global Economic Crisis: Renovation or Resignation?*, pp. 77–96. Manchester: Manchester University Press.

Carter, Zach. 2018. 'Stephanie Kelton Has the Biggest Idea in Washington', *Huffpost*, 20 May, (Accessed 31 May 2022) www.huffpost.com/entry/stephanie-kelton-economy-washington_n_5afee5eae4b0463cdba15121

Cockett, Richard. 1995. *Think the Unthinkable*. New York: HarperCollins.

Coote, Anna; and Yazici, Edanur. 2019. 'Universal Basic Income: A Union Perspective', *Public Services International*, April, (Accessed 23 June 2022) www.world-psi.org/sites/default/files/documents/research/en_ubi_full_report_2019.pdf

Desai, Radhika. 1994. *Intellectuals and Socialism: 'Social Democrats' and the Labour Party*. London: Lawrence and Wishart.

Desai, Radhika. 2006. 'Neoliberalism and Cultural Nationalism: A Danse Macabre', in Plehwe, Dieter, Walpen, Bernhard; and Nuenhoeffer, Gisela (eds), *Neo-Liberal Hegemony: A Global Critique*, pp. 222–35. New York: Routledge.

Desai, Radhika. 2011. 'The New Communists of the Commons: Twenty-First-Century Proudhonists', *International Critical Thought*, 1(2), pp. 204–23.

Desai, Radhika. 2022. 'The Long Shadow of Hiroshima: Capitalism and Nuclear Weapons', *International Critical Thought*, 8 April, pp. 1–21. https://doi.org/10.1080/21598282.2022.2051582

Eley, Geoff. 2002. *Forging Democracy: The History of the Left in Europe, 1850–2000*. Oxford: Oxford University Press.

Epstein, Gerald. 2020. 'The MMT Free Lunch Mirage Can Lead to a Perverse Outcome', *Challenge*, 63(1), pp. 2–13, https://doi.org/10.1080/05775132.2019.1684661

Felkerson, James. 2011. '$29,000,000,000,000: A Detailed Look at the Fed's Bailout By Funding Facility and Recipient', *Working Paper No. 698, Levy Economics Institute of Bard College*, pp. 1–35.

Financial Times, Editorial Board. 2020. 'Virus Lays Bare the Frailty of the Social Contract', *Financial Times*, 3 April, (Accessed 31 May 2022) www.ft.com/content/7eff769a-74dd-11ea-95fe-fcd274e920ca

Gowan, Peter. 2001. 'Neoliberal Cosmopolitanism', *New Left Review*, 11(Sept/Oct). https://newleftreview.org/issues/ii11/articles/peter-gowan-neoliberal-cosmopolitanism

Hall, Peter A. 2015. 'Varieties of Capitalism', *Emerging Trends in the Social and Behavioral Sciences: An Interdisciplinary, Searchable, and Linkable Resource*, pp. 1–15.

Henwood, Doug. 2019. 'Modern Monetary Theory isn't Helping', *Jacobin*, 21 February, (Accessed 31 May 2022) https://jacobin.com/2019/02/modern-monetary-theory-isnt-helping

Hirschman, Albert O. 1991. *The Rhetoric of Reaction*. Cambridge, MA: Harvard University Press.

Hornstein, Andreas; and Kudlyak, Marianna. 2022. 'The Pandemic's Impact on Unemployment and Labor Force Participation Trends', *Federal Reserve Bank of Richmond*, nos. 22–12. www.richmondfed.org/publications/research/economic_brief/2022/eb_22-12

Huws, Ursula. 2020. *Reinventing the Welfare State: Digital Platforms and Public Policies*. London: Pluto Press.

Joll, James. 1955. 'Failure of a Revolution: Germany in 1918–19', *International Affairs*, October 1955, 31(4), pp. 511–12, https://doi.org/10.2307/2604870

Kelton, Stephanie. 2020. *The Deficit Myth: Modern Monetary Theory and the Birth of the People's Economy*. New York: Public Affairs.

Lenin, Vladimir. 1916/1970. *Imperialism, the Highest Stage of Capitalism, a Popular Outline*. Moscow: Progress Publishers.

Macqueen, Rory. 2020. 'UK Workers Hit By the Economic Pain of Coronavirus Need an Income Guarantee', *The Guardian*, 7 April, (Accessed 1 June 2022) www.theguardian.

com/commentisfree/2020/apr/07/uk-workers-economic-coronavirus-guarantee-universal-basic-income

Mair, Peter. 2006. 'Ruling the Void', *New Left Review*, 42(Nov/Dec), https://newleftreview.org/issues/ii42/articles/peter-mair-ruling-the-void

Mair, Peter. 2013. *Ruling the Void: The Hollowing of Western Democracy*. London & New York: Verso.

Mannheim, Karl. 1954/2018. *Ideology and Utopia: An Introduction to the Sociology of Knowledge*. London: Forgotten Books.

Marx, Karl. 1847. *The Poverty of Philosophy*.London: Martin Lawrence.

Marx, Karl; and Engels, Fredrick. 1848/1967. *The Communist Manifesto*. Translated by Samuel Moore. With an Introduction by A.J.P. Taylor. London: Penguin.

Marx, Karl. 1867/1977. *Capital* (Vol. 1). London: Penguin.

Mazzucato, Mariana. 2021. *Mission Economy: A Moonshot Guide to Changing Capitalism*. London: Penguin.

McDonnell, John. 2020. 'The Revelations in the Leaked Labour Report Are a Genuine Scandal', *The Guardian*, 21 April, (Accessed 5 June 2022) www.theguardian.com/commentisfree/2020/apr/21/revelations-leaked-labour-report-genuine-scandal

McKenzie, Robert Trelford. 1968. *Angels in Marble: Working Class Conservatives in Urban England*. Portsmouth: Heinemann Educational.

Mirsky, Dimitry. 1935. *The Intelligentsia of Great Britain*. London: Victor Gollancz.

Morozov, Evgeny. 2016. 'Silicon Valley Talks a Good Game on 'Basic Income', But Its Words Are Empty', *The Guardian*, 28 February, (Accessed 1 June 2022) www.theguardian.com/commentisfree/2016/feb/28/silicon-valley-basic-income

Muir-Harmony, Teasel. 2020. *Operation Moonglow: A Political History of Project Apollo*. New York: Basic Books.

Murphy, Craig. 1984. *The Emergence of the NIEO Ideology*. Boulder, CO: Westview.

Patnaik, Prabhat. 2009. 'Finance Capital and Fiscal Deficits', *MRonline*, 24 May, (Accessed 1 June 2022) https://mronline.org/2009/05/24/finance-capital-and-fiscal-deficits/

Patnaik, Utsa; and Patnaik, Prabhat. 2017. *A Theory of Imperialism*. New York: Columbia University Press.

Patnaik, Utsa; and Patnaik, Prabhat. 2021. *Capital and Imperialism: Theory, History, and the Present*. New York: Monthly Review Press.

Perkin, Harold. 1989. *The Rise of Professional Society: England Since 1880*. New York: Routledge.

Reich, Robert B. 2020. 'Resurrect Antitrust', *Project Syndicate*, 23 April, (Accessed 31 May 2022) www.project-syndicate.org/onpoint/break-up-big-tech-companies-by-robert-b-reich-2020-04?barrier=accesspaylog

Roberts, Michael. 2021. 'Mission Impossible', *Michael Roberts Blog*, 20 February, (accessed 31 May 2022) https://thenextrecession.wordpress.com/2021/02/20/mission-impossible/

Rogoff, Kenneth. 2020. 'The Case for Deeply Negative Interest Rates', *Project Syndicate*, 4 May, (Accessed 31 May 2022) www.project-syndicate.org/commentary/advanced-economies-need-deeply-negative-interest-rates-by-kenneth-rogoff-2020–05?barrier=accesspaylog

Ryner, Magnus. 2014. 'Why the Financial Crisis Has Not Generated a Social Democratic Alternative in Europe?', in Bailey, David; Escalona, Fabien; de Waele, Jean-Michel; and Vieira, Mathieu (eds) *European Social Democracy During the Global Economic Crisis*, pp. 60–76. Manchester: Manchester University Press.

Skidelsky, Robert. 2016. 'Basic Income Revisited', *Project Syndicate*, 23 June, (Accessed 31 May 2022) www.project-syndicate.org/commentary/unconditional-basic-income-revisited-by-robert-skidelsky-2016-06?barrier=accesspaylog

Soros, George. 2020. 'Spain Is Leading the Way on Perpetual Bonds', *Project Syndicate*, 22 April, (Accessed 5 June 2022) www.project-syndicate.org/commentary/spain-leading-europe-on-covid19-response-with-perpetual-bonds-by-george-soros-2020-04?barrier=accesspaylog

Stone, Jon. 2020. 'Anti-Corbyn Labour Officials Worked to Lose General Election to Oust Leader, Leaked Dossier Finds', *Independent*, 13 April, (Accessed 1 June 2022) www.independent.co.uk/news/uk/politics/labour-leak-report-corbyn-election-whatsapp-antisemitism-tories-yougov-poll-a9462456.html

Tcherneva, Pavlina R. 2016. 'Money, Power, and Monetary Regimes', *Levy Economics Institute, Working Paper*, (861), https://deliverypdf.ssrn.com/delivery.php?ID=908065002113090029028025004117018092002057081068083017073028117026123027111000077025031050122061114096018114066005087027095071000023046060084076124014083080072087041015095127065087005083002080120009110075124095086078019112007019028089080094126006022&EXT=pdf&INDEX=TRUE

Van der Pijl, Kees. 2020. 'Democracy, Planning, and Big Data', *Monthly Review*, 1 April (Accessed 1 June 2022) https://monthlyreview.org/2020/04/01/democracy-planning-and-big-data/

Van Parijs, Philippe. 1992. *Arguing for Basic Income* (Vol. 995). London: Verso.

Varoufakis, Yanis. 2016. 'The Universal Right to Capital Income', *Project Syndicate*, 31 October, (Accessed 5 June 2022) www.project-syndicate.org/commentary/basic-income-funded-by-capital-income-by-yanis-varoufakis-2016-10?barrier=accesspaylog

Wray, L.R. 2020. 'The "Kansas City" Approach to Modern Money Theory', *Levy Economics Institute of Bard College, Working Paper 961*, pp. 1–40. https://dx.doi.org/10.2139/ssrn.3650357

INDEX

Headnote: Figures and tables are in **bold** type.

Abbreviations used:
ICT - information and communications technologies
MMT - Modern Monetary Theory
UBI - Universal Basic Income
UCD - uneven and combined development

FSC
www.fsc.org
MIX
Papier | Fördert gute Waldnutzung
FSC® C083411

Kolibri 360 GmbH
Ferdinand-Jühlke-Straße 7
99095 Erfurt, Deutschland
produktsicherheit@kolibri360.de